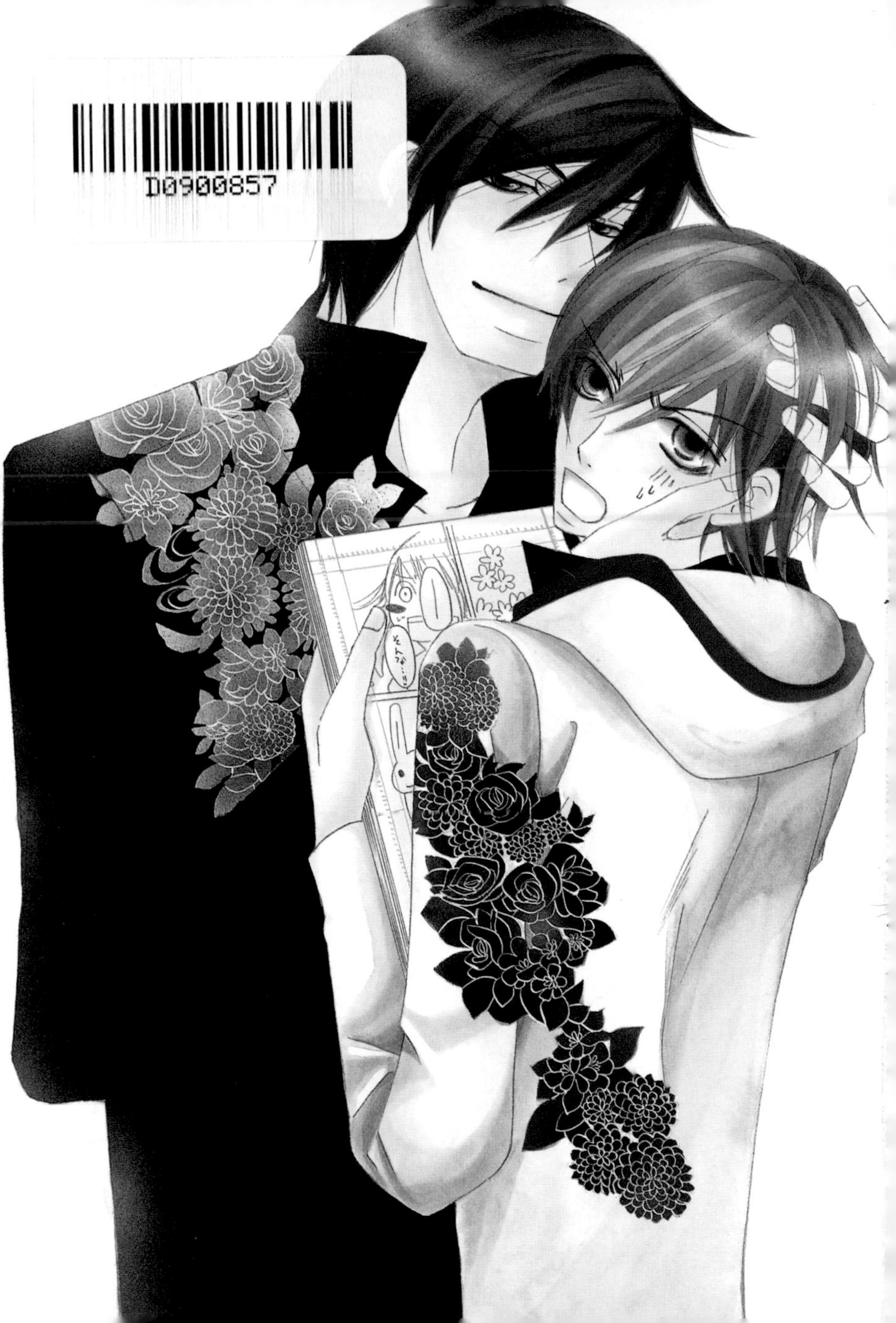
そんな…!!

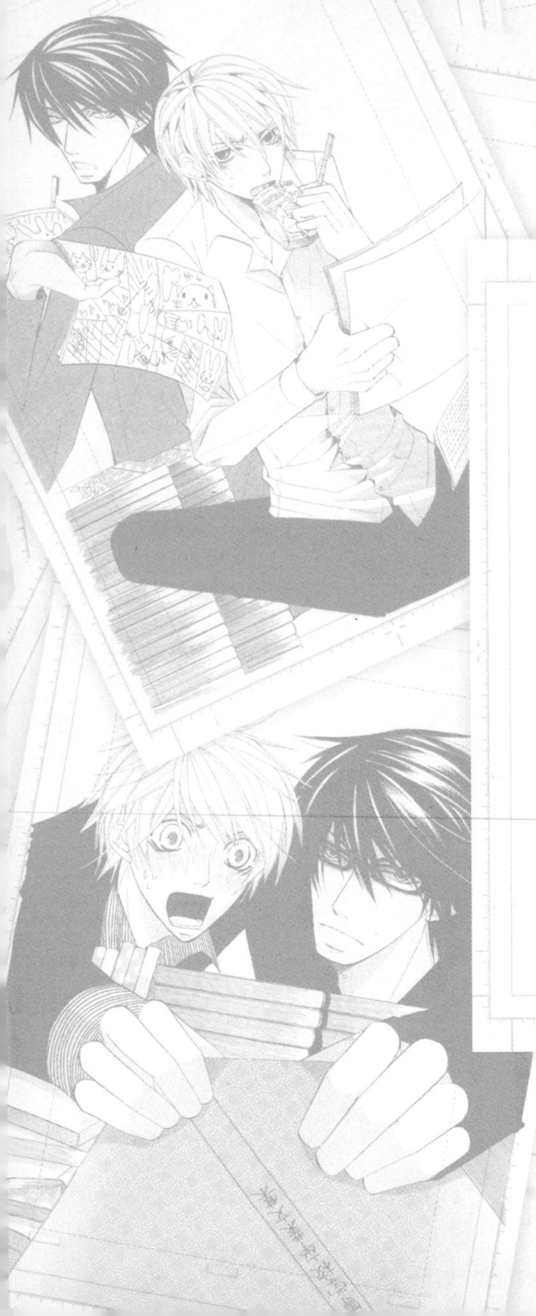

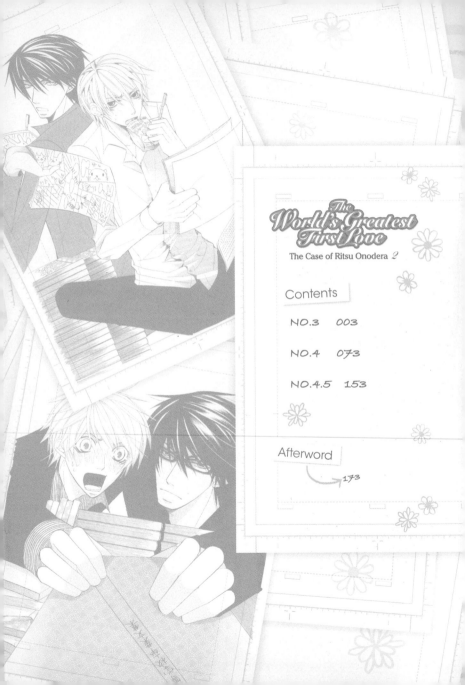

The World's Greatest First Love

The Case of Ritsu Onodera 2

Contents

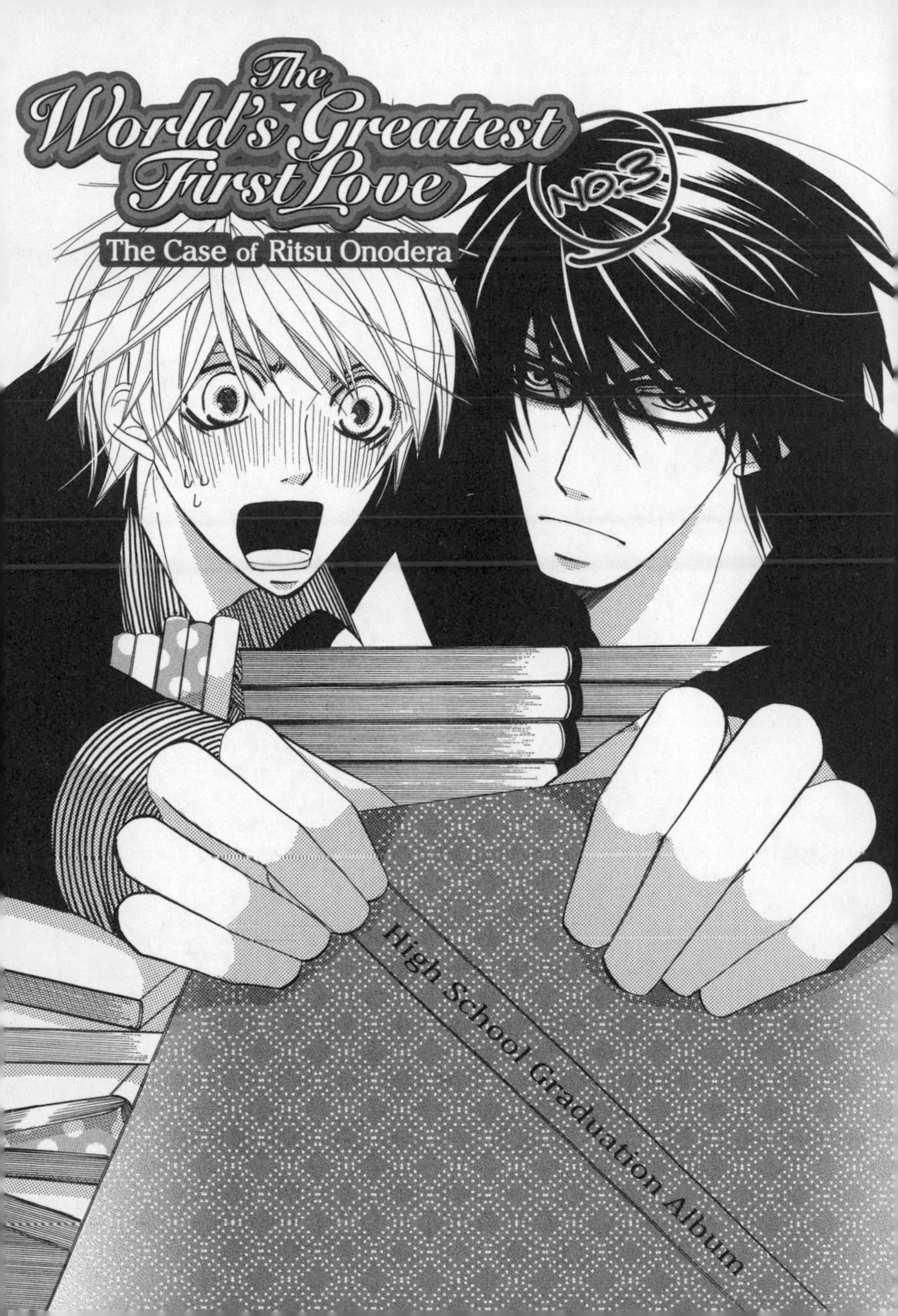
The World's Greatest First Love
No.3
The Case of Ritsu Onodera
High School Graduation Album

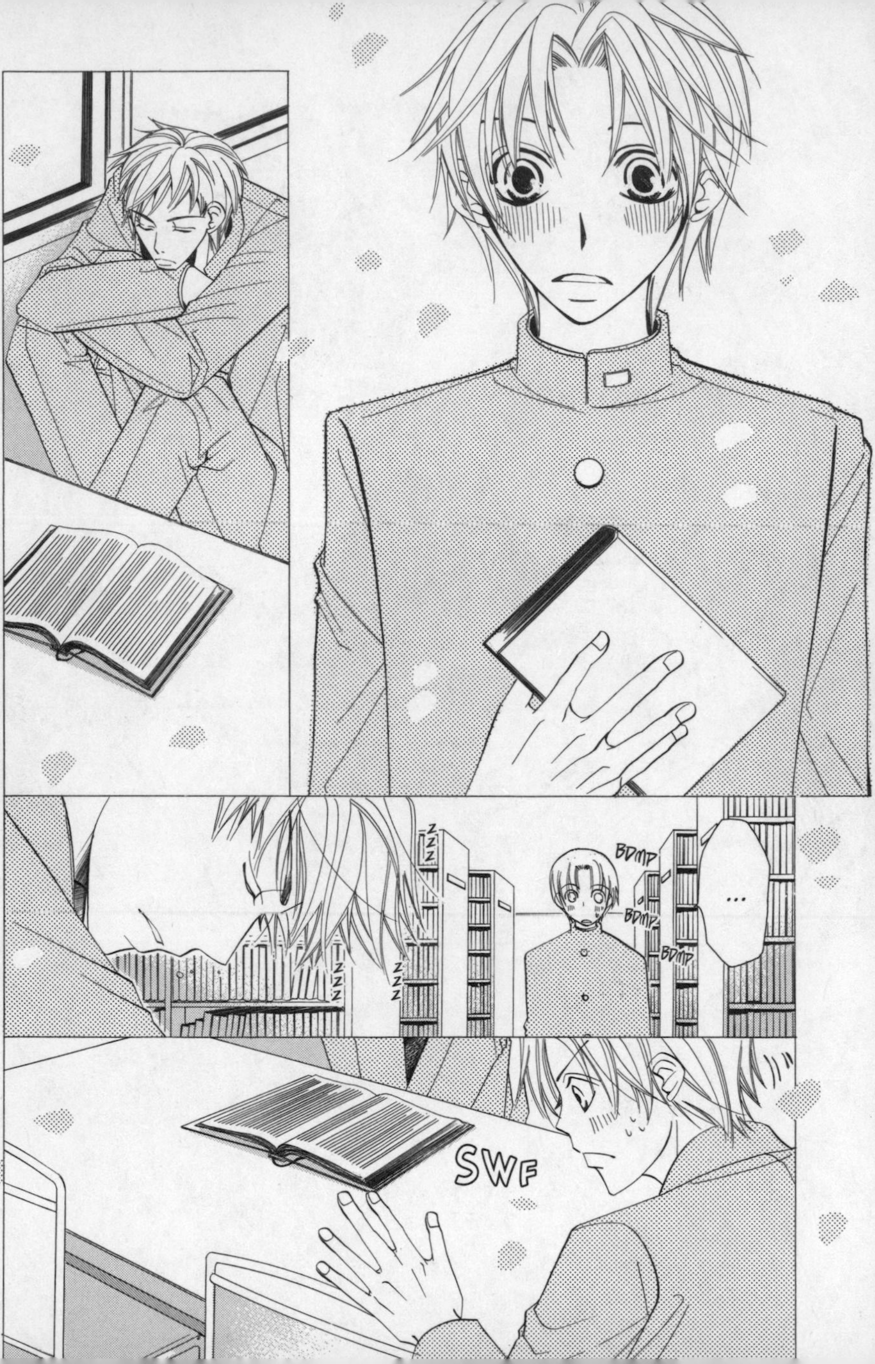
...
BDMP
BDMP
BDMP
ZZZ
ZZZ
ZZZ
SWF

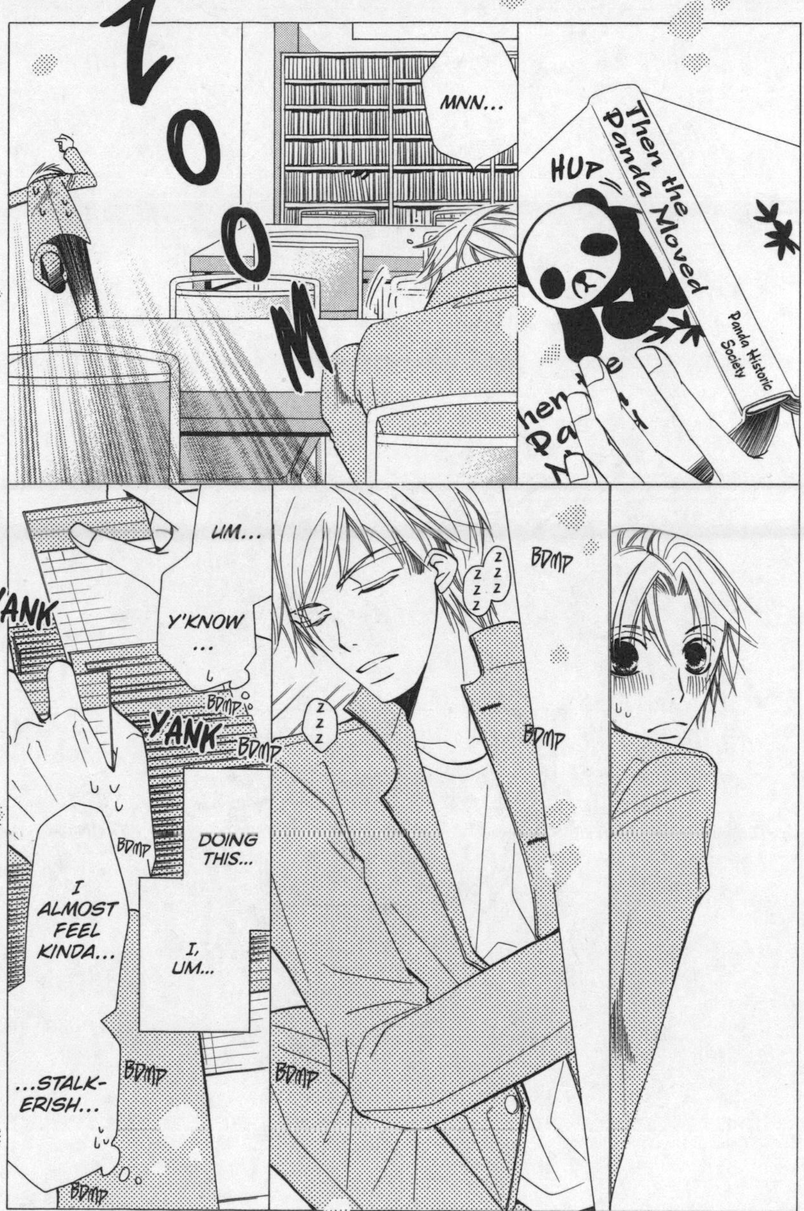

HUP
Then the Panda Moved
Panda Historic Society
MNN...
ZOOM
BDMP
BDMP
ZZZZZ
ZZZ
BDMP
UM...
Y'KNOW...
YANK
YANK
BDMP
BDMP
DOING THIS...
I, UM...
BDMP
I ALMOST FEEL KINDA...
...STALK-ERISH...
BDMP
BDMP

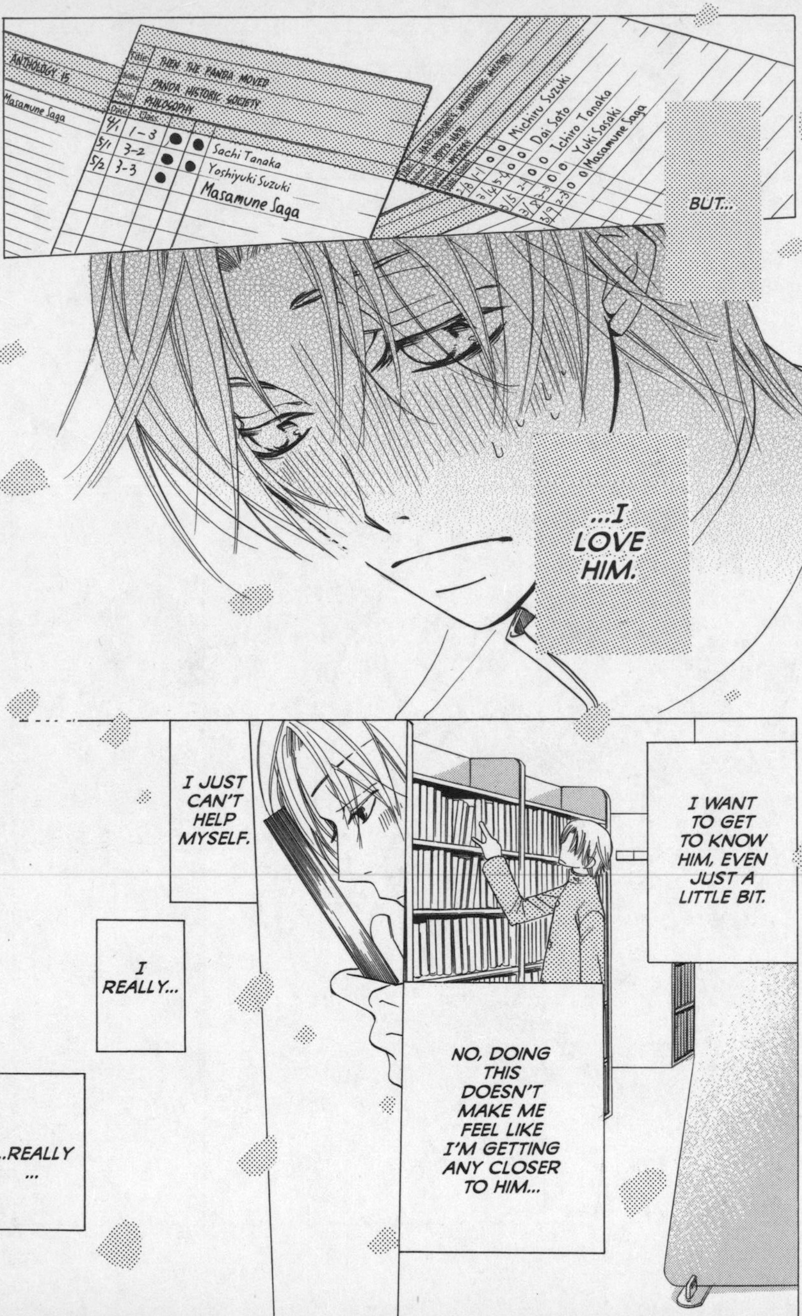

Michiru Suzuki
Dai Sato
Ichiro Tanaka
Yuki Sasaki
Masamune Saga
ANTHOLOGY 15
Masamune Saga
Title: THEN THE PANDA MOVED
Author: PANDA HISTORIC SOCIETY
Shelf: PHILOSOPHY
Date Class
4/1 1-3
5/1 3-2 Sachi Tanaka
5/2 3-3 Yoshiyuki Suzuki
Masamune Saga
BUT...
...I LOVE HIM.
I WANT TO GET TO KNOW HIM, EVEN JUST A LITTLE BIT.
I JUST CAN'T HELP MYSELF.
NO, DOING THIS DOESN'T MAKE ME FEEL LIKE I'M GETTING ANY CLOSER TO HIM...
I REALLY...
...REALLY ...

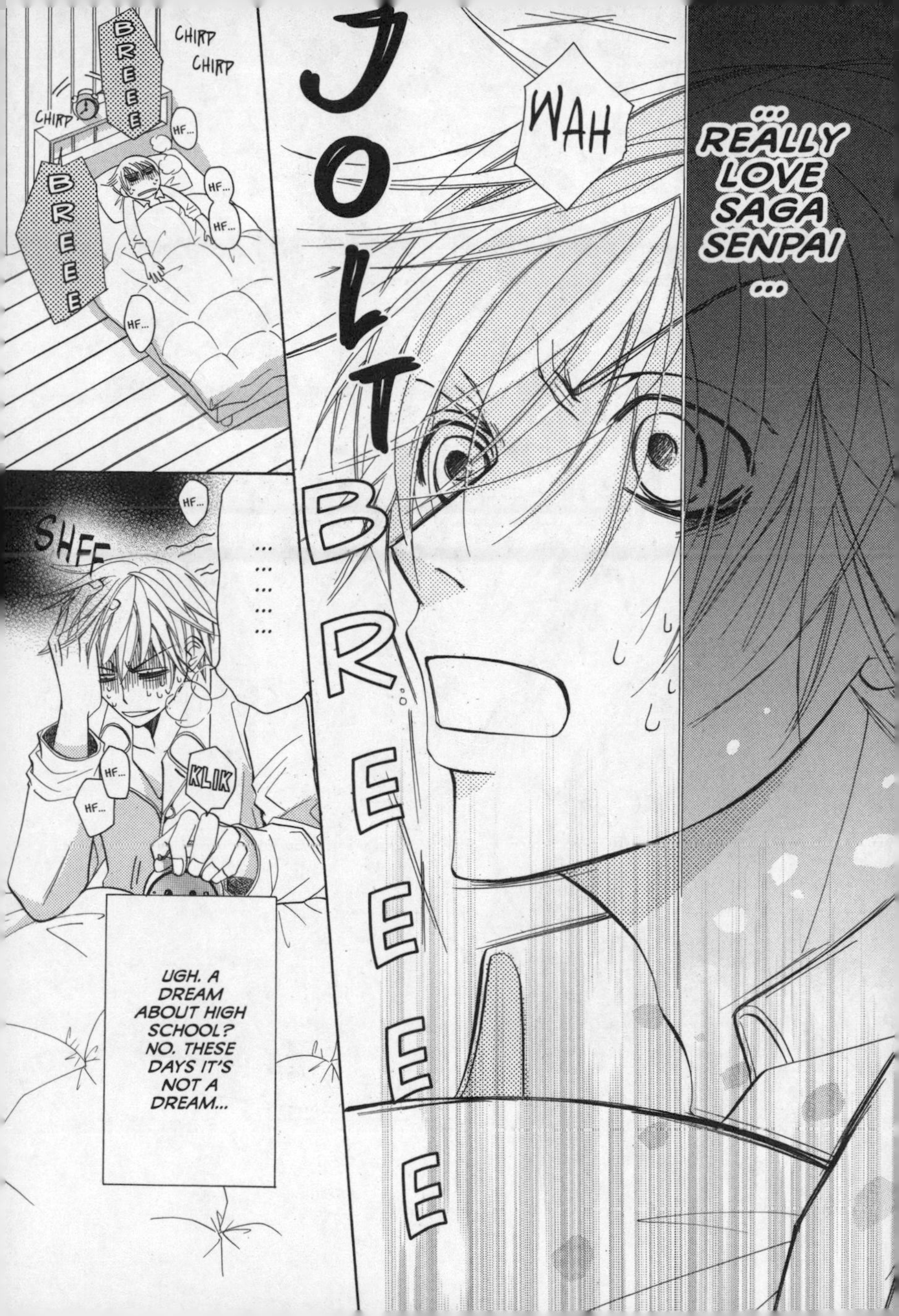

...REALLY LOVE SAGA SENPAI...
WAH
JOLT
BREEEE
BREEE
CHIRP
CHIRP
CHIRP
HF...
BREEEE
HF...
HF...
HF...
HF...
SHFF
......
KLIK
HF...
HF...
UGH. A DREAM ABOUT HIGH SCHOOL? NO. THESE DAYS IT'S NOT A DREAM...

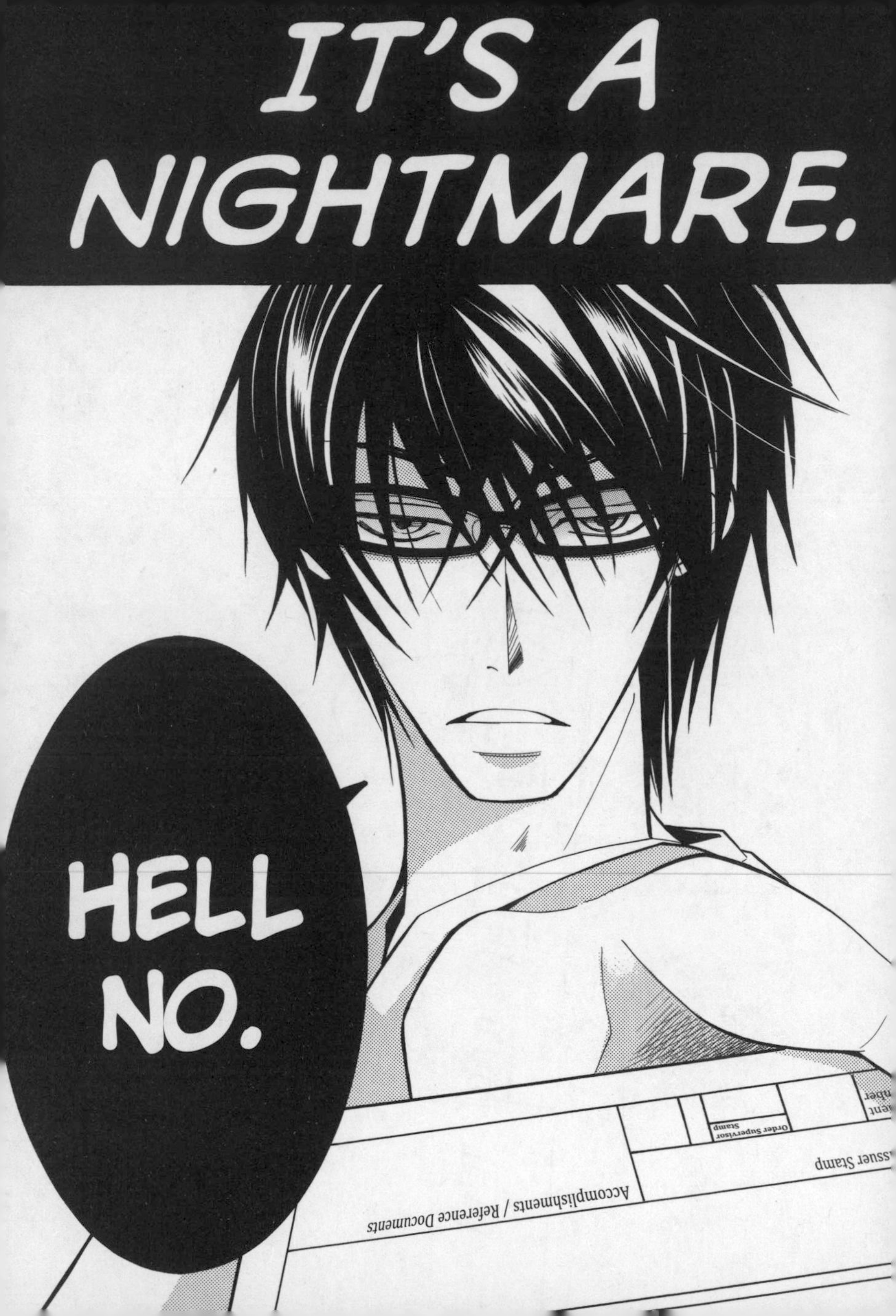
IT'S A NIGHTMARE.
HELL NO.
Order Supervisor Stamp
Accomplishments / Reference Documents

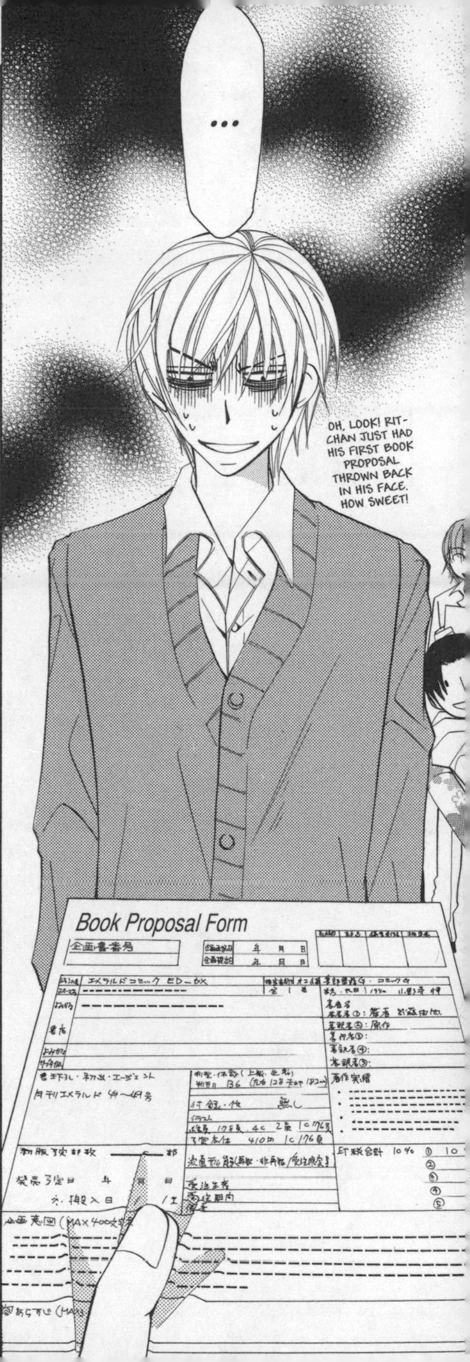
...
OH, LOOK! RIT-CHAN JUST HAD HIS FIRST BOOK PROPOSAL THROWN BACK IN HIS FACE. HOW SWEET!
Book Proposal Form

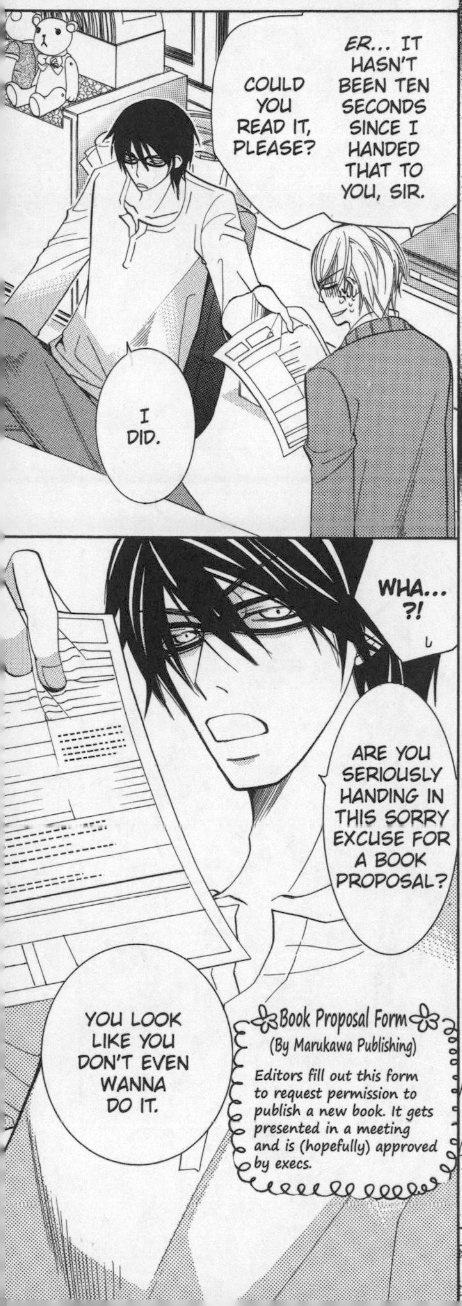
ER... IT HASN'T BEEN TEN SECONDS SINCE I HANDED THAT TO YOU, SIR.
COULD YOU READ IT, PLEASE?
I DID.
WHA...?!
ARE YOU SERIOUSLY HANDING IN THIS SORRY EXCUSE FOR A BOOK PROPOSAL?
YOU LOOK LIKE YOU DON'T EVEN WANNA DO IT.
Book Proposal Form
(By Marukawa Publishing)
Editors fill out this form to request permission to publish a new book. It gets presented in a meeting and is (hopefully) approved by execs.

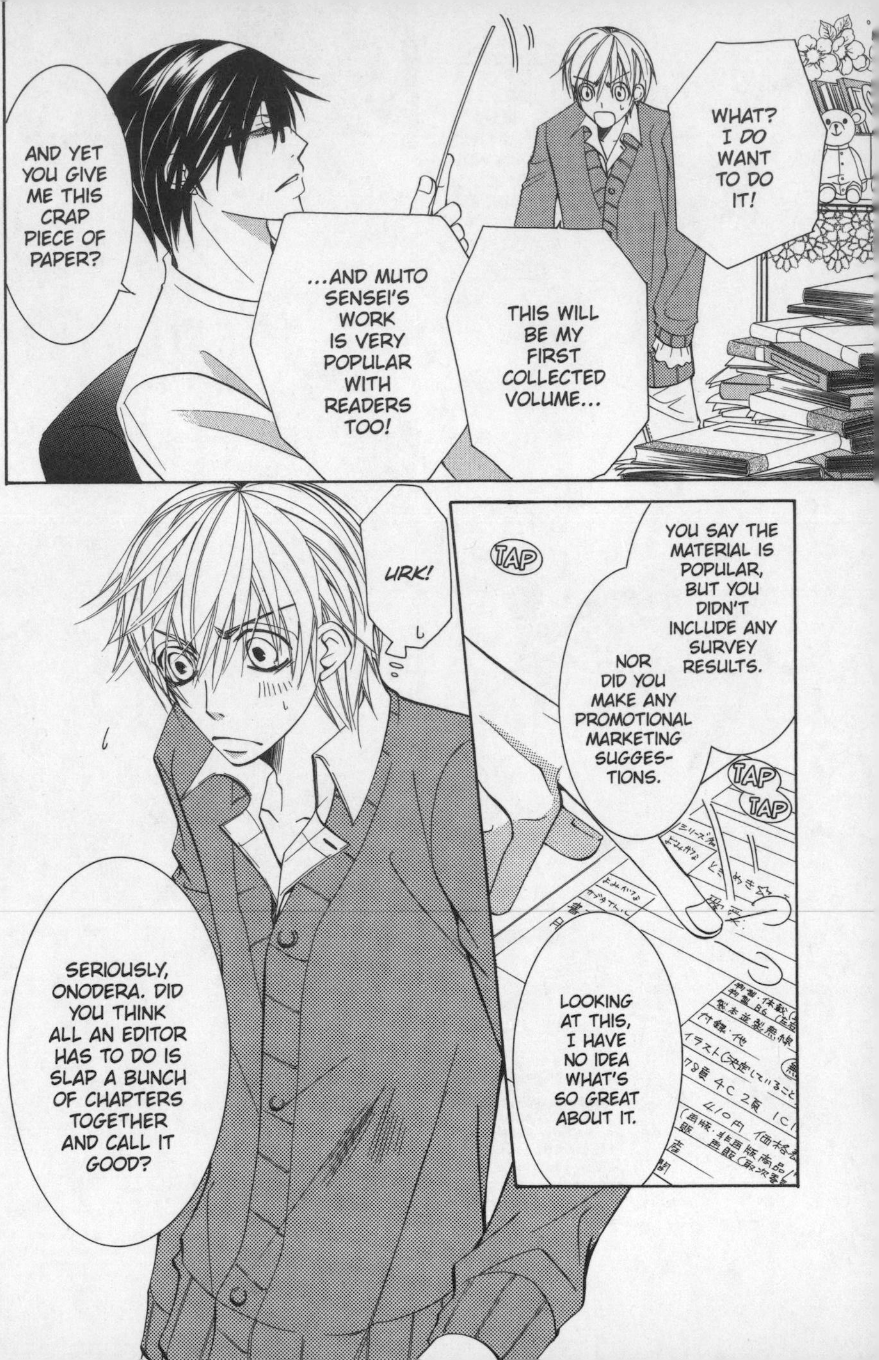
WHAT? I DO WANT TO DO IT!
THIS WILL BE MY FIRST COLLECTED VOLUME...
...AND MUTO SENSEI'S WORK IS VERY POPULAR WITH READERS TOO!
AND YET YOU GIVE ME THIS CRAP PIECE OF PAPER?
TAP
YOU SAY THE MATERIAL IS POPULAR, BUT YOU DIDN'T INCLUDE ANY SURVEY RESULTS.
NOR DID YOU MAKE ANY PROMOTIONAL MARKETING SUGGES-TIONS.
TAP
TAP
LOOKING AT THIS, I HAVE NO IDEA WHAT'S SO GREAT ABOUT IT.
URK!
SERIOUSLY, ONODERA. DID YOU THINK ALL AN EDITOR HAS TO DO IS SLAP A BUNCH OF CHAPTERS TOGETHER AND CALL IT GOOD?

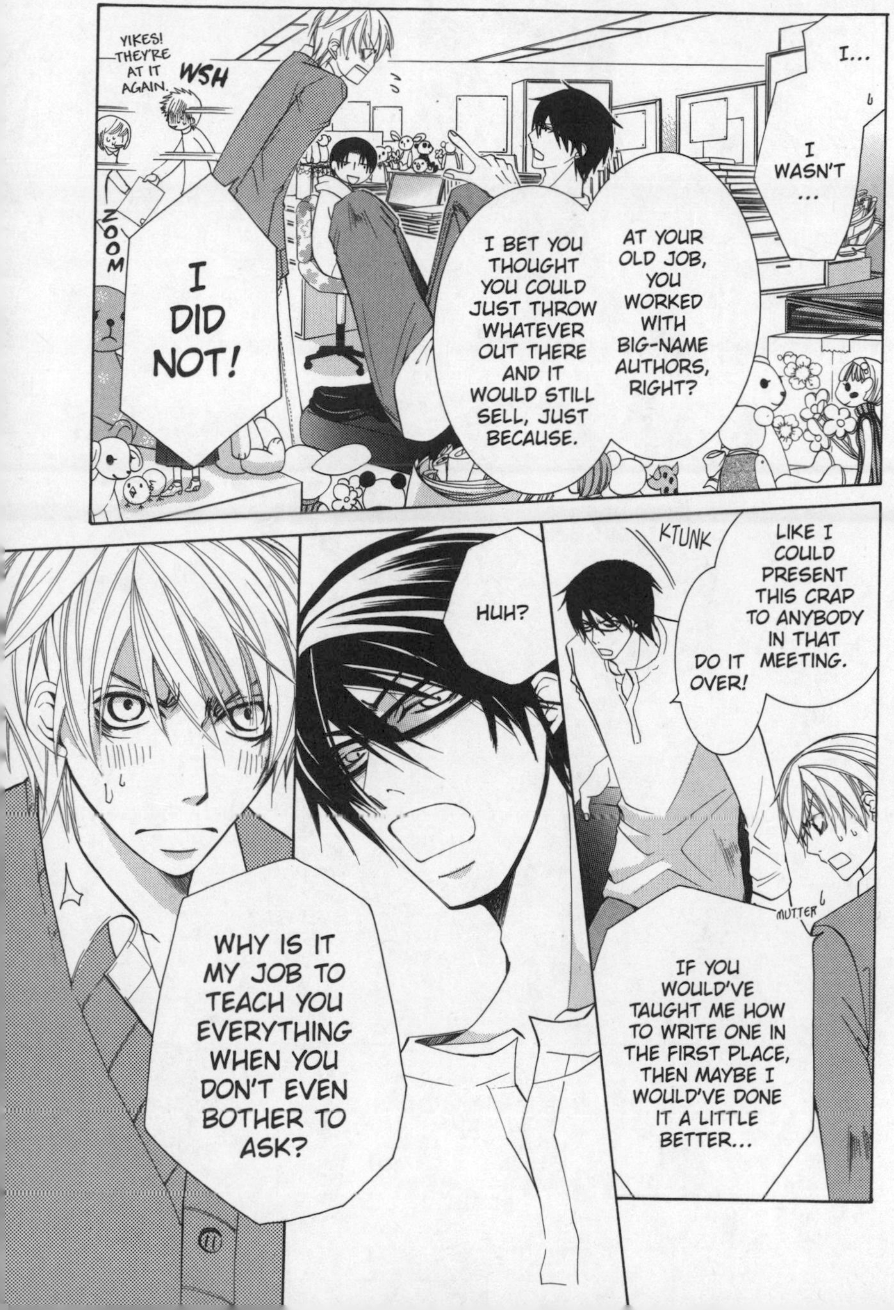
I...
I WASN'T ...
AT YOUR OLD JOB, YOU WORKED WITH BIG-NAME AUTHORS, RIGHT?
I BET YOU THOUGHT YOU COULD JUST THROW WHATEVER OUT THERE AND IT WOULD STILL SELL, JUST BECAUSE.
I DID NOT!
WSH
YIKES! THEY'RE AT IT AGAIN.
ZOOM
KTUNK
LIKE I COULD PRESENT THIS CRAP TO ANYBODY IN THAT MEETING.
DO IT OVER!
MUTTER
IF YOU WOULD'VE TAUGHT ME HOW TO WRITE ONE IN THE FIRST PLACE, THEN MAYBE I WOULD'VE DONE IT A LITTLE BETTER...
HUH?
WHY IS IT MY JOB TO TEACH YOU EVERYTHING WHEN YOU DON'T EVEN BOTHER TO ASK?

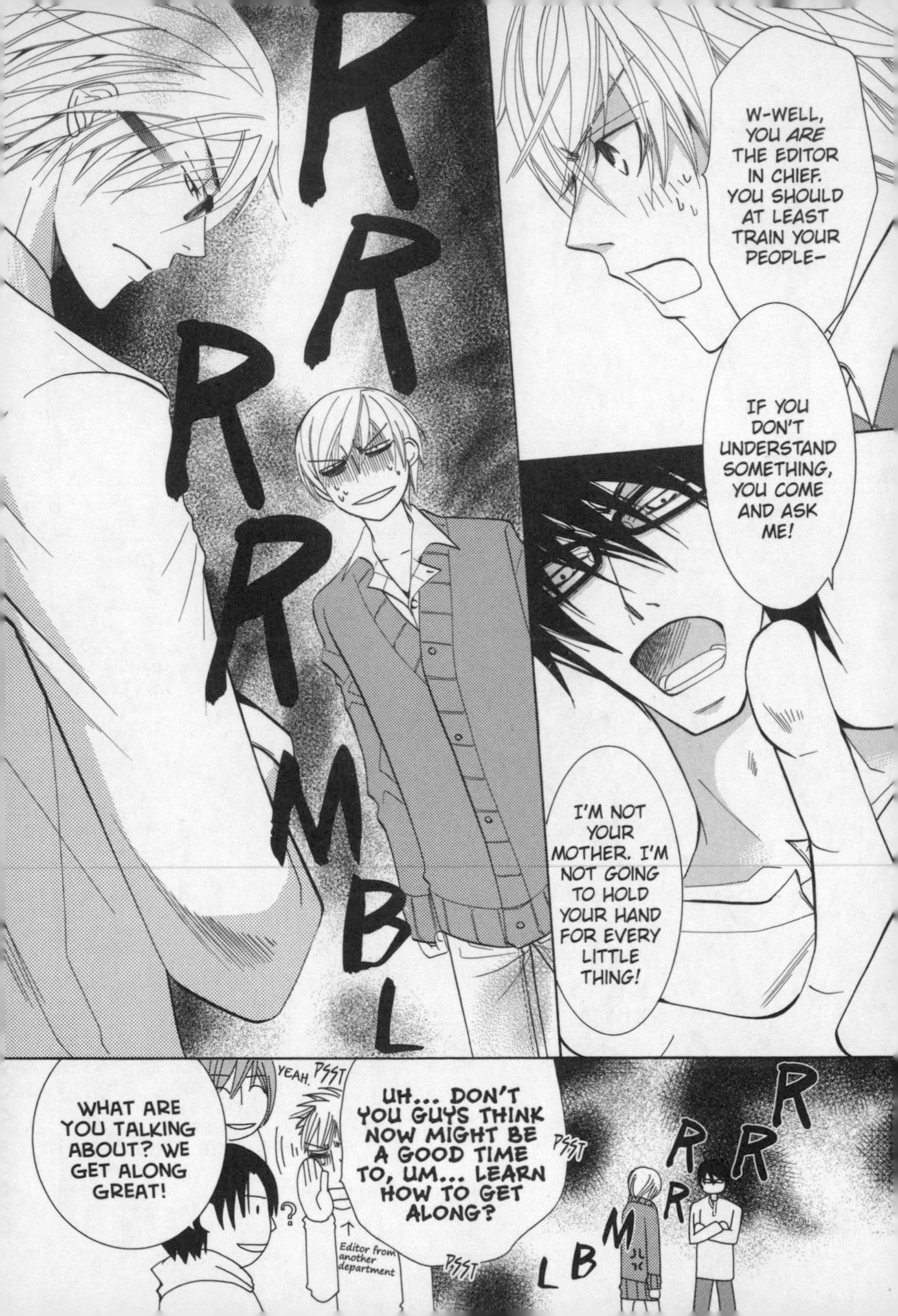
W-WELL, YOU *ARE* THE EDITOR IN CHIEF. YOU SHOULD AT LEAST TRAIN YOUR PEOPLE-
IF YOU DON'T UNDERSTAND SOMETHING, YOU COME AND ASK ME!
I'M NOT YOUR MOTHER. I'M NOT GOING TO HOLD YOUR HAND FOR EVERY LITTLE THING!
RRRRMBL
RRRRMBL
PSST
UH... DON'T YOU GUYS THINK NOW MIGHT BE A GOOD TIME TO, UM... LEARN HOW TO GET ALONG?
PSST
PSST
YEAH.
Editor from another department
WHAT ARE YOU TALKING ABOUT? WE GET ALONG GREAT!

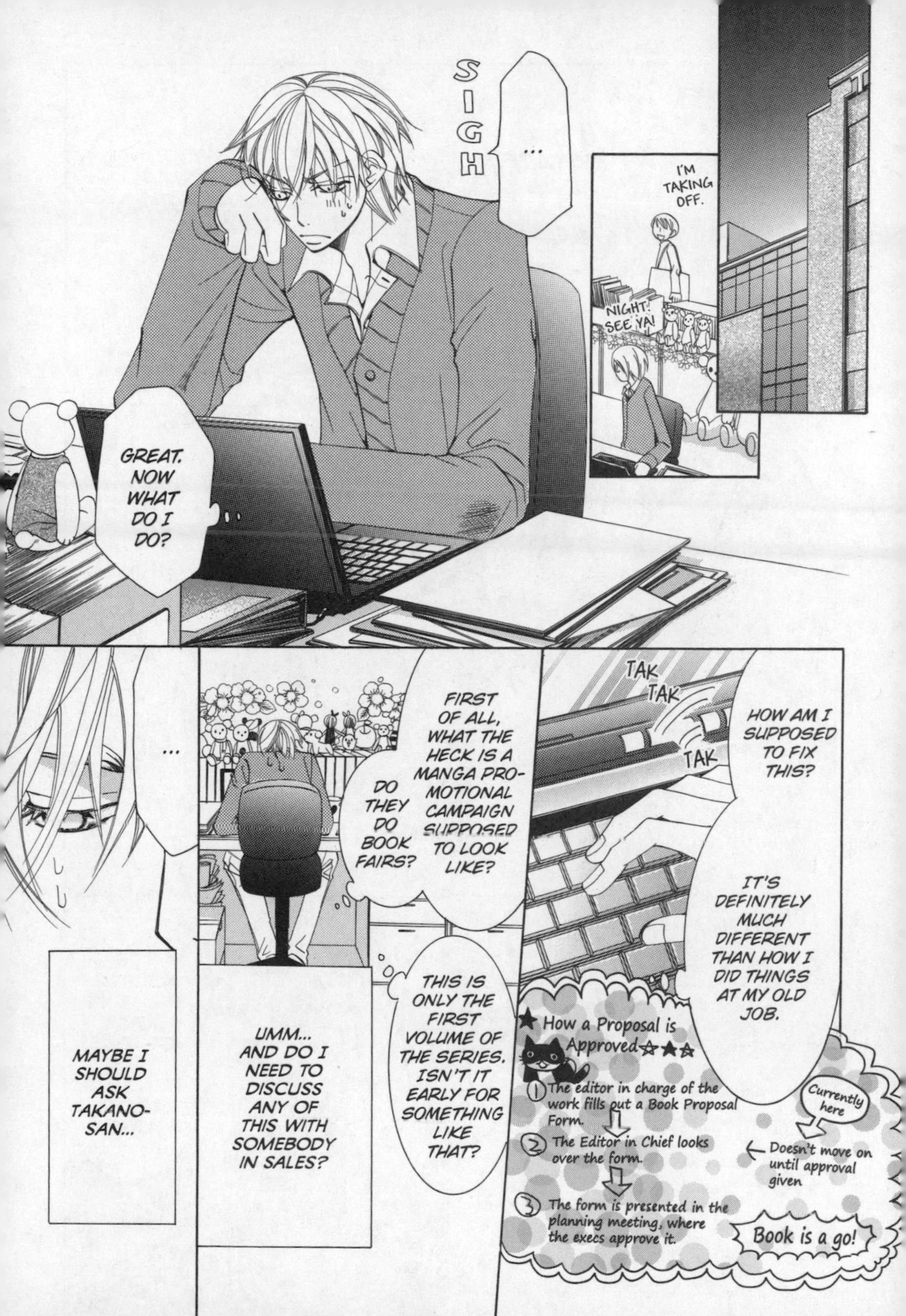
I'M TAKING OFF.
NIGHT! SEE YA!
SIGH
...
GREAT. NOW WHAT DO I DO?
TAK TAK TAK
HOW AM I SUPPOSED TO FIX THIS?
IT'S DEFINITELY MUCH DIFFERENT THAN HOW I DID THINGS AT MY OLD JOB.
★ How a Proposal is Approved☆★☆
① The editor in charge of the work fills out a Book Proposal Form.
② The Editor in Chief looks over the form.
③ The form is presented in the planning meeting, where the execs approve it.
Currently here
← Doesn't move on until approval given
Book is a go!
FIRST OF ALL, WHAT THE HECK IS A MANGA PROMOTIONAL CAMPAIGN SUPPOSED TO LOOK LIKE?
DO THEY DO BOOK FAIRS?
THIS IS ONLY THE FIRST VOLUME OF THE SERIES. ISN'T IT EARLY FOR SOMETHING LIKE THAT?
UMM... AND DO I NEED TO DISCUSS ANY OF THIS WITH SOMEBODY IN SALES?
...
MAYBE I SHOULD ASK TAKANO-SAN...

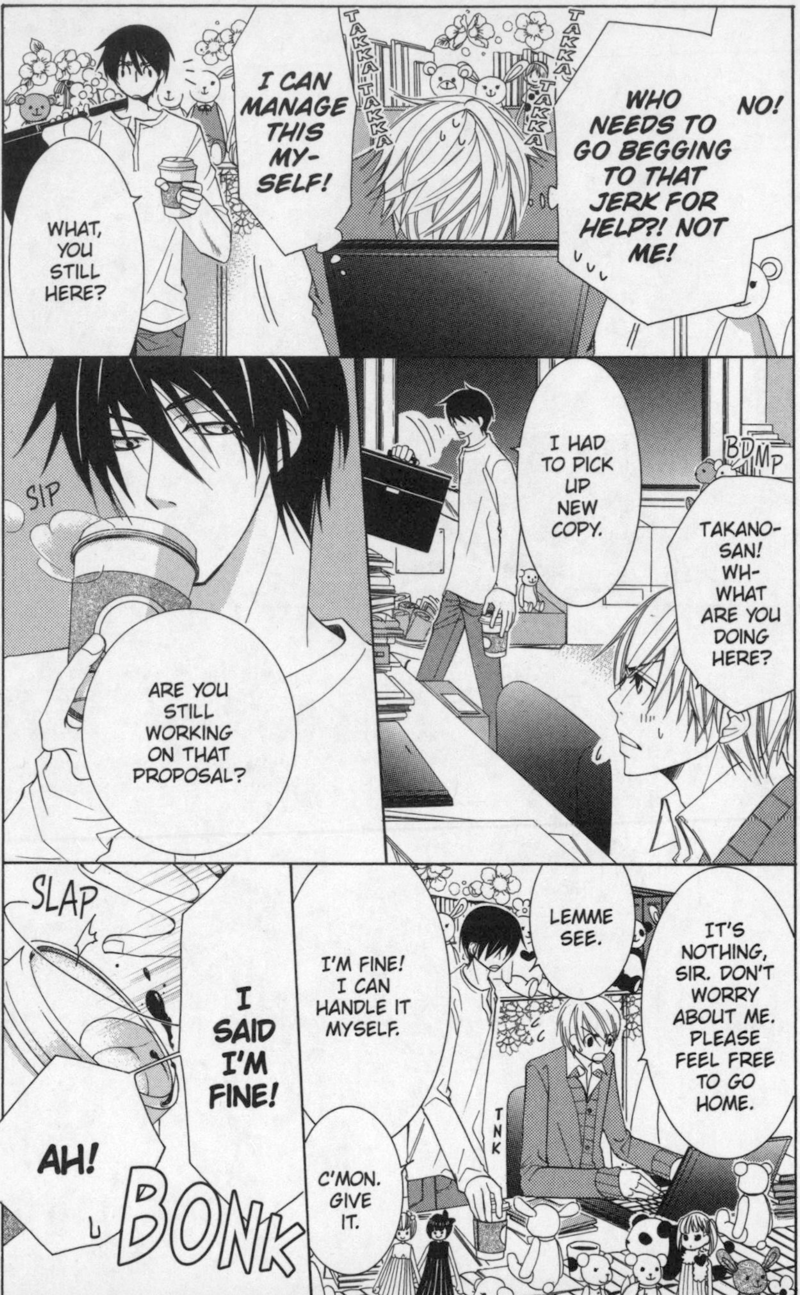
NO!
WHO NEEDS TO GO BEGGING TO THAT JERK FOR HELP?! NOT ME!
TAKKA TAKKA
I CAN MANAGE THIS MY-SELF!
TAKKA TAKKA
WHAT, YOU STILL HERE?
BDMP
TAKANO-SAN! WH-WHAT ARE YOU DOING HERE?
I HAD TO PICK UP NEW COPY.
SIP
ARE YOU STILL WORKING ON THAT PROPOSAL?
IT'S NOTHING, SIR. DON'T WORRY ABOUT ME. PLEASE FEEL FREE TO GO HOME.
LEMME SEE.
I'M FINE! I CAN HANDLE IT MYSELF.
TNK
C'MON. GIVE IT.
SLAP
I SAID I'M FINE!
AH!
BONK

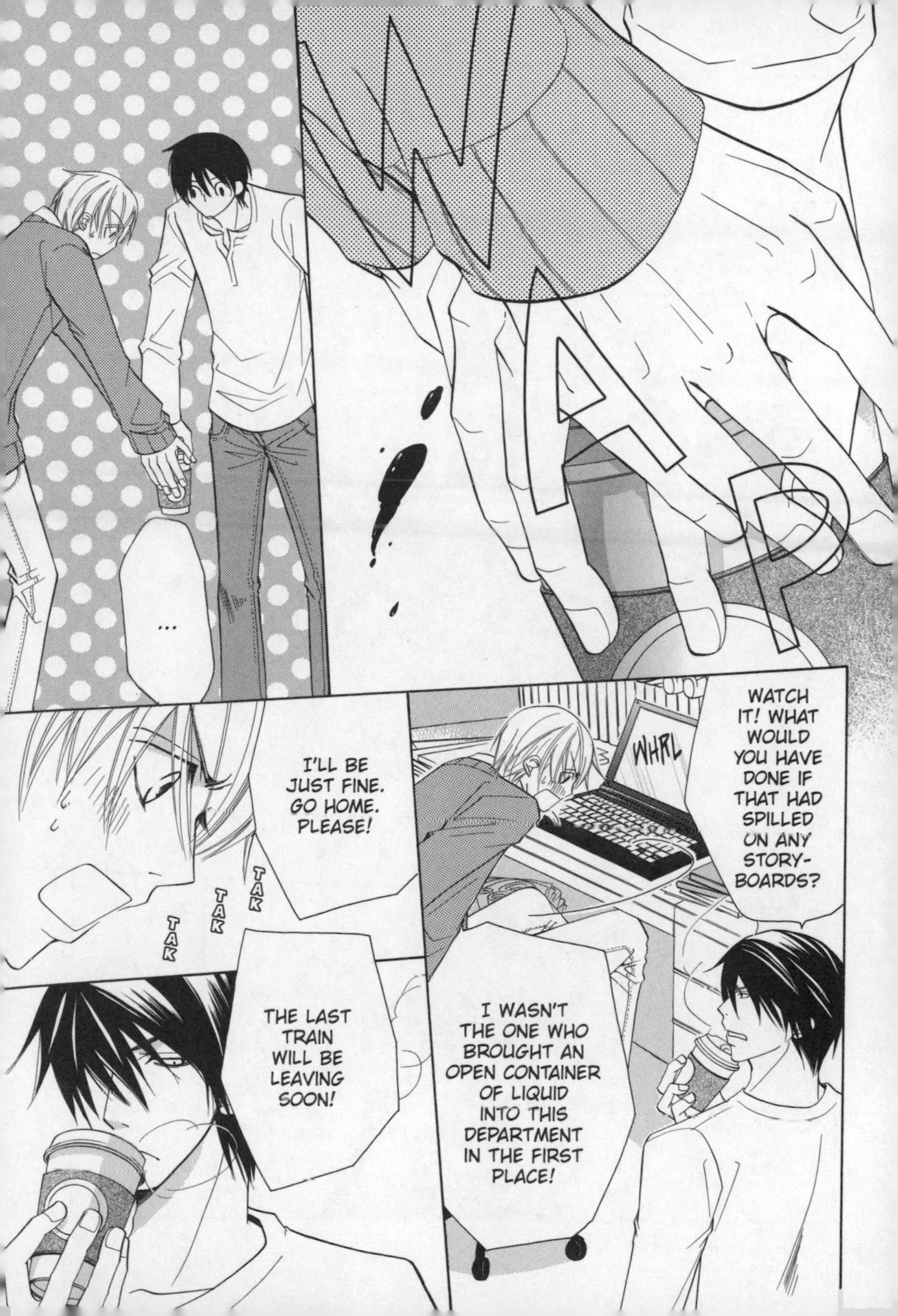
WAP
...
WHRL
WATCH IT! WHAT WOULD YOU HAVE DONE IF THAT HAD SPILLED ON ANY STORY-BOARDS?
I WASN'T THE ONE WHO BROUGHT AN OPEN CONTAINER OF LIQUID INTO THIS DEPARTMENT IN THE FIRST PLACE!
I'LL BE JUST FINE. GO HOME. PLEASE!
TAK
TAK
TAK
THE LAST TRAIN WILL BE LEAVING SOON!

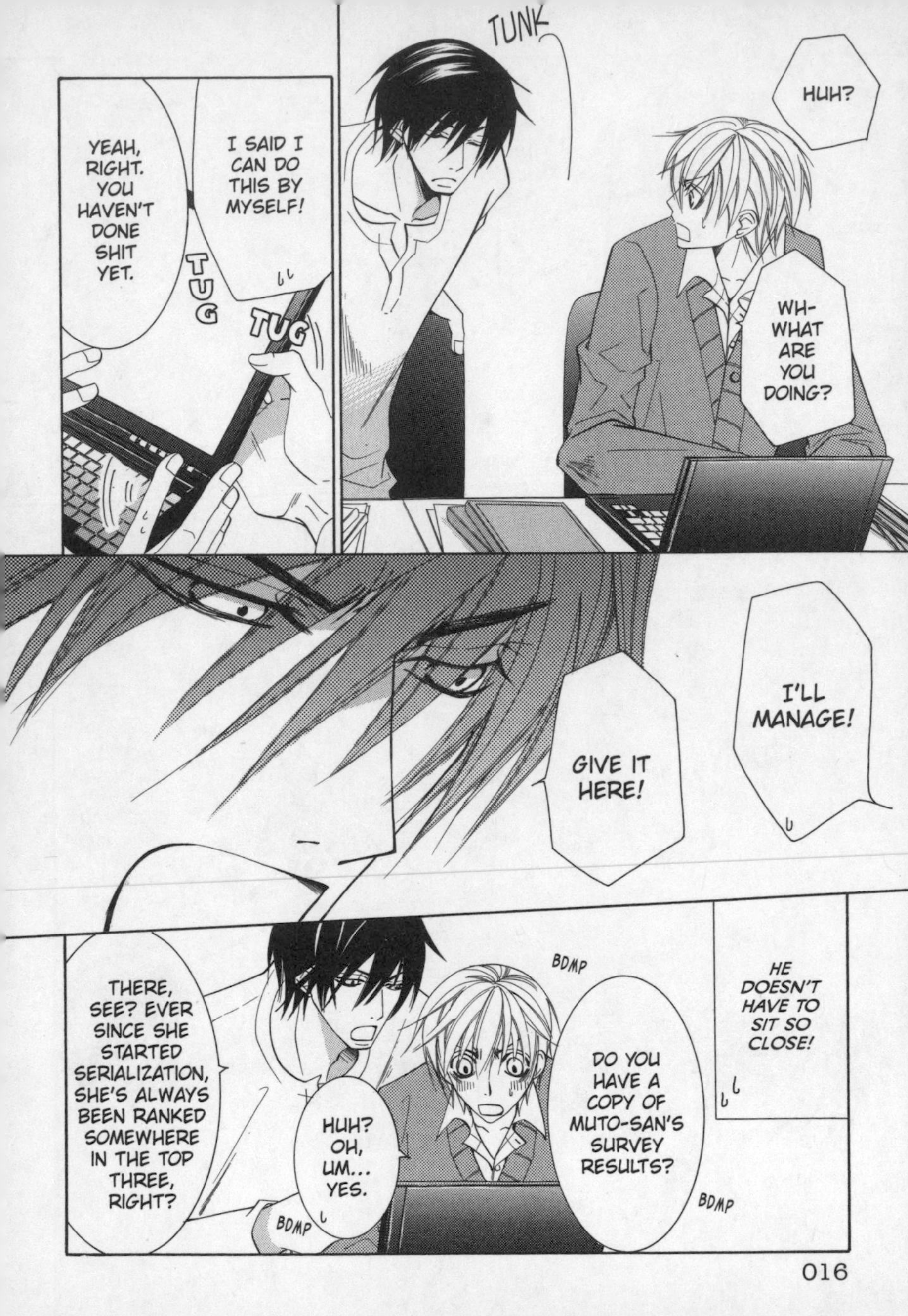
TUNK
HUH?
WH- WHAT ARE YOU DOING?
I SAID I CAN DO THIS BY MYSELF!
YEAH, RIGHT. YOU HAVEN'T DONE SHIT YET.
TUG
TUG
I'LL MANAGE!
GIVE IT HERE!
HE DOESN'T HAVE TO SIT SO CLOSE!
BDMP
DO YOU HAVE A COPY OF MUTO-SAN'S SURVEY RESULTS?
BDMP
HUH? OH, UM... YES.
THERE, SEE? EVER SINCE SHE STARTED SERIALIZATION, SHE'S ALWAYS BEEN RANKED SOMEWHERE IN THE TOP THREE, RIGHT?
BDMP

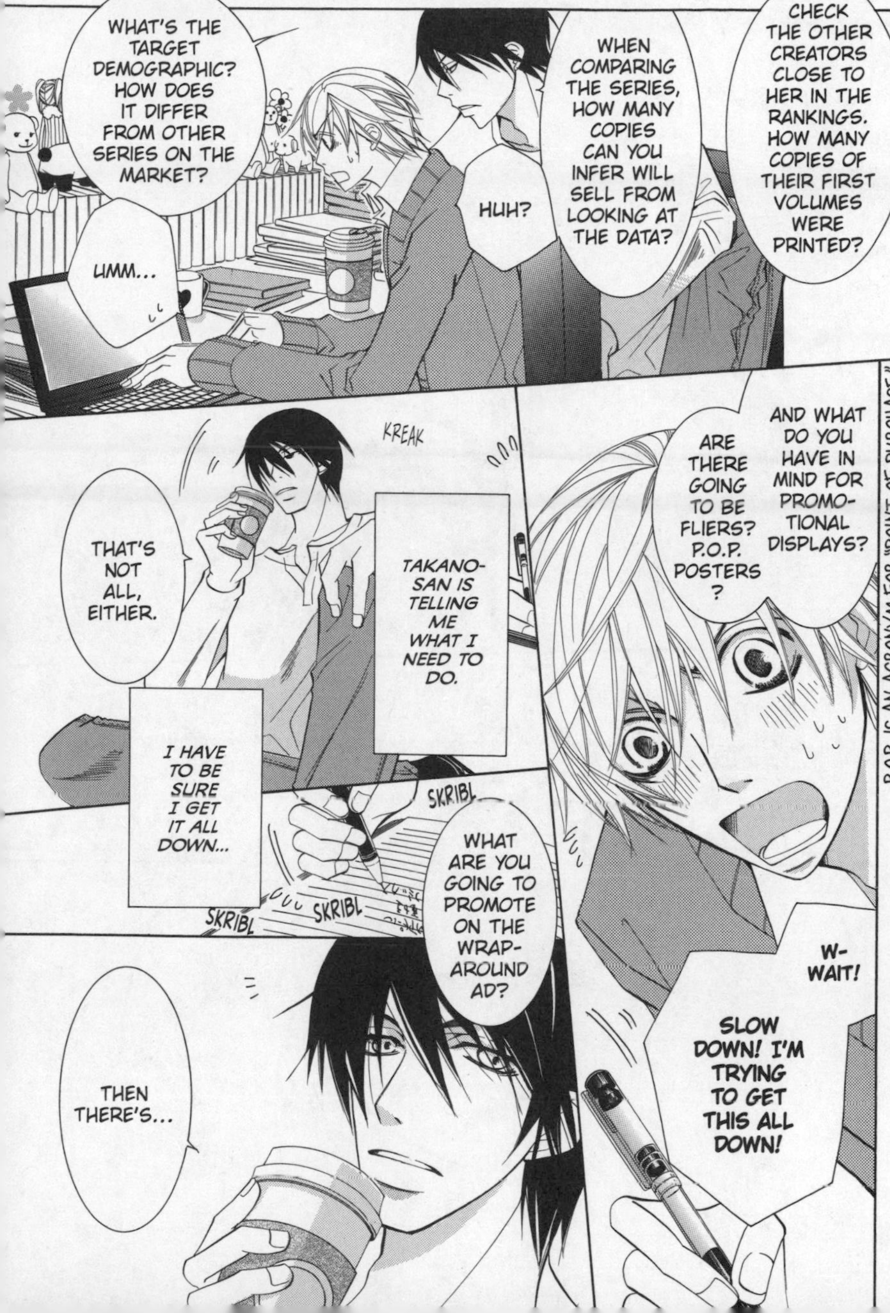
CHECK THE OTHER CREATORS CLOSE TO HER IN THE RANKINGS. HOW MANY COPIES OF THEIR FIRST VOLUMES WERE PRINTED?
WHEN COMPARING THE SERIES, HOW MANY COPIES CAN YOU INFER WILL SELL FROM LOOKING AT THE DATA?
HUH?
WHAT'S THE TARGET DEMOGRAPHIC? HOW DOES IT DIFFER FROM OTHER SERIES ON THE MARKET?
UMM...
AND WHAT DO YOU HAVE IN MIND FOR PROMOTIONAL DISPLAYS?
ARE THERE GOING TO BE FLIERS? P.O.P. POSTERS?
KREAK
TAKANO-SAN IS TELLING ME WHAT I NEED TO DO.
THAT'S NOT ALL, EITHER.
I HAVE TO BE SURE I GET IT ALL DOWN...
SKRIBL
SKRIBL
SKRIBL
WHAT ARE YOU GOING TO PROMOTE ON THE WRAP-AROUND AD?
THEN THERE'S...
W-WAIT!
SLOW DOWN! I'M TRYING TO GET THIS ALL DOWN!

P.O.P. IS AN ACRONYM FOR "POINT OF PURCHASE."

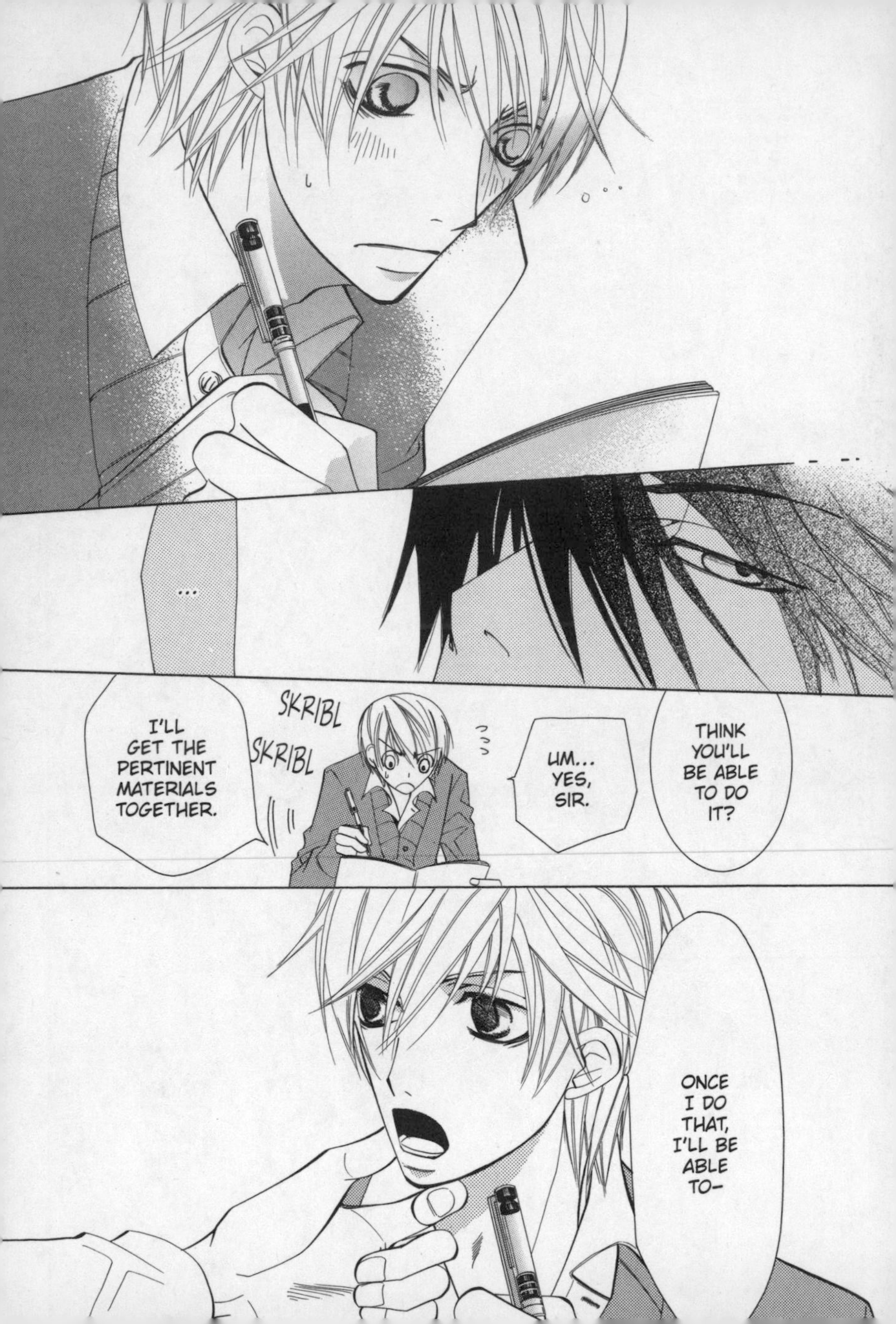
...
THINK YOU'LL BE ABLE TO DO IT?
UM... YES, SIR.
SKRIBL
SKRIBL
I'LL GET THE PERTINENT MATERIALS TOGETHER.
ONCE I DO THAT, I'LL BE ABLE TO–

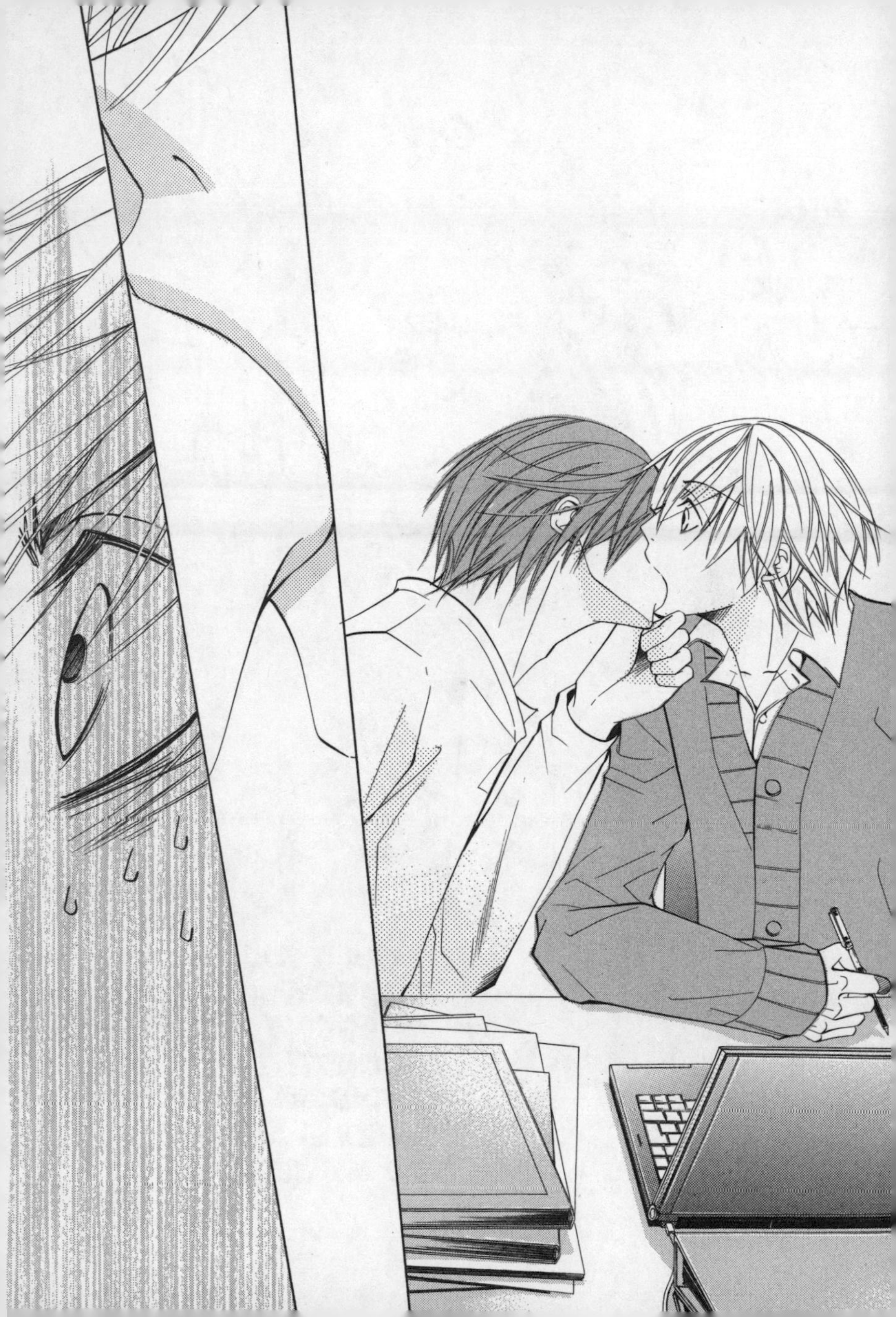

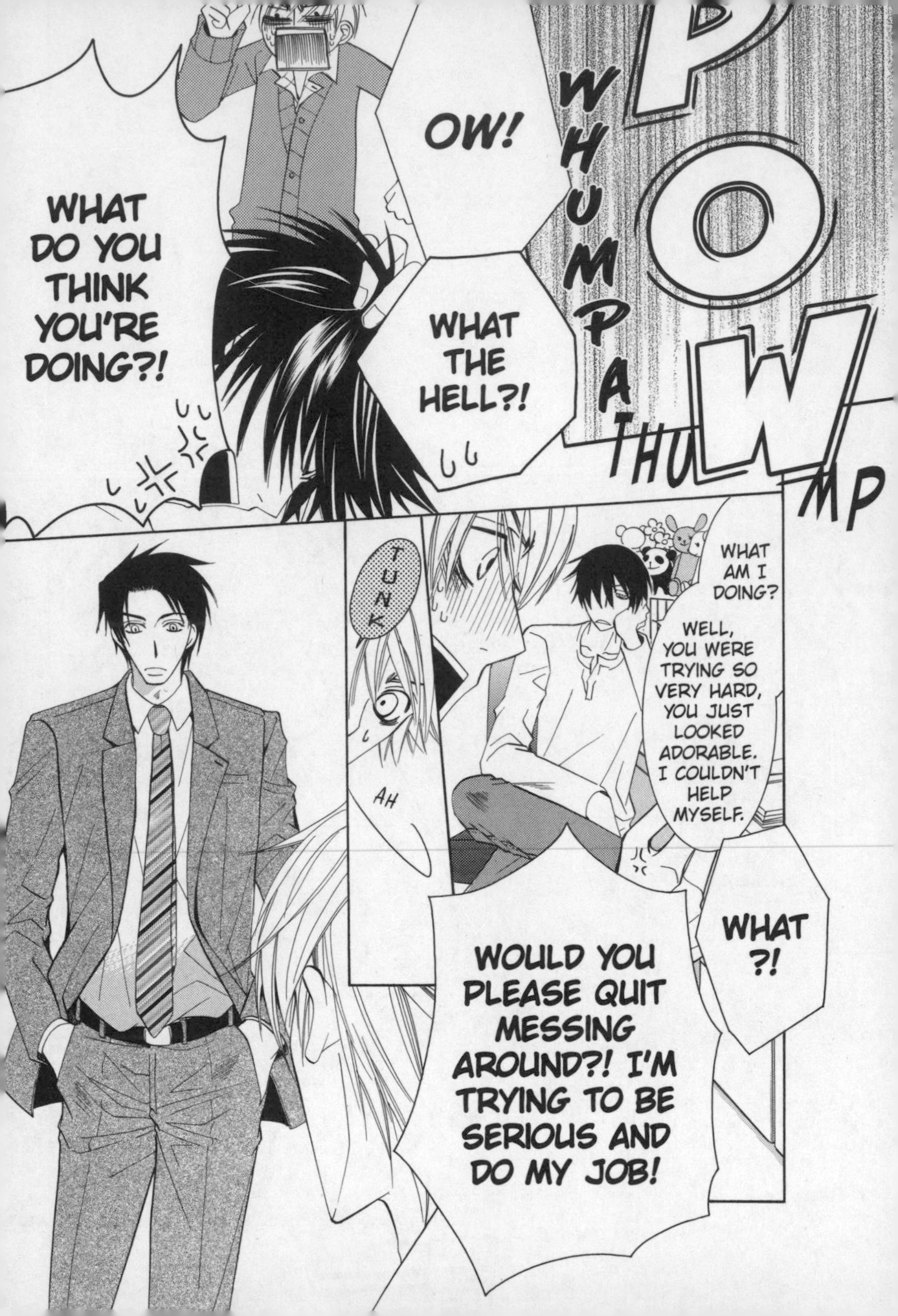
POW
WHUMPA
THUMP
OW!
WHAT THE HELL?!
WHAT DO YOU THINK YOU'RE DOING?!
WHAT AM I DOING?
WELL, YOU WERE TRYING SO VERY HARD, YOU JUST LOOKED ADORABLE. I COULDN'T HELP MYSELF.
TUNK
AH
WHAT ?!
WOULD YOU PLEASE QUIT MESSING AROUND?! I'M TRYING TO BE SERIOUS AND DO MY JOB!

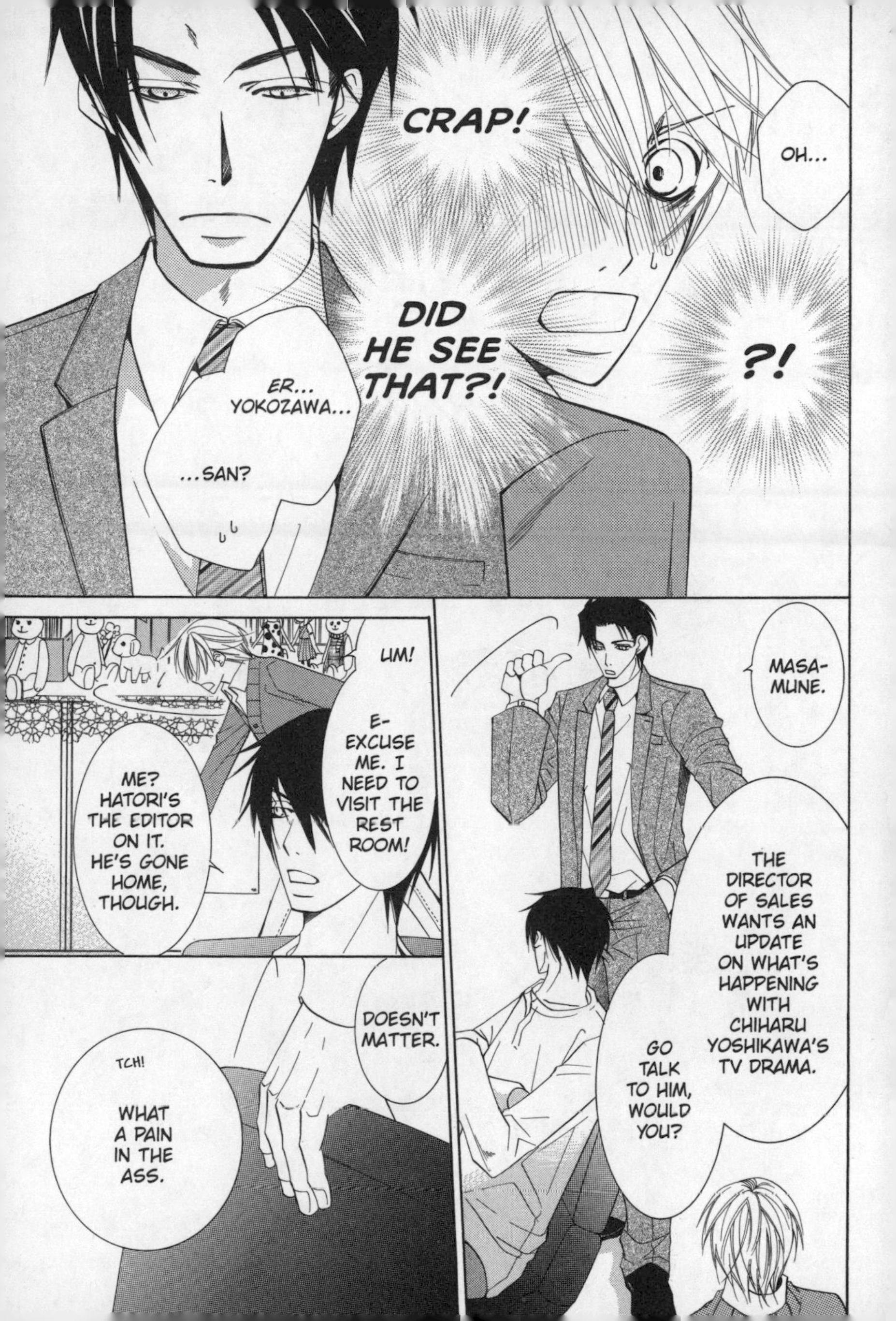
OH...
CRAP!
?!
DID HE SEE THAT?!
ER... YOKOZAWA...
...SAN?
MASA-MUNE.
THE DIRECTOR OF SALES WANTS AN UPDATE ON WHAT'S HAPPENING WITH CHIHARU YOSHIKAWA'S TV DRAMA.
GO TALK TO HIM, WOULD YOU?
UM!
E-EXCUSE ME. I NEED TO VISIT THE REST ROOM!
ME? HATORI'S THE EDITOR ON IT. HE'S GONE HOME, THOUGH.
DOESN'T MATTER.
TCH!
WHAT A PAIN IN THE ASS.

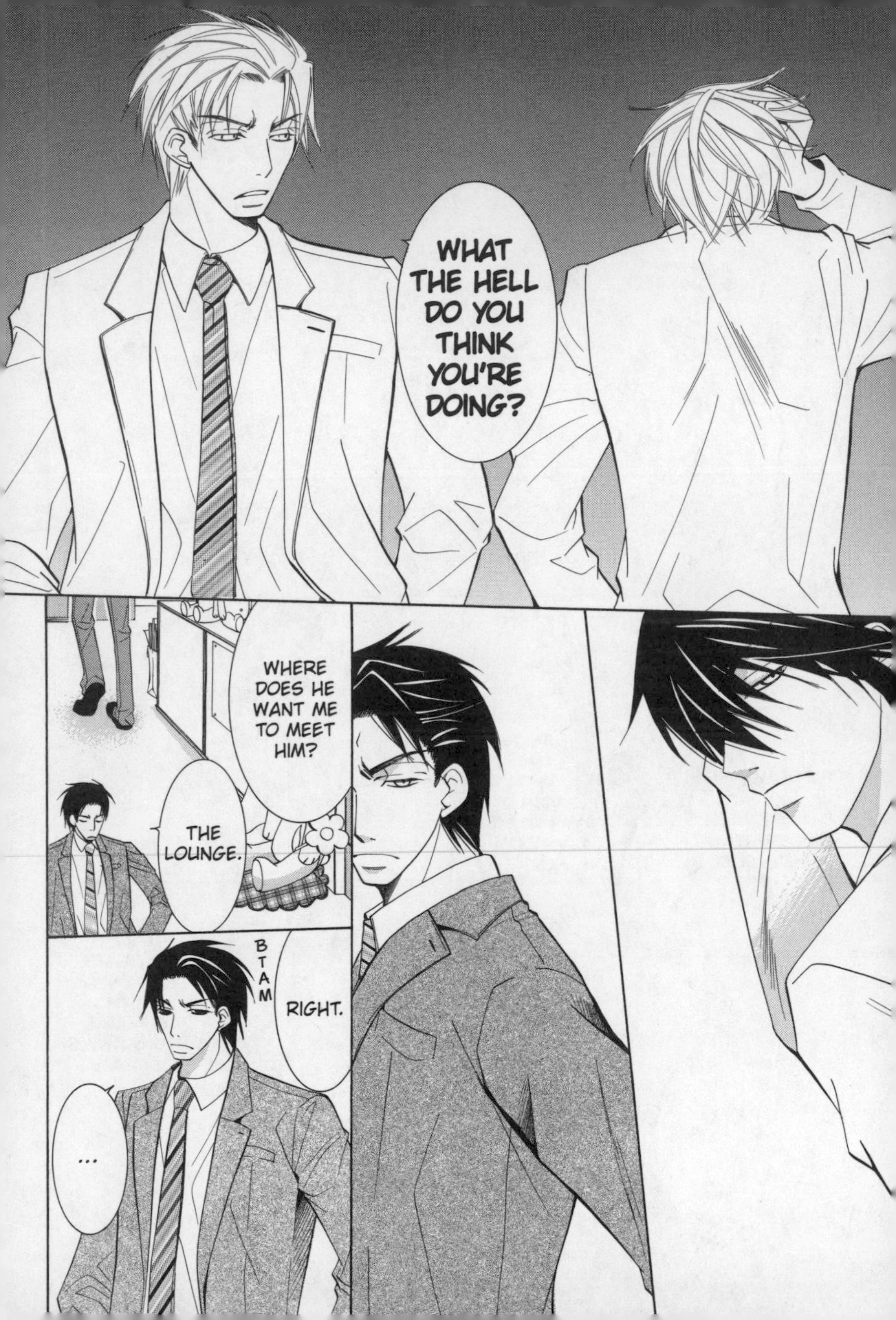
WHAT THE HELL DO YOU THINK YOU'RE DOING?
WHERE DOES HE WANT ME TO MEET HIM?
THE LOUNGE.
BTAM
RIGHT.
...

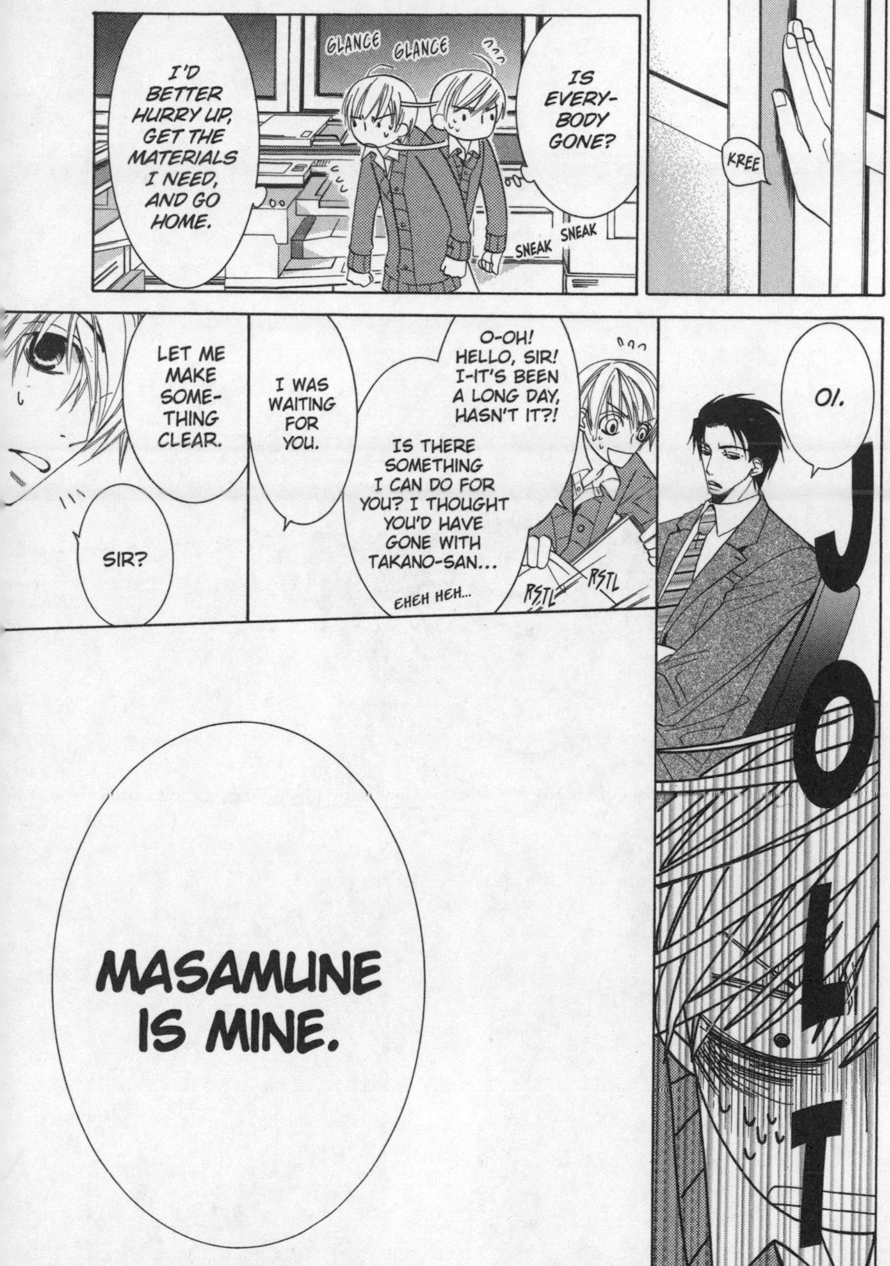
KREE
IS EVERY-BODY GONE?
GLANCE GLANCE
I'D BETTER HURRY UP, GET THE MATERIALS I NEED, AND GO HOME.
SNEAK SNEAK
OI.
JOLT
O-OH! HELLO, SIR! I-IT'S BEEN A LONG DAY, HASN'T IT?!
IS THERE SOMETHING I CAN DO FOR YOU? I THOUGHT YOU'D HAVE GONE WITH TAKANO-SAN...
EHEH HEH...
RSTL RSTL
I WAS WAITING FOR YOU.
LET ME MAKE SOME-THING CLEAR.
SIR?
MASAMUNE IS MINE.

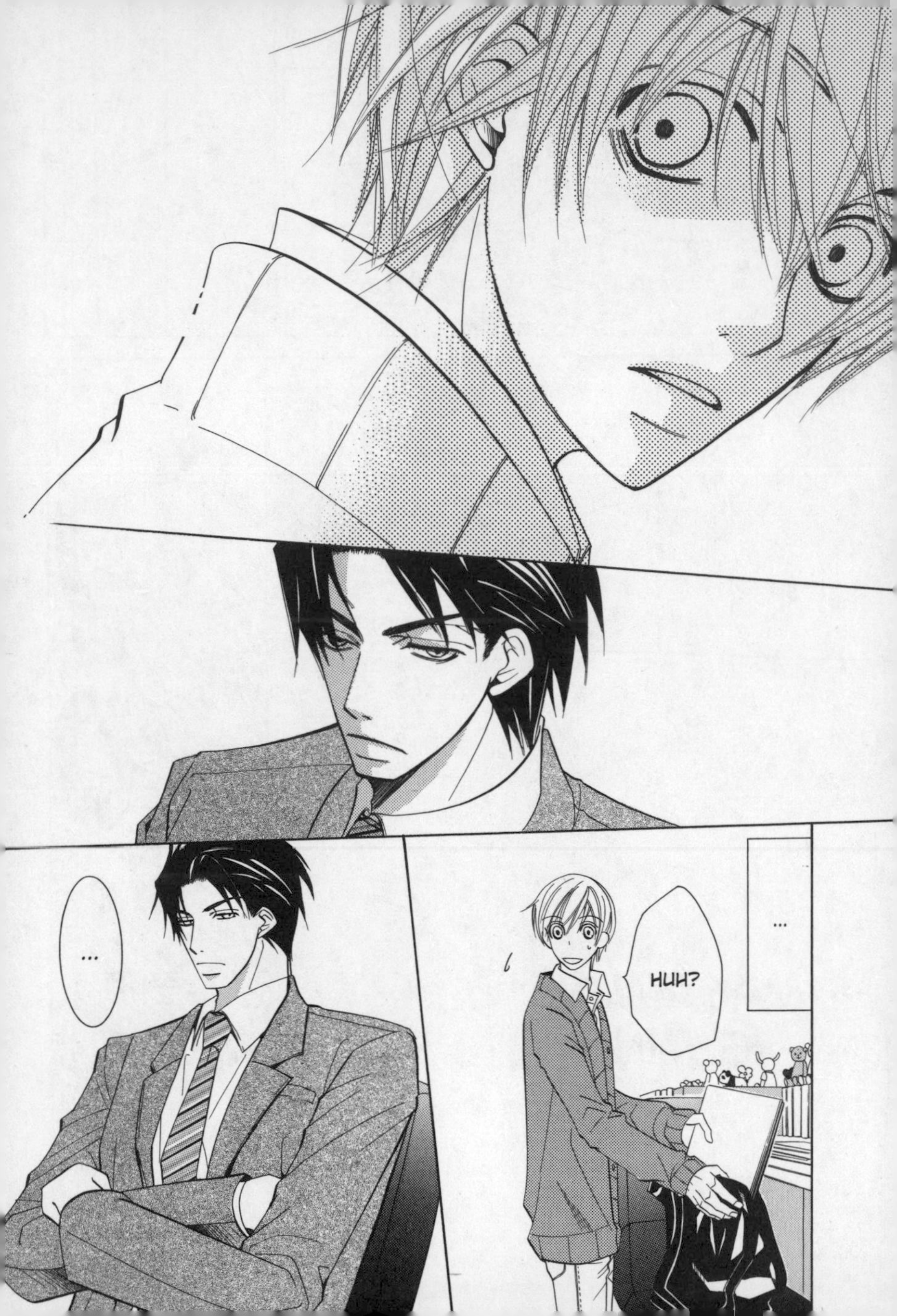
...
HUH?
...

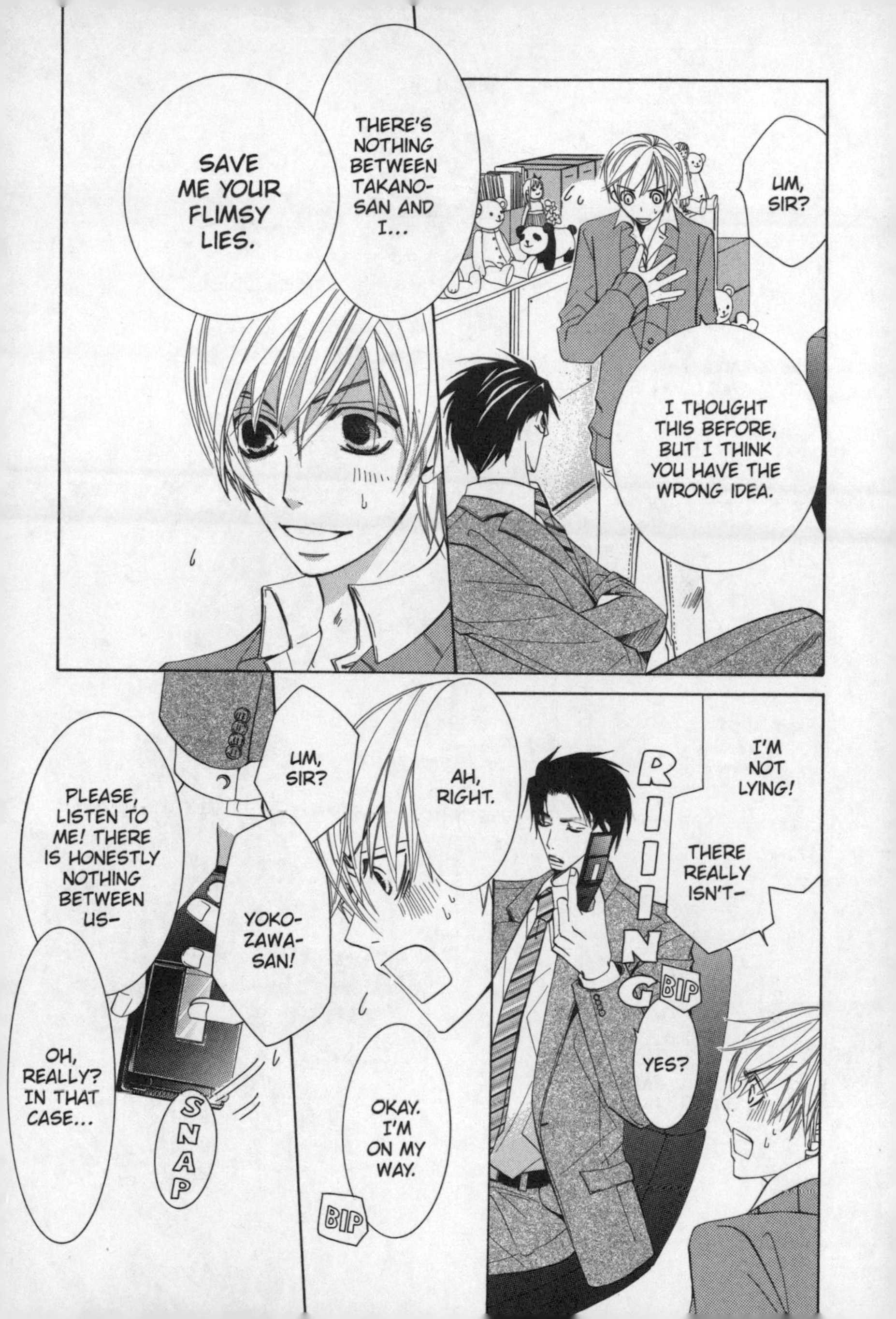
UM, SIR?
I THOUGHT THIS BEFORE, BUT I THINK YOU HAVE THE WRONG IDEA.
THERE'S NOTHING BETWEEN TAKANO-SAN AND I...
SAVE ME YOUR FLIMSY LIES.
I'M NOT LYING!
THERE REALLY ISN'T-
RIIIING
BIP
YES?
AH, RIGHT.
UM, SIR?
OKAY. I'M ON MY WAY.
BIP
PLEASE, LISTEN TO ME! THERE IS HONESTLY NOTHING BETWEEN US-
YOKO-ZAWA-SAN!
SNAP
OH, REALLY? IN THAT CASE...

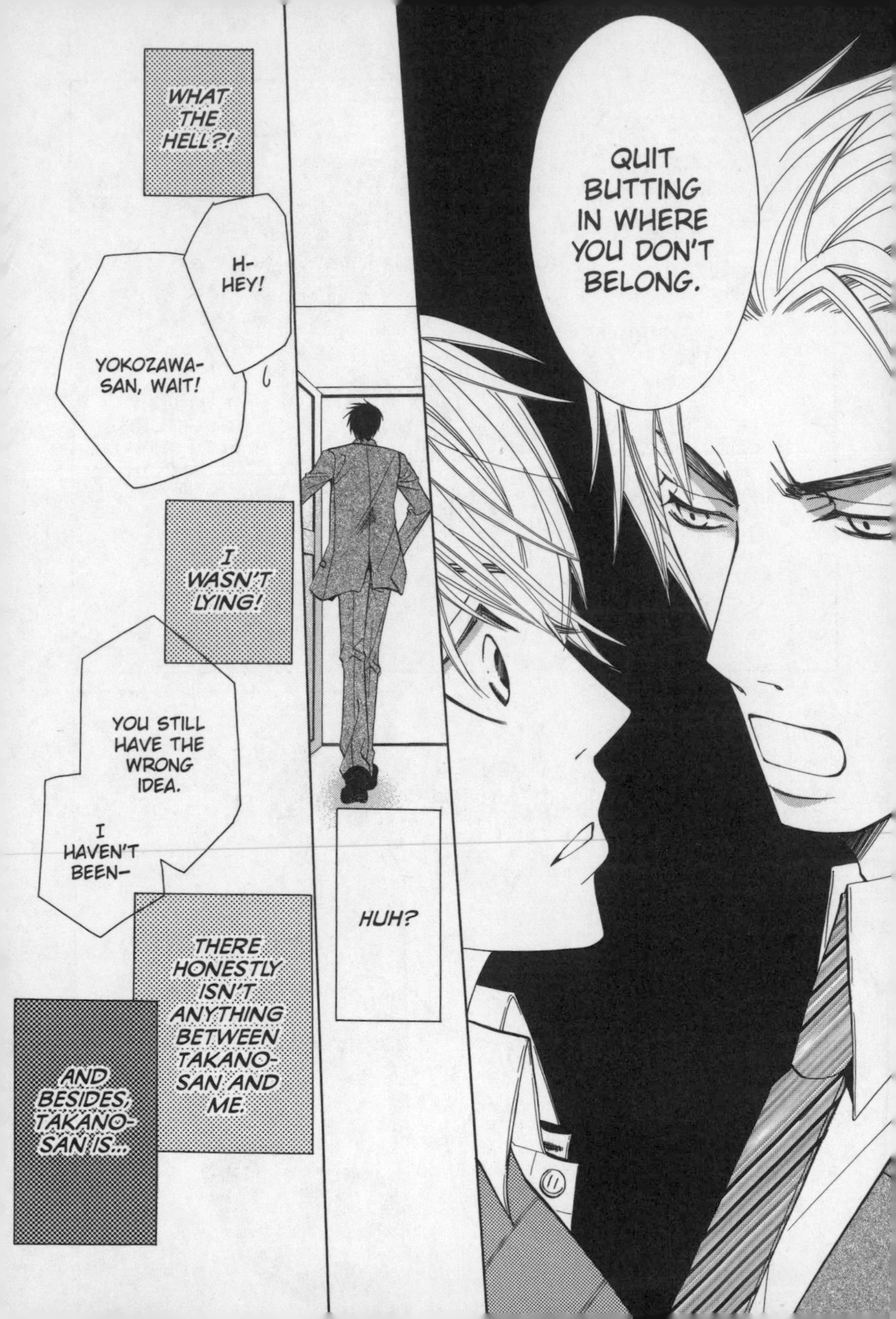
QUIT BUTTING IN WHERE YOU DON'T BELONG.
HUH?
WHAT THE HELL?!
H-HEY!
YOKOZAWA-SAN, WAIT!
I WASN'T LYING!
YOU STILL HAVE THE WRONG IDEA.
I HAVEN'T BEEN-
THERE HONESTLY ISN'T ANYTHING BETWEEN TAKANO-SAN AND ME.
AND BESIDES, TAKANO-SAN IS...

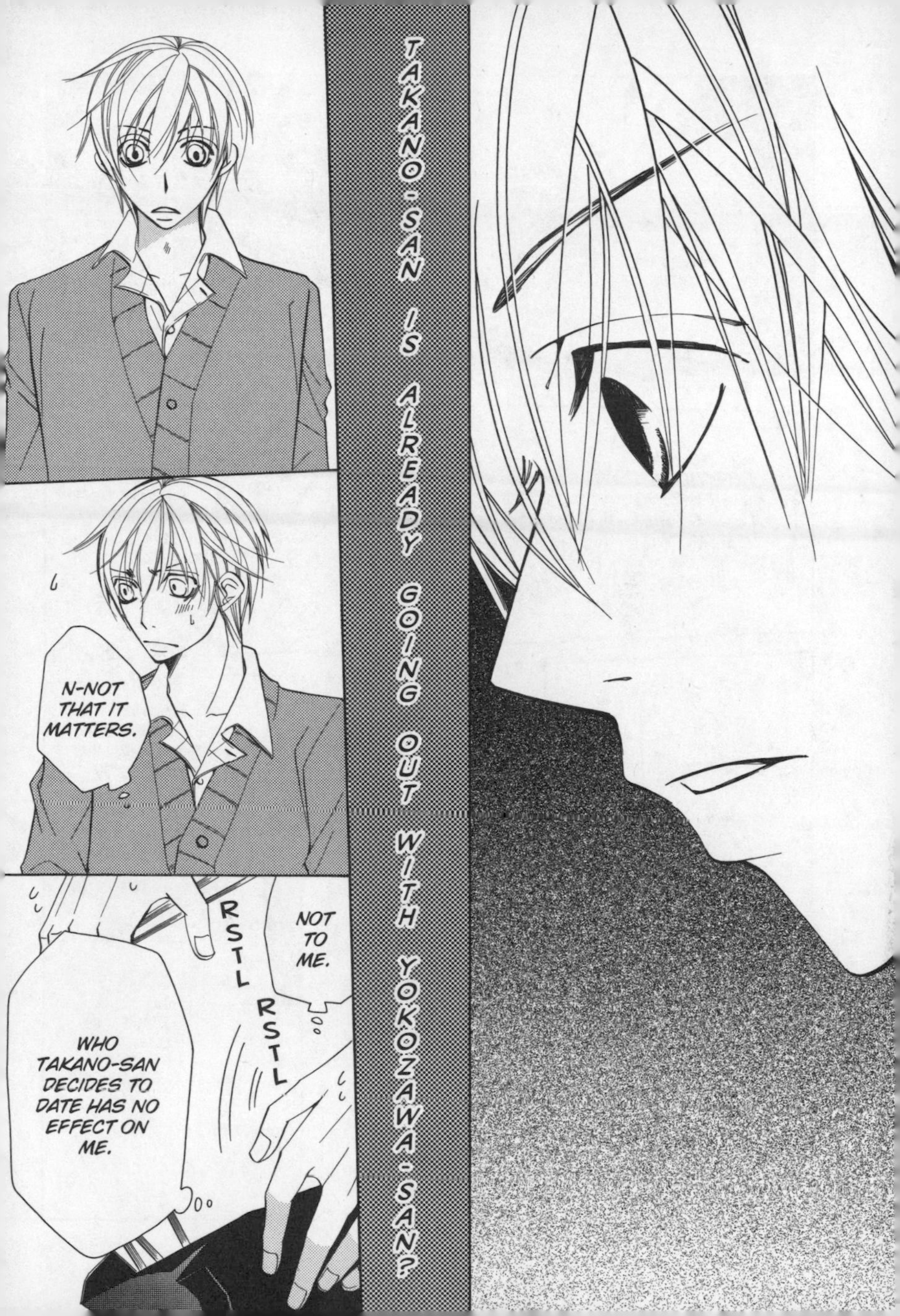
TAKANO-SAN IS ALREADY GOING OUT WITH YOKOZAWA-SAN?
N-NOT THAT IT MATTERS.
NOT TO ME.
RSTL RSTL
WHO TAKANO-SAN DECIDES TO DATE HAS NO EFFECT ON ME.

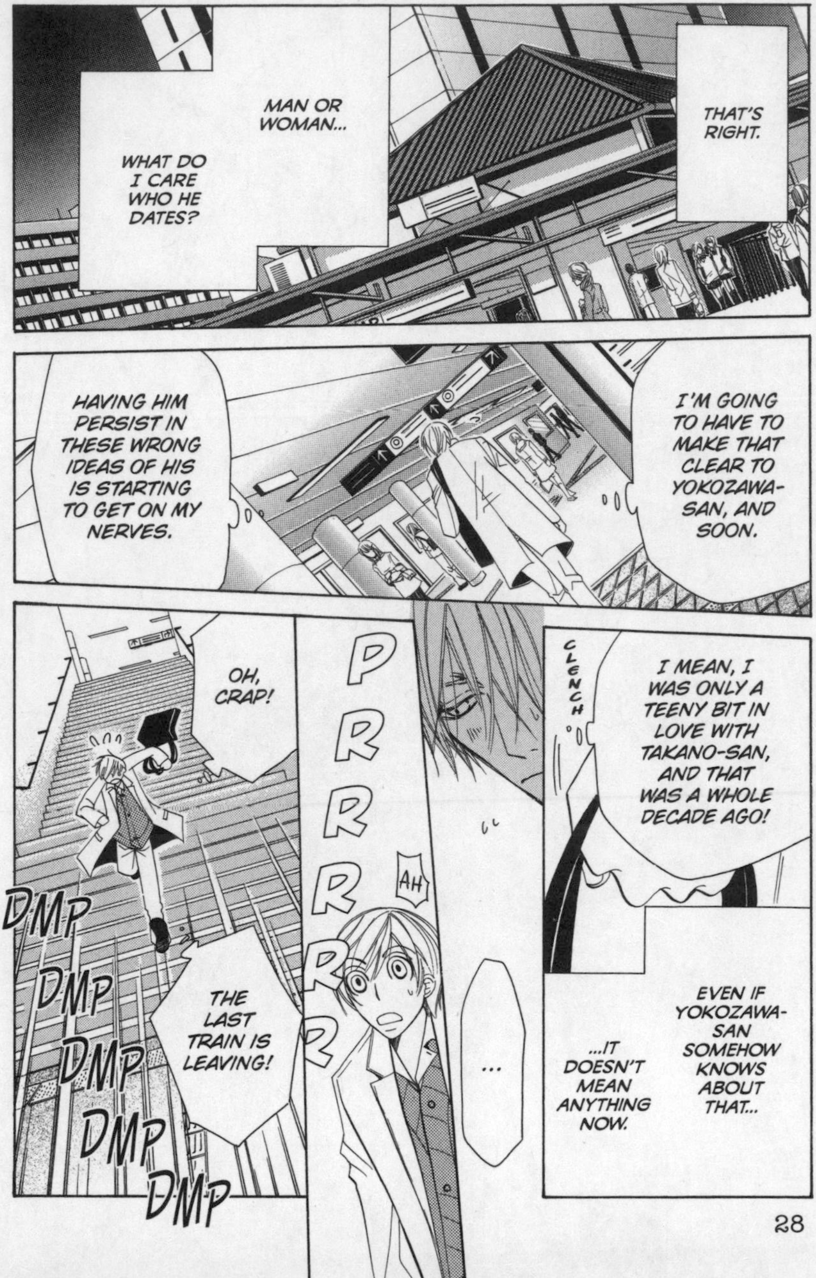
THAT'S RIGHT.
MAN OR WOMAN...
WHAT DO I CARE WHO HE DATES?
I'M GOING TO HAVE TO MAKE THAT CLEAR TO YOKOZAWA-SAN, AND SOON.
HAVING HIM PERSIST IN THESE WRONG IDEAS OF HIS IS STARTING TO GET ON MY NERVES.
CLENCH
I MEAN, I WAS ONLY A TEENY BIT IN LOVE WITH TAKANO-SAN, AND THAT WAS A WHOLE DECADE AGO!
EVEN IF YOKOZAWA-SAN SOMEHOW KNOWS ABOUT THAT...
...IT DOESN'T MEAN ANYTHING NOW.
...
AH
PRRRRR
OH, CRAP!
THE LAST TRAIN IS LEAVING!
DMP
DMP
DMP
DMP
DMP

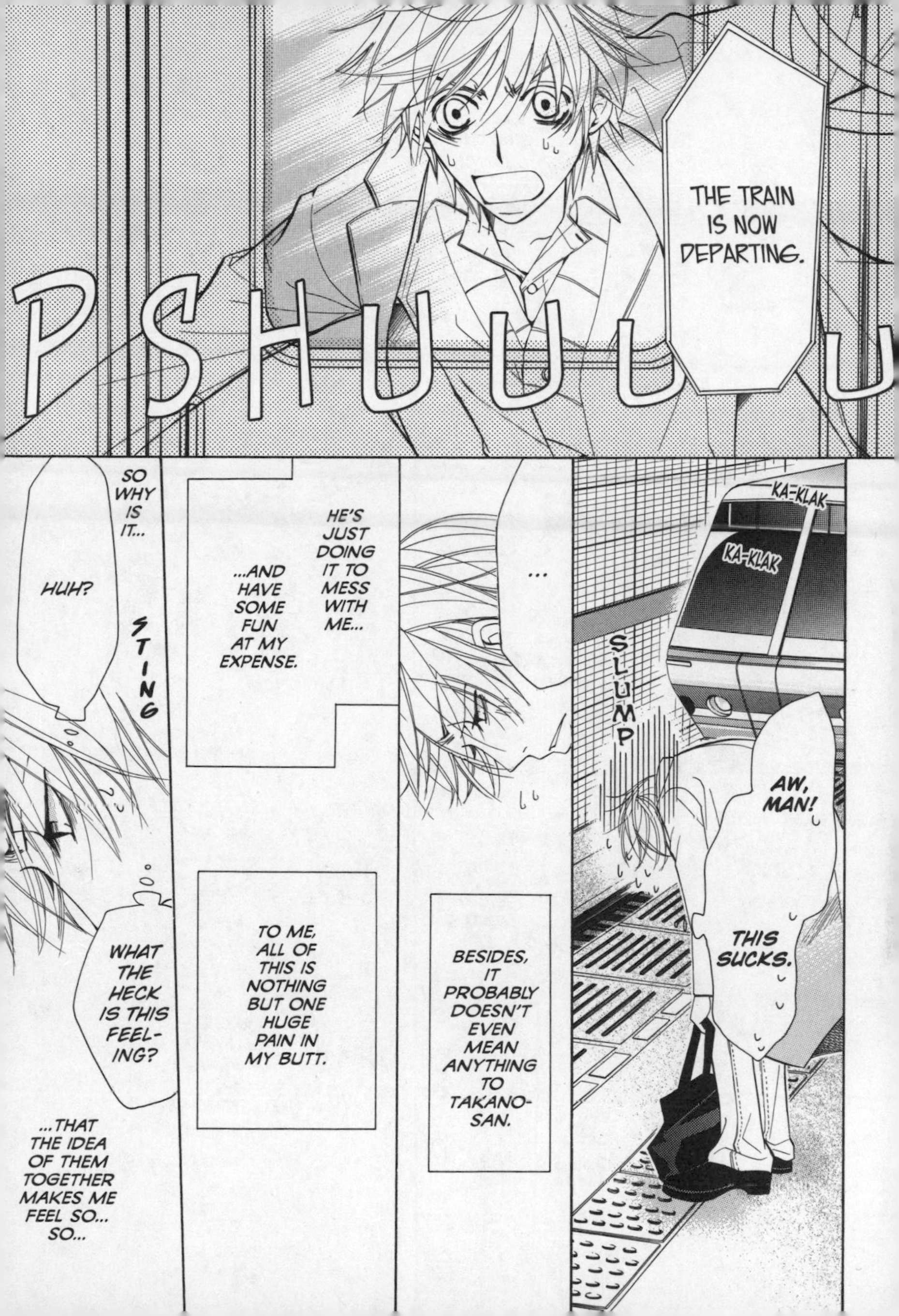
THE TRAIN IS NOW DEPARTING.
PSHUUUU
KA-KLAK
KA-KLAK
SLUMP
AW, MAN!
THIS SUCKS.
...
BESIDES, IT PROBABLY DOESN'T EVEN MEAN ANYTHING TO TAKANO-SAN.
HE'S JUST DOING IT TO MESS WITH ME...
...AND HAVE SOME FUN AT MY EXPENSE.
TO ME, ALL OF THIS IS NOTHING BUT ONE HUGE PAIN IN MY BUTT.
SO WHY IS IT...
...THAT THE IDEA OF THEM TOGETHER MAKES ME FEEL SO... SO...
HUH?
STING
WHAT THE HECK IS THIS FEEL-ING?

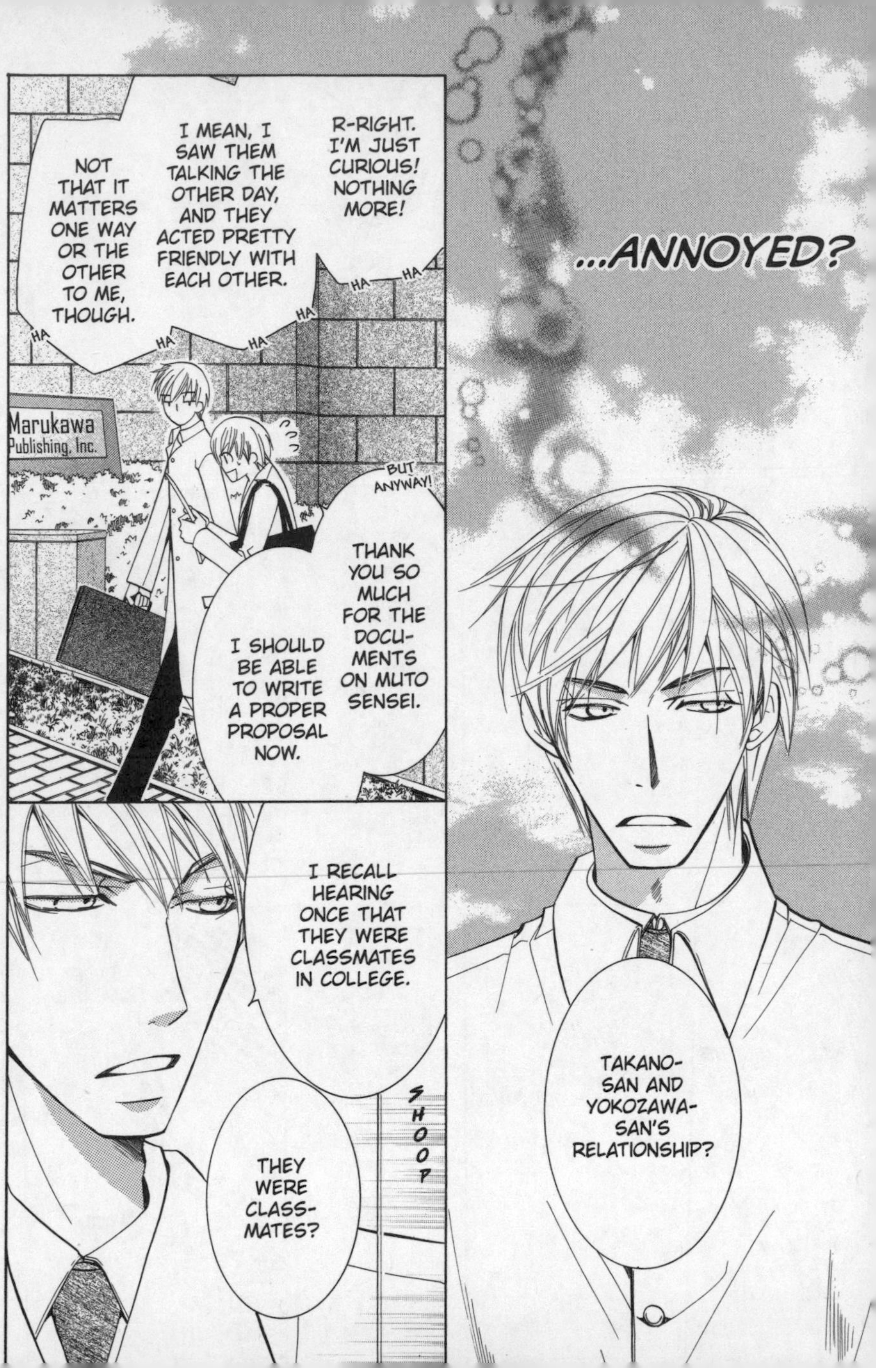
...ANNOYED?
TAKANO-SAN AND YOKOZAWA-SAN'S RELATIONSHIP?
R-RIGHT. I'M JUST CURIOUS! NOTHING MORE!
I MEAN, I SAW THEM TALKING THE OTHER DAY, AND THEY ACTED PRETTY FRIENDLY WITH EACH OTHER.
NOT THAT IT MATTERS ONE WAY OR THE OTHER TO ME, THOUGH.
HA HA HA HA HA HA
Marukawa Publishing, Inc.
BUT ANYWAY!
THANK YOU SO MUCH FOR THE DOCUMENTS ON MUTO SENSEI.
I SHOULD BE ABLE TO WRITE A PROPER PROPOSAL NOW.
I RECALL HEARING ONCE THAT THEY WERE CLASSMATES IN COLLEGE.
SHOOP
THEY WERE CLASSMATES?

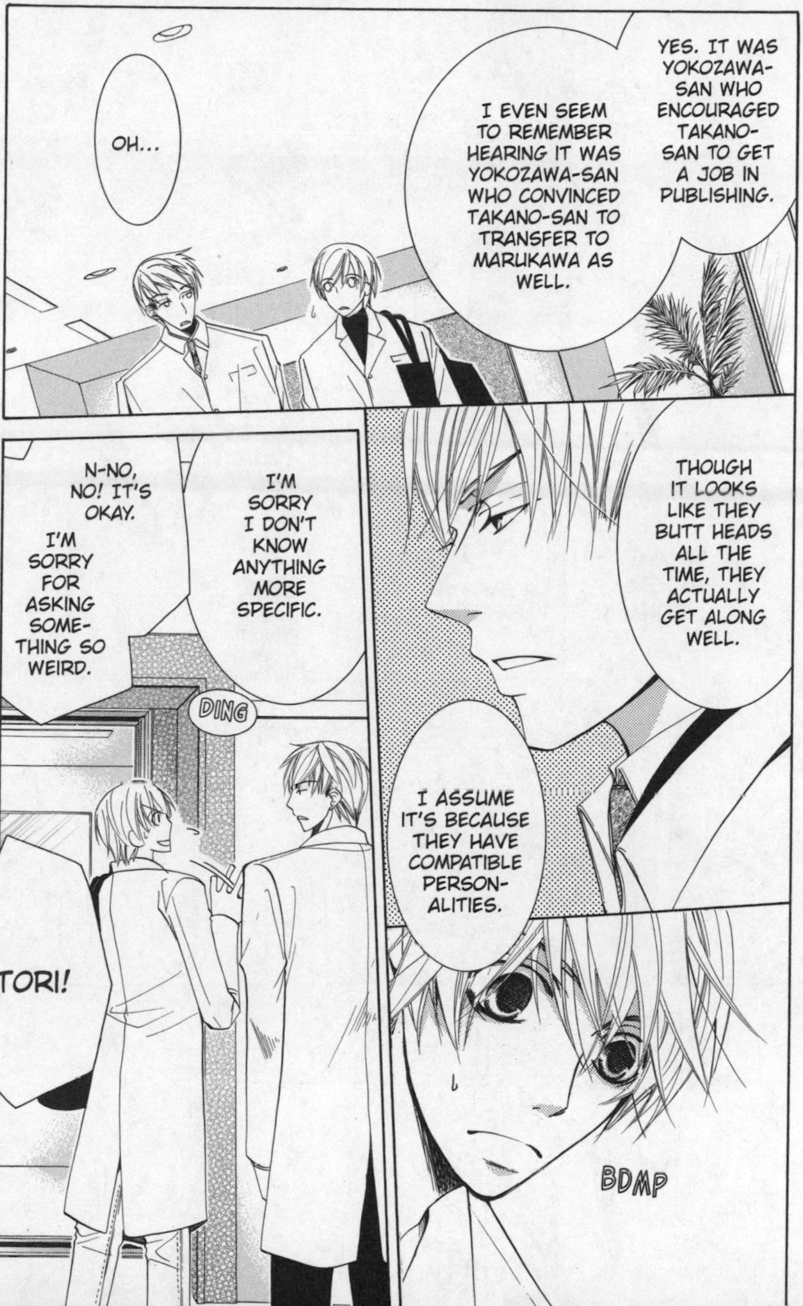
YES. IT WAS YOKOZAWA-SAN WHO ENCOURAGED TAKANO-SAN TO GET A JOB IN PUBLISHING.
I EVEN SEEM TO REMEMBER HEARING IT WAS YOKOZAWA-SAN WHO CONVINCED TAKANO-SAN TO TRANSFER TO MARUKAWA AS WELL.
OH...
THOUGH IT LOOKS LIKE THEY BUTT HEADS ALL THE TIME, THEY ACTUALLY GET ALONG WELL.
I ASSUME IT'S BECAUSE THEY HAVE COMPATIBLE PERSON-ALITIES.
I'M SORRY I DON'T KNOW ANYTHING MORE SPECIFIC.
N-NO, NO! IT'S OKAY.
I'M SORRY FOR ASKING SOME-THING SO WEIRD.
DING
TORI!
BDMP

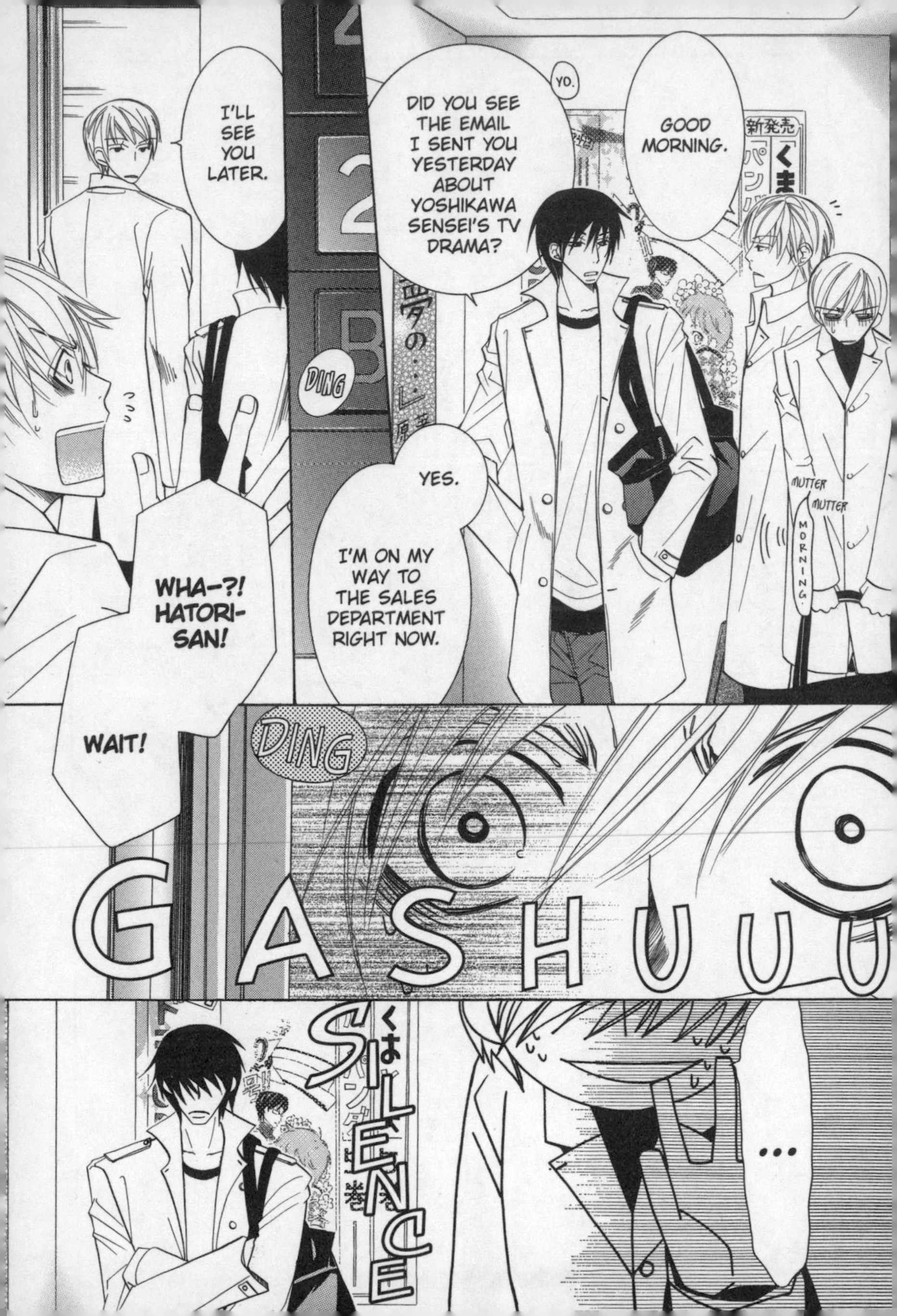
新発売
GOOD MORNING.
YO.
DID YOU SEE THE EMAIL I SENT YOU YESTERDAY ABOUT YOSHIKAWA SENSEI'S TV DRAMA?
MUTTER
MUTTER
MORNING.
DING
YES.
I'M ON MY WAY TO THE SALES DEPARTMENT RIGHT NOW.
I'LL SEE YOU LATER.
WHA-?! HATORI-SAN!
WAIT!
DING
GASHUUU
...
SILENCE

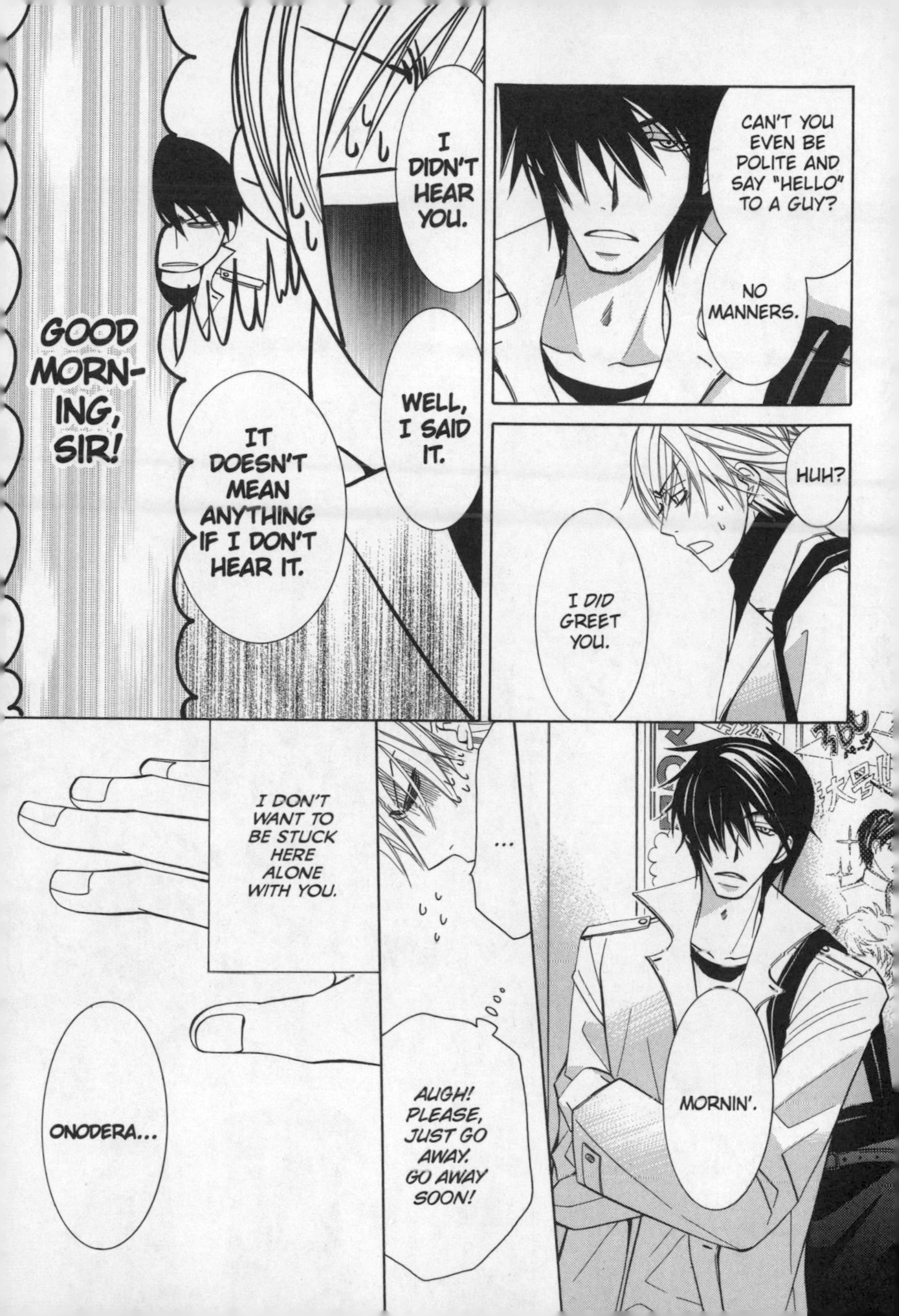
CAN'T YOU EVEN BE POLITE AND SAY "HELLO" TO A GUY?
NO MANNERS.
HUH?
I *DID* GREET YOU.
I DIDN'T HEAR YOU.
WELL, I SAID IT.
IT DOESN'T MEAN ANYTHING IF I DON'T HEAR IT.
GOOD MORNING, SIR!
MORNIN'.
...
AUGH! PLEASE, JUST GO AWAY. GO AWAY SOON!
I DON'T WANT TO BE STUCK HERE ALONE WITH YOU.
ONODERA...

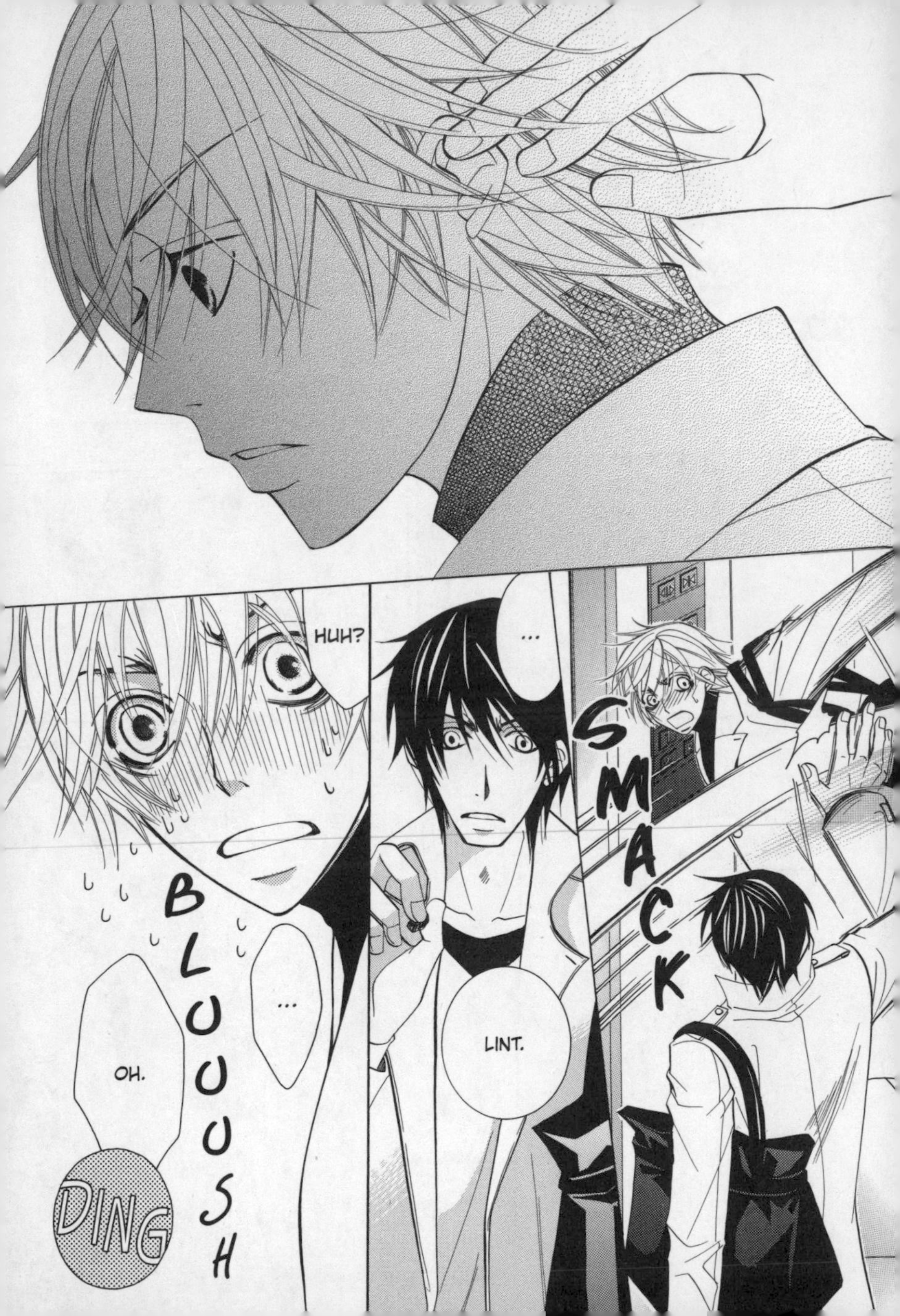
SMACK
...
LINT.
HUH?
...
OH.
BLUUUSH
DING

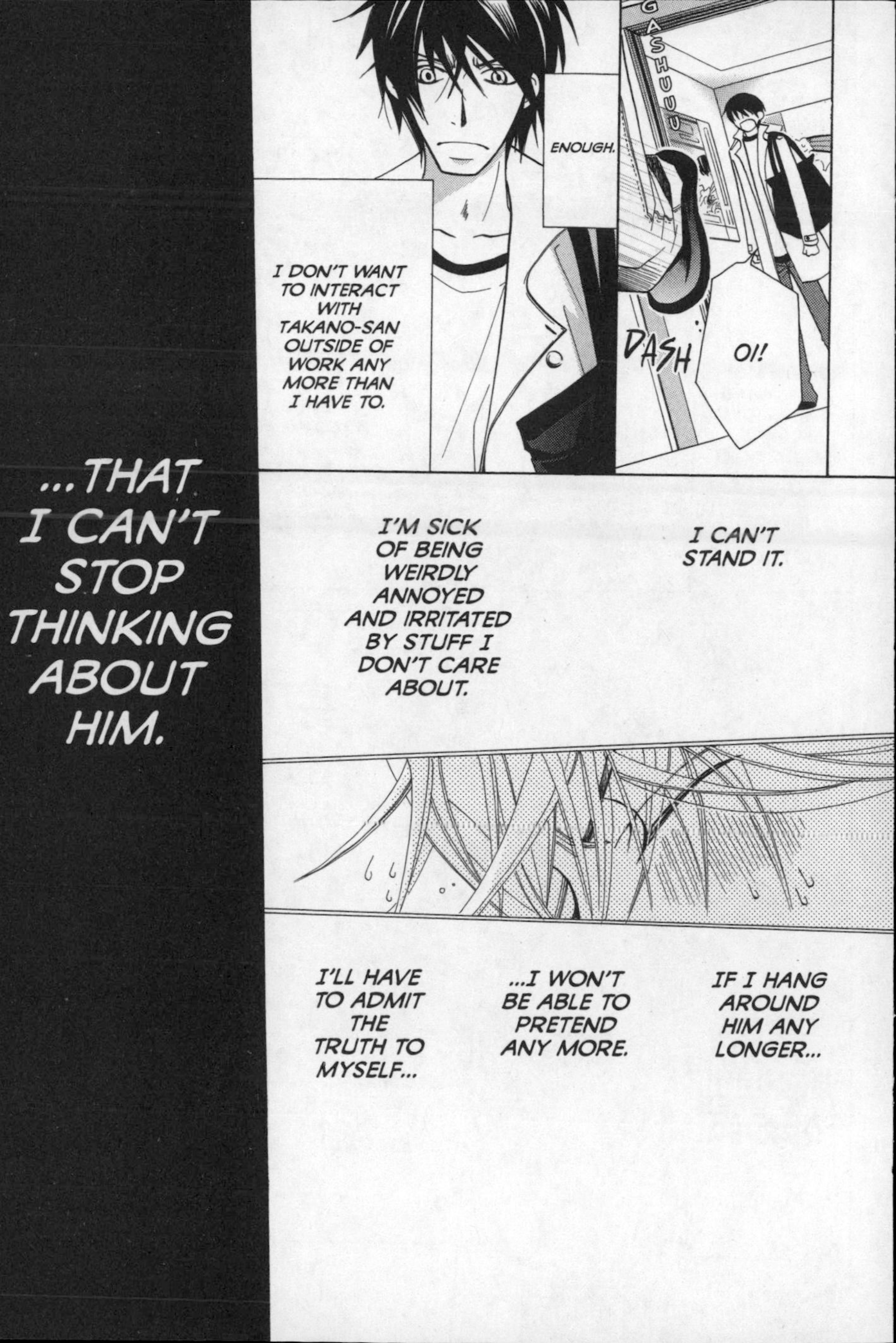
GASHUUU
OI!
DASH
ENOUGH.
I DON'T WANT TO INTERACT WITH TAKANO-SAN OUTSIDE OF WORK ANY MORE THAN I HAVE TO.
I CAN'T STAND IT.
I'M SICK OF BEING WEIRDLY ANNOYED AND IRRITATED BY STUFF I DON'T CARE ABOUT.
IF I HANG AROUND HIM ANY LONGER...
...I WON'T BE ABLE TO PRETEND ANY MORE.
I'LL HAVE TO ADMIT THE TRUTH TO MYSELF...
...THAT I CAN'T STOP THINKING ABOUT HIM.

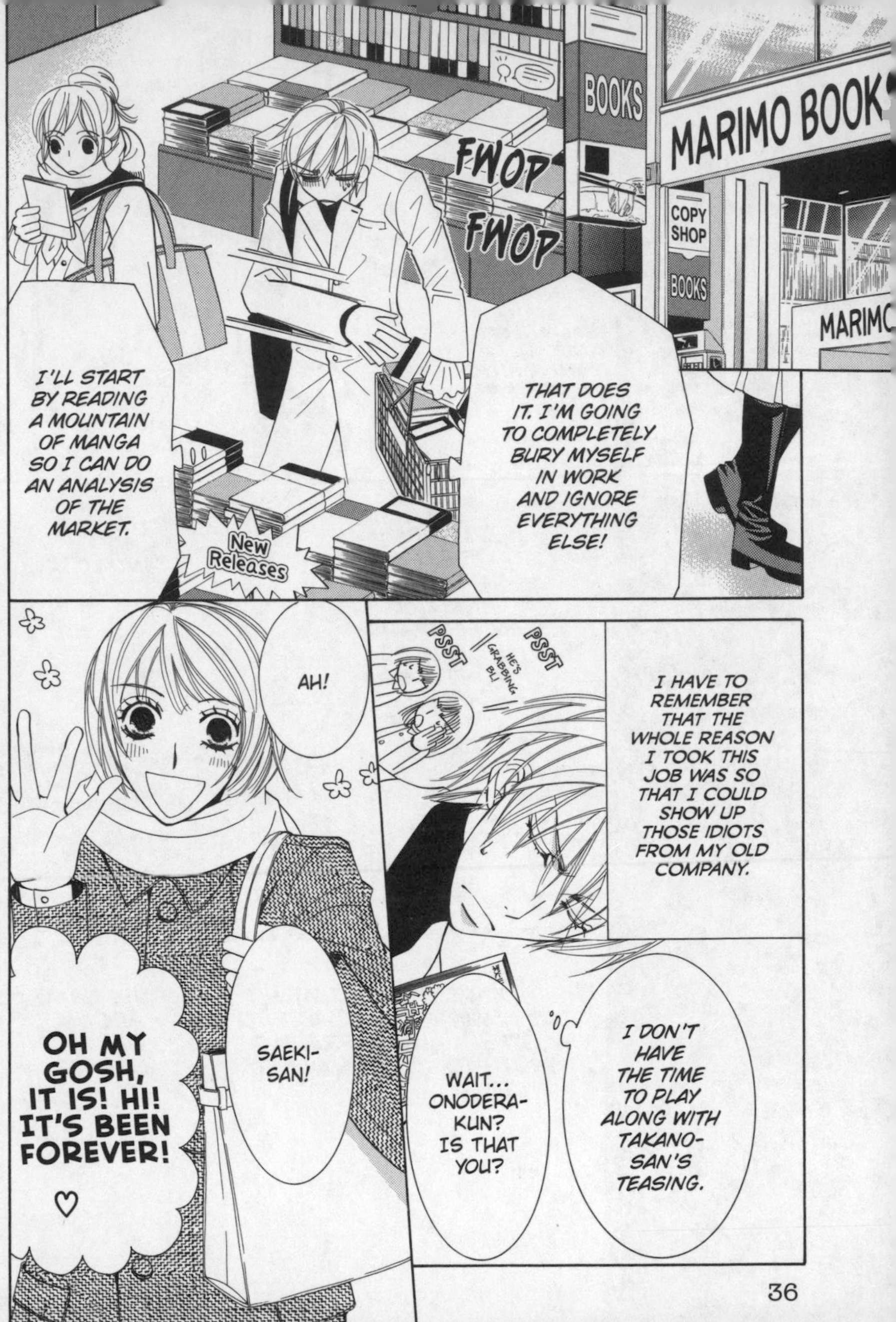
MARIMO BOOKS
BOOKS
COPY SHOP
BOOKS
MARIMO
FWOP
FWOP
THAT DOES IT. I'M GOING TO COMPLETELY BURY MYSELF IN WORK AND IGNORE EVERYTHING ELSE!
I'LL START BY READING A MOUNTAIN OF MANGA SO I CAN DO AN ANALYSIS OF THE MARKET.
New Releases
I HAVE TO REMEMBER THAT THE WHOLE REASON I TOOK THIS JOB WAS SO THAT I COULD SHOW UP THOSE IDIOTS FROM MY OLD COMPANY.
PSST
HE'S GRABBING BL!
PSST
I DON'T HAVE THE TIME TO PLAY ALONG WITH TAKANO-SAN'S TEASING.
WAIT... ONODERA-KUN? IS THAT YOU?
AH!
SAEKI-SAN!
OH MY GOSH, IT IS! HI! IT'S BEEN FOREVER! ♡

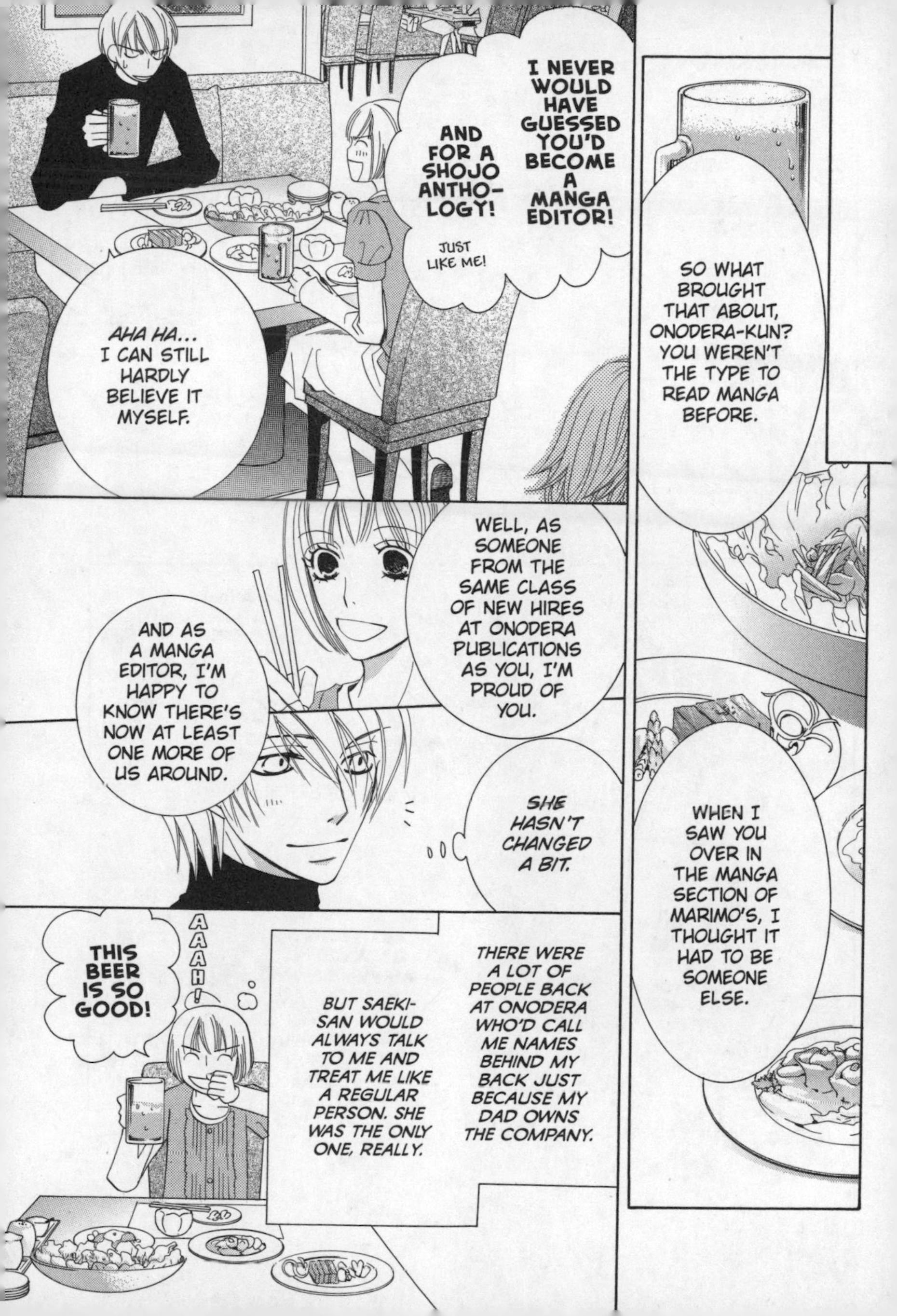
I NEVER WOULD HAVE GUESSED YOU'D BECOME A MANGA EDITOR!
AND FOR A SHOJO ANTHOLOGY!
JUST LIKE ME!
AHA HA... I CAN STILL HARDLY BELIEVE IT MYSELF.
SO WHAT BROUGHT THAT ABOUT, ONODERA-KUN? YOU WEREN'T THE TYPE TO READ MANGA BEFORE.
WHEN I SAW YOU OVER IN THE MANGA SECTION OF MARIMO'S, I THOUGHT IT HAD TO BE SOMEONE ELSE.
WELL, AS SOMEONE FROM THE SAME CLASS OF NEW HIRES AT ONODERA PUBLICATIONS AS YOU, I'M PROUD OF YOU.
AND AS A MANGA EDITOR, I'M HAPPY TO KNOW THERE'S NOW AT LEAST ONE MORE OF US AROUND.
SHE HASN'T CHANGED A BIT.
THERE WERE A LOT OF PEOPLE BACK AT ONODERA WHO'D CALL ME NAMES BEHIND MY BACK JUST BECAUSE MY DAD OWNS THE COMPANY.
BUT SAEKI-SAN WOULD ALWAYS TALK TO ME AND TREAT ME LIKE A REGULAR PERSON. SHE WAS THE ONLY ONE, REALLY.
AAAAH!
THIS BEER IS SO GOOD!

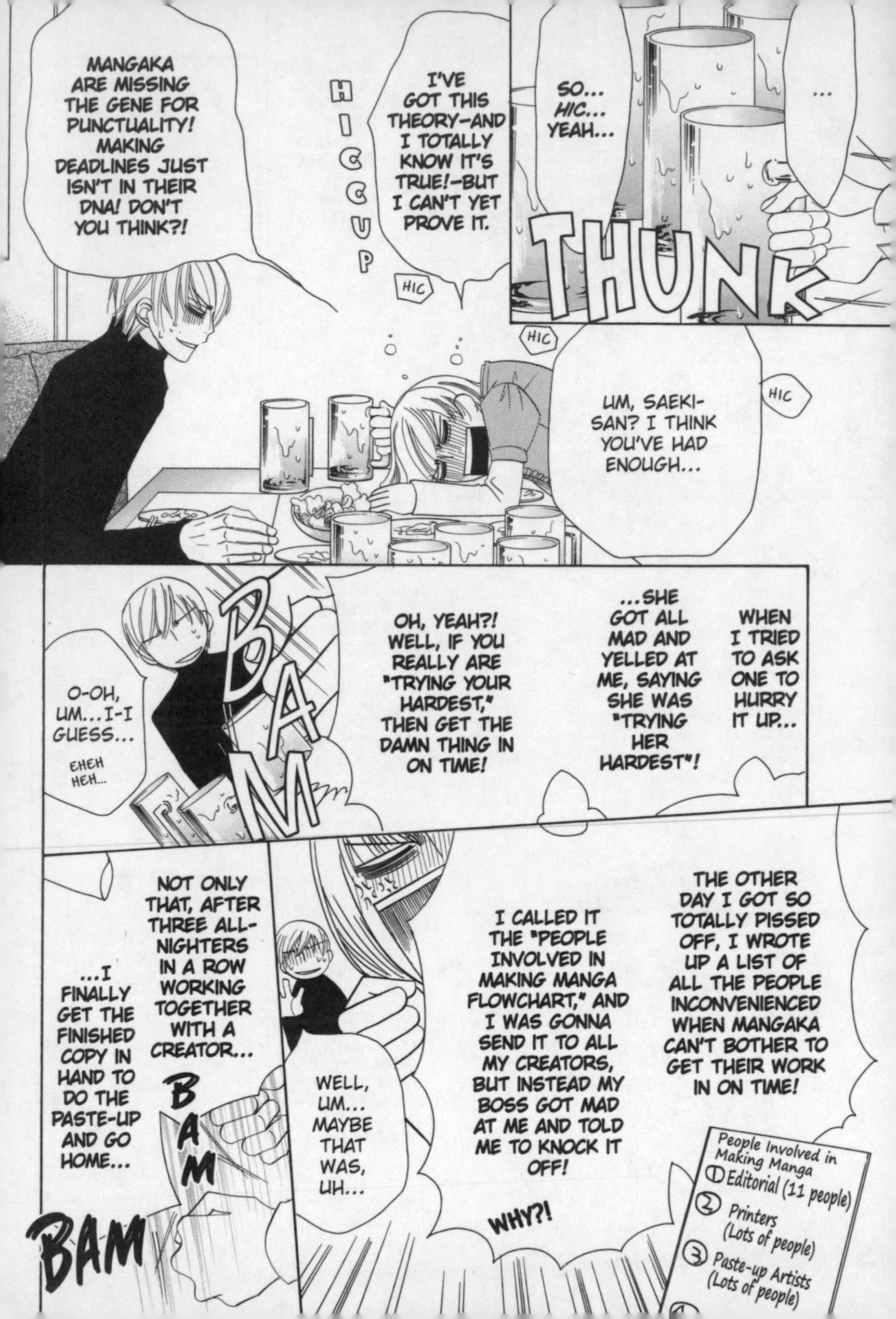
...
SO... HIC... YEAH...
THUNK
I'VE GOT THIS THEORY—AND I TOTALLY KNOW IT'S TRUE!—BUT I CAN'T YET PROVE IT.
HICCUP
HIC
MANGAKA ARE MISSING THE GENE FOR PUNCTUALITY! MAKING DEADLINES JUST ISN'T IN THEIR DNA! DON'T YOU THINK?!
HIC
HIC
UM, SAEKI-SAN? I THINK YOU'VE HAD ENOUGH...
WHEN I TRIED TO ASK ONE TO HURRY IT UP...
...SHE GOT ALL MAD AND YELLED AT ME, SAYING SHE WAS "TRYING HER HARDEST"!
OH, YEAH?! WELL, IF YOU REALLY ARE "TRYING YOUR HARDEST," THEN GET THE DAMN THING IN ON TIME!
BAM
O-OH, UM...I-I GUESS...
EHEH HEH...
THE OTHER DAY I GOT SO TOTALLY PISSED OFF, I WROTE UP A LIST OF ALL THE PEOPLE INCONVENIENCED WHEN MANGAKA CAN'T BOTHER TO GET THEIR WORK IN ON TIME!
People Involved in Making Manga
① Editorial (11 people)
② Printers (Lots of people)
③ Paste-up Artists (Lots of people)
I CALLED IT THE "PEOPLE INVOLVED IN MAKING MANGA FLOWCHART," AND I WAS GONNA SEND IT TO ALL MY CREATORS, BUT INSTEAD MY BOSS GOT MAD AT ME AND TOLD ME TO KNOCK IT OFF!
WHY?!
WELL, UM... MAYBE THAT WAS, UH...
NOT ONLY THAT, AFTER THREE ALL-NIGHTERS IN A ROW WORKING TOGETHER WITH A CREATOR...
...I FINALLY GET THE FINISHED COPY IN HAND TO DO THE PASTE-UP AND GO HOME...
BAM
BAM

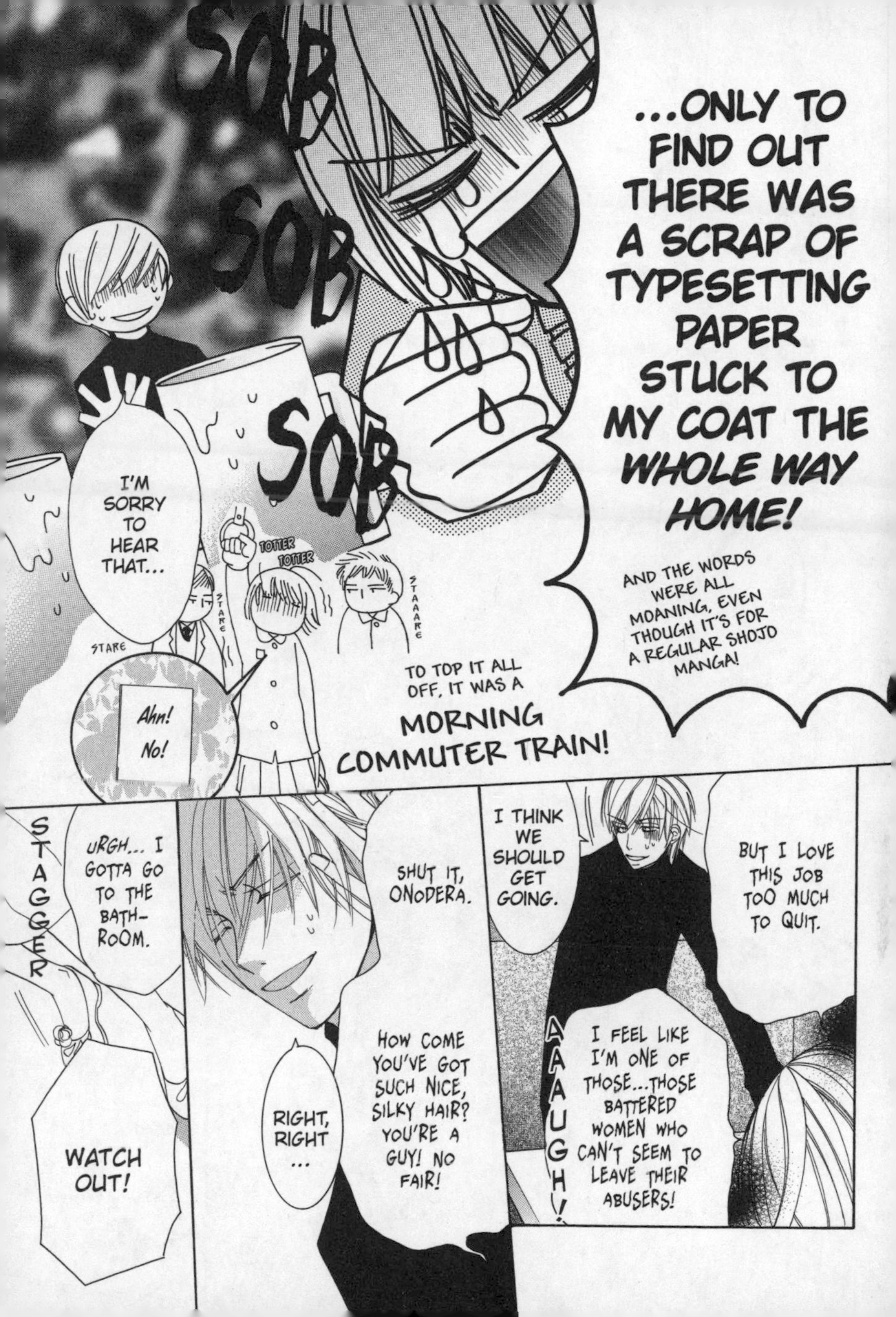
...ONLY TO FIND OUT THERE WAS A SCRAP OF TYPESETTING PAPER STUCK TO MY COAT THE *WHOLE WAY HOME!*
AND THE WORDS WERE ALL MOANING, EVEN THOUGH IT'S FOR A REGULAR SHOJO MANGA!
SOB
SOB
SOB
TO TOP IT ALL OFF, IT WAS A MORNING COMMUTER TRAIN!
TOTTER TOTTER
STAAARE
STARE
I'M SORRY TO HEAR THAT...
STARE
Ahn! No!
BUT I LOVE THIS JOB TOO MUCH TO QUIT.
I THINK WE SHOULD GET GOING.
I FEEL LIKE I'M ONE OF THOSE...THOSE BATTERED WOMEN WHO CAN'T SEEM TO LEAVE THEIR ABUSERS!
AAAUGH!
SHUT IT, ONODERA.
HOW COME YOU'VE GOT SUCH NICE, SILKY HAIR? YOU'RE A GUY! NO FAIR!
RIGHT, RIGHT...
URGH... I GOTTA GO TO THE BATH-ROOM.
STAGGER
WATCH OUT!

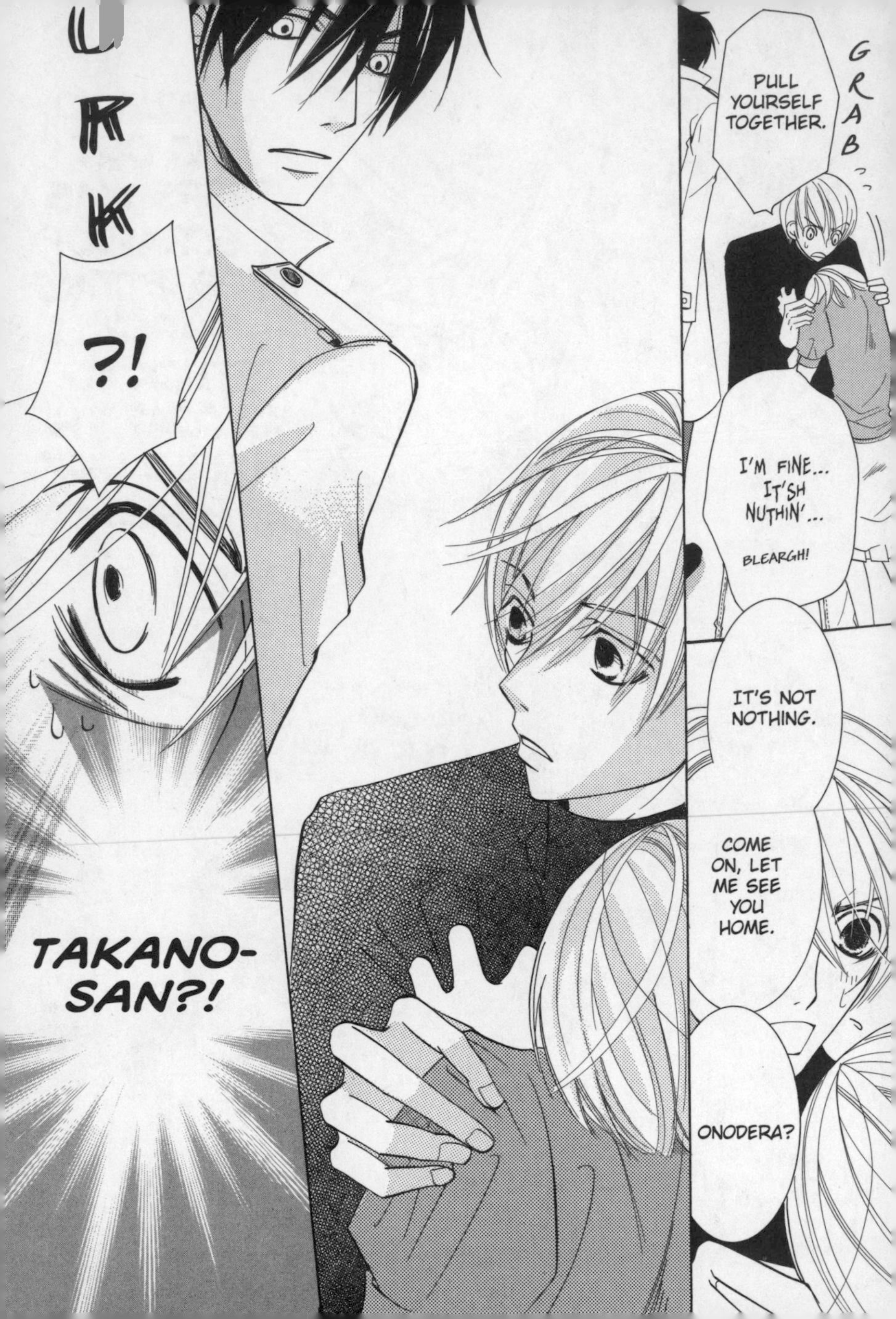
PULL YOURSELF TOGETHER.
GRAB
I'M FINE... IT'SH NUTHIN'...
BLEARGH!
IT'S NOT NOTHING.
COME ON, LET ME SEE YOU HOME.
ONODERA?
URRK
?!
TAKANO-SAN?!

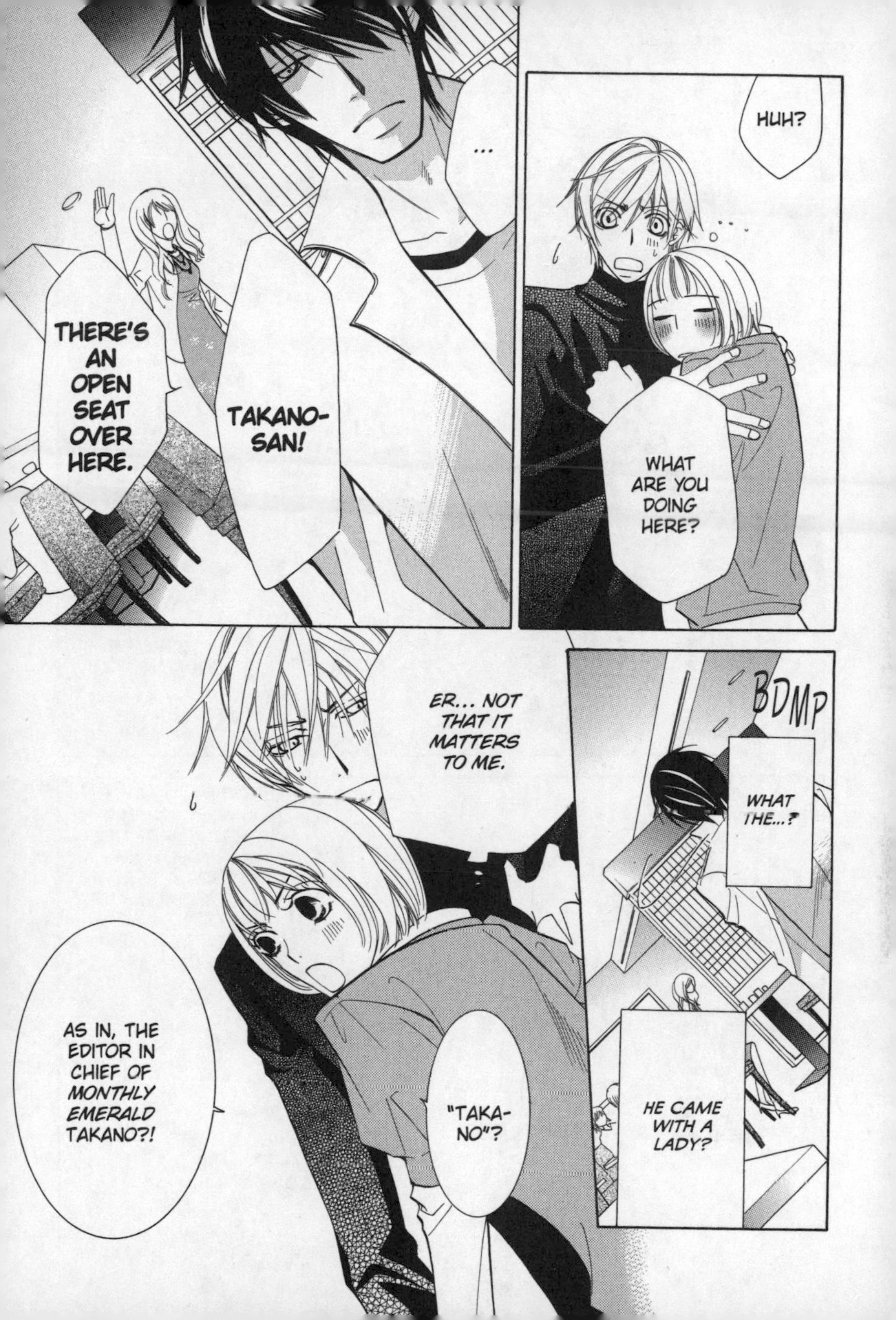
HUH?
WHAT ARE YOU DOING HERE?
...
TAKANO-SAN!
THERE'S AN OPEN SEAT OVER HERE.
BDMP
WHAT THE...?
HE CAME WITH A LADY?
ER... NOT THAT IT MATTERS TO ME.
"TAKA-NO"?
AS IN, THE EDITOR IN CHIEF OF *MONTHLY EMERALD* TAKANO?!

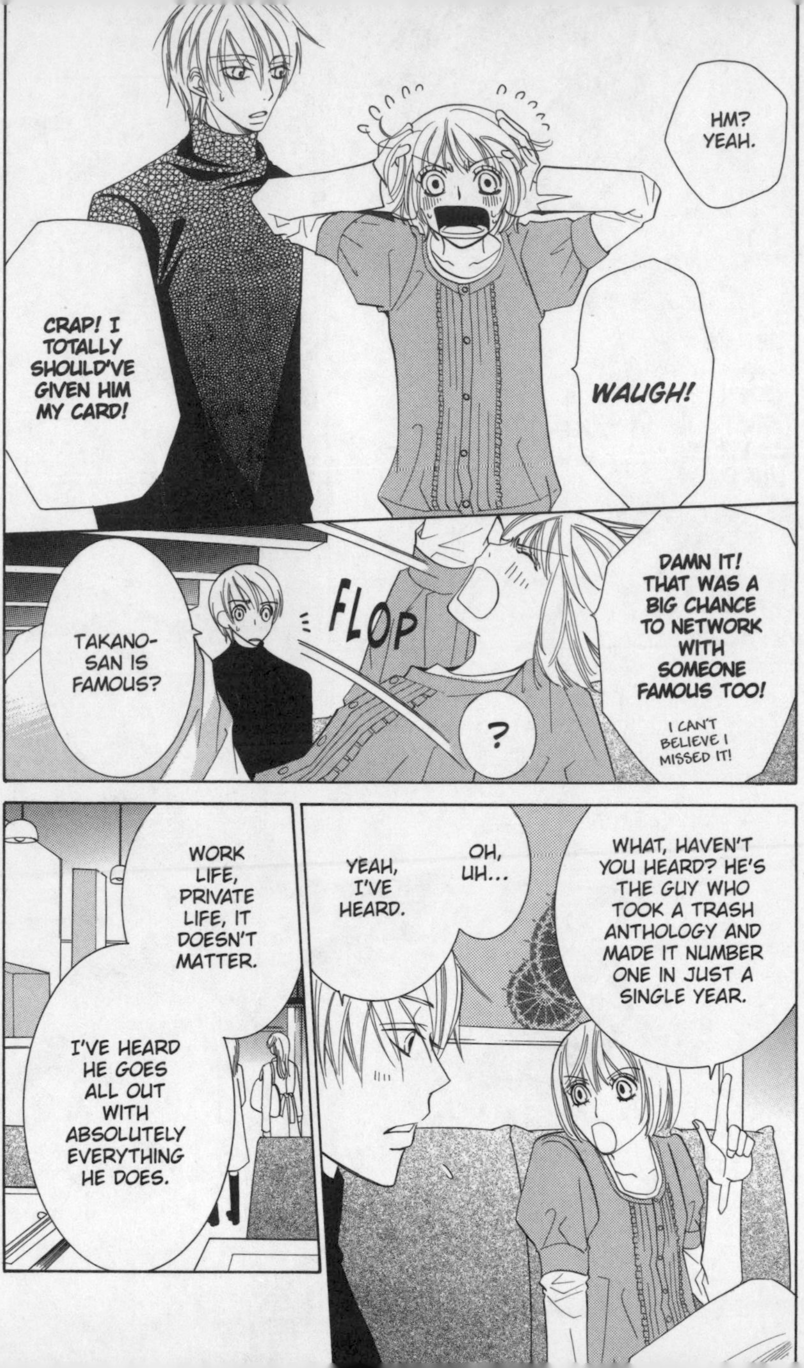
HM? YEAH.
WAUGH!
CRAP! I TOTALLY SHOULD'VE GIVEN HIM MY CARD!
DAMN IT! THAT WAS A BIG CHANCE TO NETWORK WITH SOMEONE FAMOUS TOO!
I CAN'T BELIEVE I MISSED IT!
FLOP
?
TAKANO-SAN IS FAMOUS?
WHAT, HAVEN'T YOU HEARD? HE'S THE GUY WHO TOOK A TRASH ANTHOLOGY AND MADE IT NUMBER ONE IN JUST A SINGLE YEAR.
OH, UH...
YEAH, I'VE HEARD.
WORK LIFE, PRIVATE LIFE, IT DOESN'T MATTER.
I'VE HEARD HE GOES ALL OUT WITH ABSOLUTELY EVERYTHING HE DOES.

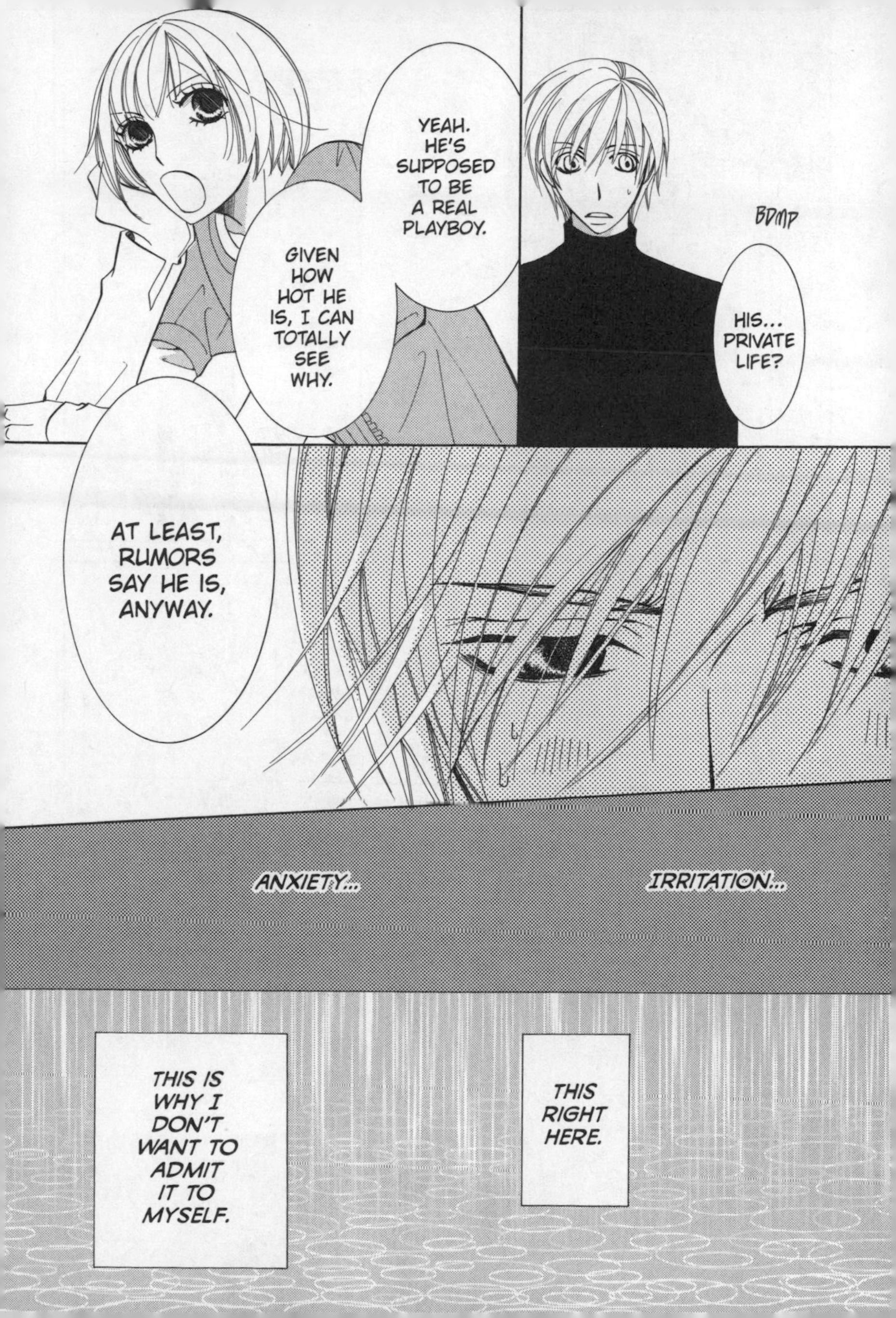
BDMP
HIS... PRIVATE LIFE?
YEAH. HE'S SUPPOSED TO BE A REAL PLAYBOY.
GIVEN HOW HOT HE IS, I CAN TOTALLY SEE WHY.
AT LEAST, RUMORS SAY HE IS, ANYWAY.
IRRITATION...
ANXIETY...
THIS RIGHT HERE.
THIS IS WHY I DON'T WANT TO ADMIT IT TO MYSELF.

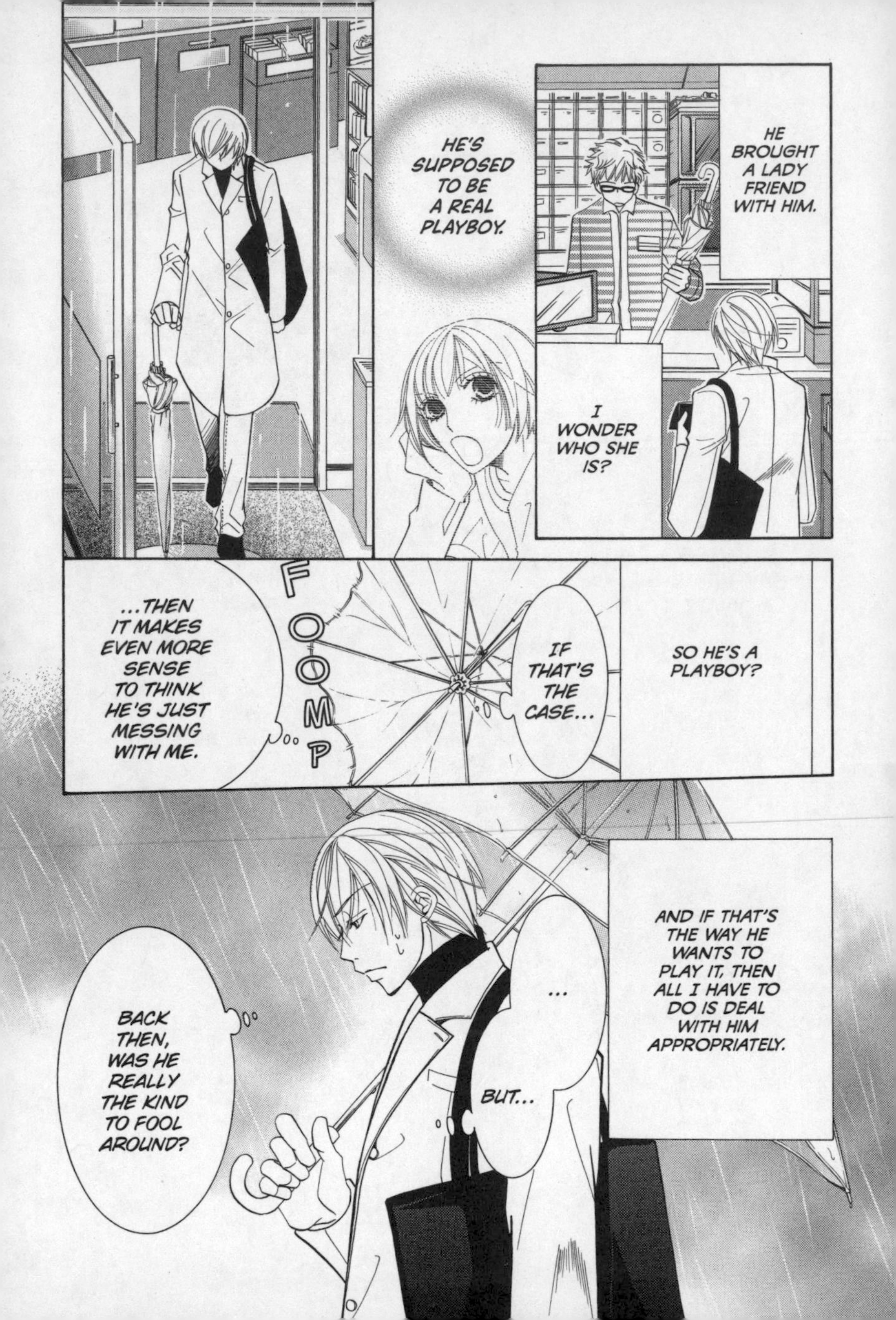
HE BROUGHT A LADY FRIEND WITH HIM.
I WONDER WHO SHE IS?
HE'S SUPPOSED TO BE A REAL PLAYBOY.
SO HE'S A PLAYBOY?
IF THAT'S THE CASE...
FOOMP
...THEN IT MAKES EVEN MORE SENSE TO THINK HE'S JUST MESSING WITH ME.
AND IF THAT'S THE WAY HE WANTS TO PLAY IT, THEN ALL I HAVE TO DO IS DEAL WITH HIM APPROPRIATELY.
...
BUT...
BACK THEN, WAS HE REALLY THE KIND TO FOOL AROUND?

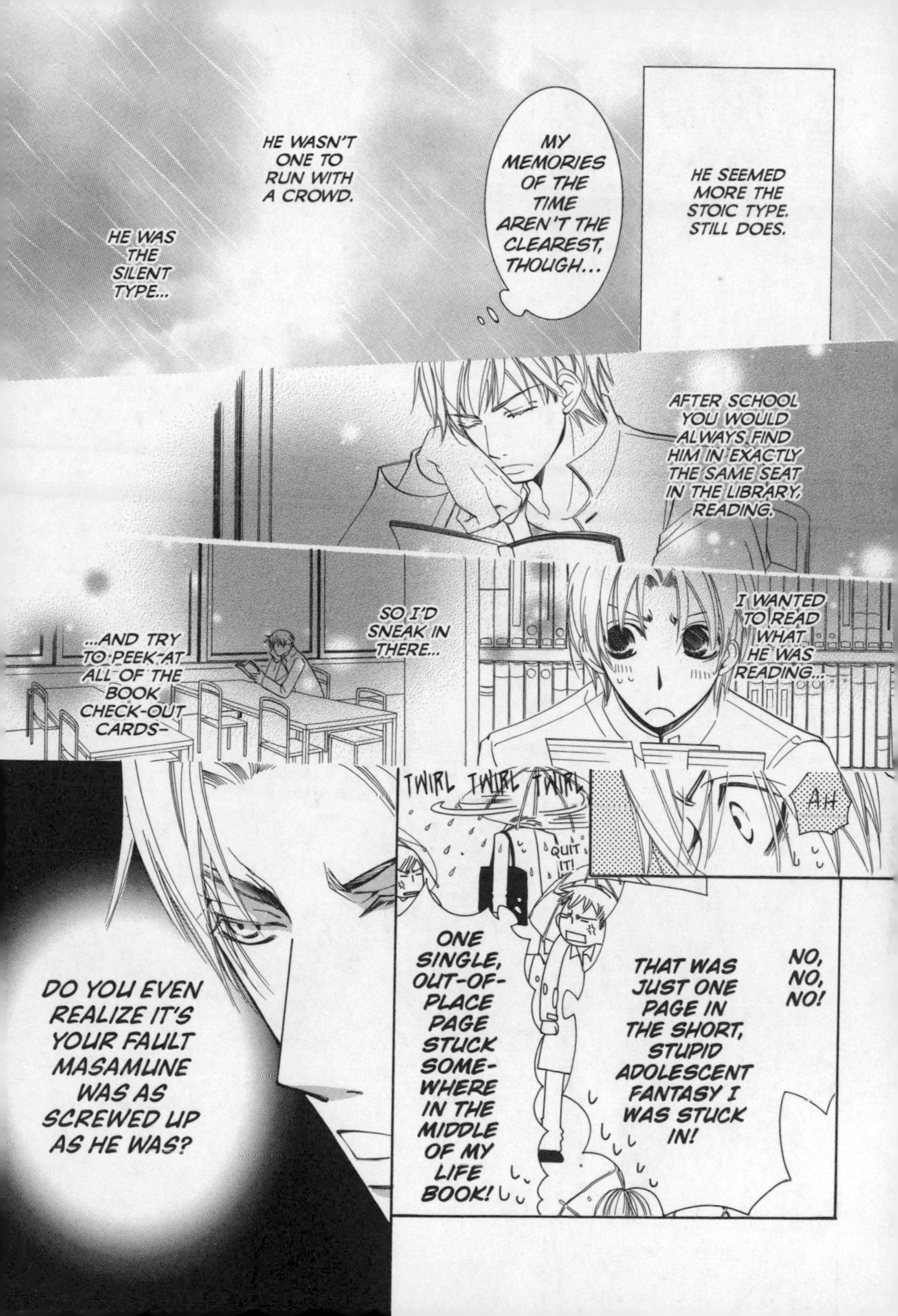
HE SEEMED MORE THE STOIC TYPE. STILL DOES.
MY MEMORIES OF THE TIME AREN'T THE CLEAREST, THOUGH...
HE WASN'T ONE TO RUN WITH A CROWD.
HE WAS THE SILENT TYPE...
AFTER SCHOOL YOU WOULD ALWAYS FIND HIM IN EXACTLY THE SAME SEAT IN THE LIBRARY, READING.
I WANTED TO READ WHAT HE WAS READING...
SO I'D SNEAK IN THERE...
...AND TRY TO PEEK AT ALL OF THE BOOK CHECK-OUT CARDS-
AH
TWIRL TWIRL TWIRL
QUIT IT!
NO, NO, NO!
THAT WAS JUST ONE PAGE IN THE SHORT, STUPID ADOLESCENT FANTASY I WAS STUCK IN!
ONE SINGLE, OUT-OF-PLACE PAGE STUCK SOME-WHERE IN THE MIDDLE OF MY LIFE BOOK!
DO YOU EVEN REALIZE IT'S YOUR FAULT MASAMUNE WAS AS SCREWED UP AS HE WAS?

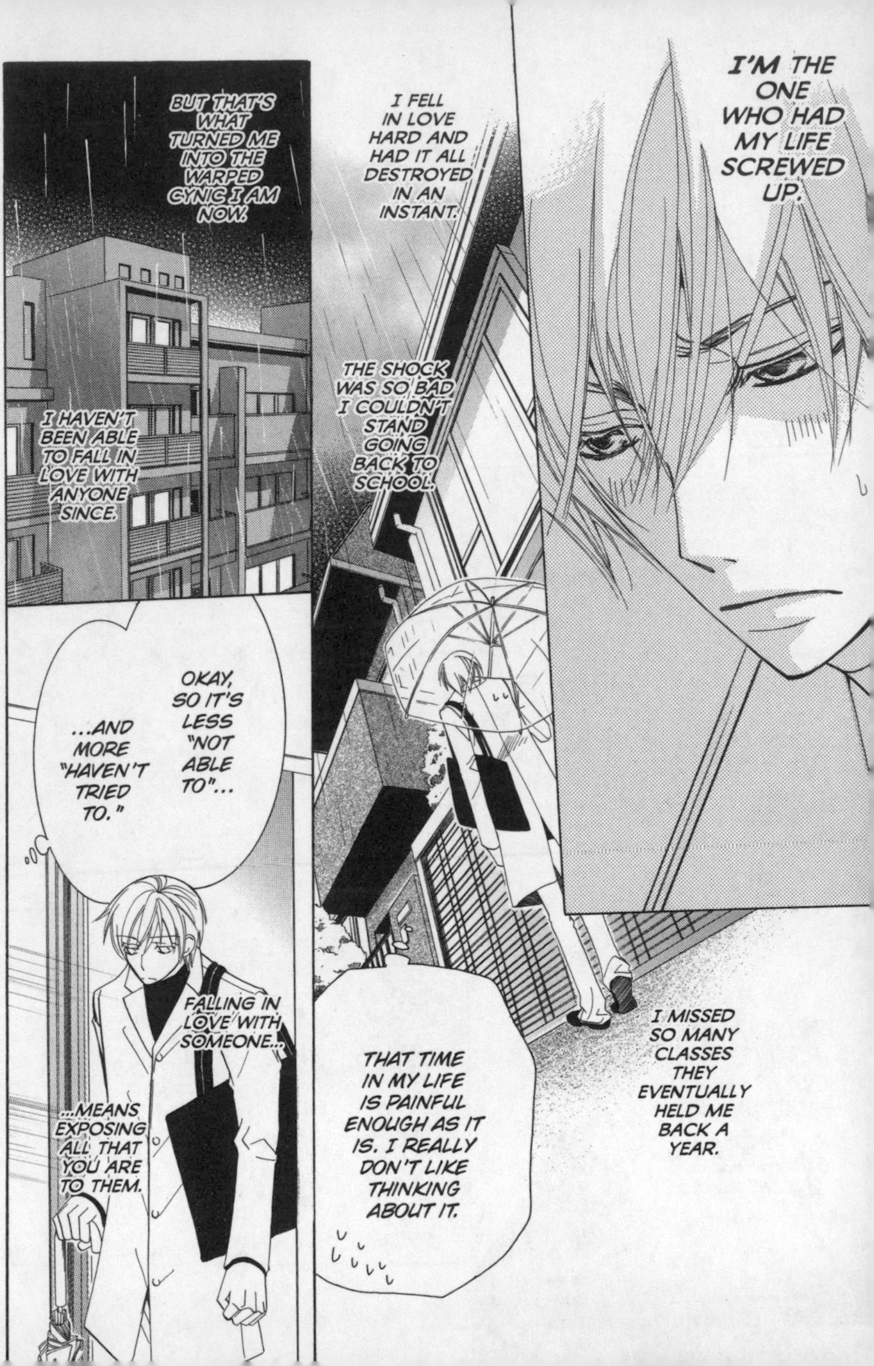

I'M THE ONE WHO HAD MY LIFE SCREWED UP.
I FELL IN LOVE HARD AND HAD IT ALL DESTROYED IN AN INSTANT.
THE SHOCK WAS SO BAD I COULDN'T STAND GOING BACK TO SCHOOL.
I MISSED SO MANY CLASSES THEY EVENTUALLY HELD ME BACK A YEAR.
THAT TIME IN MY LIFE IS PAINFUL ENOUGH AS IT IS. I REALLY DON'T LIKE THINKING ABOUT IT.
BUT THAT'S WHAT TURNED ME INTO THE WARPED CYNIC I AM NOW.
I HAVEN'T BEEN ABLE TO FALL IN LOVE WITH ANYONE SINCE.
OKAY, SO IT'S LESS "NOT ABLE TO"...
...AND MORE "HAVEN'T TRIED TO."
FALLING IN LOVE WITH SOMEONE...
...MEANS EXPOSING ALL THAT YOU ARE TO THEM.

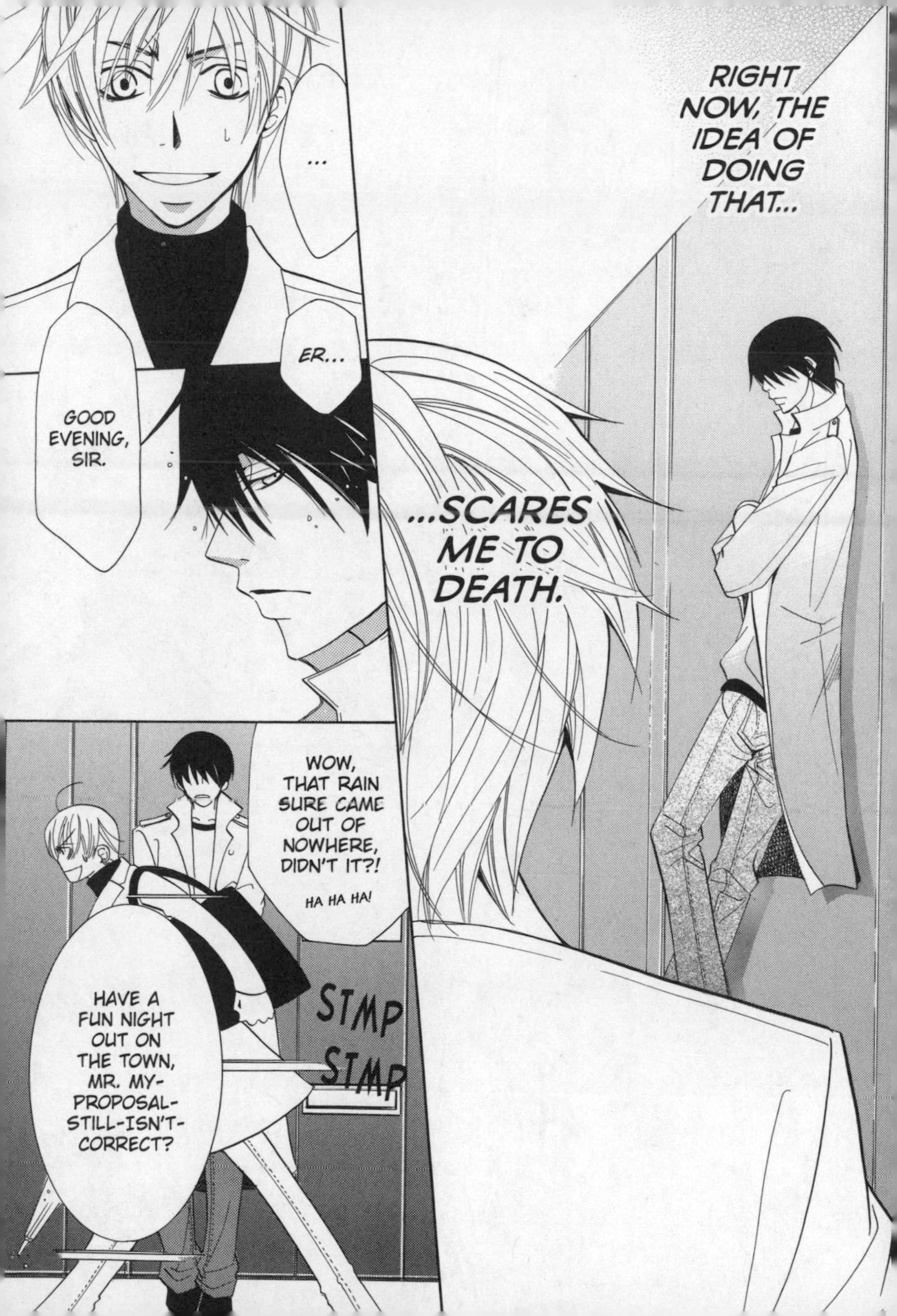
RIGHT NOW, THE IDEA OF DOING THAT...
...SCARES ME TO DEATH.
...
ER...
GOOD EVENING, SIR.
WOW, THAT RAIN SURE CAME OUT OF NOWHERE, DIDN'T IT?!
HA HA HA!
STMP STMP
HAVE A FUN NIGHT OUT ON THE TOWN, MR. MY-PROPOSAL-STILL-ISN'T-CORRECT?

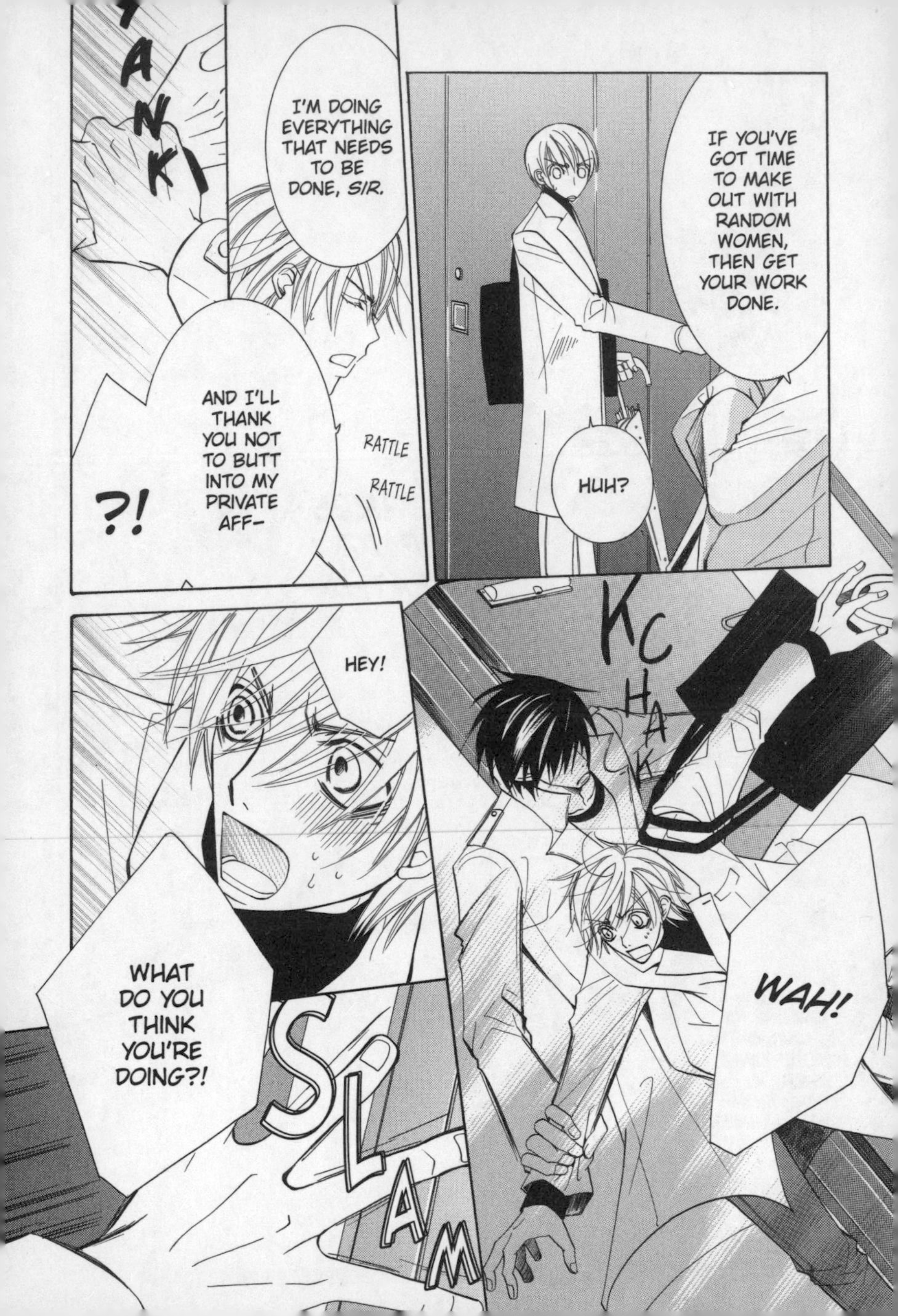
IF YOU'VE GOT TIME TO MAKE OUT WITH RANDOM WOMEN, THEN GET YOUR WORK DONE.
HUH?
YANK
I'M DOING EVERYTHING THAT NEEDS TO BE DONE, SIR.
AND I'LL THANK YOU NOT TO BUTT INTO MY PRIVATE AFF–
RATTLE
RATTLE
?!
KCHAK
WAH!
SLAM
HEY!
WHAT DO YOU THINK YOU'RE DOING?!

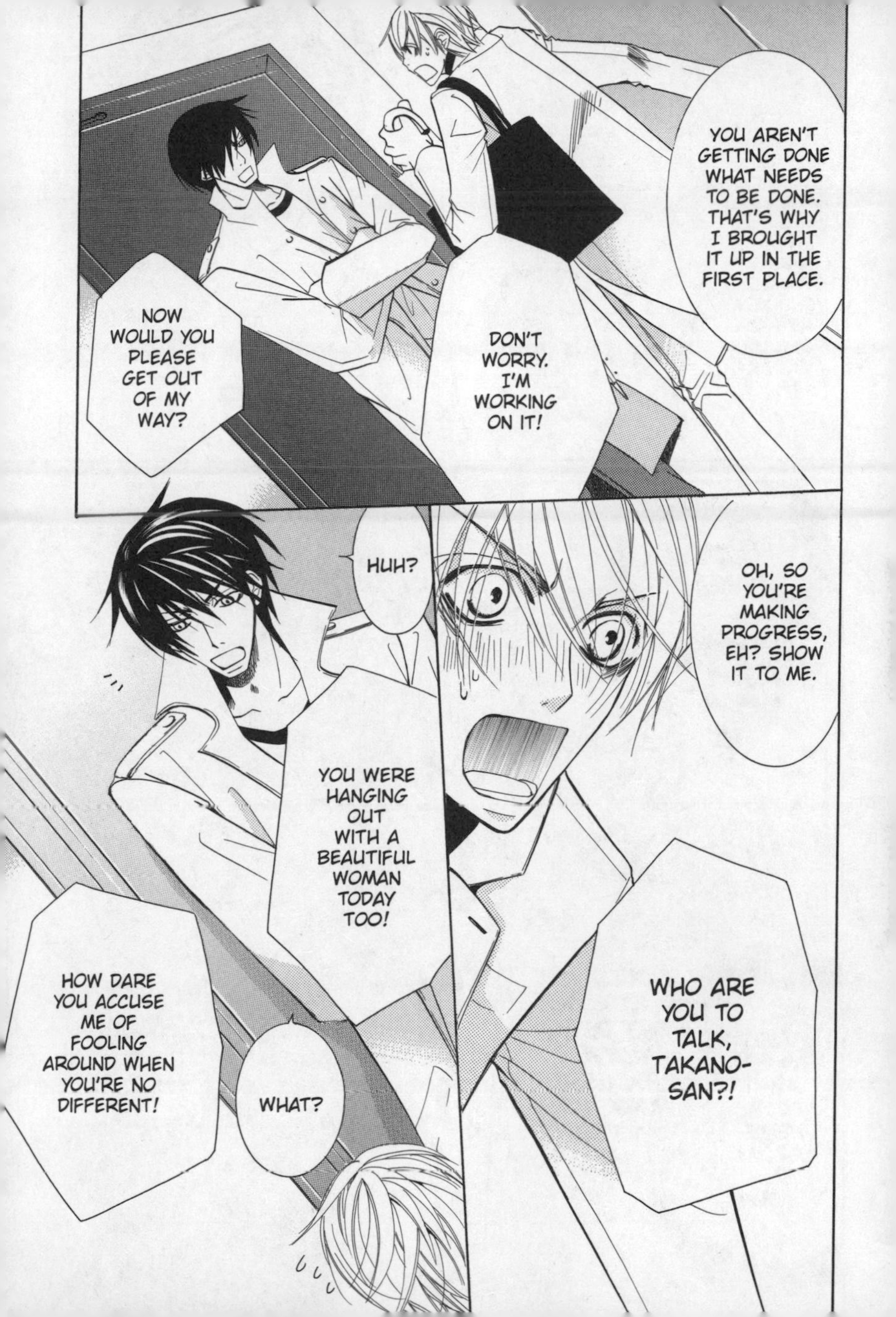
YOU AREN'T GETTING DONE WHAT NEEDS TO BE DONE. THAT'S WHY I BROUGHT IT UP IN THE FIRST PLACE.
DON'T WORRY. I'M WORKING ON IT!
NOW WOULD YOU PLEASE GET OUT OF MY WAY?
OH, SO YOU'RE MAKING PROGRESS, EH? SHOW IT TO ME.
HUH?
WHO ARE YOU TO TALK, TAKANO-SAN?!
YOU WERE HANGING OUT WITH A BEAUTIFUL WOMAN TODAY TOO!
WHAT?
HOW DARE YOU ACCUSE ME OF FOOLING AROUND WHEN YOU'RE NO DIFFERENT!

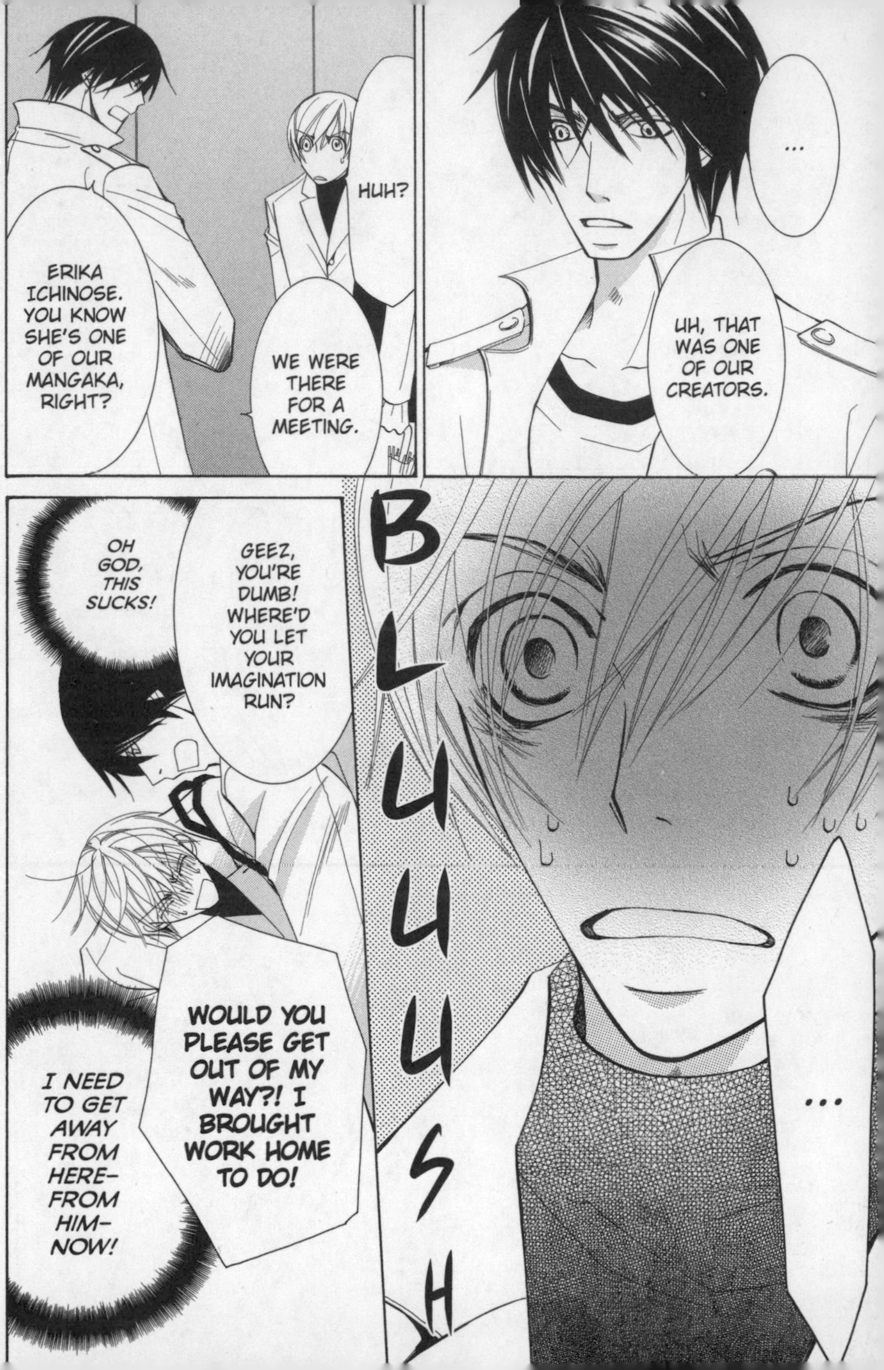
...
UH, THAT WAS ONE OF OUR CREATORS.
HUH?
ERIKA ICHINOSE. YOU KNOW SHE'S ONE OF OUR MANGAKA, RIGHT?
WE WERE THERE FOR A MEETING.
BLUUUUSH
...
GEEZ, YOU'RE DUMB! WHERE'D YOU LET YOUR IMAGINATION RUN?
OH GOD, THIS SUCKS!
WOULD YOU PLEASE GET OUT OF MY WAY?! I BROUGHT WORK HOME TO DO!
I NEED TO GET AWAY FROM HERE—FROM HIM—NOW!

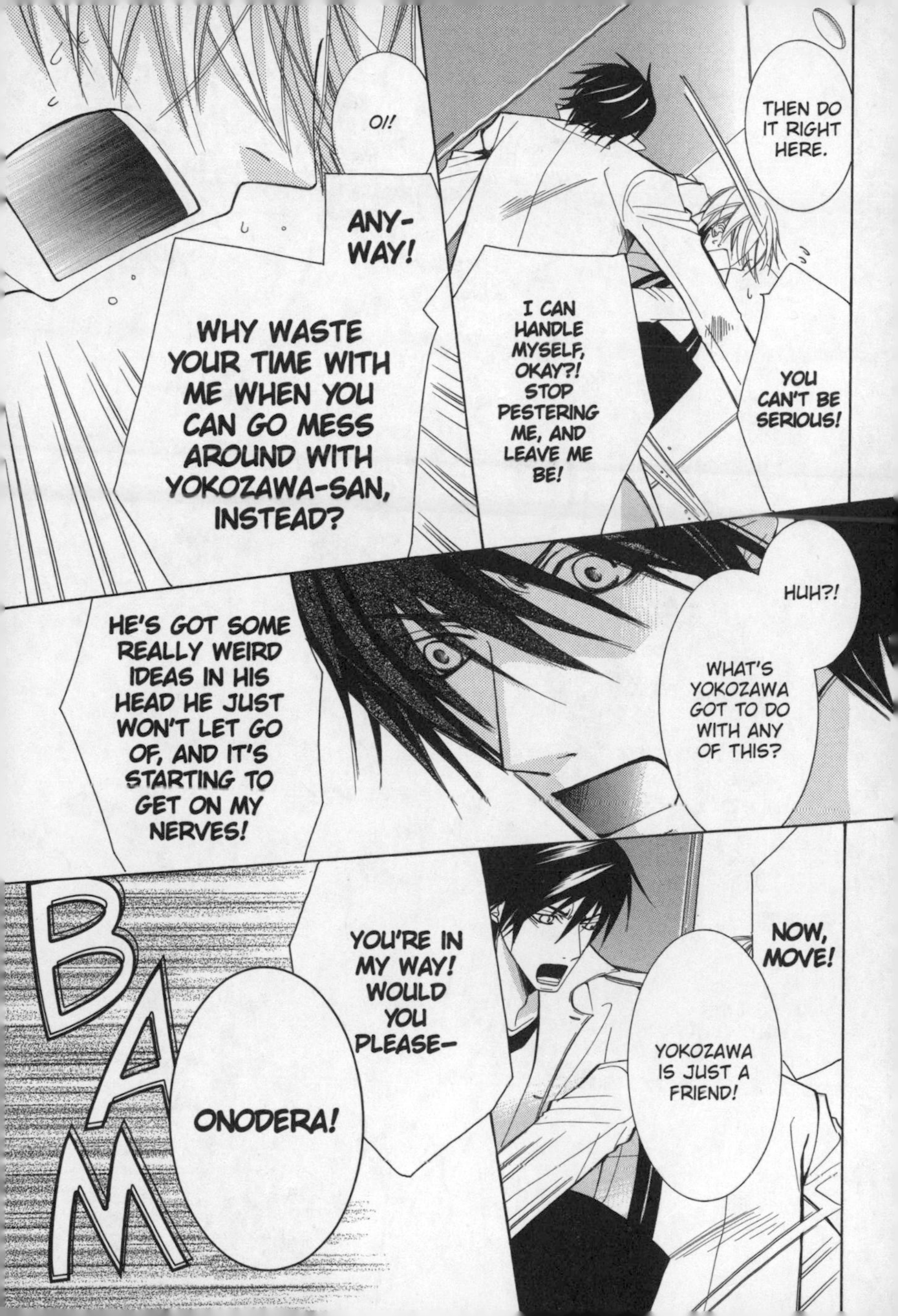
THEN DO IT RIGHT HERE.
YOU CAN'T BE SERIOUS!
OI!
ANY-WAY!
I CAN HANDLE MYSELF, OKAY?! STOP PESTERING ME, AND LEAVE ME BE!
WHY WASTE YOUR TIME WITH ME WHEN YOU CAN GO MESS AROUND WITH YOKOZAWA-SAN, INSTEAD?
HUH?!
WHAT'S YOKOZAWA GOT TO DO WITH ANY OF THIS?
HE'S GOT SOME REALLY WEIRD IDEAS IN HIS HEAD HE JUST WON'T LET GO OF, AND IT'S STARTING TO GET ON MY NERVES!
NOW, MOVE!
YOKOZAWA IS JUST A FRIEND!
YOU'RE IN MY WAY! WOULD YOU PLEASE-
ONODERA!
BAM

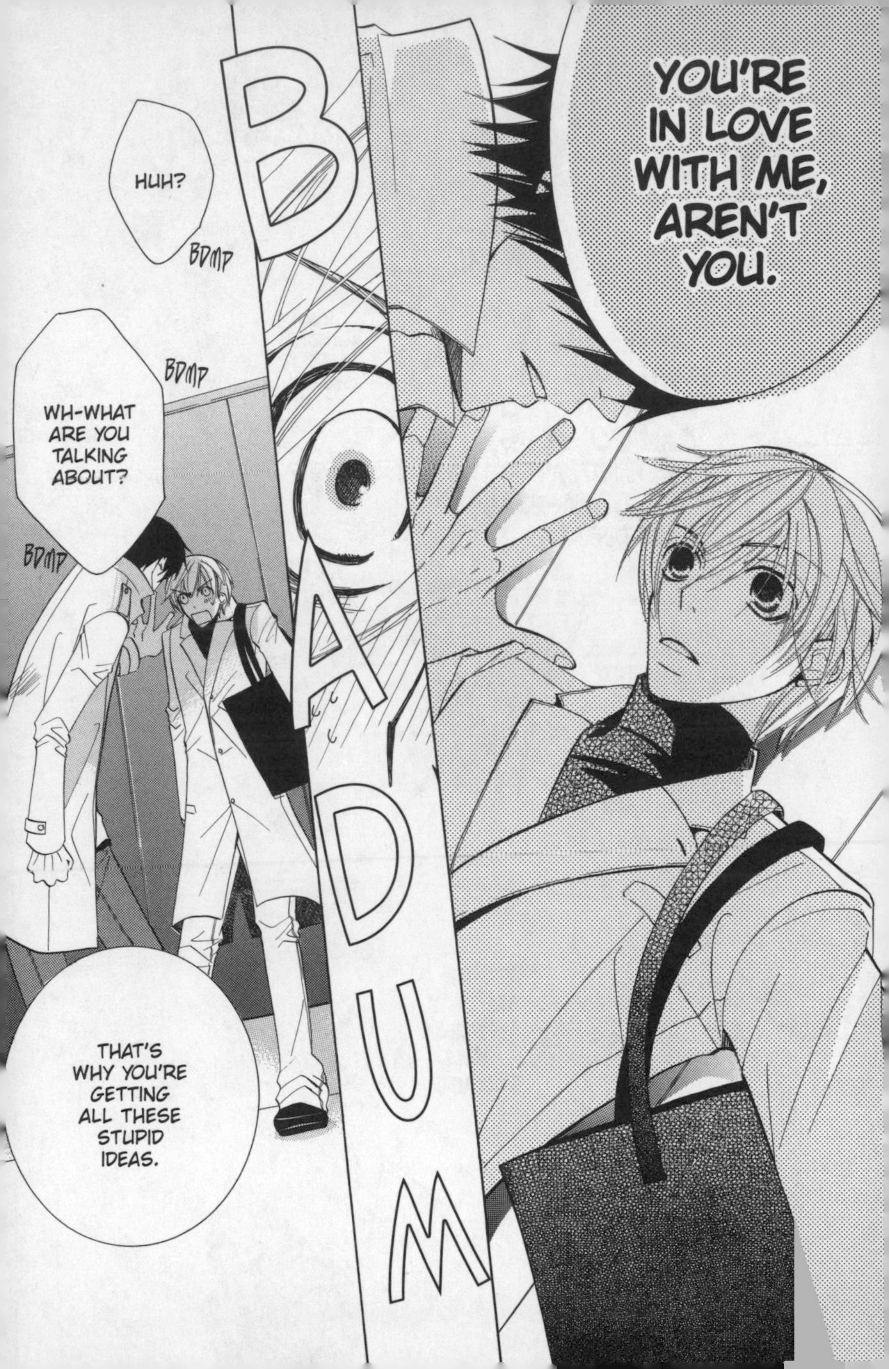
YOU'RE IN LOVE WITH ME, AREN'T YOU.
BADUM
HUH?
BDMP
WH-WHAT ARE YOU TALKING ABOUT?
BDMP
BDMP
THAT'S WHY YOU'RE GETTING ALL THESE STUPID IDEAS.

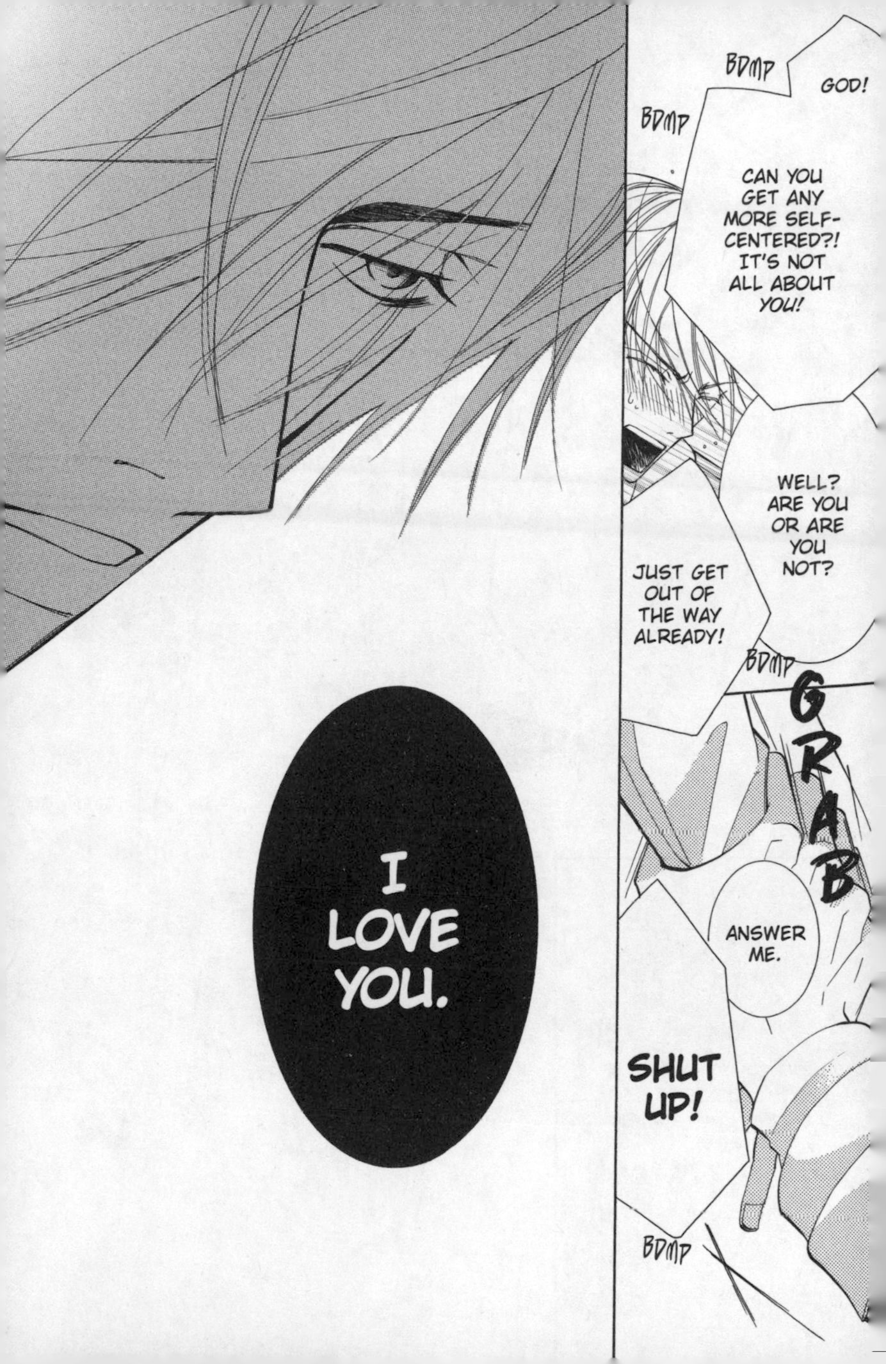
BDMP
GOD!
BDMP
CAN YOU GET ANY MORE SELF-CENTERED?! IT'S NOT ALL ABOUT *YOU!*
WELL? ARE YOU OR ARE YOU NOT?
JUST GET OUT OF THE WAY ALREADY!
BDMP
GRAB
ANSWER ME.
SHUT UP!
BDMP
I LOVE YOU.

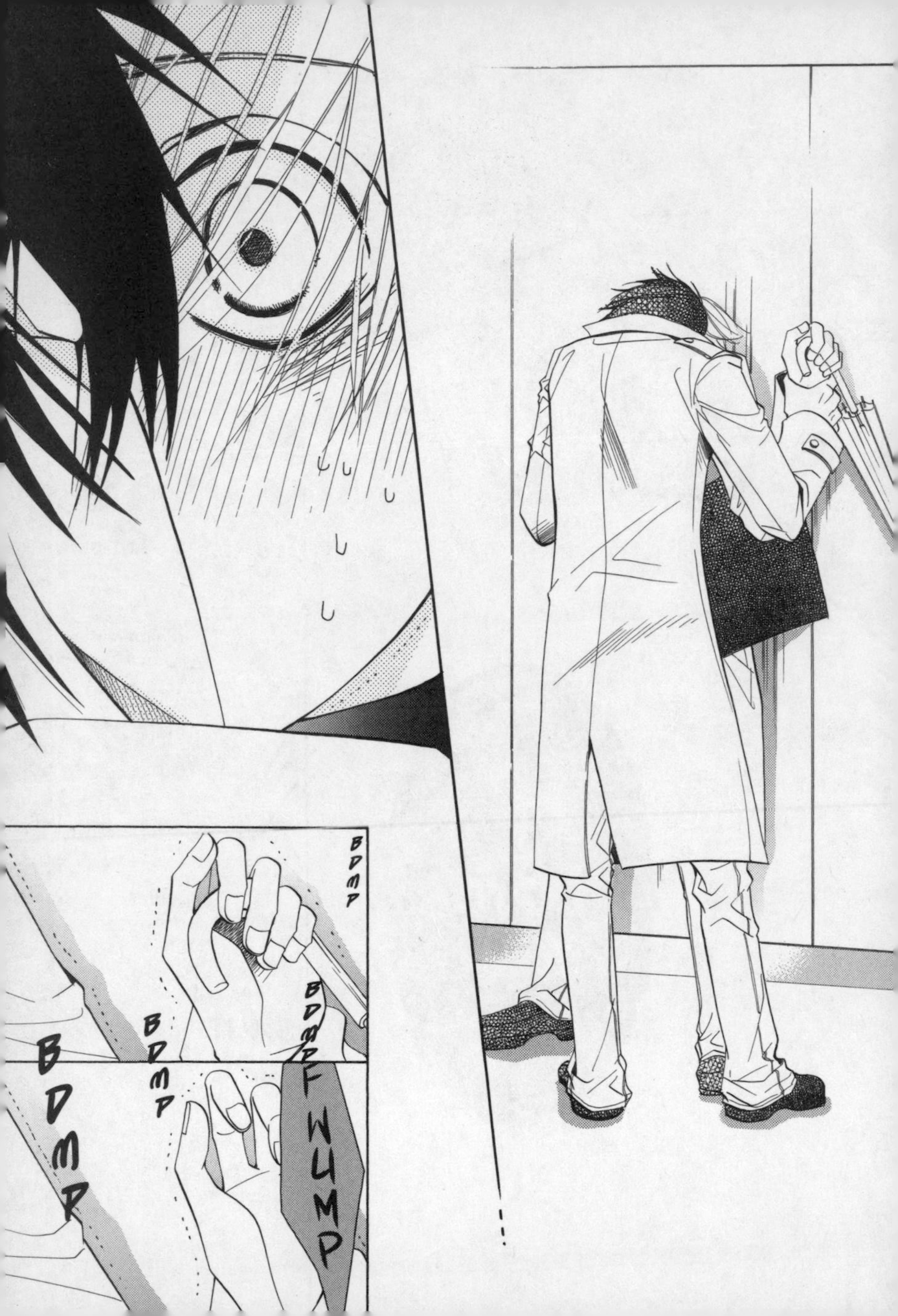

BDMP
BDMP
BDMP
BDMP
WUMP

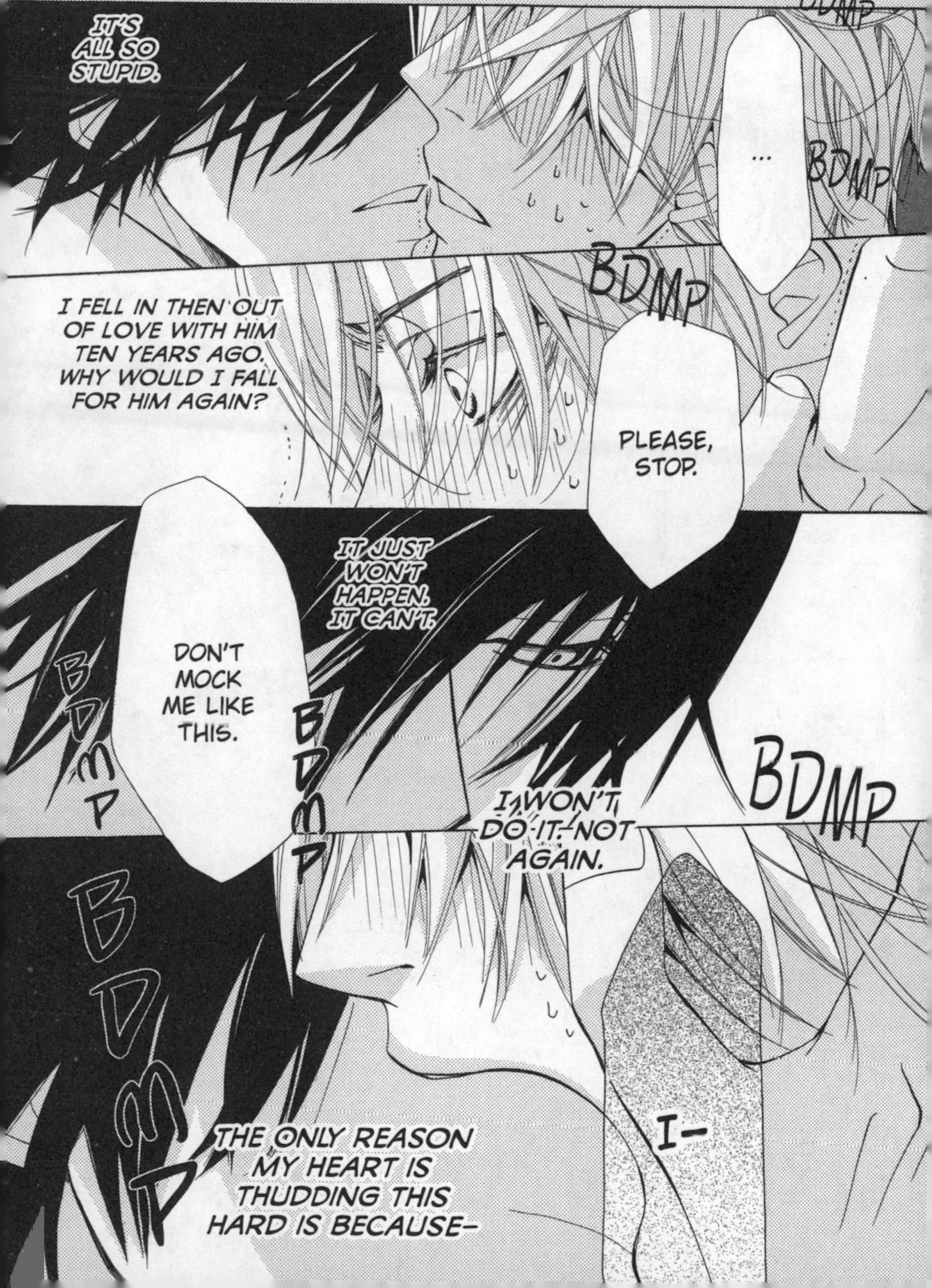
BDMP
...
BDMP
IT'S ALL SO STUPID.
BDMP
PLEASE, STOP.
I FELL IN THEN OUT OF LOVE WITH HIM TEN YEARS AGO. WHY WOULD I FALL FOR HIM AGAIN?
BDMP
I WON'T DO IT. NOT AGAIN.
IT JUST WON'T HAPPEN. IT CAN'T.
BDMP
DON'T MOCK ME LIKE THIS.
BDMP
I-
BDMP
THE ONLY REASON MY HEART IS THUDDING THIS HARD IS BECAUSE-

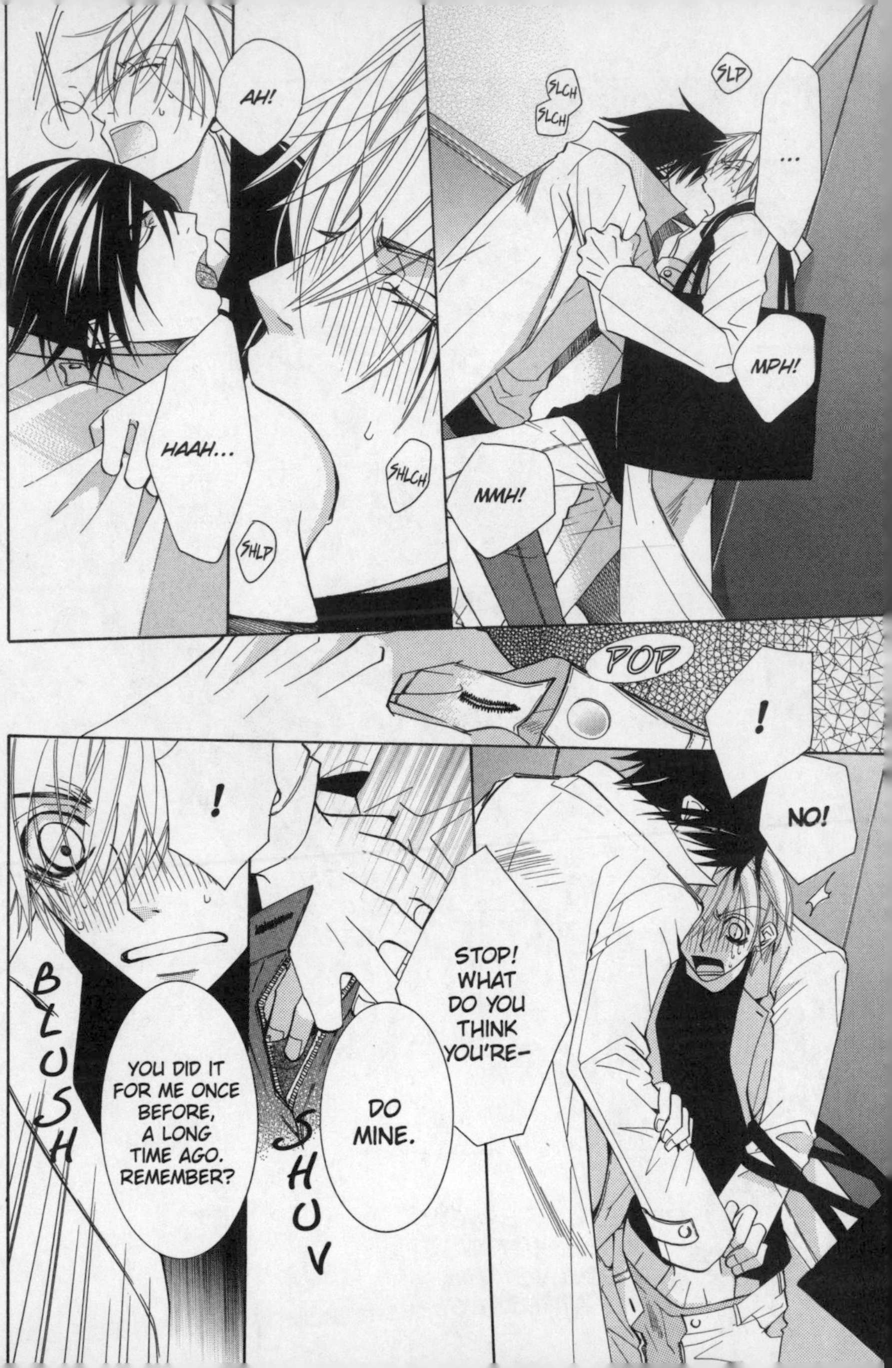
...
SLP
SLCH
SLCH
MPH!
MMH!
AH!
HAAH...
SHLCH
SHLP
POP
!
NO!
STOP! WHAT DO YOU THINK YOU'RE-
!
DO MINE.
YOU DID IT FOR ME ONCE BEFORE, A LONG TIME AGO. REMEMBER?
SHUV
BLUSH

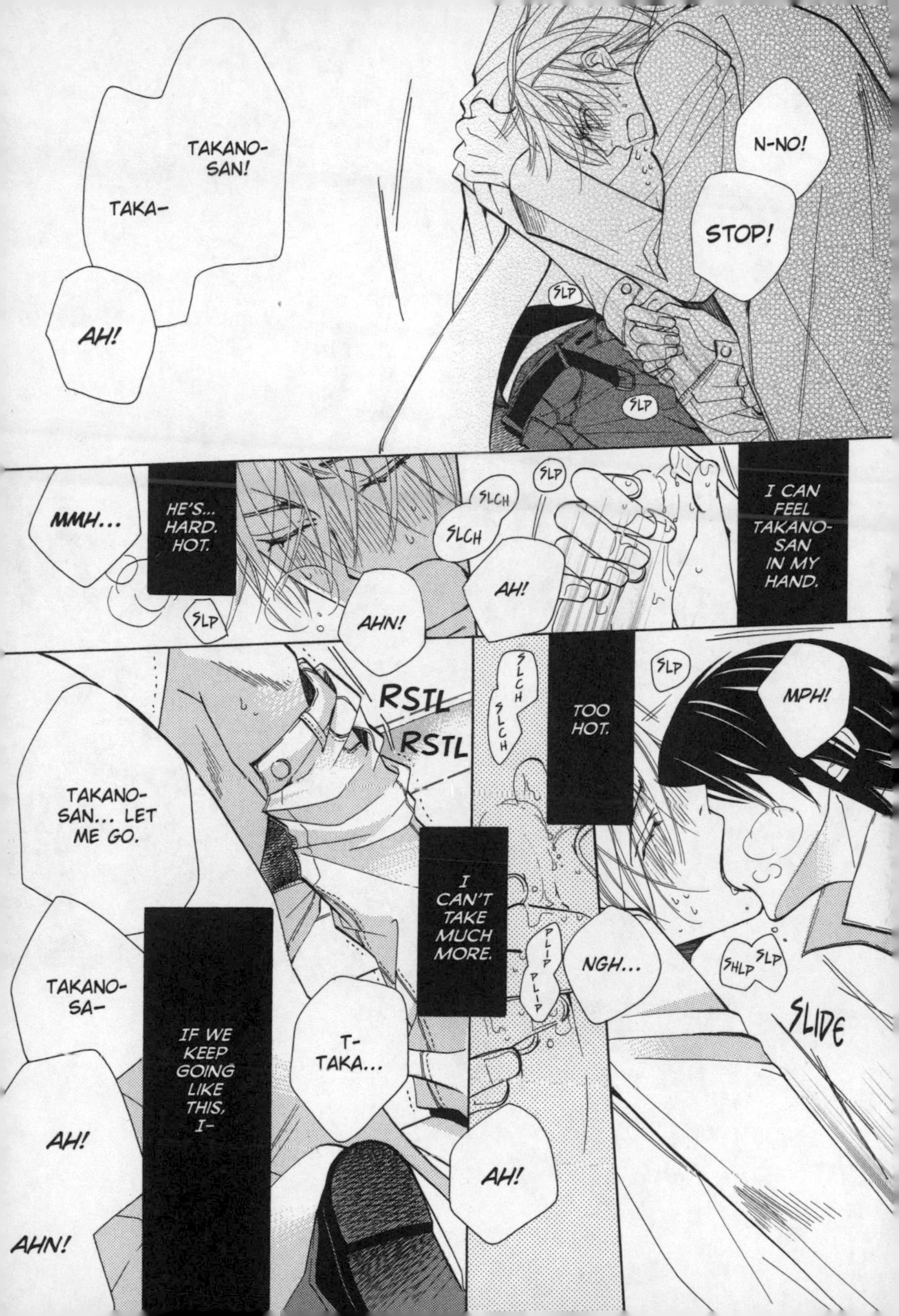
N-NO!
STOP!
TAKANO-SAN!
TAKA-
SLP
SLP
AH!
I CAN FEEL TAKANO-SAN IN MY HAND.
SLP
SLCH
SLCH
AH!
AHN!
HE'S... HARD. HOT.
MMH...
SLP
SLP
MPH!
TOO HOT.
SLCH SLCH
SHLP SLP
SLIDE
NGH...
PLIP PLIP
I CAN'T TAKE MUCH MORE.
AH!
RSTL
RSTL
TAKANO-SAN... LET ME GO.
T-TAKA...
TAKANO-SA-
IF WE KEEP GOING LIKE THIS, I-
AH!
AHN!

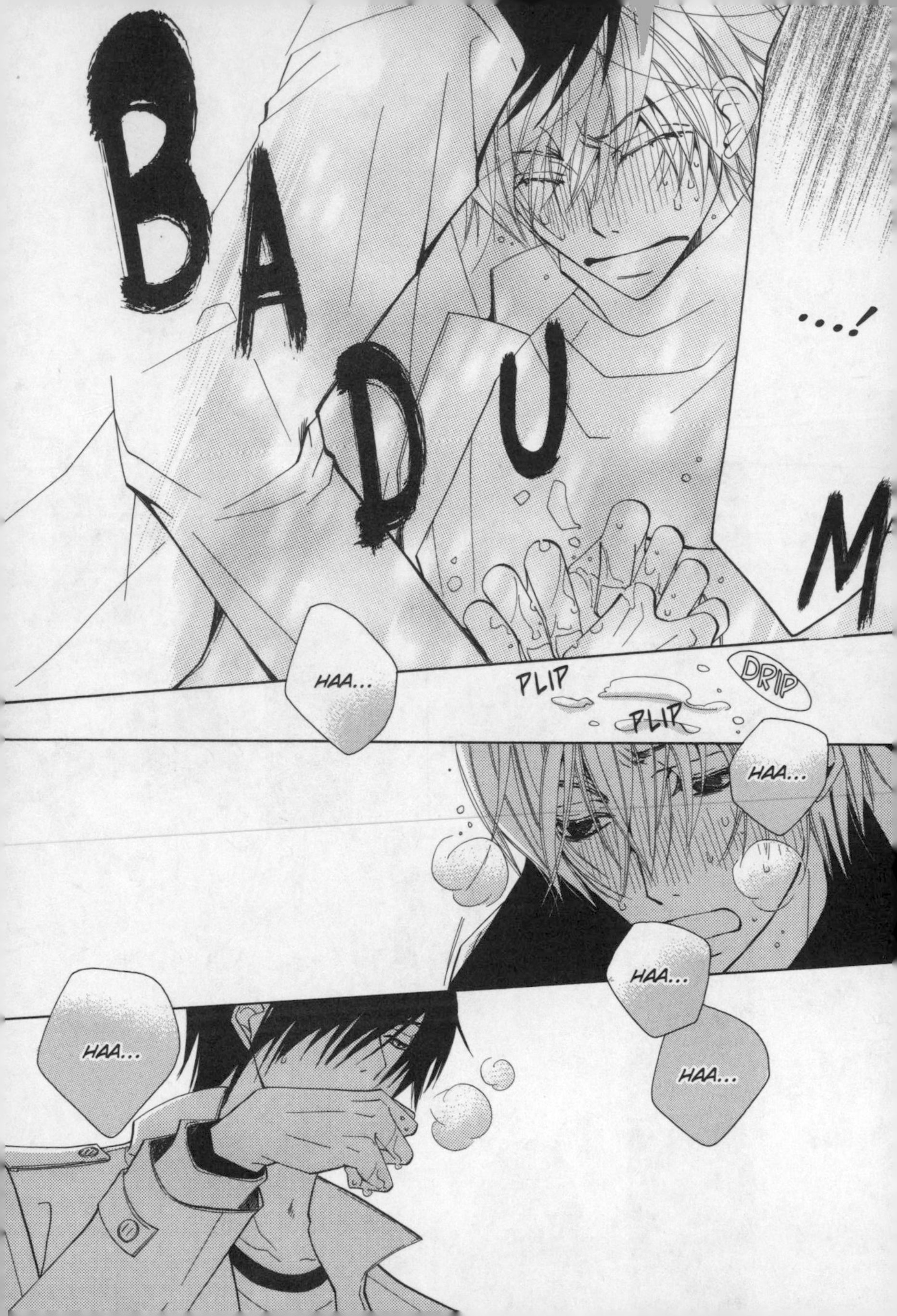
...!
BADUM
DRIP
PLIP
PLIP
HAA...
HAA...
HAA...
HAA...
HAA...

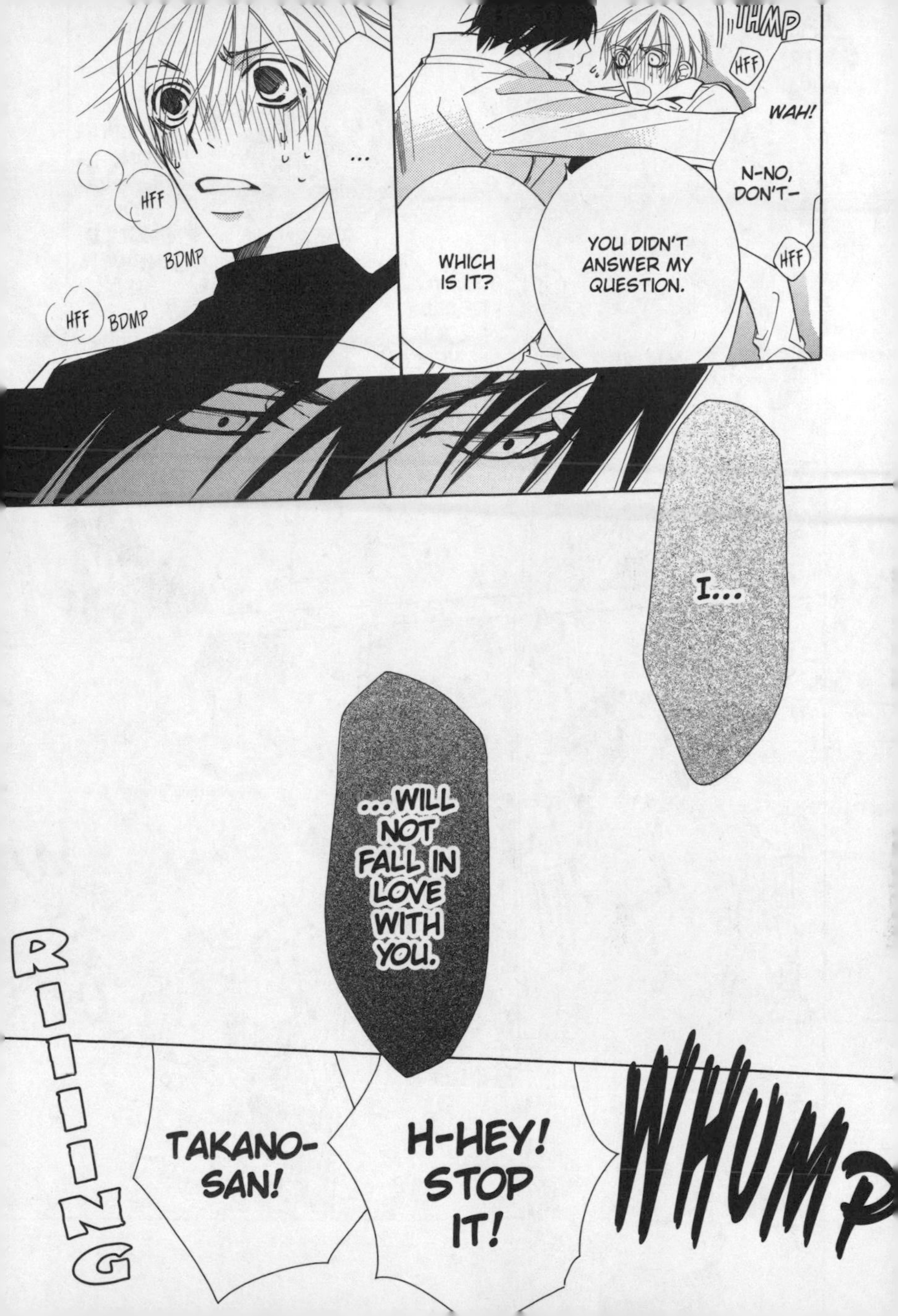
THMP
HFF
WAH!
N-NO, DON'T–
HFF
YOU DIDN'T ANSWER MY QUESTION.
WHICH IS IT?
...
HFF
BDMP
HFF
BDMP
I...
...WILL NOT FALL IN LOVE WITH YOU.
WHUMP
H-HEY! STOP IT!
TAKANO-SAN!
RIIING

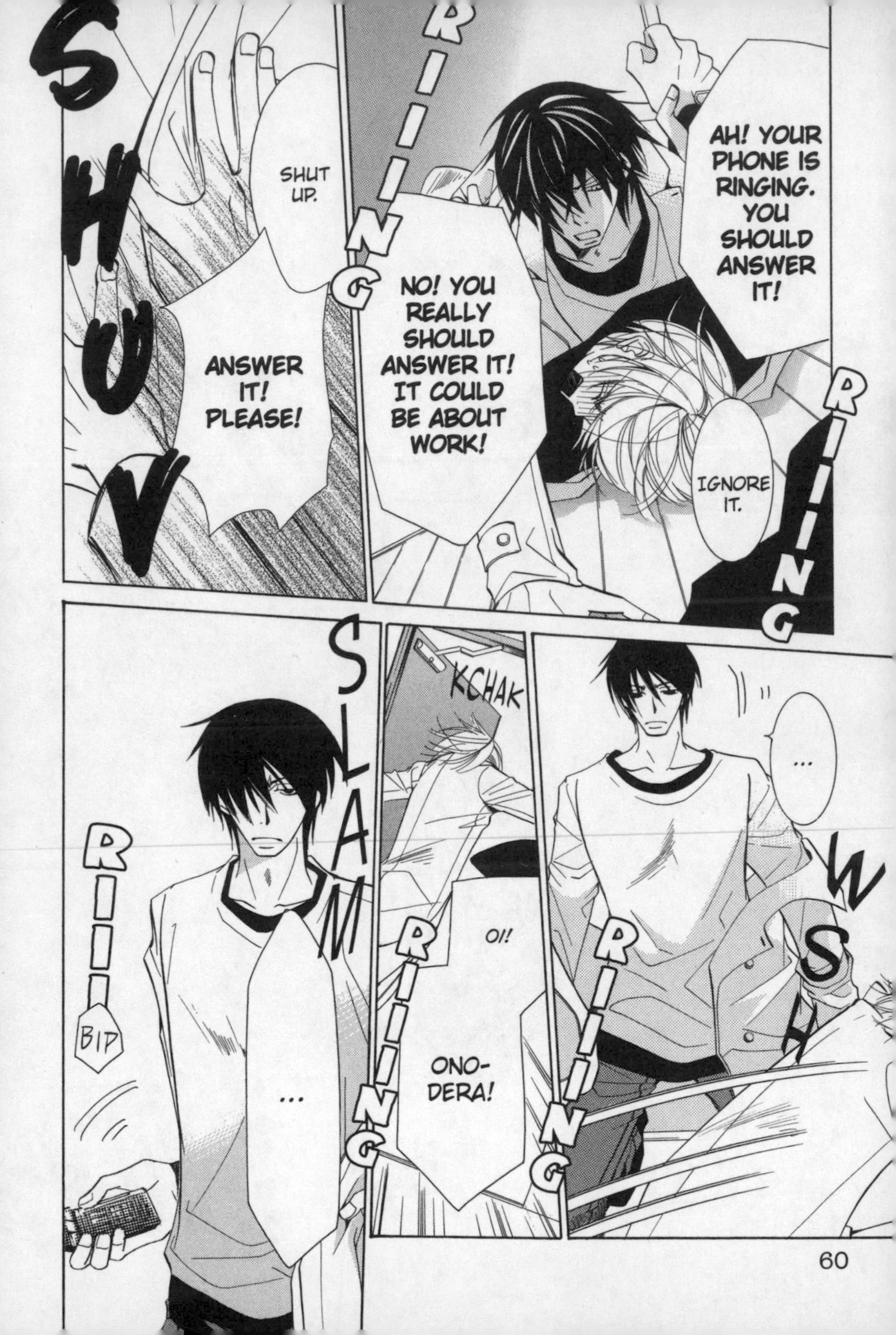
AH! YOUR PHONE IS RINGING. YOU SHOULD ANSWER IT!
IGNORE IT.
RIIIING
RIIIING
NO! YOU REALLY SHOULD ANSWER IT! IT COULD BE ABOUT WORK!
SHUV
SHUT UP.
ANSWER IT! PLEASE!
...
WSH
RIIIING
KCHAK
SLAM
OI!
ONO-DERA!
RIIIING
RIIII
BIP
...

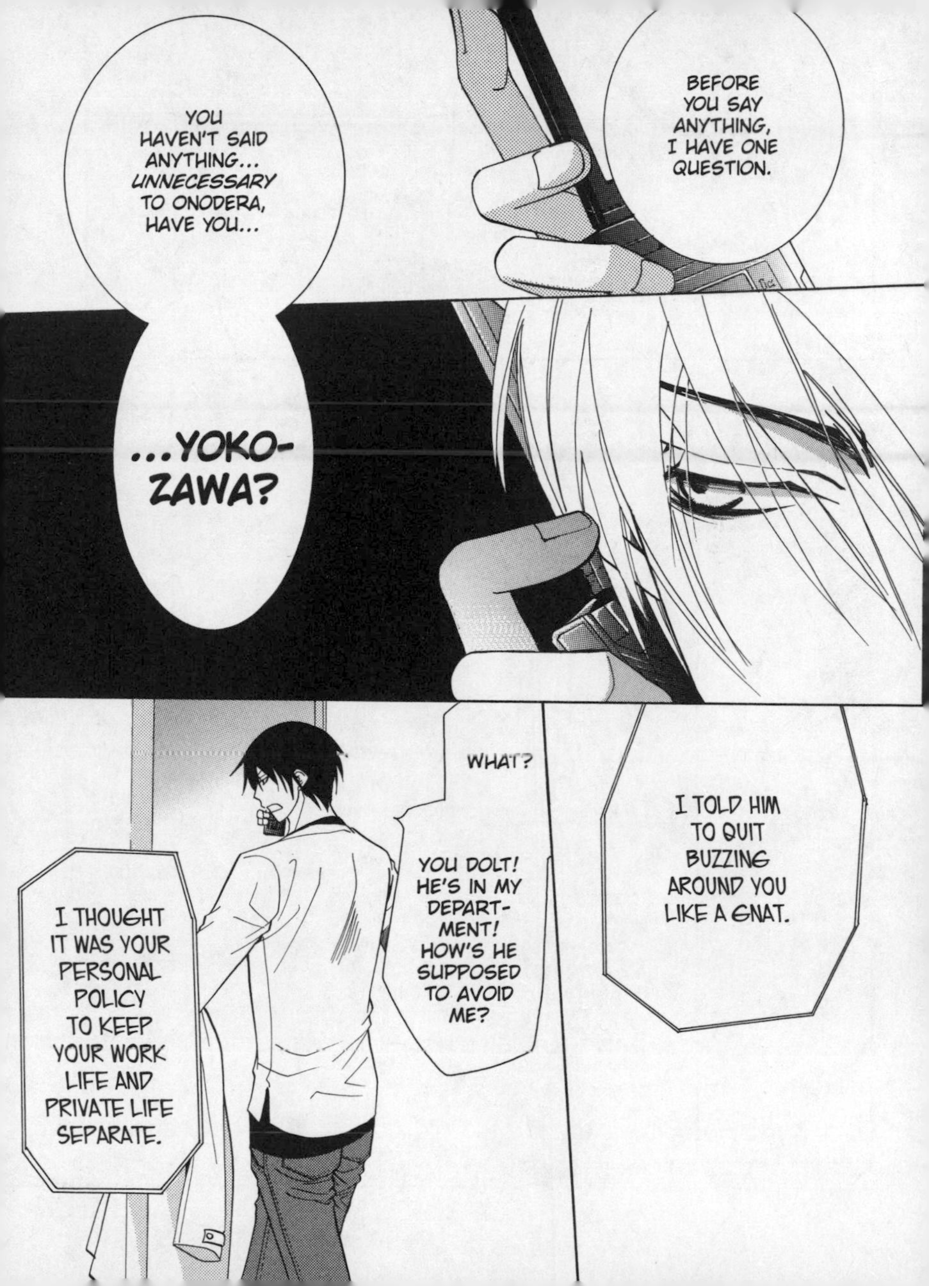
BEFORE YOU SAY ANYTHING, I HAVE ONE QUESTION.
YOU HAVEN'T SAID ANYTHING... *UNNECESSARY* TO ONODERA, HAVE YOU...
...YOKO-ZAWA?
I TOLD HIM TO QUIT BUZZING AROUND YOU LIKE A GNAT.
WHAT?
YOU DOLT! HE'S IN MY DEPART-MENT! HOW'S HE SUPPOSED TO AVOID ME?
I THOUGHT IT WAS YOUR PERSONAL POLICY TO KEEP YOUR WORK LIFE AND PRIVATE LIFE SEPARATE.

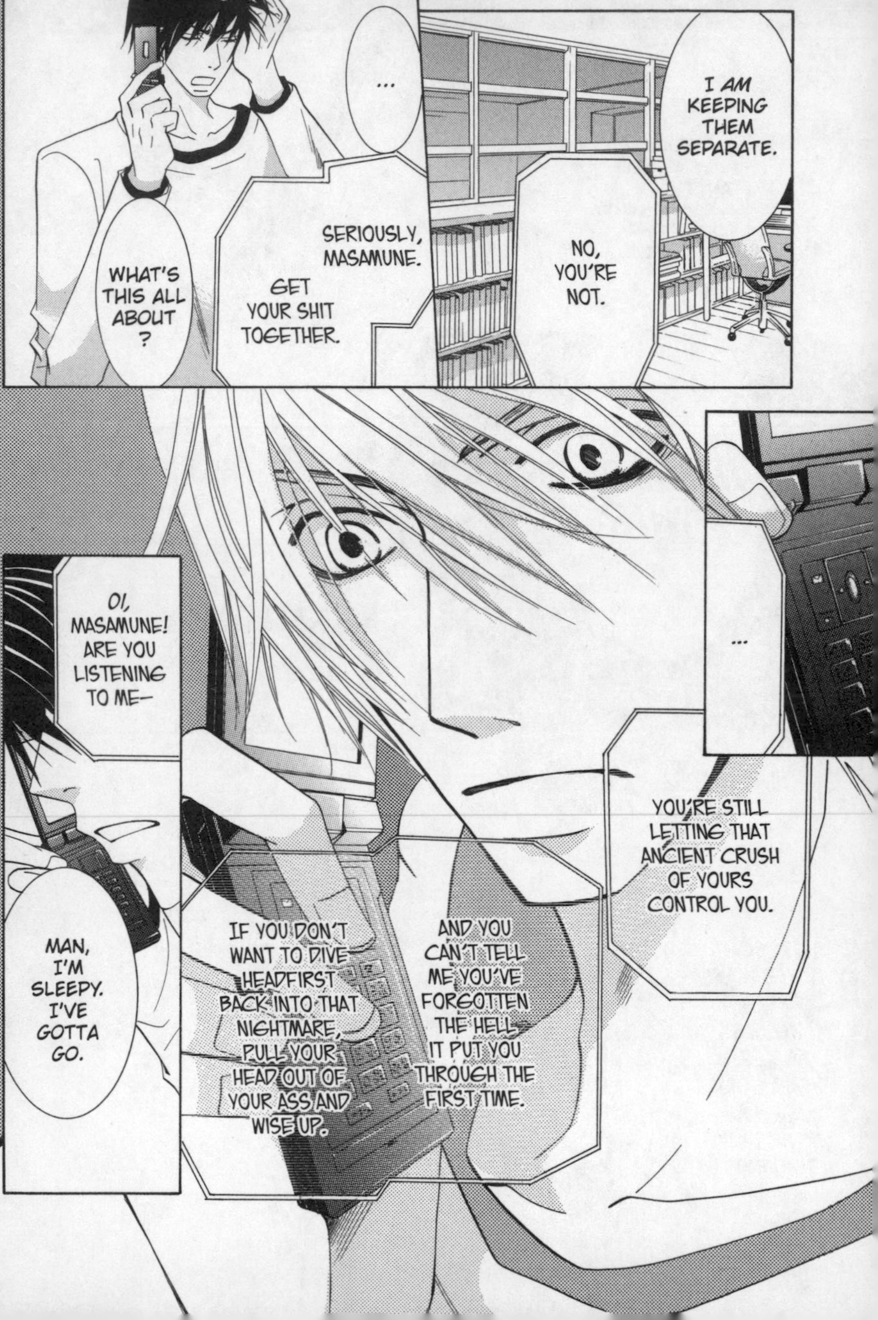
I AM KEEPING THEM SEPARATE.
NO, YOU'RE NOT.
...
SERIOUSLY, MASAMUNE.
GET YOUR SHIT TOGETHER.
WHAT'S THIS ALL ABOUT?
...
YOU'RE STILL LETTING THAT ANCIENT CRUSH OF YOURS CONTROL YOU.
AND YOU CAN'T TELL ME YOU'VE FORGOTTEN THE HELL IT PUT YOU THROUGH THE FIRST TIME.
IF YOU DON'T WANT TO DIVE HEADFIRST BACK INTO THAT NIGHTMARE, PULL YOUR HEAD OUT OF YOUR ASS AND WISE UP.
OI, MASAMUNE! ARE YOU LISTENING TO ME–
MAN, I'M SLEEPY. I'VE GOTTA GO.

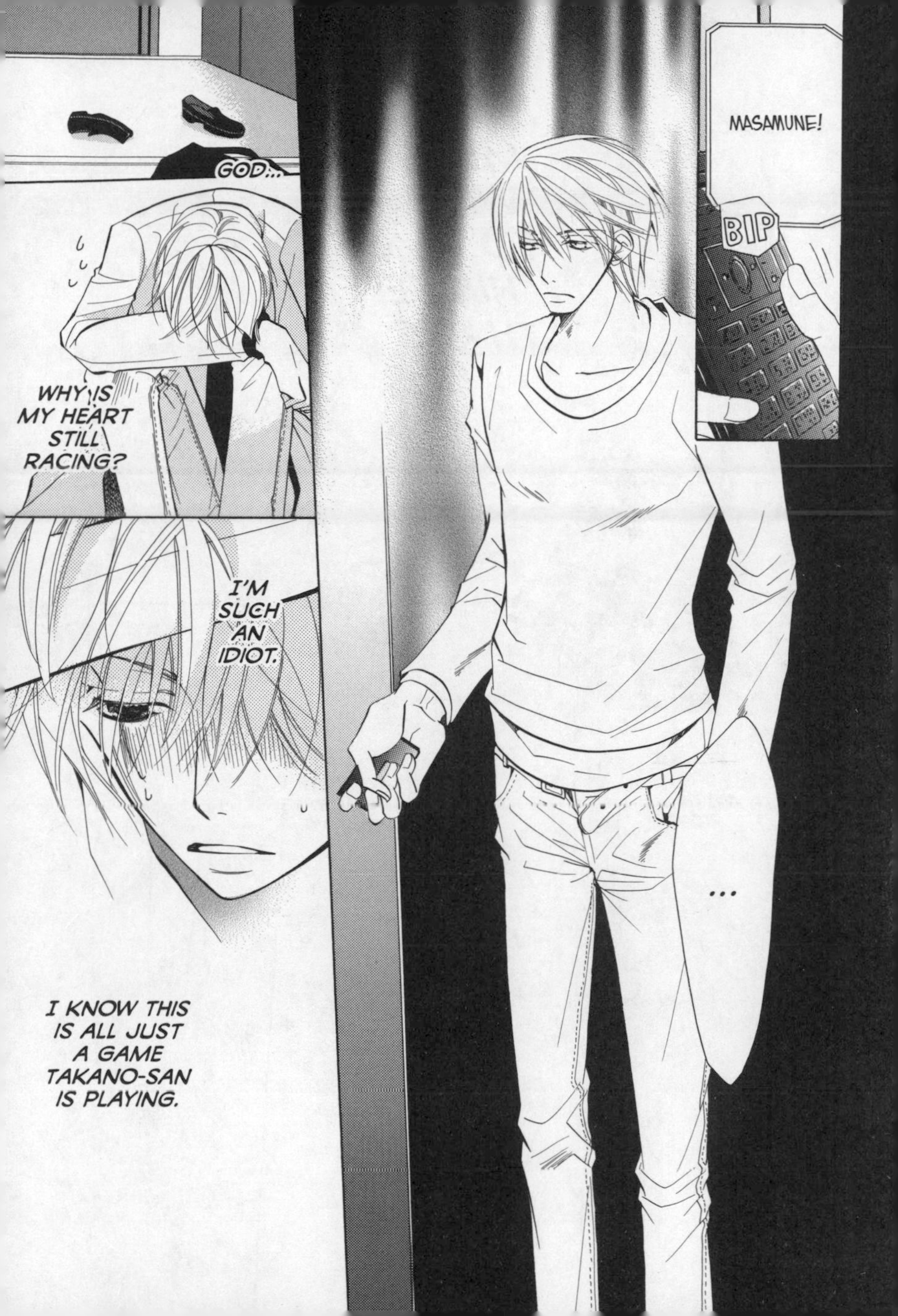
MASAMUNE!
BIP
...
GOD...
WHY IS MY HEART STILL RACING?
I'M SUCH AN IDIOT.
I KNOW THIS IS ALL JUST A GAME TAKANO-SAN IS PLAYING.

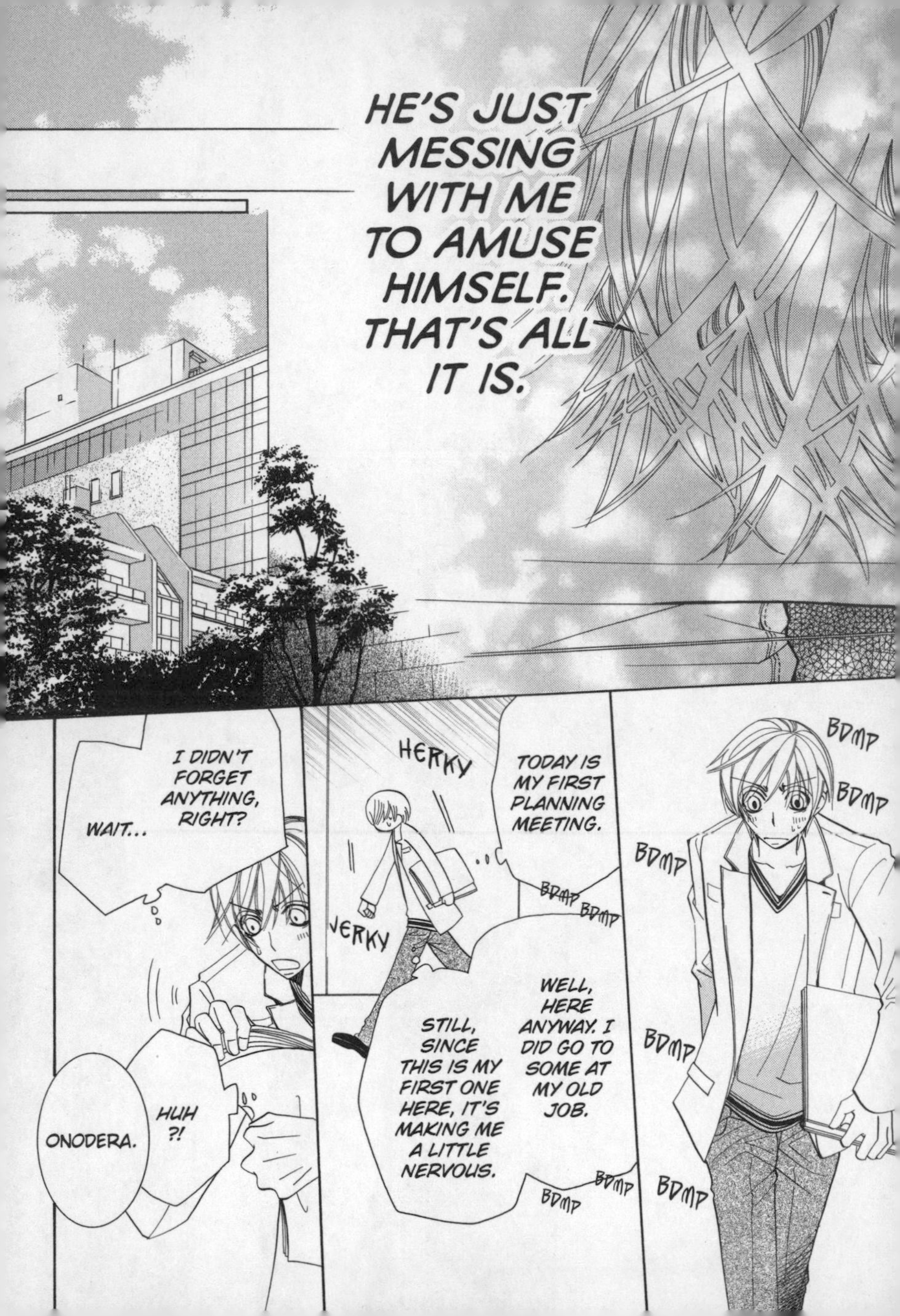
HE'S JUST MESSING WITH ME TO AMUSE HIMSELF. THAT'S ALL IT IS.
BDMP
BDMP
BDMP
BDMP
BDMP
TODAY IS MY FIRST PLANNING MEETING.
HERKY
JERKY
..
BDMP BDMP
WELL, HERE ANYWAY. I DID GO TO SOME AT MY OLD JOB.
STILL, SINCE THIS IS MY FIRST ONE HERE, IT'S MAKING ME A LITTLE NERVOUS.
BDMP
BDMP
I DIDN'T FORGET ANYTHING, RIGHT?
WAIT...
HUH ?!
ONODERA.

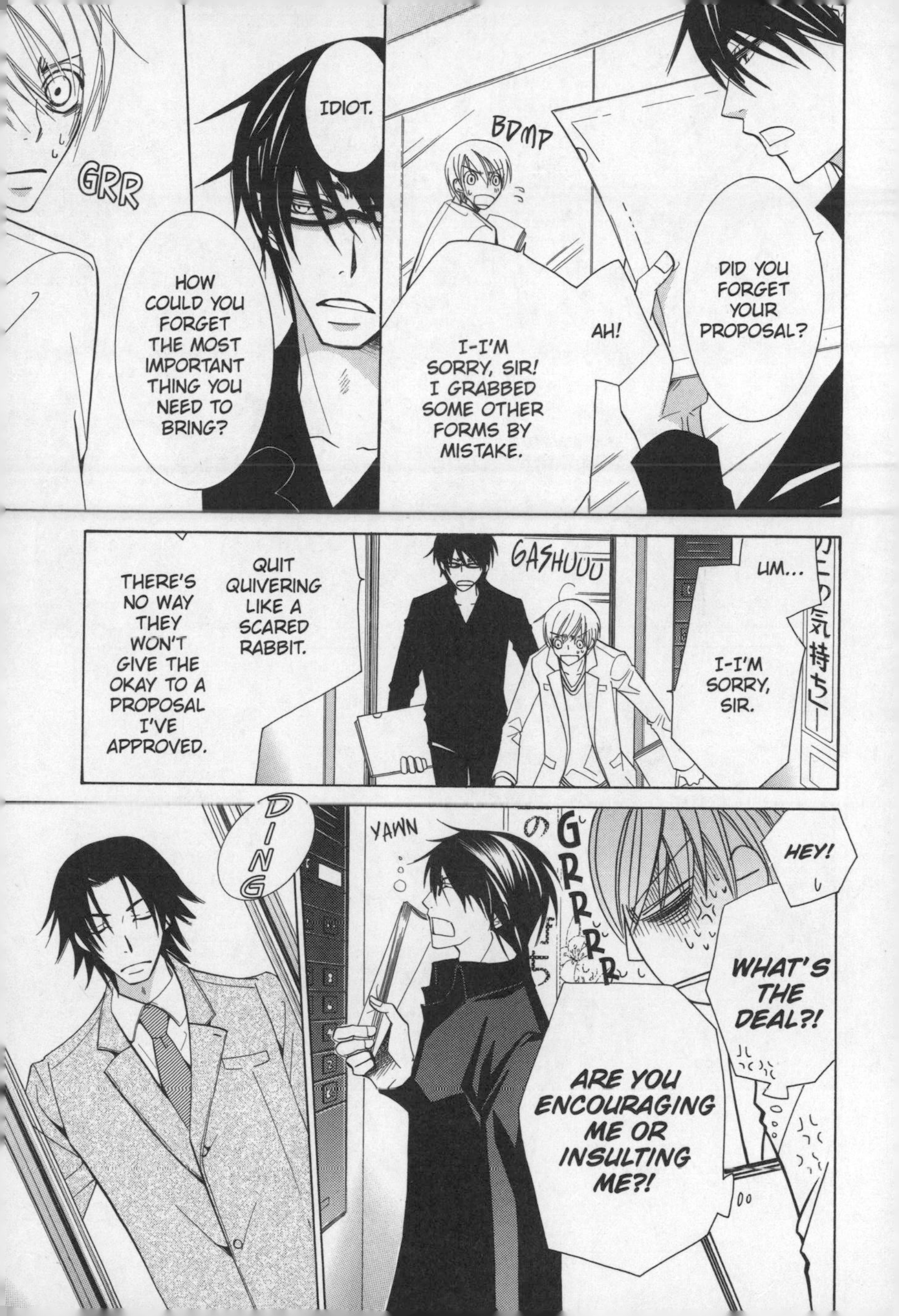
DID YOU FORGET YOUR PROPOSAL?
AH!
BDMP
I-I'M SORRY, SIR! I GRABBED SOME OTHER FORMS BY MISTAKE.
IDIOT.
HOW COULD YOU FORGET THE MOST IMPORTANT THING YOU NEED TO BRING?
GRR
UM...
I-I'M SORRY, SIR.
GASHUUU
QUIT QUIVERING LIKE A SCARED RABBIT.
THERE'S NO WAY THEY WON'T GIVE THE OKAY TO A PROPOSAL I'VE APPROVED.
HEY!
WHAT'S THE DEAL?!
ARE YOU ENCOURAGING ME OR INSULTING ME?!
GRRRRR
YAWN
DING

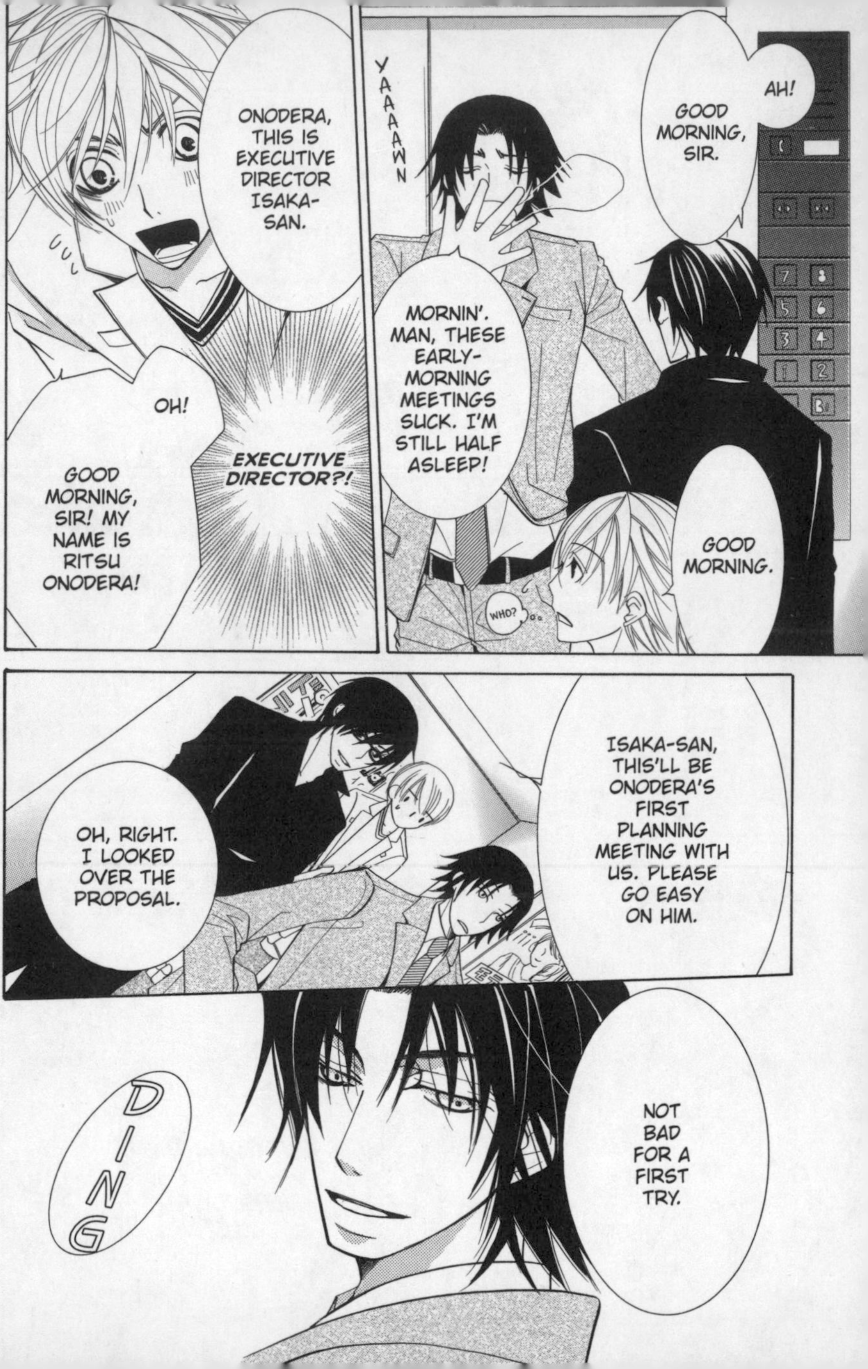
AH!
GOOD MORNING, SIR.
YAAAAAWN
MORNIN'. MAN, THESE EARLY-MORNING MEETINGS SUCK. I'M STILL HALF ASLEEP!
GOOD MORNING.
WHO?
ONODERA, THIS IS EXECUTIVE DIRECTOR ISAKA-SAN.
EXECUTIVE DIRECTOR?!
OH!
GOOD MORNING, SIR! MY NAME IS RITSU ONODERA!
ISAKA-SAN, THIS'LL BE ONODERA'S FIRST PLANNING MEETING WITH US. PLEASE GO EASY ON HIM.
OH, RIGHT. I LOOKED OVER THE PROPOSAL.
NOT BAD FOR A FIRST TRY.
DING

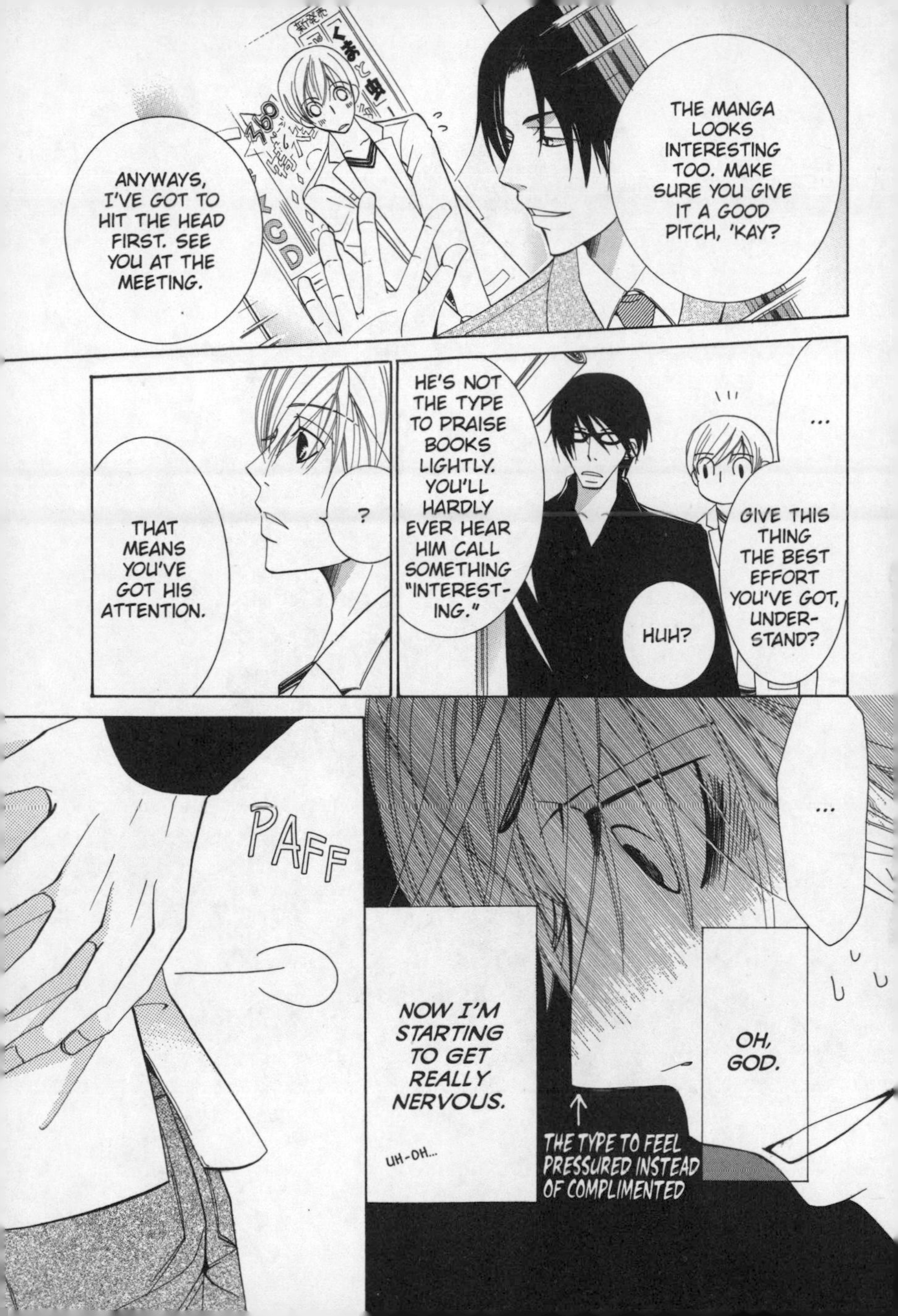
THE MANGA LOOKS INTERESTING TOO. MAKE SURE YOU GIVE IT A GOOD PITCH, 'KAY?
ANYWAYS, I'VE GOT TO HIT THE HEAD FIRST. SEE YOU AT THE MEETING.
...
GIVE THIS THING THE BEST EFFORT YOU'VE GOT, UNDERSTAND?
HUH?
HE'S NOT THE TYPE TO PRAISE BOOKS LIGHTLY. YOU'LL HARDLY EVER HEAR HIM CALL SOMETHING "INTERESTING."
?
THAT MEANS YOU'VE GOT HIS ATTENTION.
...
OH, GOD.
NOW I'M STARTING TO GET REALLY NERVOUS.
THE TYPE TO FEEL PRESSURED INSTEAD OF COMPLIMENTED
UH-OH...
PAFF

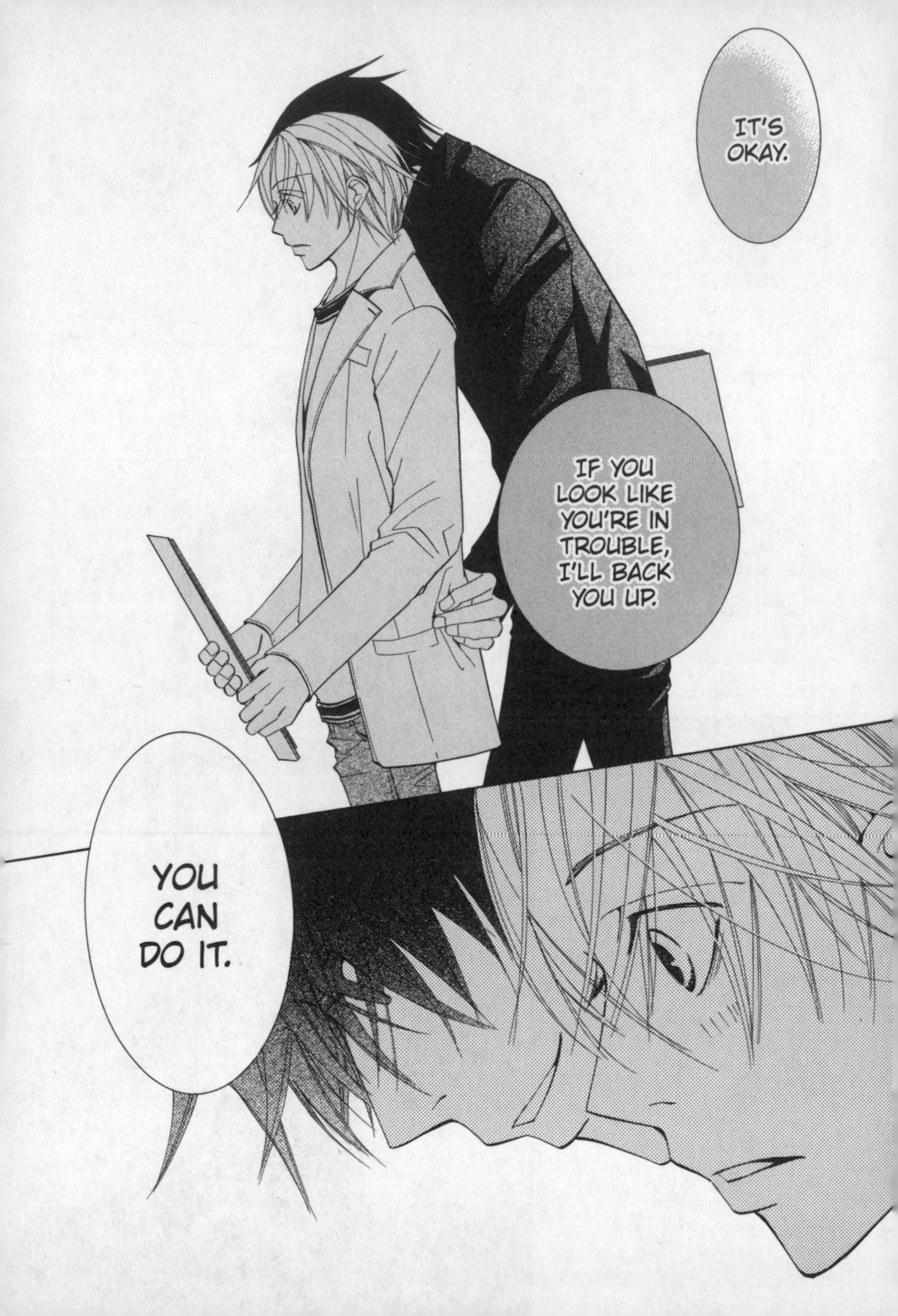
IT'S OKAY.
IF YOU LOOK LIKE YOU'RE IN TROUBLE, I'LL BACK YOU UP.
YOU CAN DO IT.

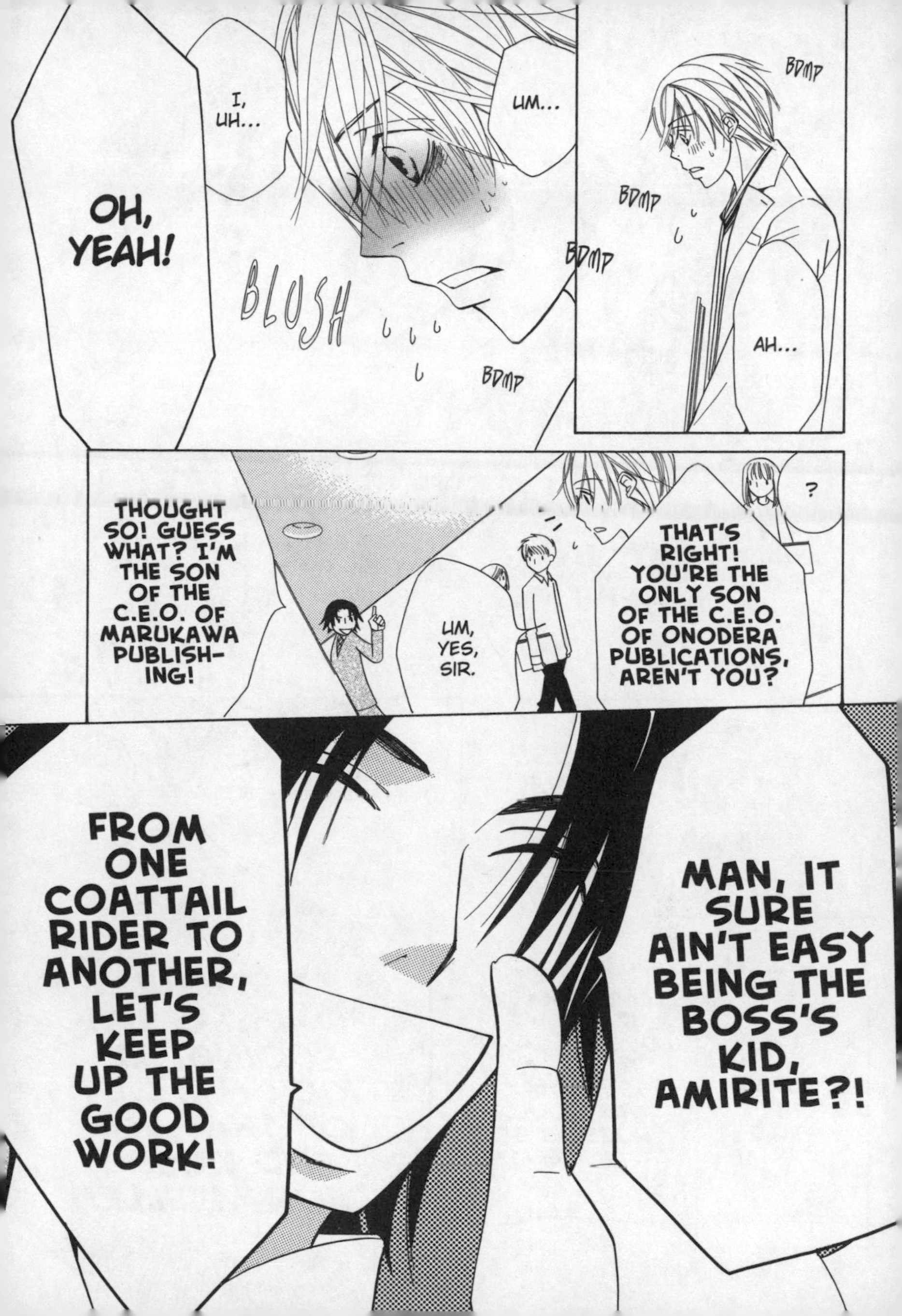
BDMP
BDMP
AH...
UM...
I, UH...
BDMP
BLUSH
BDMP
OH, YEAH!
?
THAT'S RIGHT! YOU'RE THE ONLY SON OF THE C.E.O. OF ONODERA PUBLICATIONS, AREN'T YOU?
UM, YES, SIR.
THOUGHT SO! GUESS WHAT? I'M THE SON OF THE C.E.O. OF MARUKAWA PUBLISHING!
MAN, IT SURE AIN'T EASY BEING THE BOSS'S KID, AMIRITE?!
FROM ONE COATTAIL RIDER TO ANOTHER, LET'S KEEP UP THE GOOD WORK!

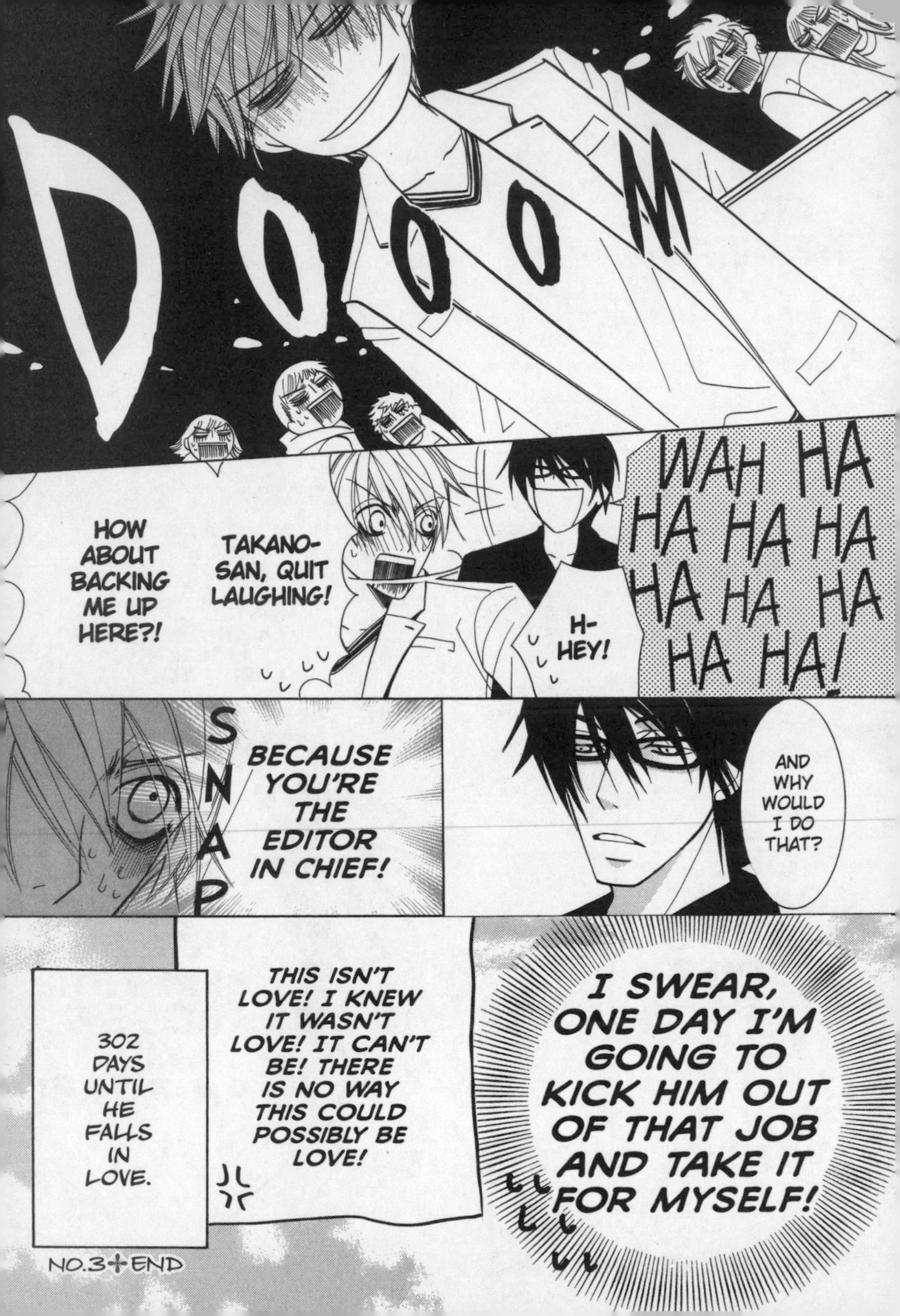
DOOOM
WAH HA HA HA HA HA HA HA HA HA HA!
H-HEY!
TAKANO-SAN, QUIT LAUGHING!
HOW ABOUT BACKING ME UP HERE?!
AND WHY WOULD I DO THAT?
SNAP
BECAUSE YOU'RE THE EDITOR IN CHIEF!
I SWEAR, ONE DAY I'M GOING TO KICK HIM OUT OF THAT JOB AND TAKE IT FOR MYSELF!
THIS ISN'T LOVE! I KNEW IT WASN'T LOVE! IT CAN'T BE! THERE IS NO WAY THIS COULD POSSIBLY BE LOVE!
302 DAYS UNTIL HE FALLS IN LOVE.
NO.3 END

MARUKAWA PUBLISHING TERMINOLOGY & JARGON (PART 5)

*NOTE: ALL OF THE TERMINOLOGY LISTED HEREIN IS SPECIFIC TO MARUKAWA PUBLISHING AND MAY NOT BE APPLICABLE TO THE GENERAL PUBLISHING INDUSTRY.

[BOOK PROPOSAL]

EDITORS, USUALLY THE ONES DIRECTLY IN CHARGE OF THE WORK, WILL FILL OUT THIS FORM TO REQUEST PERMISSION FROM THE COMPANY TO PUBLISH A NEW BOOK. IN MARUKAWA PUBLISHING'S CASE, THE FORM ASKS FOR NOT ONLY PLAN INTENT AND A SUMMARY OF THE WORK BUT ALSO FOR OTHER THINGS SUCH AS THE CREATOR'S TRACK RECORD, THE WORK'S RANKING IN POPULARITY POLLS, AND A SUGGESTED PROMOTIONAL CAMPAIGN.

[PLANNING MEETING]

IN THIS MEETING, EDITORS PRESENT THEIR NEW BOOK PROPOSAL TO COMPANY EXECUTIVES AND ASK FOR IT TO BE APPROVED. IN MARUKAWA, THE EXECUTIVE DIRECTOR ALONG WITH REPRESENTATIVES FROM SALES AND OTHER DEPARTMENTS ATTEND THE MEETING AND REVIEW THE PROPOSAL. IF THE PROPOSAL DOESN'T GET THE OKAY HERE, THE BOOK CAN'T BE MADE.

[PRINT-RUN MEETING]

ONCE A BOOK HAS BEEN APPROVED FOR PRODUCTION, THIS MEETING IS HELD TO DETERMINE HOW MANY COPIES OF THE BOOK WILL BE PRINTED. IN MARUKAWA, THE EXECUTIVE DIRECTOR AND REPRESENTATIVES FROM THE SALES DEPARTMENT, EDITING DEPARTMENT, AND DISTRIBUTION CENTER ATTEND THIS MEETING. EACH REPRESENTATIVE SUGGESTS A NUMBER, AND THEY ALL DISCUSS THE APPROPRIATE AMOUNT TO PRINT, TAKING INTO ACCOUNT THE CREATOR'S TRACK RECORD OF SALES AND THE POPULARITY OF THE WORK.

The World's Greatest First Love
The Case of Ritsu Onodera

EVERY DAY NEW AND PRETTY THINGS ARE ADDED TO THE DEPARTMENT.

MARUKAWA PUBLISHING TERMINOLOGY & JARGON (PART 6)

*NOTE: ALL OF THE TERMINOLOGY LISTED HEREIN IS SPECIFIC TO MARUKAWA PUBLISHING AND MAY NOT BE APPLICABLE TO THE GENERAL PUBLISHING INDUSTRY.

[PHOTOTYPESETTING]

A METHOD OF SETTING TYPE FOR PRINTING, THIS PHOTOGRAPHIC PROCESS IS USED TO PROJECT TEXT OR IMAGES ONTO PHOTOGRAPHIC PAPER TO CREATE BLOCK COPY FOR PRINTING. IT CAN ALSO REFER TO THE CREATED TEXT ITSELF. IN THE CASE OF MANGA, IT IS PRIMARILY USED FOR TEXT SECTIONS (SUCH AS DIALOGUE). THE PROCESS OF ATTACHING PHOTOTYPESETTING TO COPY IS KNOWN AS "PASTE-UP."

[POINT]

THE PHOTOTYPESETTING FONT SIZE IS REFERRED TO AS ITS POINT SIZE. A 1-POINT FONT IS 0.25 MILLIMETERS HIGH. THE JAPANESE WORD FOR POINT, *KYUUSUU*, IS GENERALLY ABBREVIATED TO *KYUU*, LEADING TO NOTATIONS FOR POINT SIZE COMMONLY BEING WRITTEN AS THE ENGLISH LETTER Q. FOR EXAMPLE, A 20-POINT FONT WOULD BE WRITTEN AS 20Q.

[MARUKAWA PUBLISHING MAIDEN CLUB]

THE MARUKAWA PUBLISHING COMPANY'S *EMERALD* EDITORIAL DEPARTMENT, RESPONSIBLE FOR PUBLISHING THE SHOJO MANGA ANTHOLOGY *MONTHLY EMERALD*, IS OFTEN REFERRED TO BY THIS NICKNAME. IT CAME ABOUT BECAUSE OF A POLICY OF THE DEPARTMENT'S CURRENT EDITOR IN CHIEF, WHO INSISTS ON "UNDERSTANDING A MAIDEN'S (THE ANTHOLOGY'S TARGET DEMOGRAPHIC) FEELINGS FROM THE ENVIRONMENT INWARD." IT IS RUMORED THAT NEW HIRE RITSU ONODERA IS THE MOST RECENT INVOLUNTARY INDUCTEE TO THE CLUB.

The **World's Greatest First Love**

The Case of Ritsu Onodera

HATORI-SAN, YOSHIKAWA SENSEI'S CHAPTER HAS JUST ARRIVED!

...

IMPOSSIBLE. SHE NEVER SENDS ANYTHING IN ON TIME.

CHIHARU YOSHIKAWA

TRUST LEVEL: ZERO

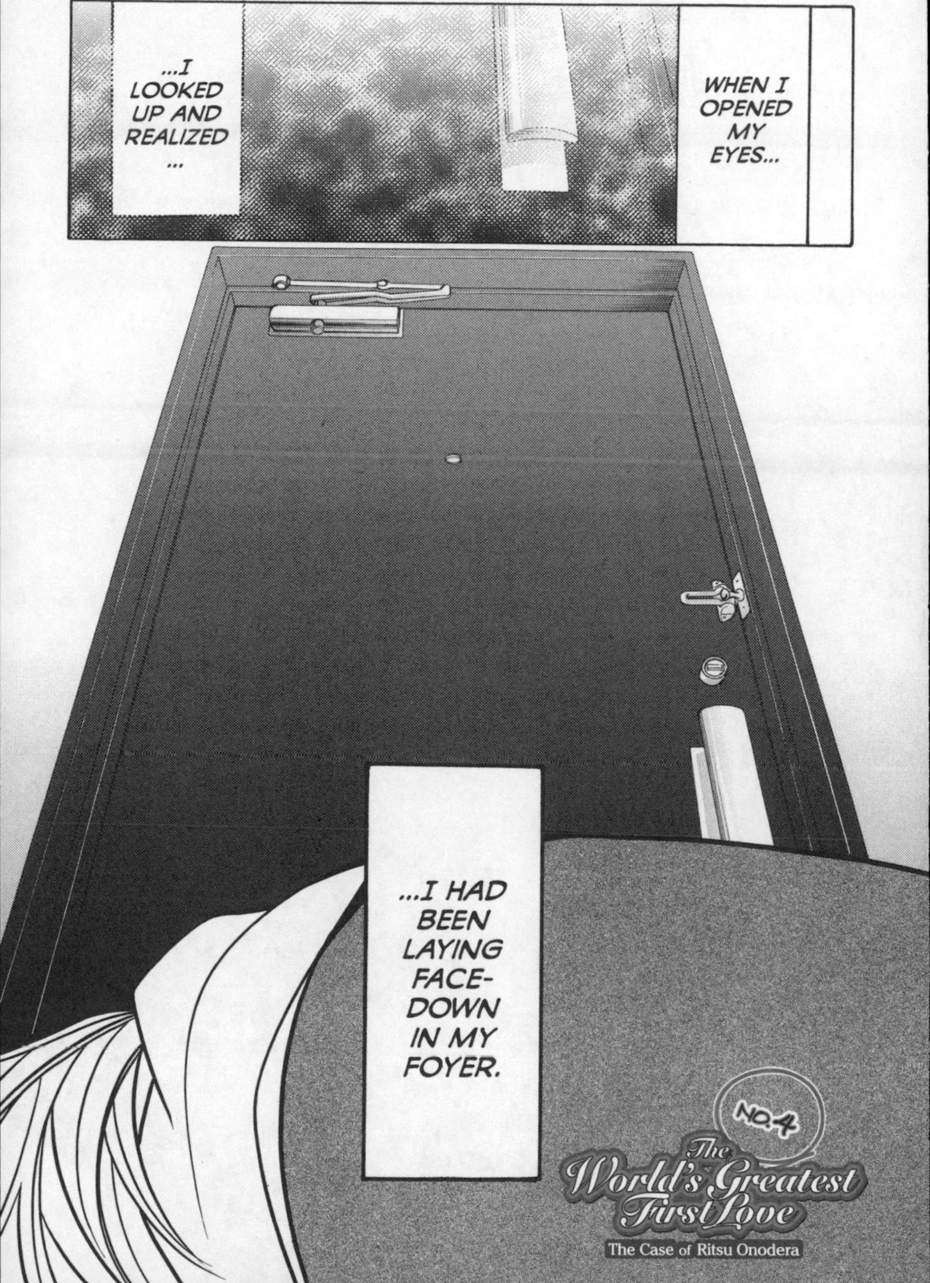
WHEN I OPENED MY EYES...
...I LOOKED UP AND REALIZED ...
...I HAD BEEN LAYING FACE-DOWN IN MY FOYER.
NO.4
The World's Greatest First Love
The Case of Ritsu Onodera

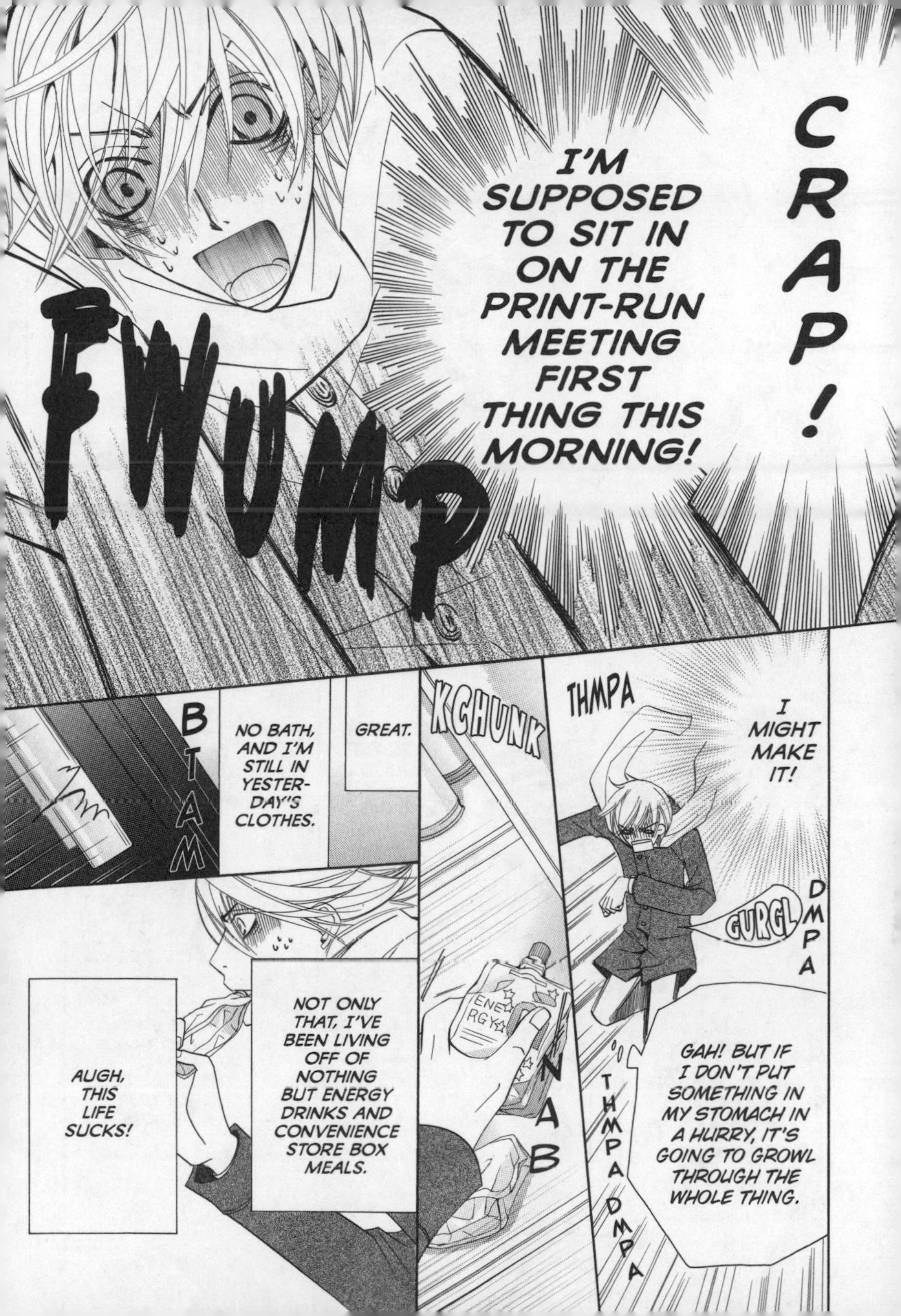
CRAP!
I'M SUPPOSED TO SIT IN ON THE PRINT-RUN MEETING FIRST THING THIS MORNING!
FWUMP
THMPA
I MIGHT MAKE IT!
DMPA DMPA
GURGL
GAH! BUT IF I DON'T PUT SOMETHING IN MY STOMACH IN A HURRY, IT'S GOING TO GROWL THROUGH THE WHOLE THING.
THMPA DMPA DMPA
KCHUNK
ENERGY
NAB
GREAT.
NO BATH, AND I'M STILL IN YESTER-DAY'S CLOTHES.
BTAM
NOT ONLY THAT, I'VE BEEN LIVING OFF OF NOTHING BUT ENERGY DRINKS AND CONVENIENCE STORE BOX MEALS.
AUGH, THIS LIFE SUCKS!

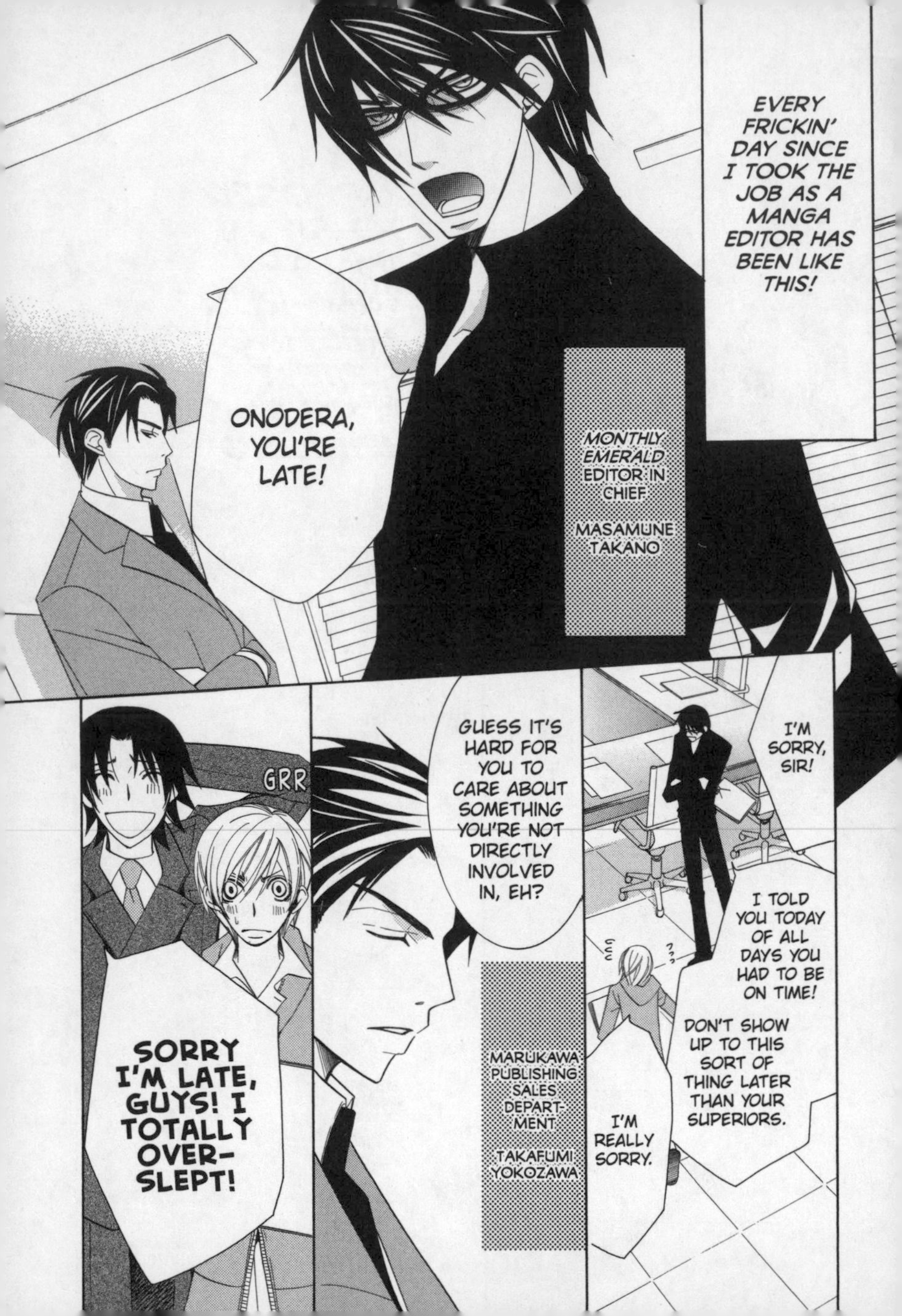
EVERY FRICKIN' DAY SINCE I TOOK THE JOB AS A MANGA EDITOR HAS BEEN LIKE THIS!
MONTHLY EMERALD EDITOR IN CHIEF
MASAMUNE TAKANO
ONODERA, YOU'RE LATE!
I'M SORRY, SIR!
I TOLD YOU TODAY OF ALL DAYS YOU HAD TO BE ON TIME!
DON'T SHOW UP TO THIS SORT OF THING LATER THAN YOUR SUPERIORS.
I'M REALLY SORRY.
GUESS IT'S HARD FOR YOU TO CARE ABOUT SOMETHING YOU'RE NOT DIRECTLY INVOLVED IN, EH?
MARUKAWA PUBLISHING SALES DEPARTMENT
TAKAFUMI YOKOZAWA
GRR
SORRY I'M LATE, GUYS! I TOTALLY OVER-SLEPT!

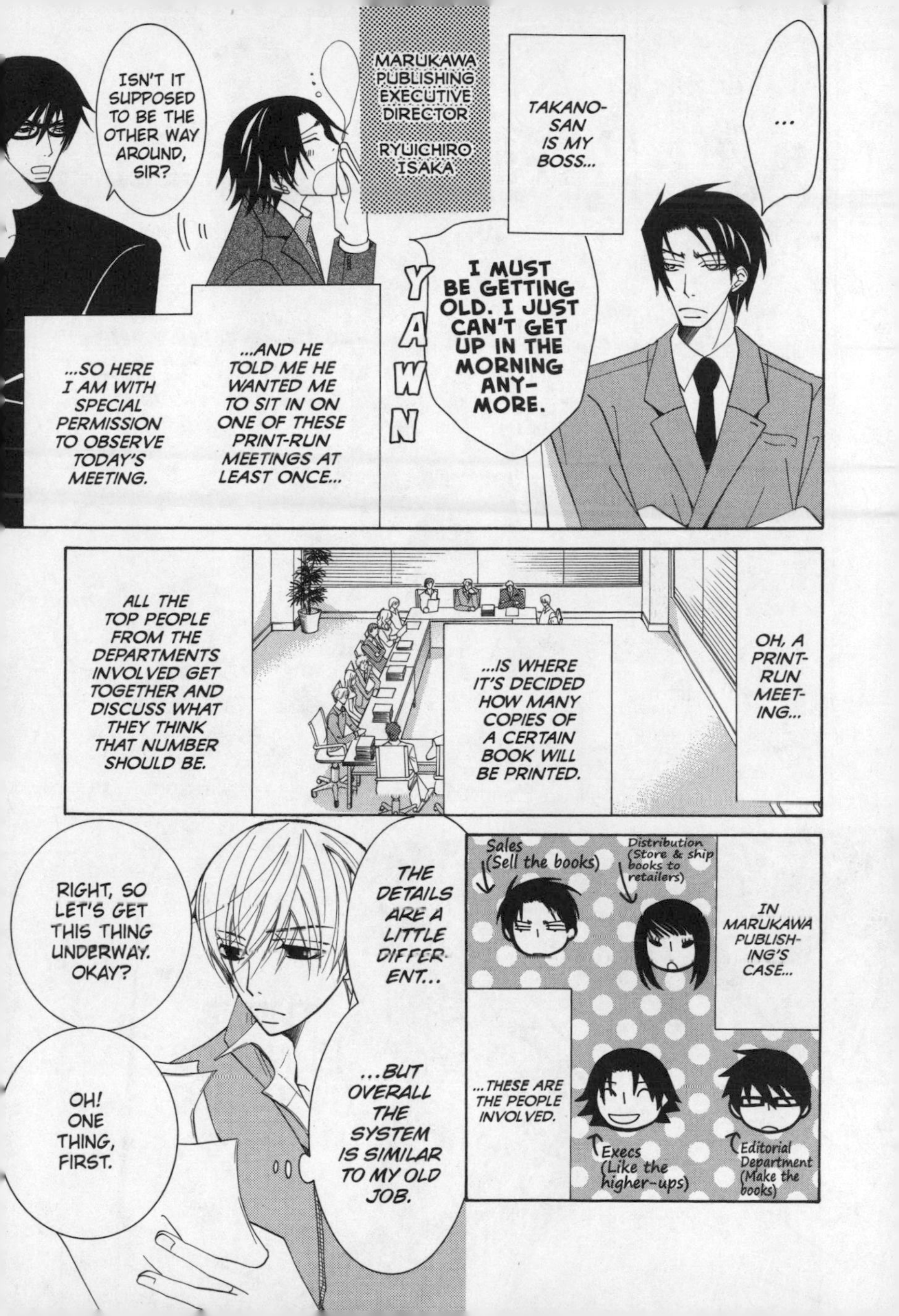
...
TAKANO-SAN IS MY BOSS...
MARUKAWA PUBLISHING EXECUTIVE DIRECTOR RYUICHIRO ISAKA
I MUST BE GETTING OLD. I JUST CAN'T GET UP IN THE MORNING ANY-MORE.
YAWN
ISN'T IT SUPPOSED TO BE THE OTHER WAY AROUND, SIR?
...AND HE TOLD ME HE WANTED ME TO SIT IN ON ONE OF THESE PRINT-RUN MEETINGS AT LEAST ONCE...
...SO HERE I AM WITH SPECIAL PERMISSION TO OBSERVE TODAY'S MEETING.
OH, A PRINT-RUN MEETING...
...IS WHERE IT'S DECIDED HOW MANY COPIES OF A CERTAIN BOOK WILL BE PRINTED.
ALL THE TOP PEOPLE FROM THE DEPARTMENTS INVOLVED GET TOGETHER AND DISCUSS WHAT THEY THINK THAT NUMBER SHOULD BE.
IN MARUKAWA PUBLISHING'S CASE...
Distribution (Store & ship books to retailers)
Sales (Sell the books)
...THESE ARE THE PEOPLE INVOLVED.
Editorial Department (Make the books)
Execs (Like the higher-ups)
THE DETAILS ARE A LITTLE DIFFERENT...
RIGHT, SO LET'S GET THIS THING UNDERWAY. OKAY?
...BUT OVERALL THE SYSTEM IS SIMILAR TO MY OLD JOB.
OH! ONE THING, FIRST.

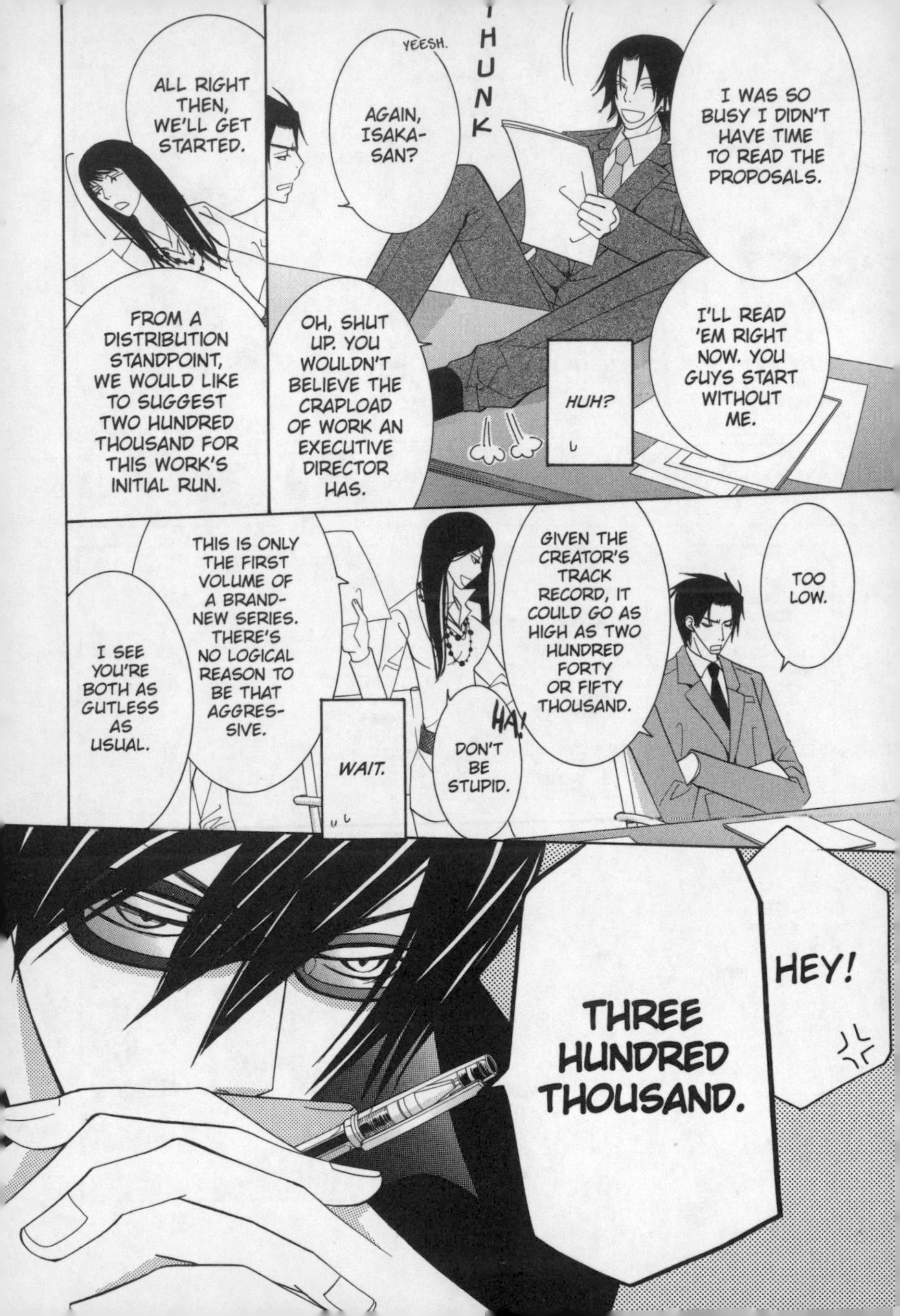
I WAS SO BUSY I DIDN'T HAVE TIME TO READ THE PROPOSALS.
THUNK
YEESH.
AGAIN, ISAKA-SAN?
I'LL READ 'EM RIGHT NOW. YOU GUYS START WITHOUT ME.
HUH?
OH, SHUT UP. YOU WOULDN'T BELIEVE THE CRAPLOAD OF WORK AN EXECUTIVE DIRECTOR HAS.
ALL RIGHT THEN, WE'LL GET STARTED.
FROM A DISTRIBUTION STANDPOINT, WE WOULD LIKE TO SUGGEST TWO HUNDRED THOUSAND FOR THIS WORK'S INITIAL RUN.
TOO LOW.
GIVEN THE CREATOR'S TRACK RECORD, IT COULD GO AS HIGH AS TWO HUNDRED FORTY OR FIFTY THOUSAND.
HA!
DON'T BE STUPID.
THIS IS ONLY THE FIRST VOLUME OF A BRAND-NEW SERIES. THERE'S NO LOGICAL REASON TO BE THAT AGGRESSIVE.
WAIT.
I SEE YOU'RE BOTH AS GUTLESS AS USUAL.
HEY!
THREE HUNDRED THOUSAND.

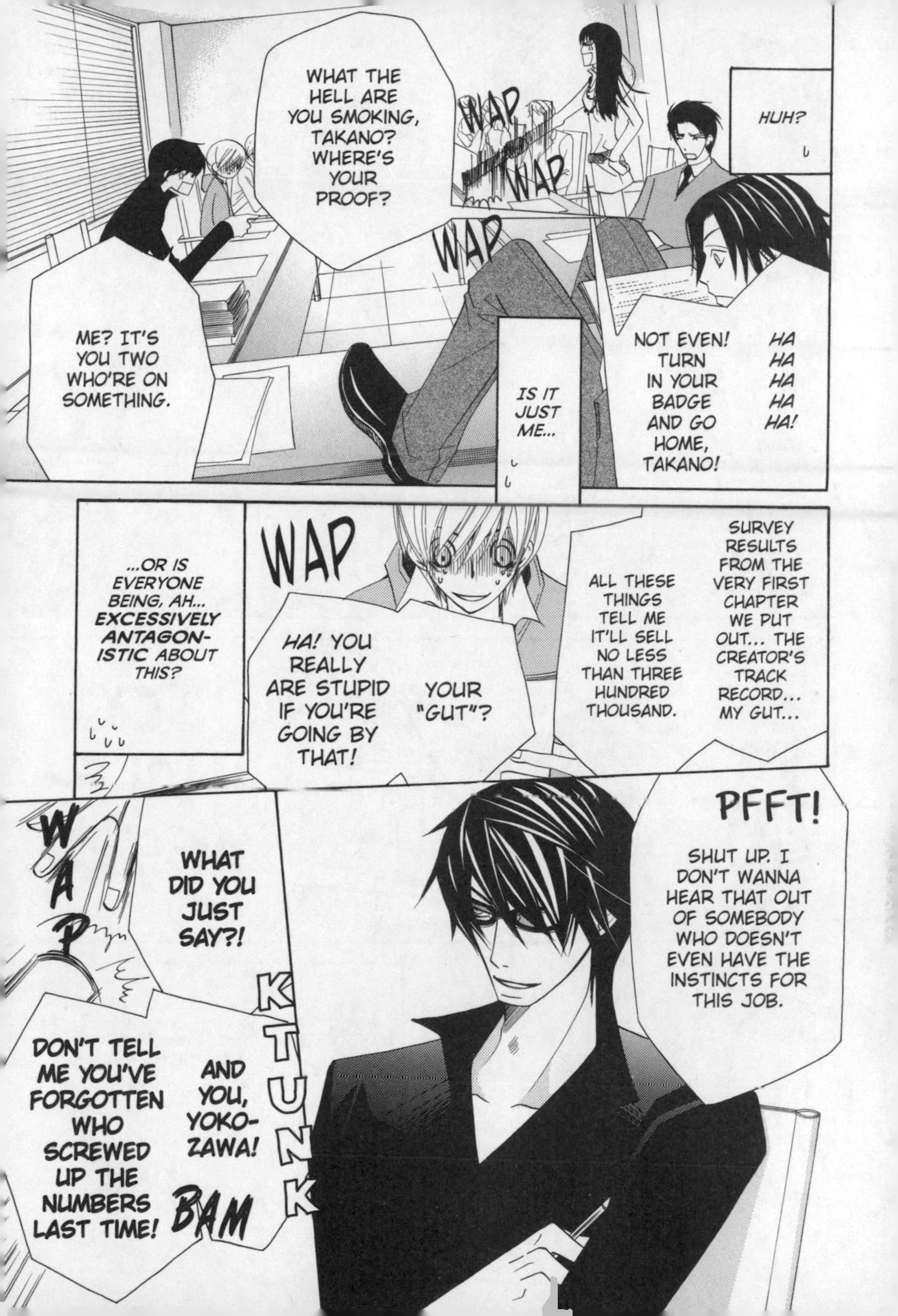
HUH?
WHAT THE HELL ARE YOU SMOKING, TAKANO? WHERE'S YOUR PROOF?
WAP WAP
WAP
HA HA HA HA HA!
NOT EVEN! TURN IN YOUR BADGE AND GO HOME, TAKANO!
IS IT JUST ME...
ME? IT'S YOU TWO WHO'RE ON SOMETHING.
SURVEY RESULTS FROM THE VERY FIRST CHAPTER WE PUT OUT... THE CREATOR'S TRACK RECORD... MY GUT...
ALL THESE THINGS TELL ME IT'LL SELL NO LESS THAN THREE HUNDRED THOUSAND.
YOUR "GUT"?
HA! YOU REALLY ARE STUPID IF YOU'RE GOING BY THAT!
WAP
...OR IS EVERYONE BEING, AH... EXCESSIVELY ANTAGONISTIC ABOUT THIS?
PFFT!
SHUT UP. I DON'T WANNA HEAR THAT OUT OF SOMEBODY WHO DOESN'T EVEN HAVE THE INSTINCTS FOR THIS JOB.
WHAT DID YOU JUST SAY?!
KTUNK
AND YOU, YOKOZAWA!
DON'T TELL ME YOU'VE FORGOTTEN WHO SCREWED UP THE NUMBERS LAST TIME!
BAM
WAP

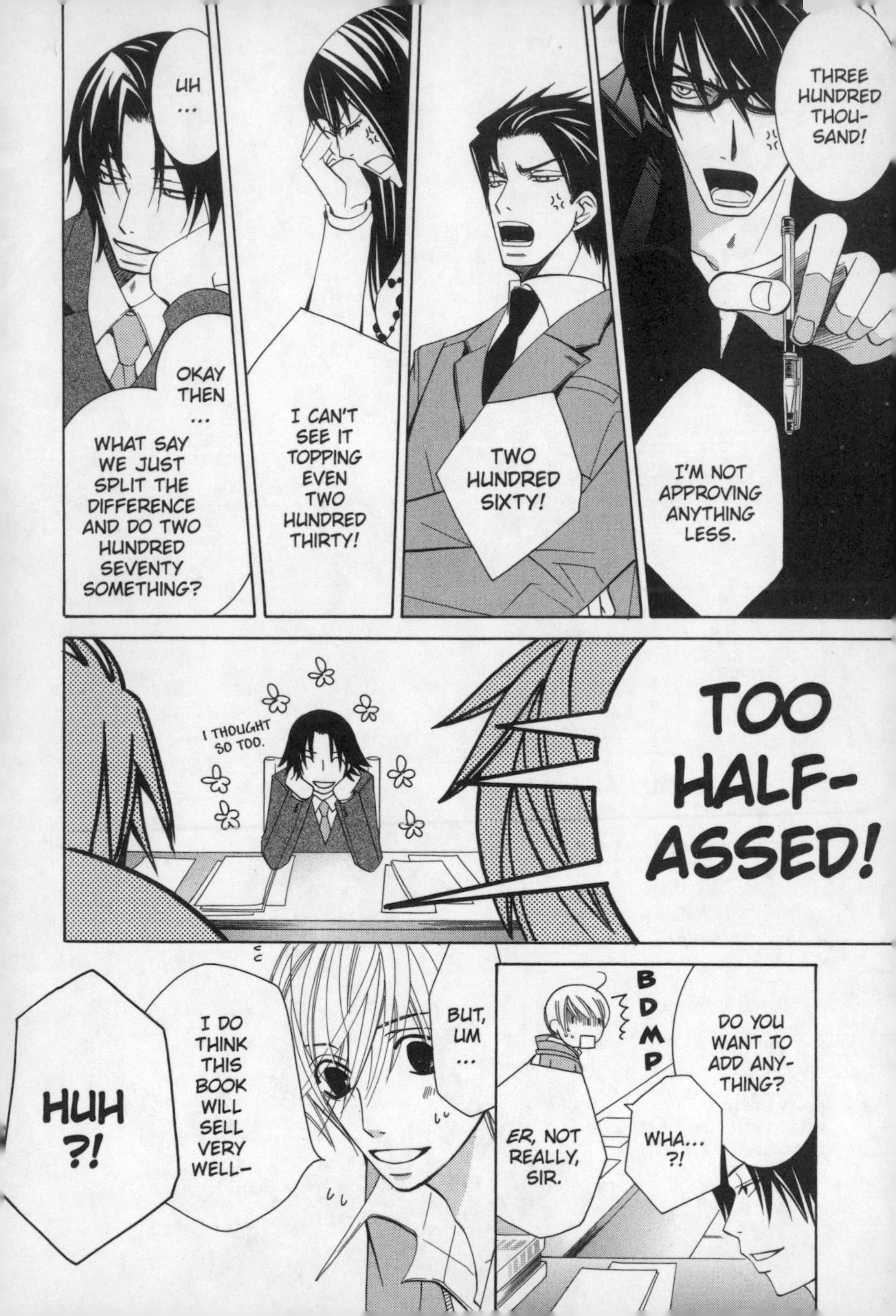
THREE HUNDRED THOUSAND!
I'M NOT APPROVING ANYTHING LESS.
TWO HUNDRED SIXTY!
I CAN'T SEE IT TOPPING EVEN TWO HUNDRED THIRTY!
UH...
OKAY THEN... WHAT SAY WE JUST SPLIT THE DIFFERENCE AND DO TWO HUNDRED SEVENTY SOMETHING?
TOO HALF-ASSED!
I THOUGHT SO TOO.
DO YOU WANT TO ADD ANYTHING?
BDMP
WHA...?!
ER, NOT REALLY, SIR.
BUT, UM...
I DO THINK THIS BOOK WILL SELL VERY WELL-
HUH?!

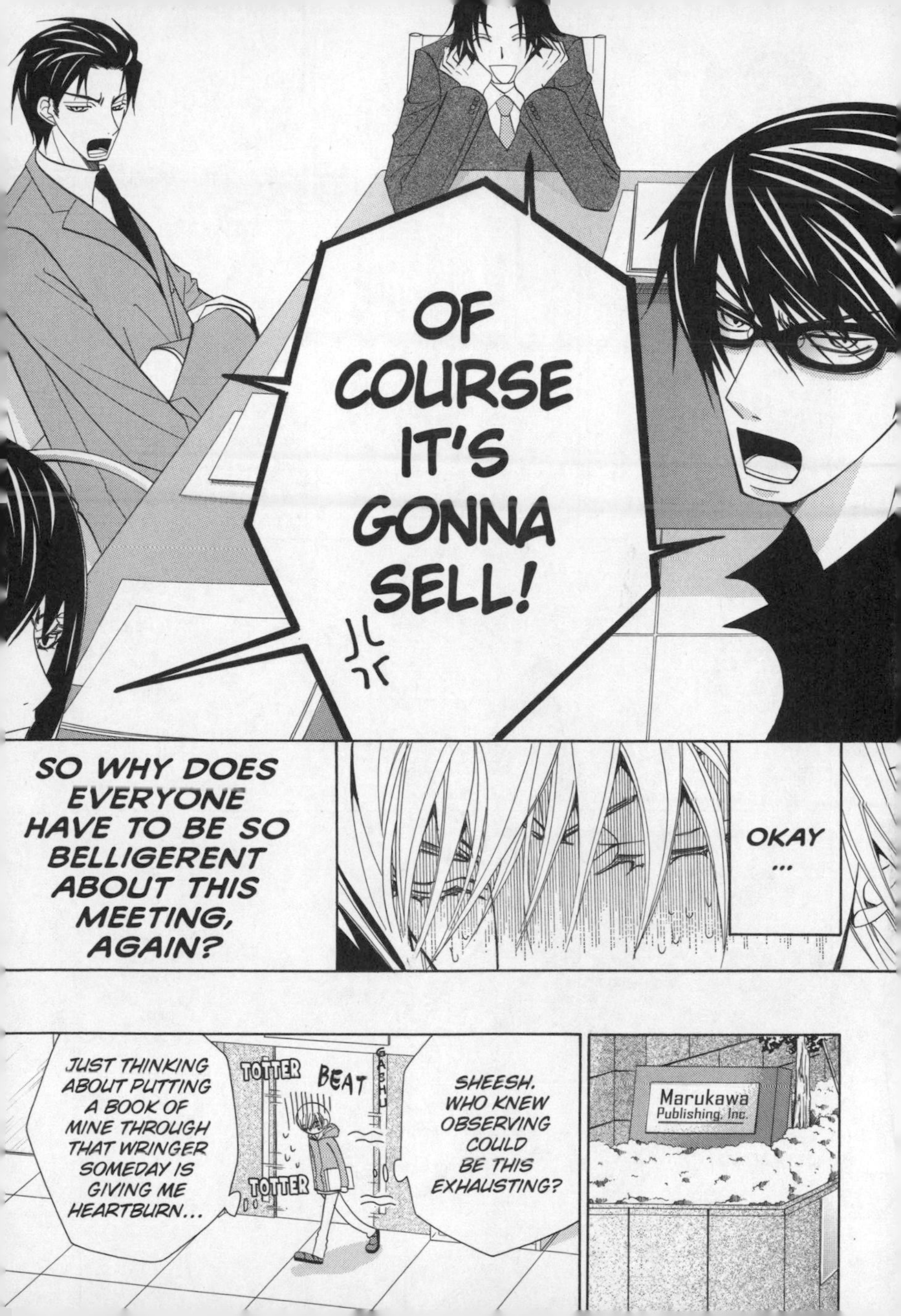
OF COURSE IT'S GONNA SELL!
OKAY ...
SO WHY DOES EVERYONE HAVE TO BE SO BELLIGERENT ABOUT THIS MEETING, AGAIN?
Marukawa Publishing, Inc.
SHEESH. WHO KNEW OBSERVING COULD BE THIS EXHAUSTING?
GASHU
BEAT
TOTTER
TOTTER
JUST THINKING ABOUT PUTTING A BOOK OF MINE THROUGH THAT WRINGER SOMEDAY IS GIVING ME HEARTBURN...

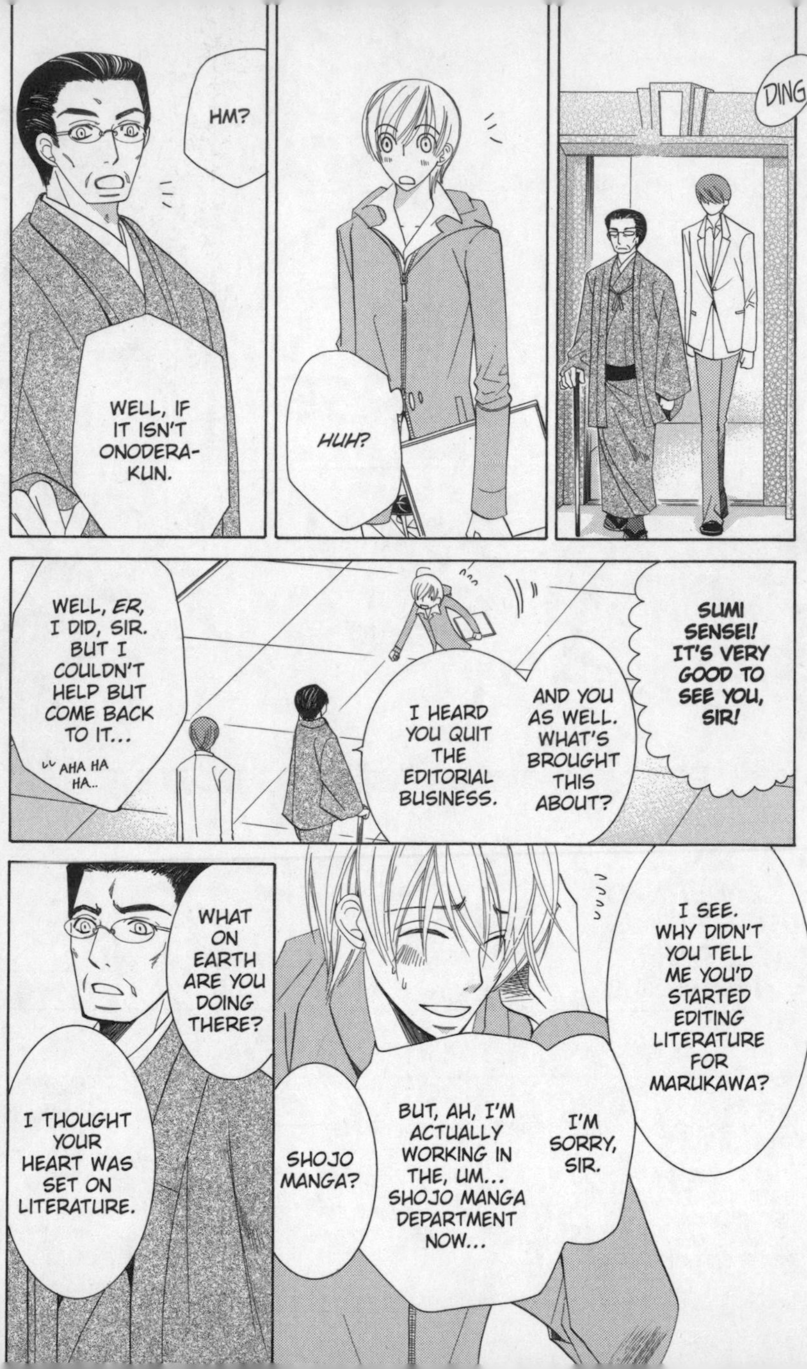
DING
HUH?
HM?
WELL, IF IT ISN'T ONODERA-KUN.
SUMI SENSEI! IT'S VERY GOOD TO SEE YOU, SIR!
AND YOU AS WELL. WHAT'S BROUGHT THIS ABOUT?
I HEARD YOU QUIT THE EDITORIAL BUSINESS.
WELL, *ER,* I DID, SIR. BUT I COULDN'T HELP BUT COME BACK TO IT...
AHA HA HA..
I SEE. WHY DIDN'T YOU TELL ME YOU'D STARTED EDITING LITERATURE FOR MARUKAWA?
I'M SORRY, SIR.
BUT, AH, I'M ACTUALLY WORKING IN THE, UM... SHOJO MANGA DEPARTMENT NOW...
SHOJO MANGA?
WHAT ON EARTH ARE YOU DOING THERE?
I THOUGHT YOUR HEART WAS SET ON LITERATURE.

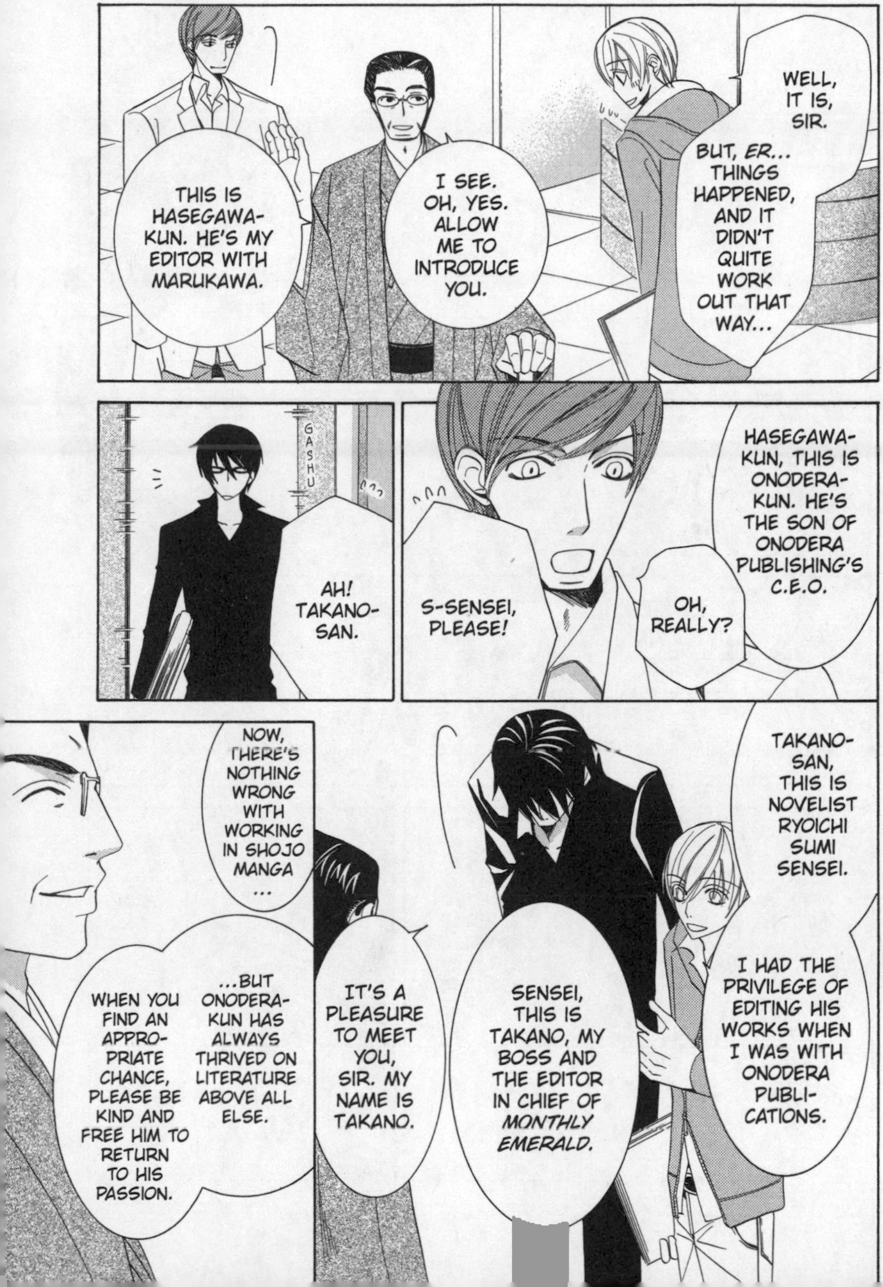
WELL, IT IS, SIR.
BUT, *ER*... THINGS HAPPENED, AND IT DIDN'T QUITE WORK OUT THAT WAY...
I SEE. OH, YES. ALLOW ME TO INTRODUCE YOU.
THIS IS HASEGAWA-KUN. HE'S MY EDITOR WITH MARUKAWA.
HASEGAWA-KUN, THIS IS ONODERA-KUN. HE'S THE SON OF ONODERA PUBLISHING'S C.E.O.
OH, REALLY?
S-SENSEI, PLEASE!
GASHU
AH! TAKANO-SAN.
TAKANO-SAN, THIS IS NOVELIST RYOICHI SUMI SENSEI.
I HAD THE PRIVILEGE OF EDITING HIS WORKS WHEN I WAS WITH ONODERA PUBLICATIONS.
SENSEI, THIS IS TAKANO, MY BOSS AND THE EDITOR IN CHIEF OF *MONTHLY EMERALD*.
IT'S A PLEASURE TO MEET YOU, SIR. MY NAME IS TAKANO.
NOW, THERE'S NOTHING WRONG WITH WORKING IN SHOJO MANGA...
...BUT ONODERA-KUN HAS ALWAYS THRIVED ON LITERATURE ABOVE ALL ELSE.
WHEN YOU FIND AN APPROPRIATE CHANCE, PLEASE BE KIND AND FREE HIM TO RETURN TO HIS PASSION.

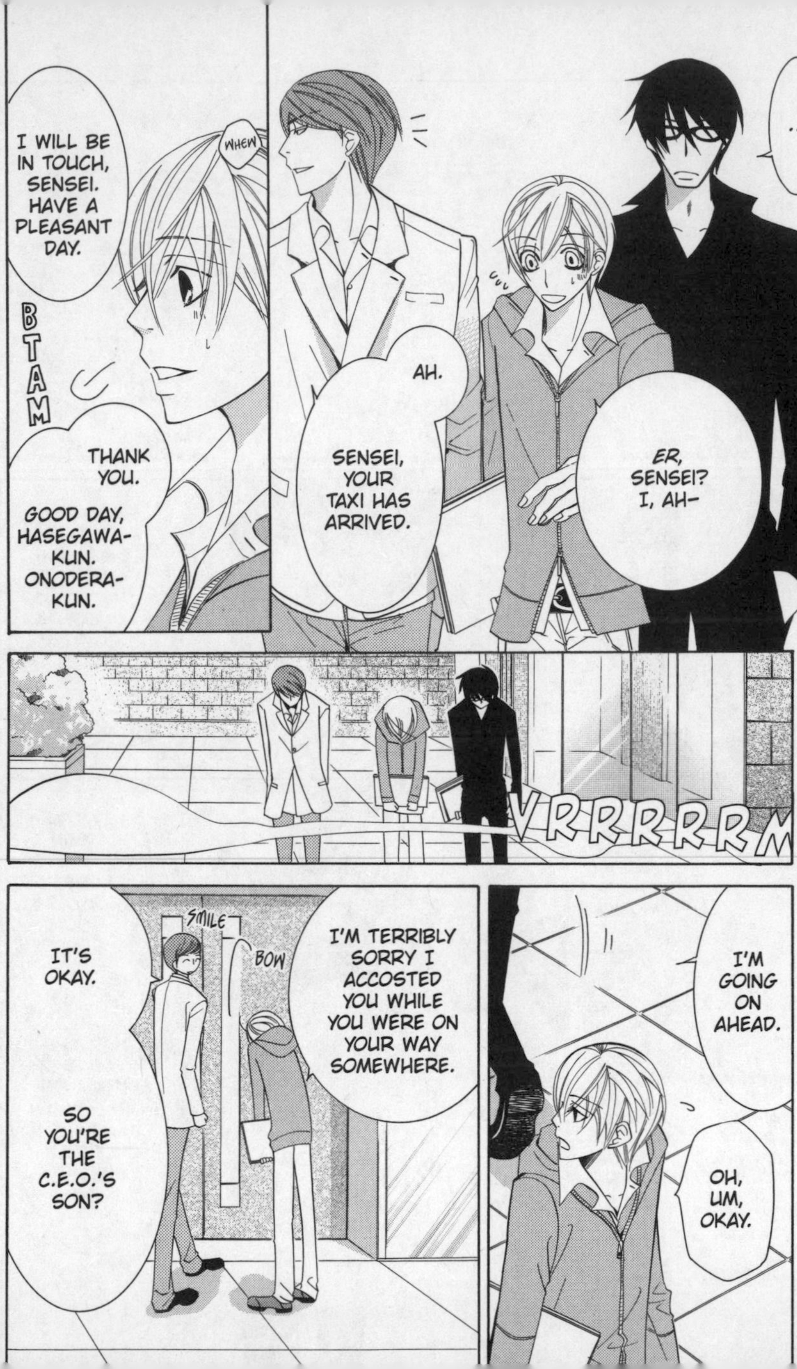
...
ER, SENSEI? I, AH-
AH.
SENSEI, YOUR TAXI HAS ARRIVED.
WHEW
I WILL BE IN TOUCH, SENSEI. HAVE A PLEASANT DAY.
BTAM
THANK YOU.
GOOD DAY, HASEGAWA-KUN. ONODERA-KUN.
VRRRRRM
I'M GOING ON AHEAD.
OH, UM, OKAY.
SMILE
BOW
I'M TERRIBLY SORRY I ACCOSTED YOU WHILE YOU WERE ON YOUR WAY SOMEWHERE.
IT'S OKAY.
SO YOU'RE THE C.E.O.'S SON?

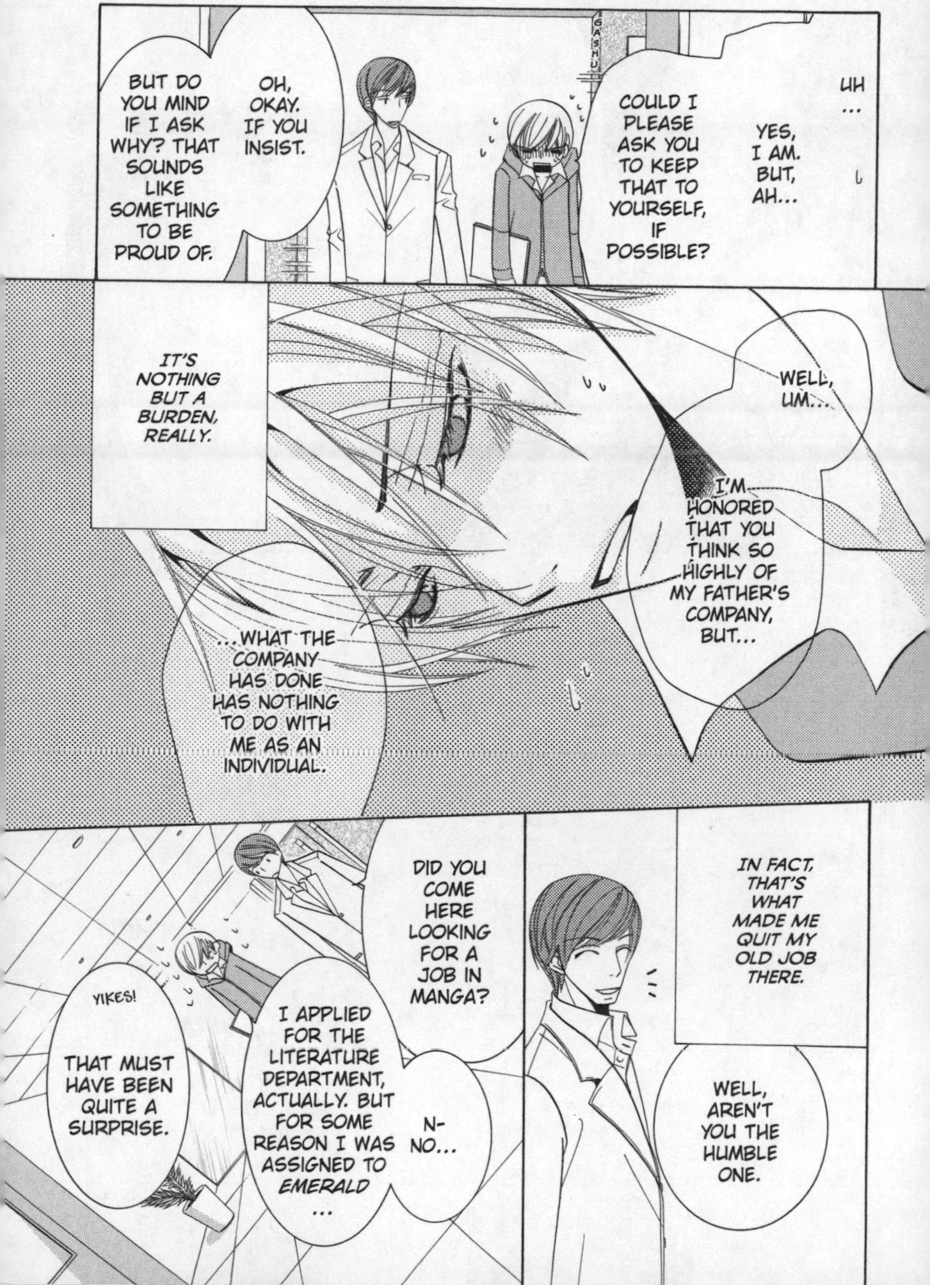
GASHU
UH ...
YES, I AM. BUT, AH...
COULD I PLEASE ASK YOU TO KEEP THAT TO YOURSELF, IF POSSIBLE?
OH, OKAY. IF YOU INSIST.
BUT DO YOU MIND IF I ASK WHY? THAT SOUNDS LIKE SOMETHING TO BE PROUD OF.
WELL, UM...
I'M HONORED THAT YOU THINK SO HIGHLY OF MY FATHER'S COMPANY, BUT...
IT'S NOTHING BUT A BURDEN, REALLY.
...WHAT THE COMPANY HAS DONE HAS NOTHING TO DO WITH ME AS AN INDIVIDUAL.
IN FACT, THAT'S WHAT MADE ME QUIT MY OLD JOB THERE.
WELL, AREN'T YOU THE HUMBLE ONE.
DID YOU COME HERE LOOKING FOR A JOB IN MANGA?
N-NO...
I APPLIED FOR THE LITERATURE DEPARTMENT, ACTUALLY. BUT FOR SOME REASON I WAS ASSIGNED TO *EMERALD* ...
YIKES!
THAT MUST HAVE BEEN QUITE A SURPRISE.

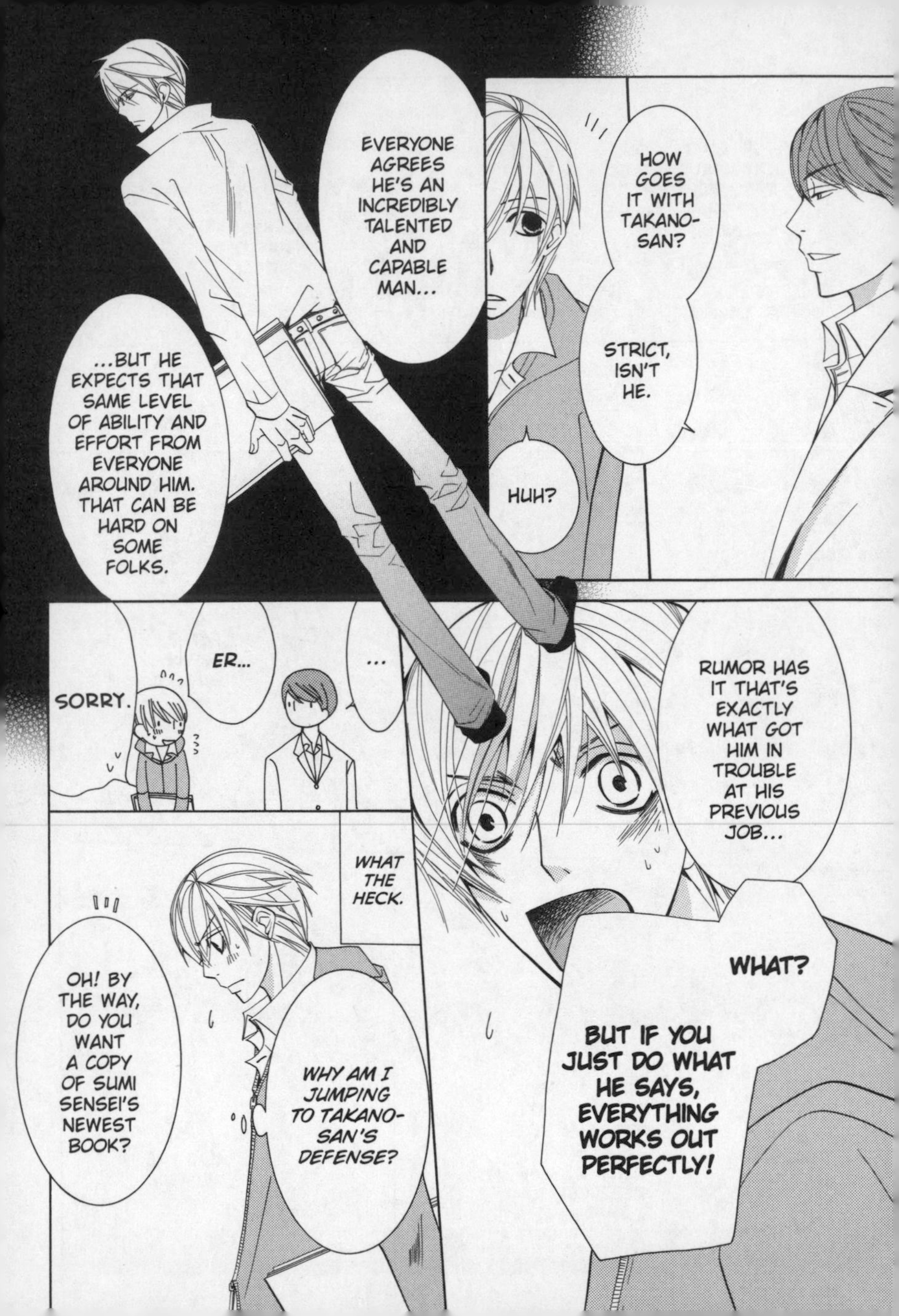
HOW GOES IT WITH TAKANO-SAN?
STRICT, ISN'T HE.
HUH?
EVERYONE AGREES HE'S AN INCREDIBLY TALENTED AND CAPABLE MAN...
...BUT HE EXPECTS THAT SAME LEVEL OF ABILITY AND EFFORT FROM EVERYONE AROUND HIM. THAT CAN BE HARD ON SOME FOLKS.
RUMOR HAS IT THAT'S EXACTLY WHAT GOT HIM IN TROUBLE AT HIS PREVIOUS JOB...
WHAT?
BUT IF YOU JUST DO WHAT HE SAYS, EVERYTHING WORKS OUT PERFECTLY!
...
ER...
SORRY.
WHAT THE HECK.
WHY AM I JUMPING TO TAKANO-SAN'S DEFENSE?
OH! BY THE WAY, DO YOU WANT A COPY OF SUMI SENSEI'S NEWEST BOOK?

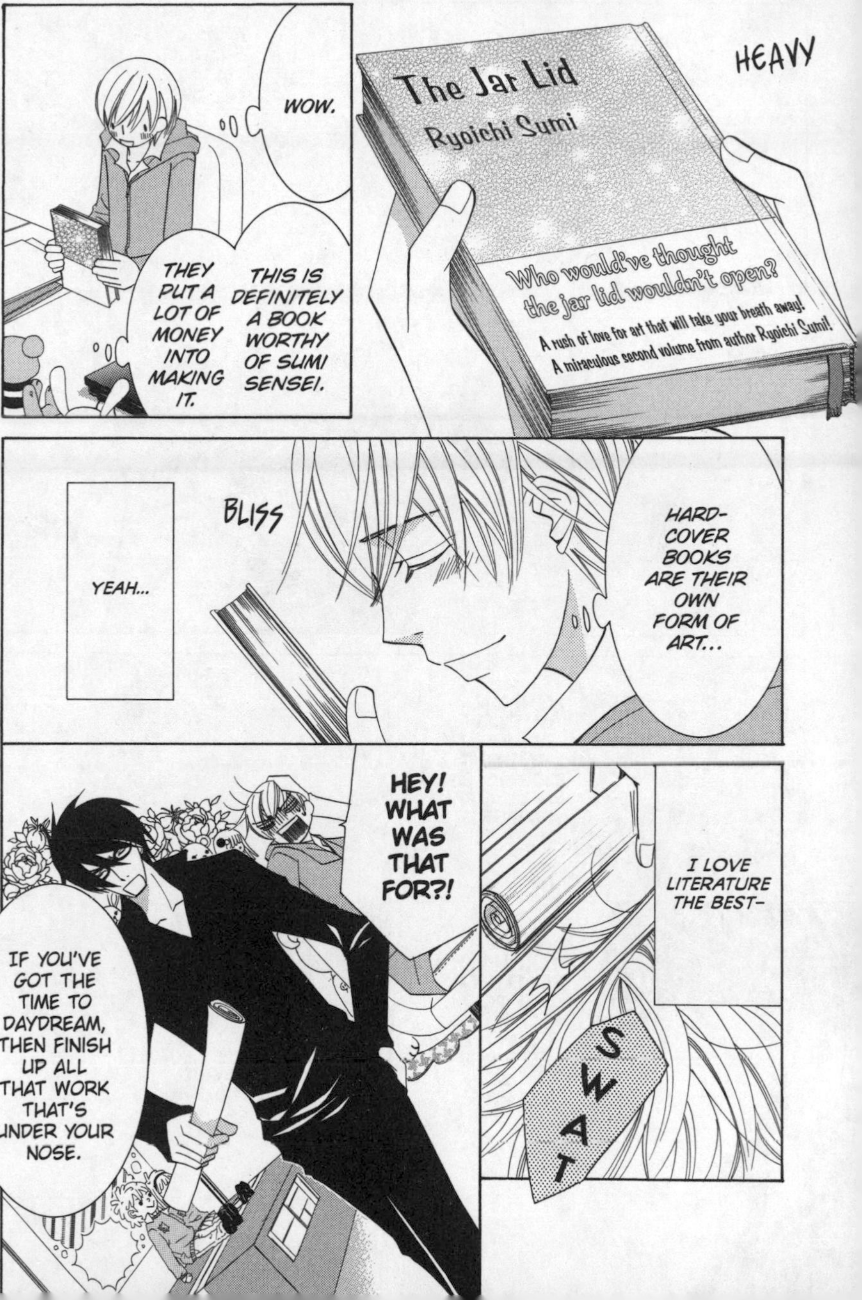
HEAVY
The Jar Lid
Ryoichi Sumi
Who would've thought the jar lid wouldn't open?
A rush of love for art that will take your breath away!
A miraculous second volume from author Ryoichi Sumi!
WOW.
THIS IS DEFINITELY A BOOK WORTHY OF SUMI SENSEI.
THEY PUT A LOT OF MONEY INTO MAKING IT.
HARD-COVER BOOKS ARE THEIR OWN FORM OF ART...
BLISS
YEAH...
I LOVE LITERATURE THE BEST–
SWAT
HEY! WHAT WAS THAT FOR?!
IF YOU'VE GOT THE TIME TO DAYDREAM, THEN FINISH UP ALL THAT WORK THAT'S UNDER YOUR NOSE.

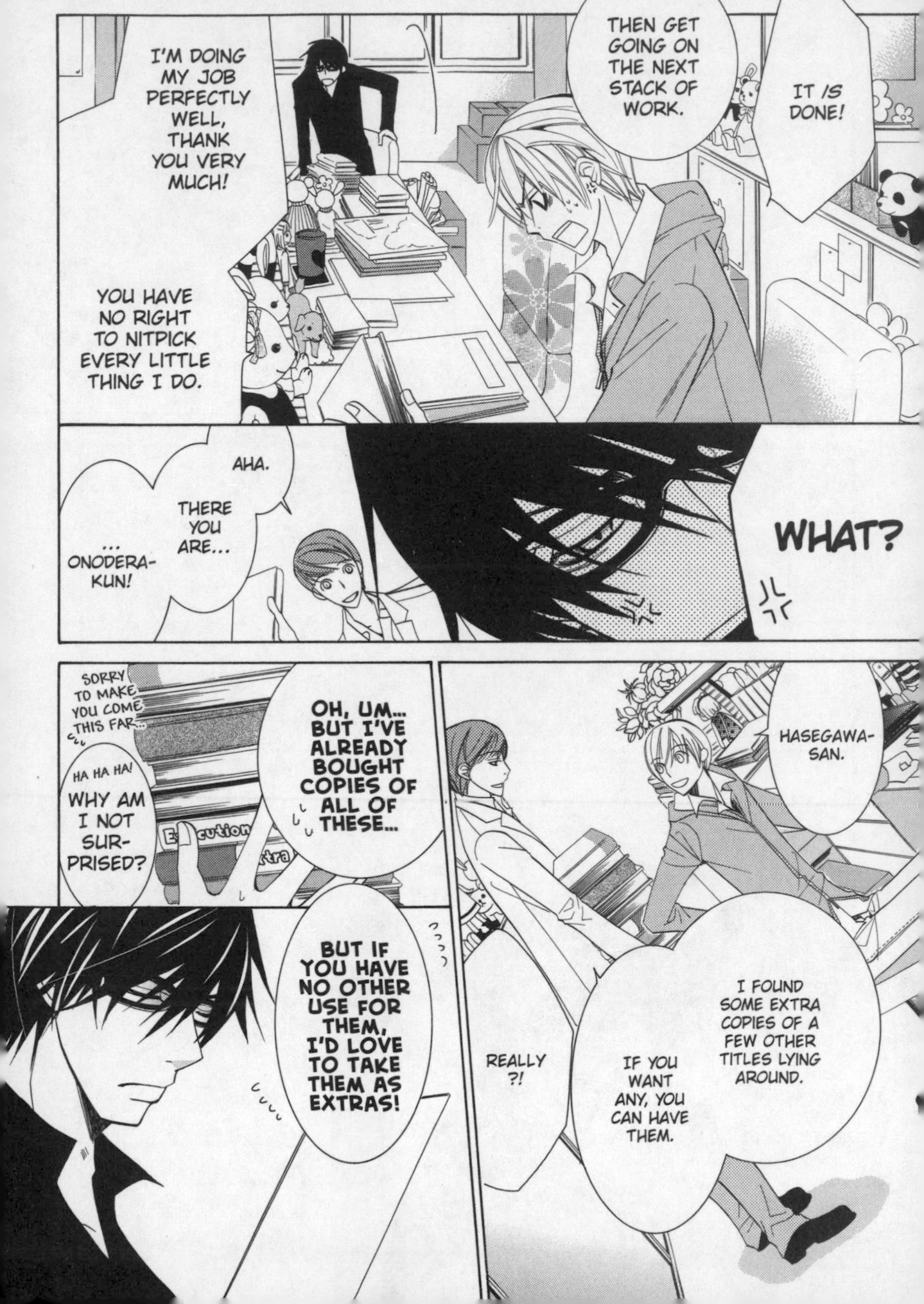
IT IS DONE!
THEN GET GOING ON THE NEXT STACK OF WORK.
I'M DOING MY JOB PERFECTLY WELL, THANK YOU VERY MUCH!
YOU HAVE NO RIGHT TO NITPICK EVERY LITTLE THING I DO.
WHAT?
AHA.
THERE YOU ARE...
...ONODERA-KUN!
HASEGAWA-SAN.
OH, UM... BUT I'VE ALREADY BOUGHT COPIES OF ALL OF THESE...
SORRY TO MAKE YOU COME THIS FAR...
HA HA HA!
WHY AM I NOT SUR-PRISED?
I FOUND SOME EXTRA COPIES OF A FEW OTHER TITLES LYING AROUND.
IF YOU WANT ANY, YOU CAN HAVE THEM.
REALLY?!
BUT IF YOU HAVE NO OTHER USE FOR THEM, I'D LOVE TO TAKE THEM AS EXTRAS!

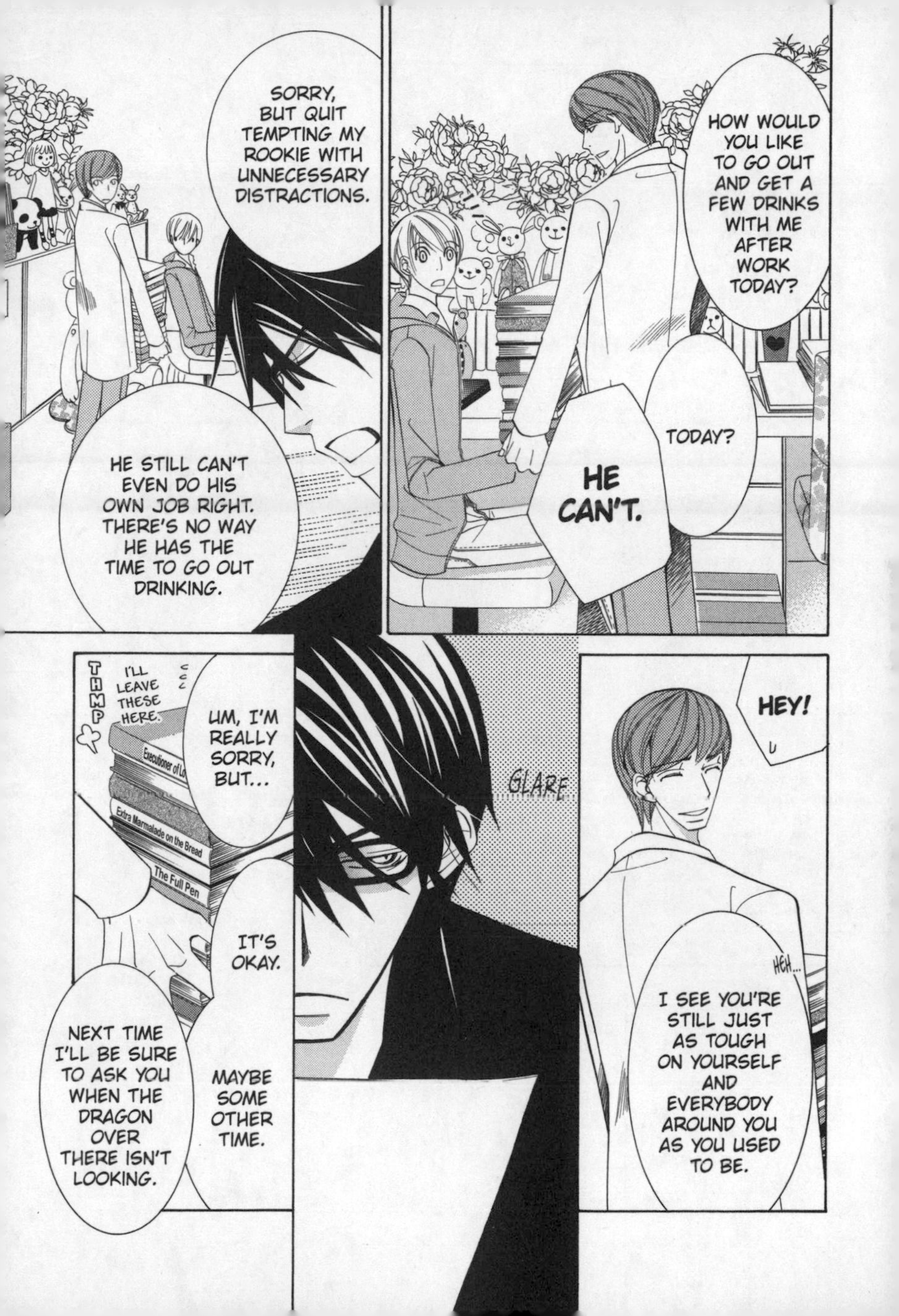
HOW WOULD YOU LIKE TO GO OUT AND GET A FEW DRINKS WITH ME AFTER WORK TODAY?
TODAY?
HE CAN'T.
SORRY, BUT QUIT TEMPTING MY ROOKIE WITH UNNECESSARY DISTRACTIONS.
HE STILL CAN'T EVEN DO HIS OWN JOB RIGHT. THERE'S NO WAY HE HAS THE TIME TO GO OUT DRINKING.
HEY!
HEH...
I SEE YOU'RE STILL JUST AS TOUGH ON YOURSELF AND EVERYBODY AROUND YOU AS YOU USED TO BE.
GLARE
THMP
I'LL LEAVE THESE HERE.
UM, I'M REALLY SORRY, BUT...
Extra Marmalade on the Bread
The Full Pen
IT'S OKAY.
MAYBE SOME OTHER TIME.
NEXT TIME I'LL BE SURE TO ASK YOU WHEN THE DRAGON OVER THERE ISN'T LOOKING.

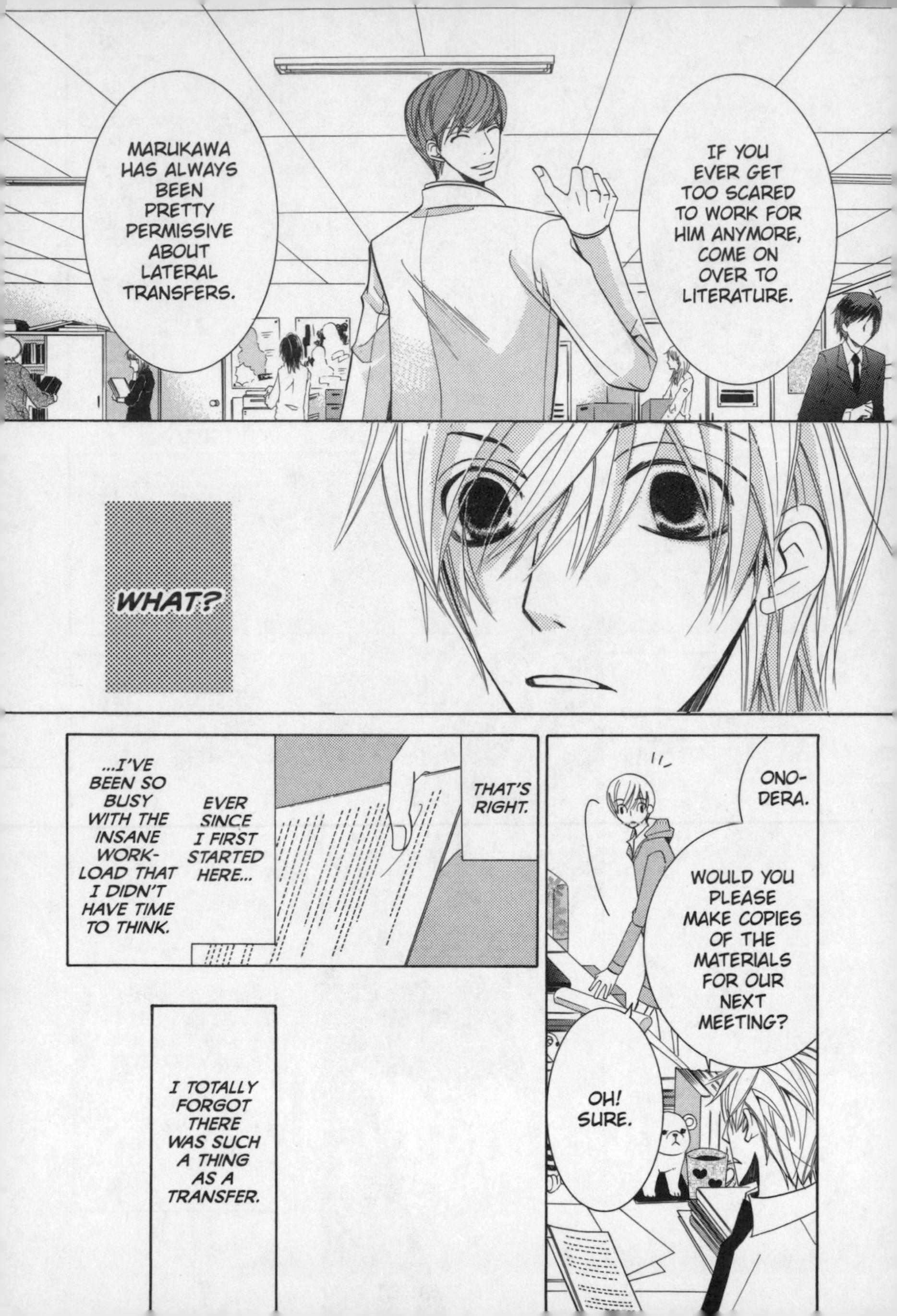
IF YOU EVER GET TOO SCARED TO WORK FOR HIM ANYMORE, COME ON OVER TO LITERATURE.
MARUKAWA HAS ALWAYS BEEN PRETTY PERMISSIVE ABOUT LATERAL TRANSFERS.
WHAT?
ONO-DERA.
WOULD YOU PLEASE MAKE COPIES OF THE MATERIALS FOR OUR NEXT MEETING?
OH! SURE.
THAT'S RIGHT.
EVER SINCE I FIRST STARTED HERE...
...I'VE BEEN SO BUSY WITH THE INSANE WORK-LOAD THAT I DIDN'T HAVE TIME TO THINK.
I TOTALLY FORGOT THERE WAS SUCH A THING AS A TRANSFER.

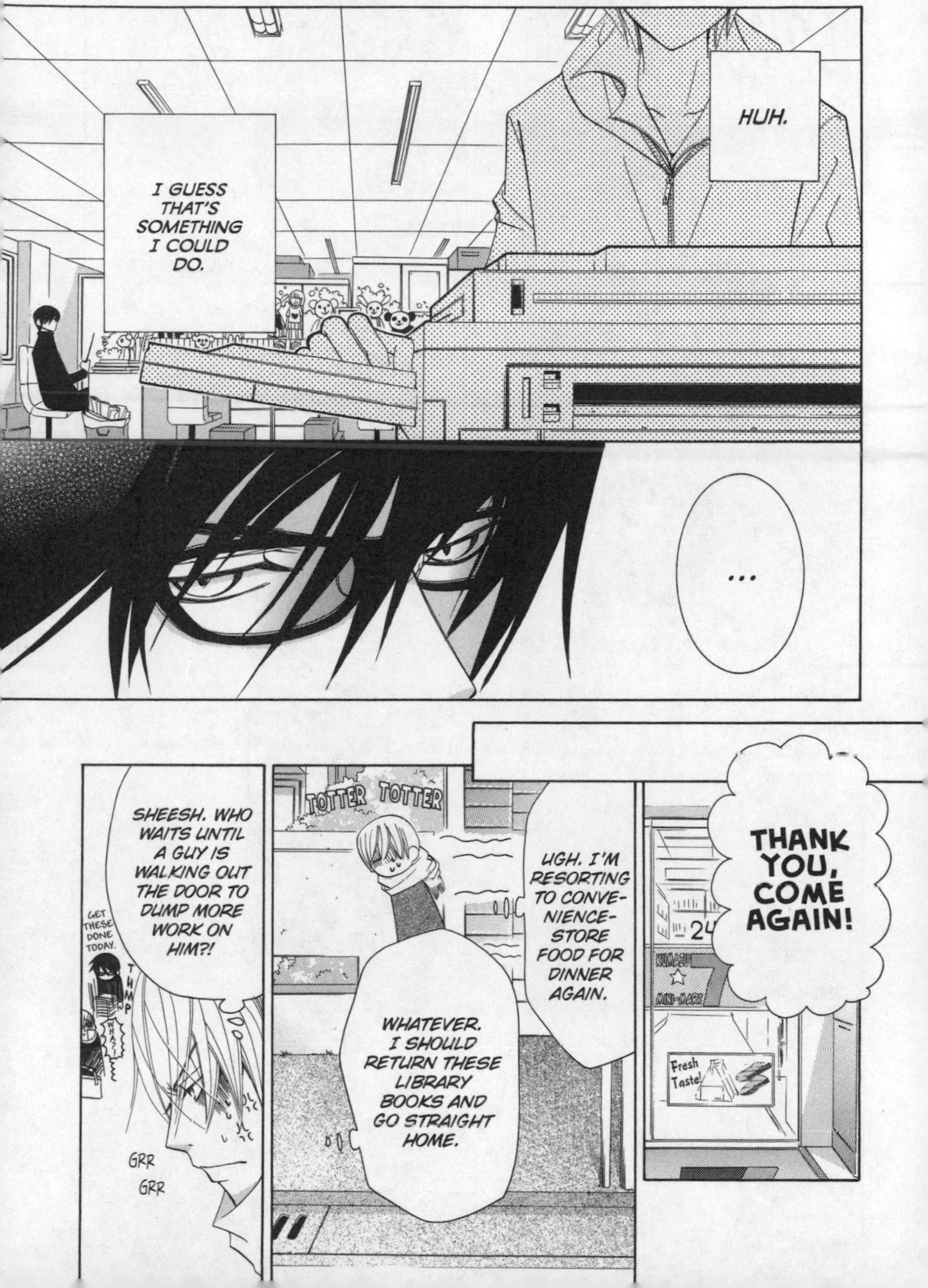
HUH.
I GUESS THAT'S SOMETHING I COULD DO.
THANK YOU, COME AGAIN!
24
KUMAZU MINI-MART
Fresh Taste!
TOTTER TOTTER
UGH. I'M RESORTING TO CONVENIENCE-STORE FOOD FOR DINNER AGAIN.
WHATEVER. I SHOULD RETURN THESE LIBRARY BOOKS AND GO STRAIGHT HOME.
SHEESH. WHO WAITS UNTIL A GUY IS WALKING OUT THE DOOR TO DUMP MORE WORK ON HIM?!
GET THESE DONE TODAY.
THUMP
WHA?!
GRR
GRR

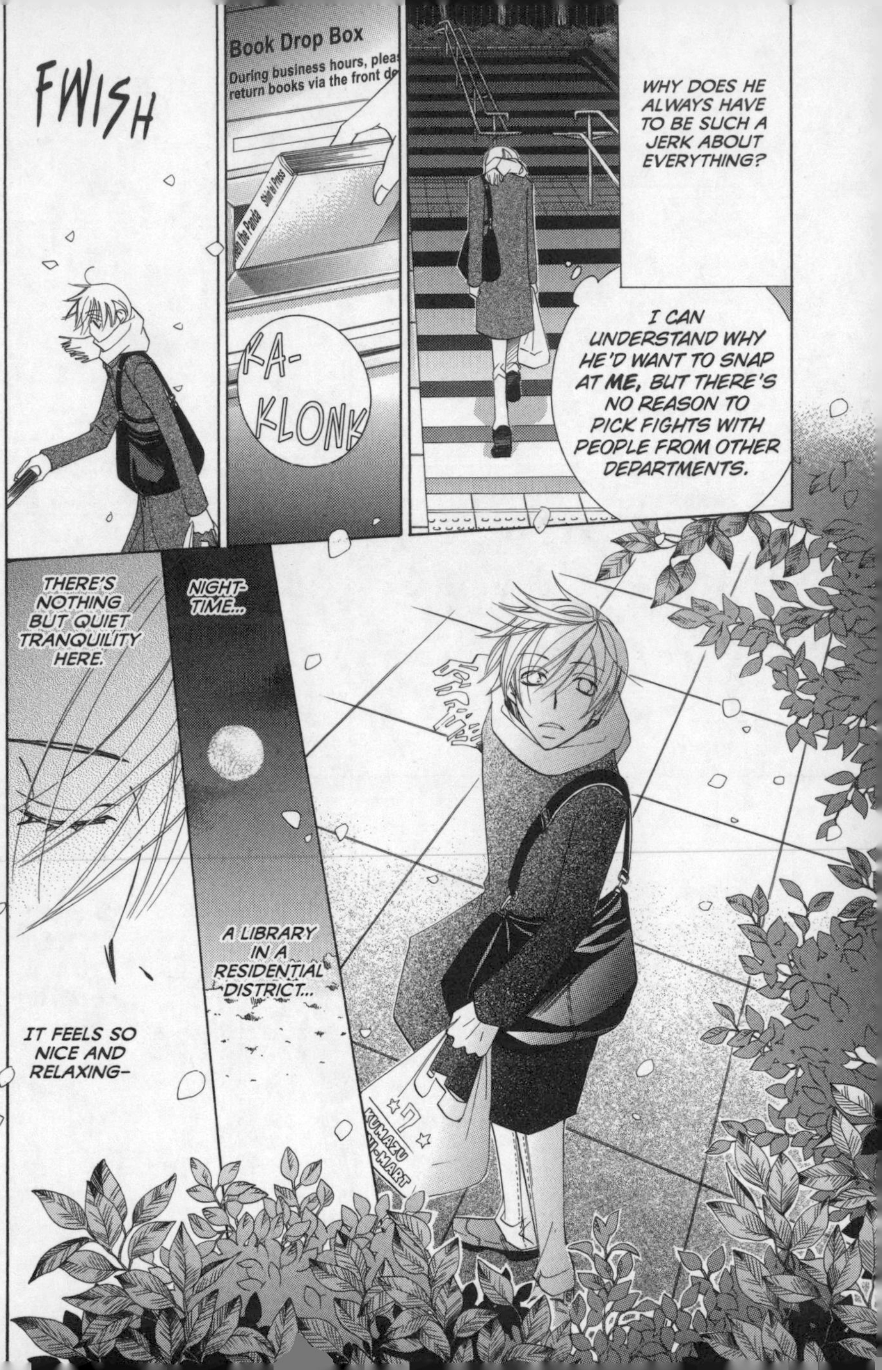

WHY DOES HE ALWAYS HAVE TO BE SUCH A JERK ABOUT EVERYTHING?
I CAN UNDERSTAND WHY HE'D WANT TO SNAP AT ME, BUT THERE'S NO REASON TO PICK FIGHTS WITH PEOPLE FROM OTHER DEPARTMENTS.
Book Drop Box
KA-KLONK
FWISH
NIGHT-TIME...
A LIBRARY IN A RESIDENTIAL DISTRICT...
THERE'S NOTHING BUT QUIET TRANQUILITY HERE.
IT FEELS SO NICE AND RELAXING-

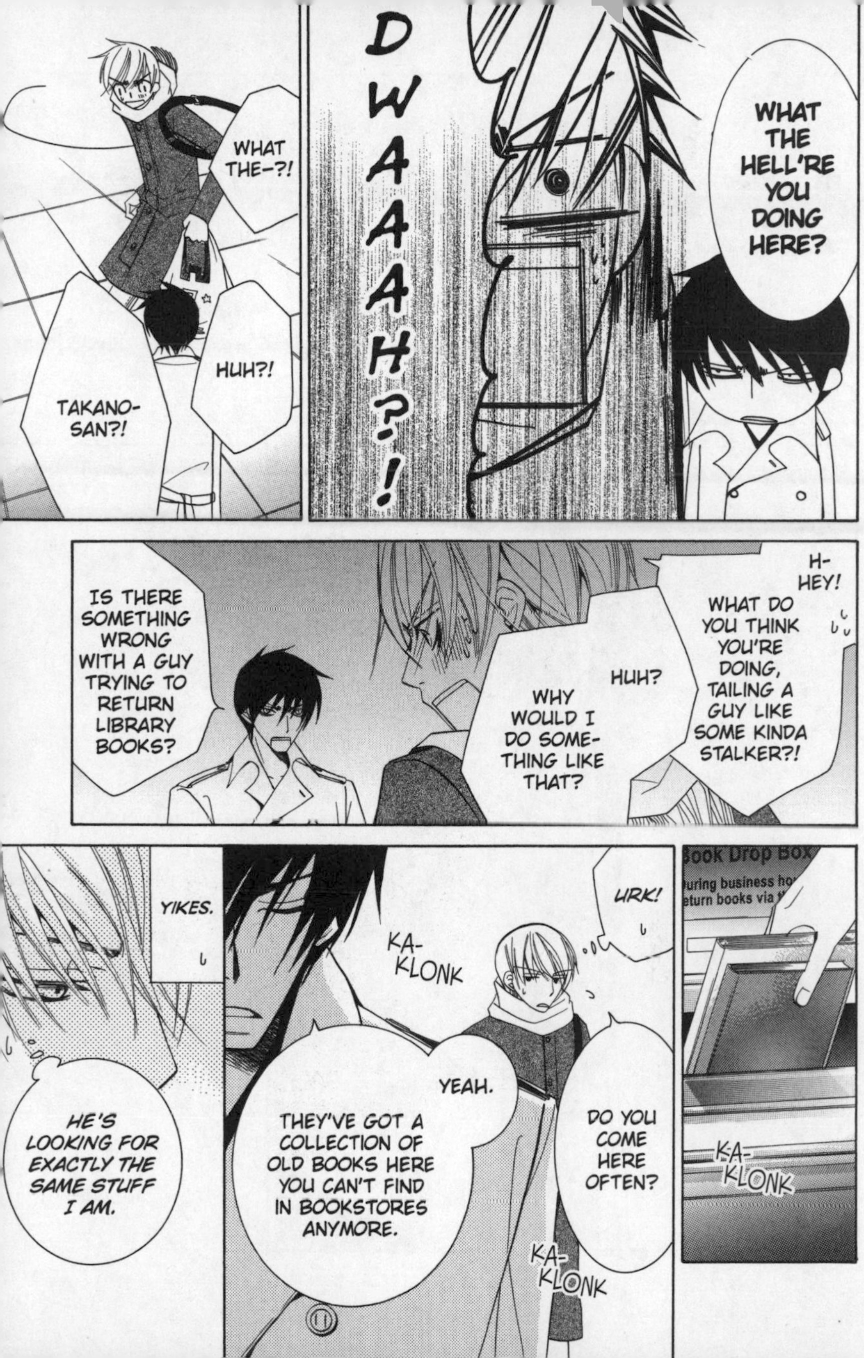
WHAT THE HELL'RE YOU DOING HERE?
DWAAAH?!
WHAT THE-?!
HUH?!
TAKANO-SAN?!
H-HEY! WHAT DO YOU THINK YOU'RE DOING, TAILING A GUY LIKE SOME KINDA STALKER?!
HUH? WHY WOULD I DO SOMETHING LIKE THAT?
IS THERE SOMETHING WRONG WITH A GUY TRYING TO RETURN LIBRARY BOOKS?
KA-KLONK
URK!
KA-KLONK
DO YOU COME HERE OFTEN?
YEAH.
THEY'VE GOT A COLLECTION OF OLD BOOKS HERE YOU CAN'T FIND IN BOOKSTORES ANYMORE.
KA-KLONK
YIKES.
HE'S LOOKING FOR EXACTLY THE SAME STUFF I AM.

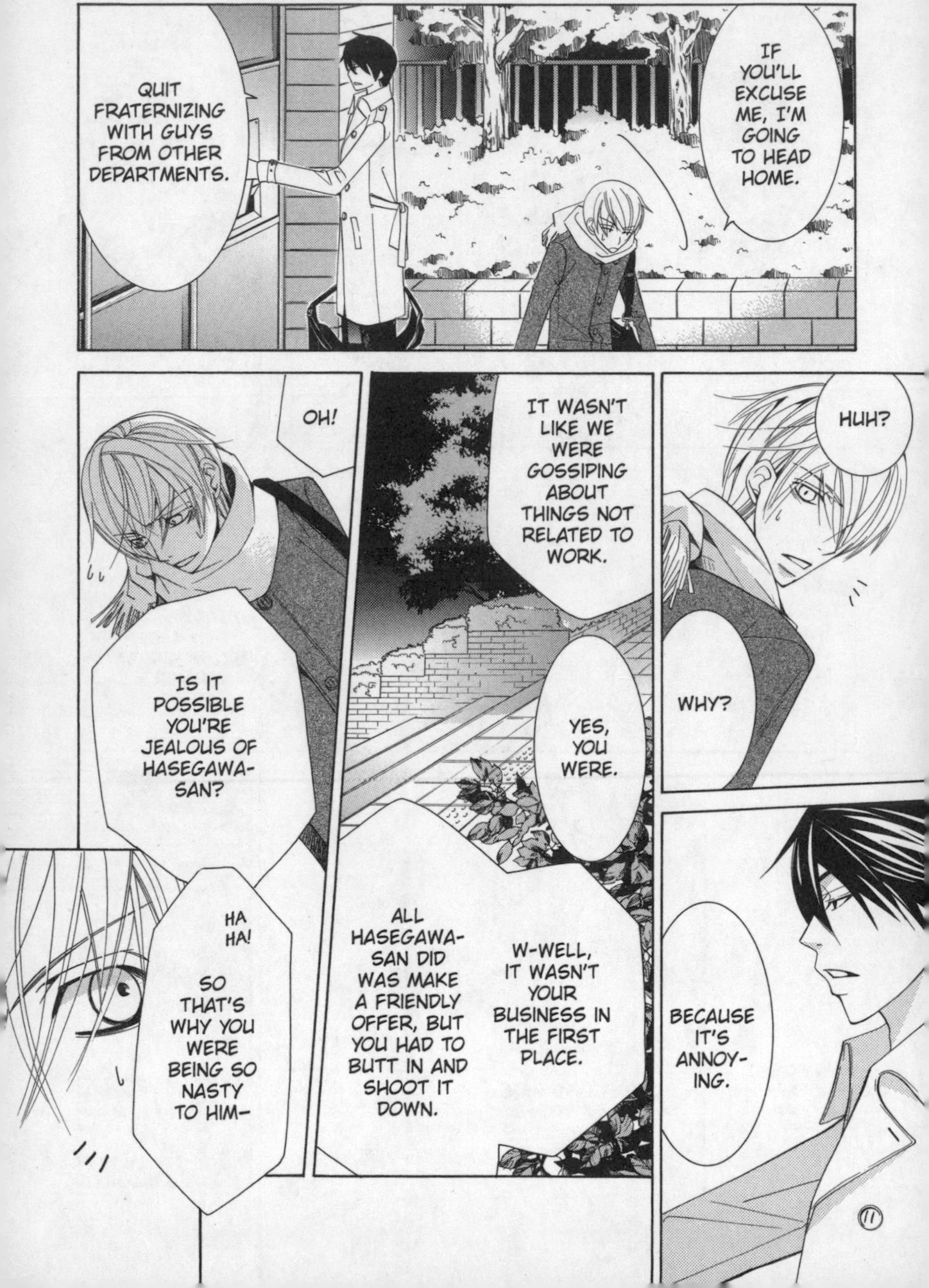
IF YOU'LL EXCUSE ME, I'M GOING TO HEAD HOME.
QUIT FRATERNIZING WITH GUYS FROM OTHER DEPARTMENTS.
HUH?
WHY?
BECAUSE IT'S ANNOY-ING.
IT WASN'T LIKE WE WERE GOSSIPING ABOUT THINGS NOT RELATED TO WORK.
YES, YOU WERE.
W-WELL, IT WASN'T YOUR BUSINESS IN THE FIRST PLACE.
ALL HASEGAWA-SAN DID WAS MAKE A FRIENDLY OFFER, BUT YOU HAD TO BUTT IN AND SHOOT IT DOWN.
OH!
IS IT POSSIBLE YOU'RE JEALOUS OF HASEGAWA-SAN?
HA HA!
SO THAT'S WHY YOU WERE BEING SO NASTY TO HIM-

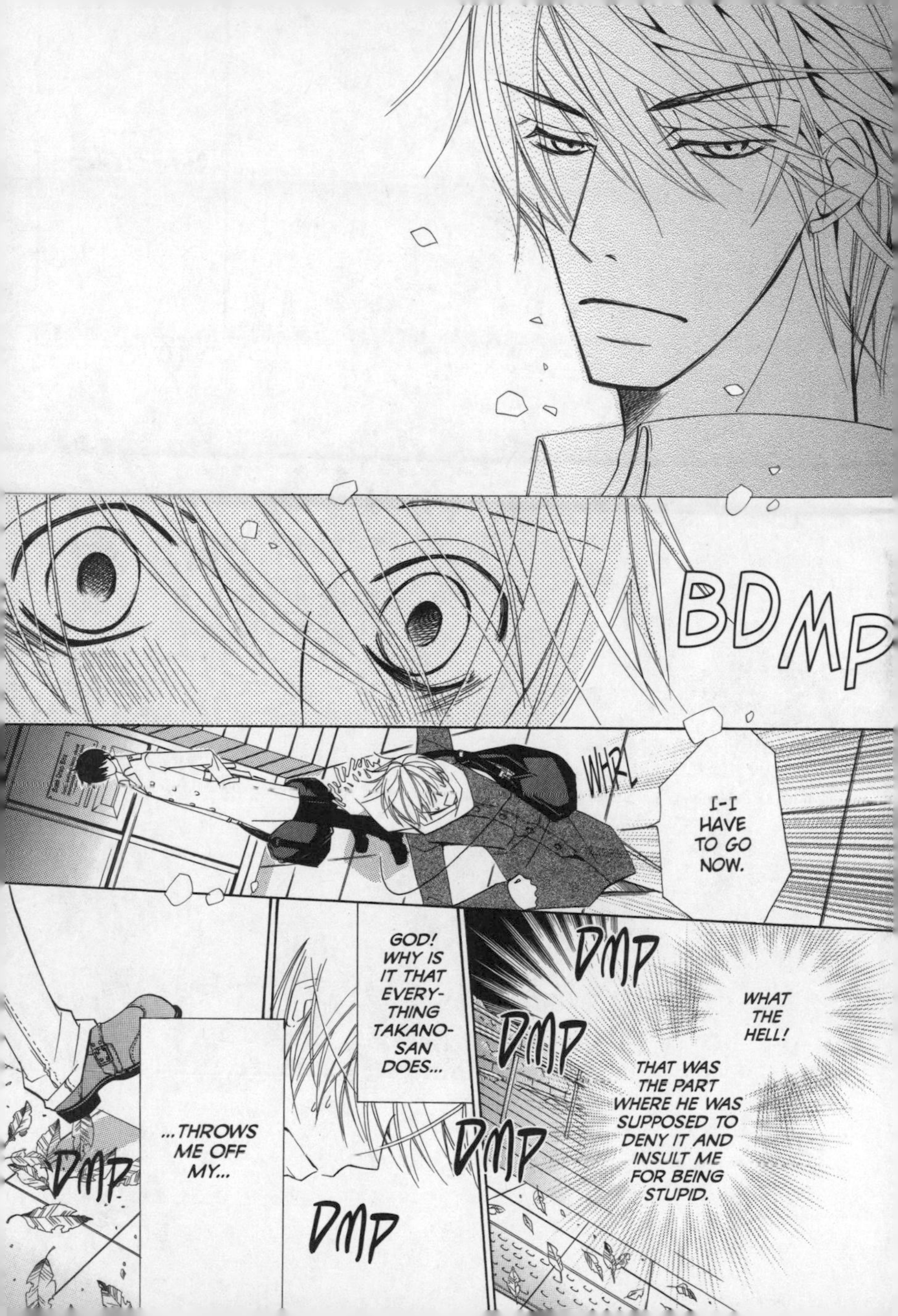
BDMP
I-I HAVE TO GO NOW.
WHRL
WHAT THE HELL!
DMP
DMP
THAT WAS THE PART WHERE HE WAS SUPPOSED TO DENY IT AND INSULT ME FOR BEING STUPID.
DMP
GOD! WHY IS IT THAT EVERY-THING TAKANO-SAN DOES...
...THROWS ME OFF MY...
DMP
DMP

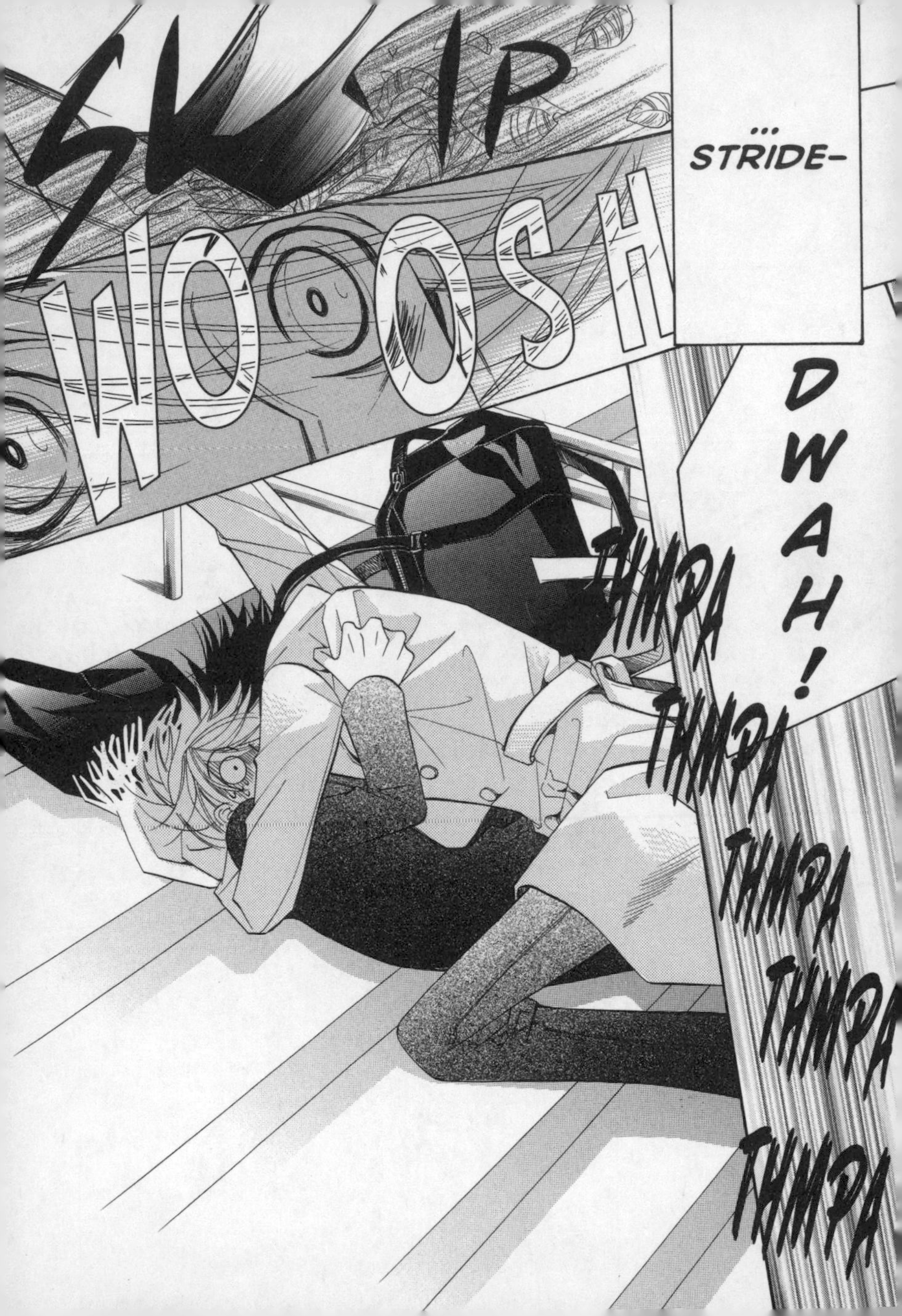
...STRIDE-
WOOOSH
DWAH!
THMPA
THMPA
THMPA
THMPA
THMPA

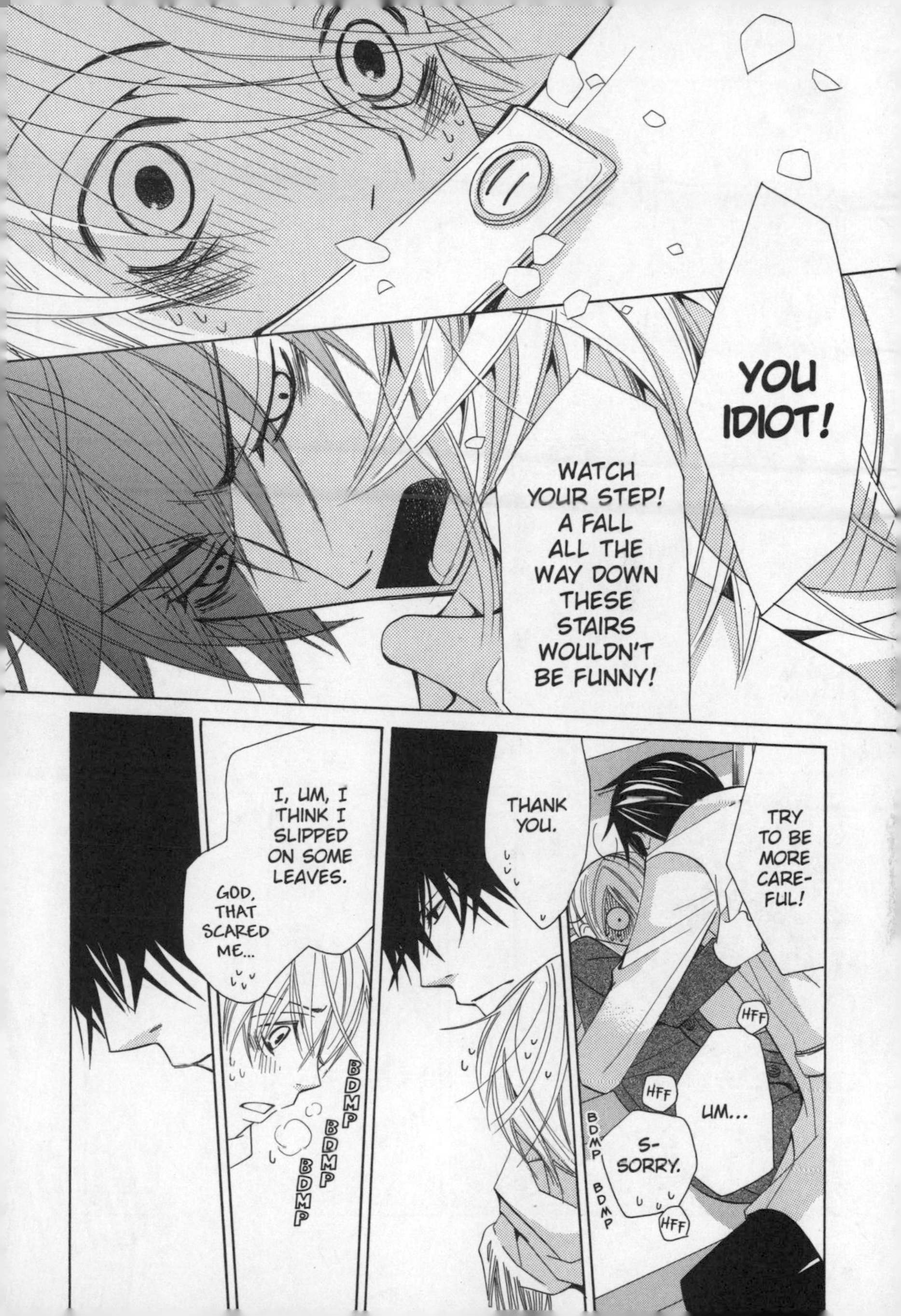
YOU IDIOT!
WATCH YOUR STEP! A FALL ALL THE WAY DOWN THESE STAIRS WOULDN'T BE FUNNY!
TRY TO BE MORE CARE-FUL!
HFF
HFF
UM...
S- SORRY.
BDMP
BDMP
HFF
THANK YOU.
I, UM, I THINK I SLIPPED ON SOME LEAVES.
GOD, THAT SCARED ME...
BDMP
BDMP
BDMP

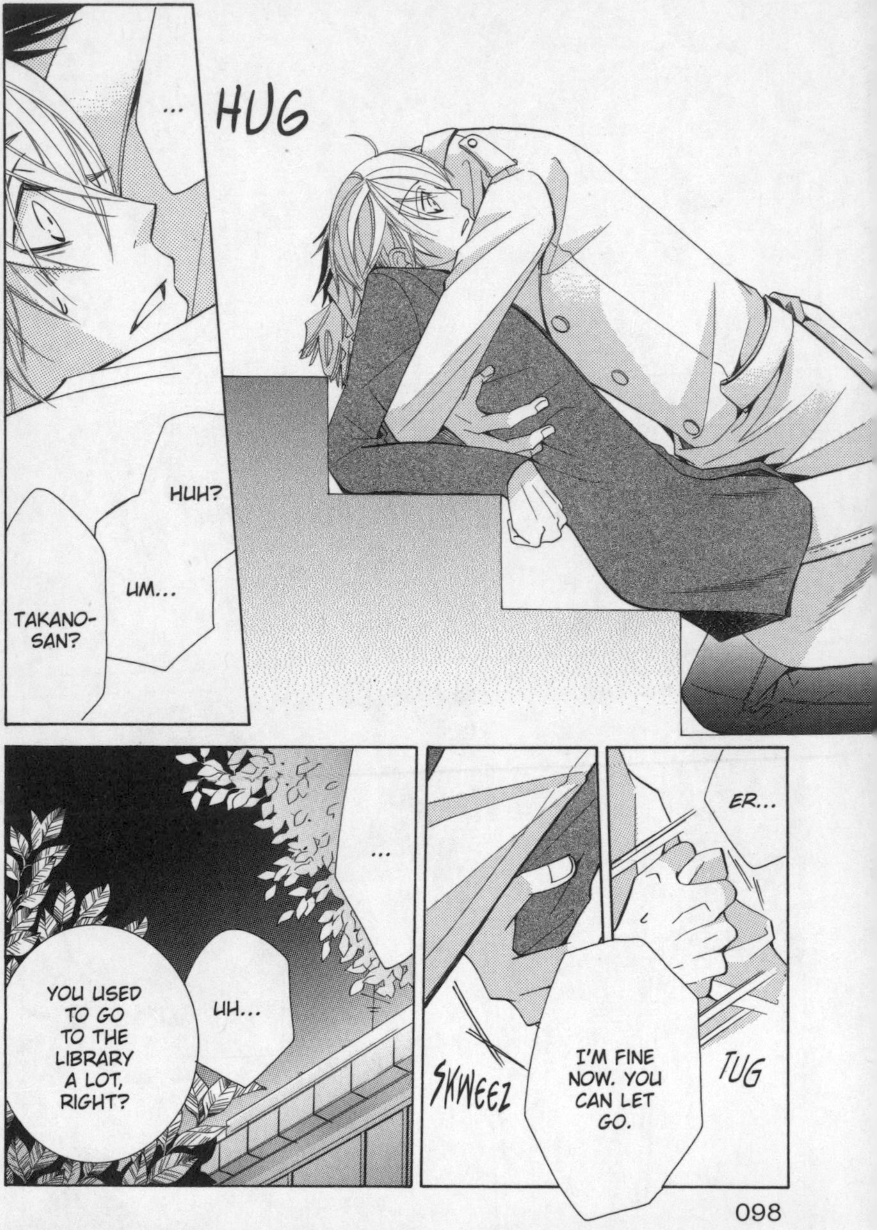
HUG
...
HUH?
UM...
TAKANO-SAN?
ER...
TUG
SKWEEZ
I'M FINE NOW. YOU CAN LET GO.
...
UH...
YOU USED TO GO TO THE LIBRARY A LOT, RIGHT?

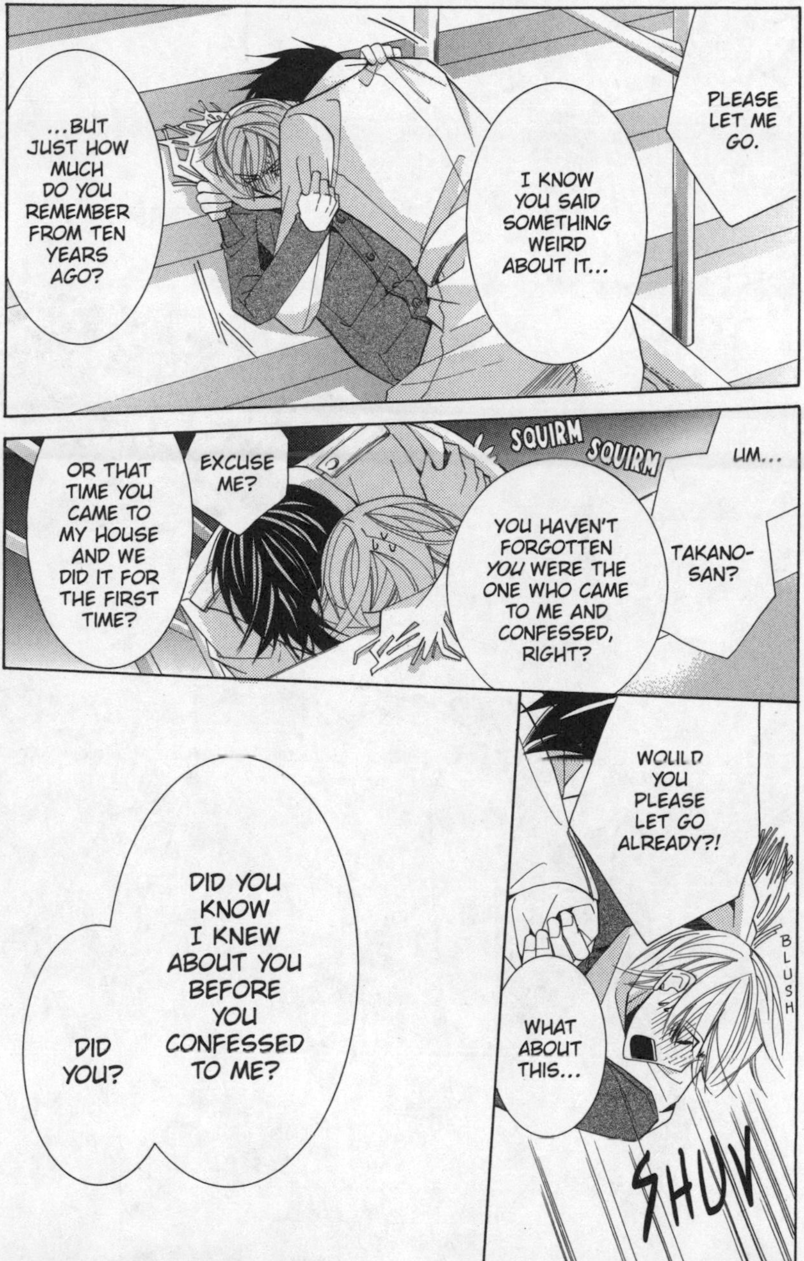
PLEASE LET ME GO.
I KNOW YOU SAID SOMETHING WEIRD ABOUT IT...
...BUT JUST HOW MUCH DO YOU REMEMBER FROM TEN YEARS AGO?
UM...
TAKANO-SAN?
SQUIRM SQUIRM
YOU HAVEN'T FORGOTTEN *YOU* WERE THE ONE WHO CAME TO ME AND CONFESSED, RIGHT?
EXCUSE ME?
OR THAT TIME YOU CAME TO MY HOUSE AND WE DID IT FOR THE FIRST TIME?
WOULD YOU PLEASE LET GO ALREADY?!
BLUSH
SHUV
WHAT ABOUT THIS...
DID YOU KNOW I KNEW ABOUT YOU BEFORE YOU CONFESSED TO ME?
DID YOU?

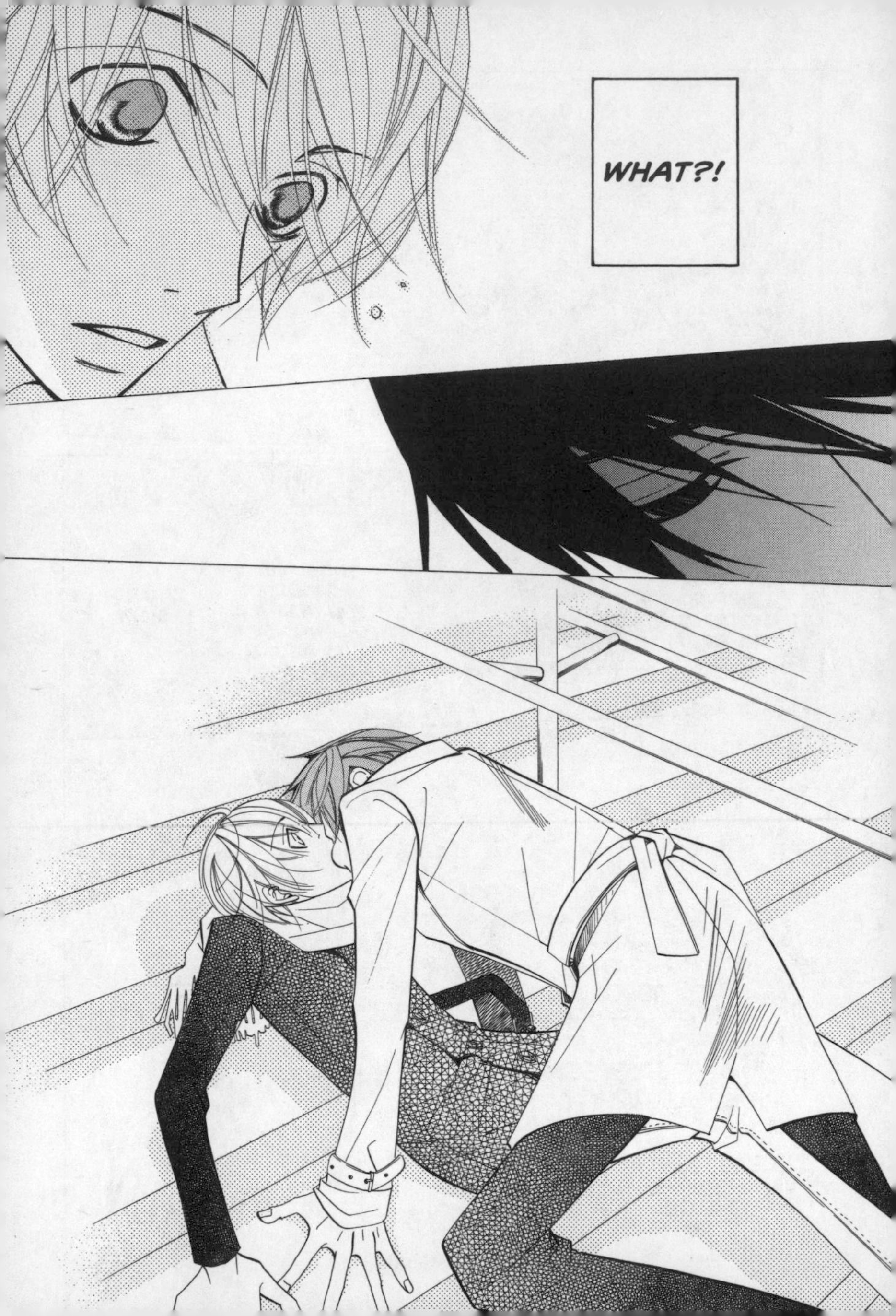
WHAT?!

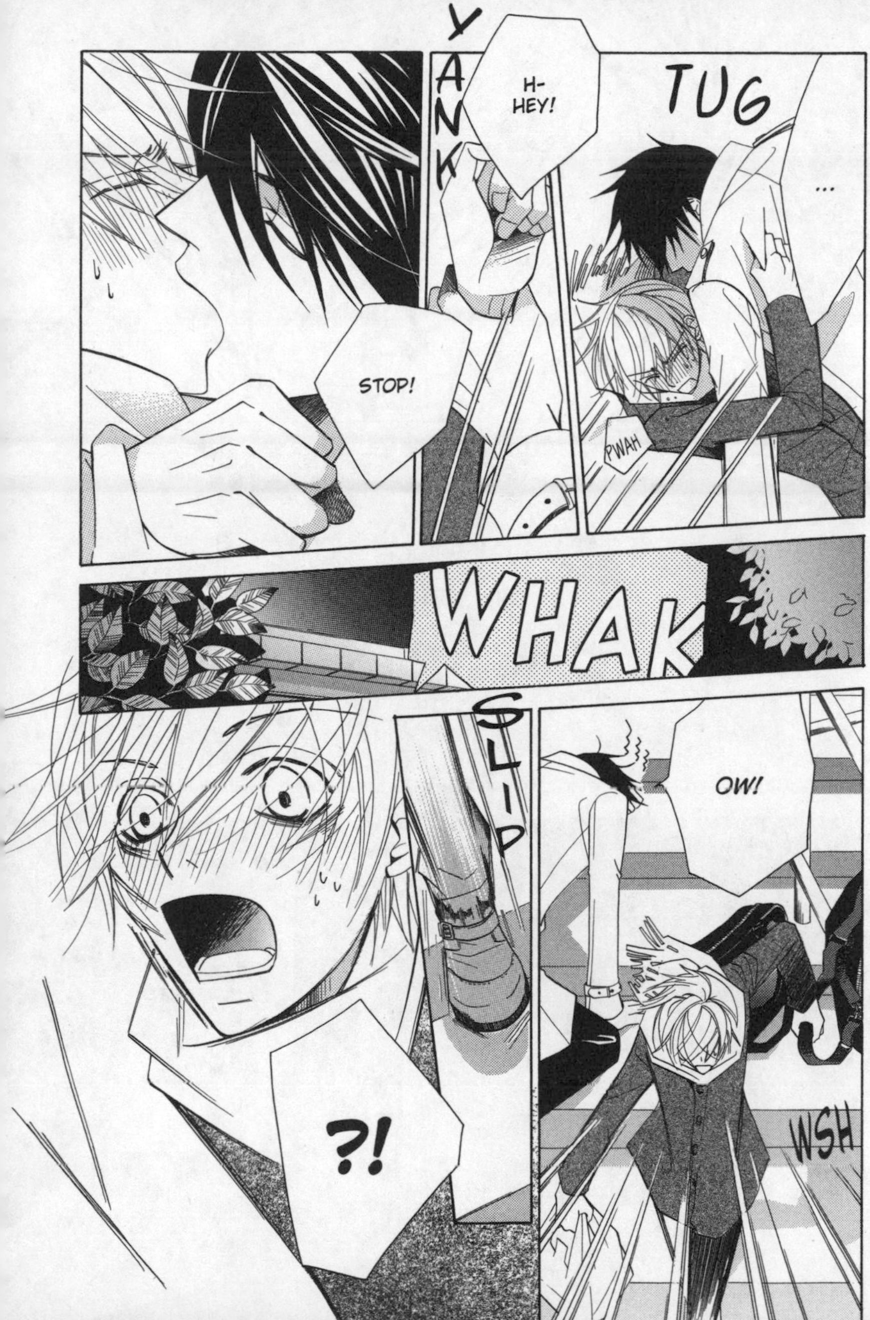
TUG
...
PWAH
YANK
H-HEY!
STOP!
WHAK
OW!
WSH
SLIP
?!

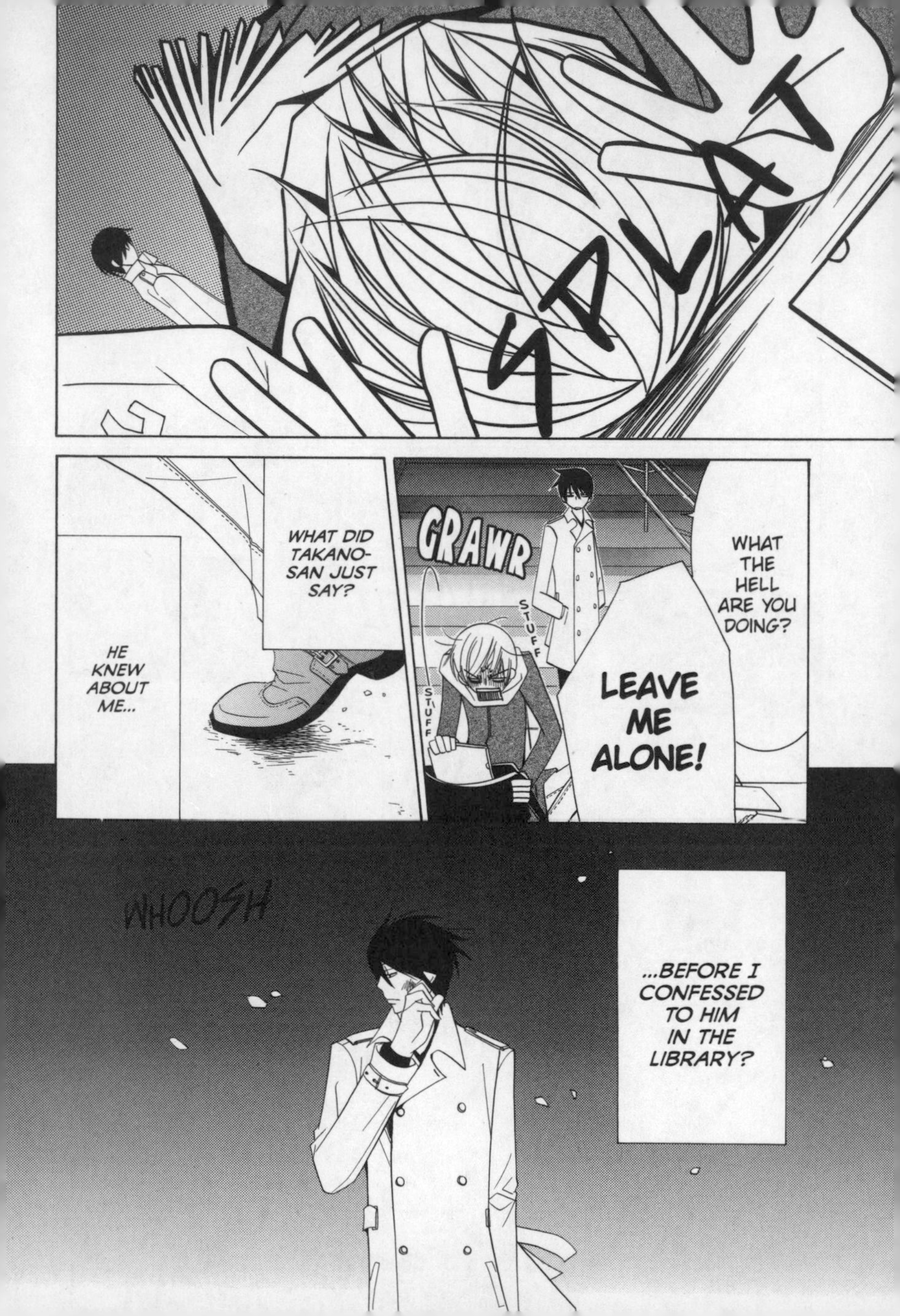
SPLAT
WHAT THE HELL ARE YOU DOING?
LEAVE ME ALONE!
GRAWR
STUFF
STUFF
WHAT DID TAKANO-SAN JUST SAY?
HE KNEW ABOUT ME...
...BEFORE I CONFESSED TO HIM IN THE LIBRARY?
WHOOSH

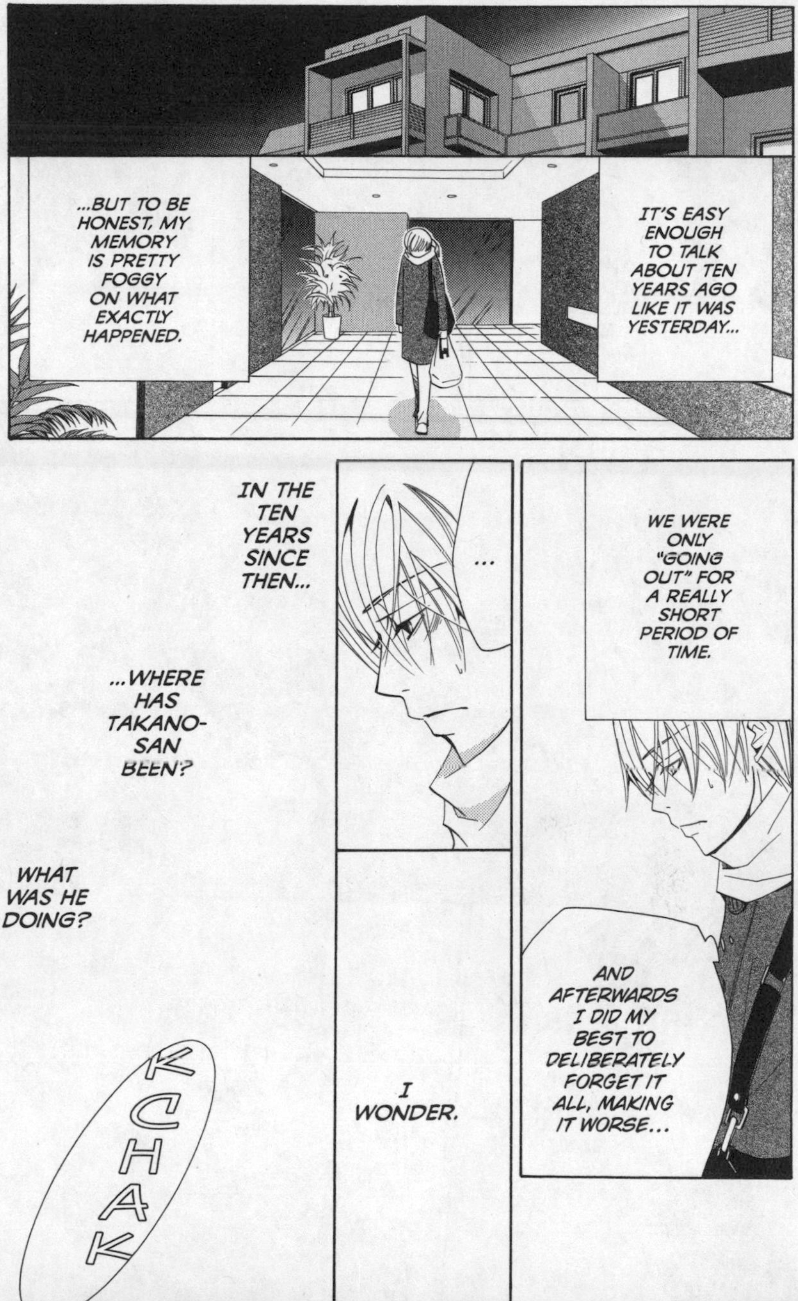
IT'S EASY ENOUGH TO TALK ABOUT TEN YEARS AGO LIKE IT WAS YESTERDAY...
...BUT TO BE HONEST, MY MEMORY IS PRETTY FOGGY ON WHAT EXACTLY HAPPENED.
WE WERE ONLY "GOING OUT" FOR A REALLY SHORT PERIOD OF TIME.
AND AFTERWARDS I DID MY BEST TO DELIBERATELY FORGET IT ALL, MAKING IT WORSE...
...
IN THE TEN YEARS SINCE THEN...
...WHERE HAS TAKANO-SAN BEEN?
WHAT WAS HE DOING?
I WONDER.
KCHAK

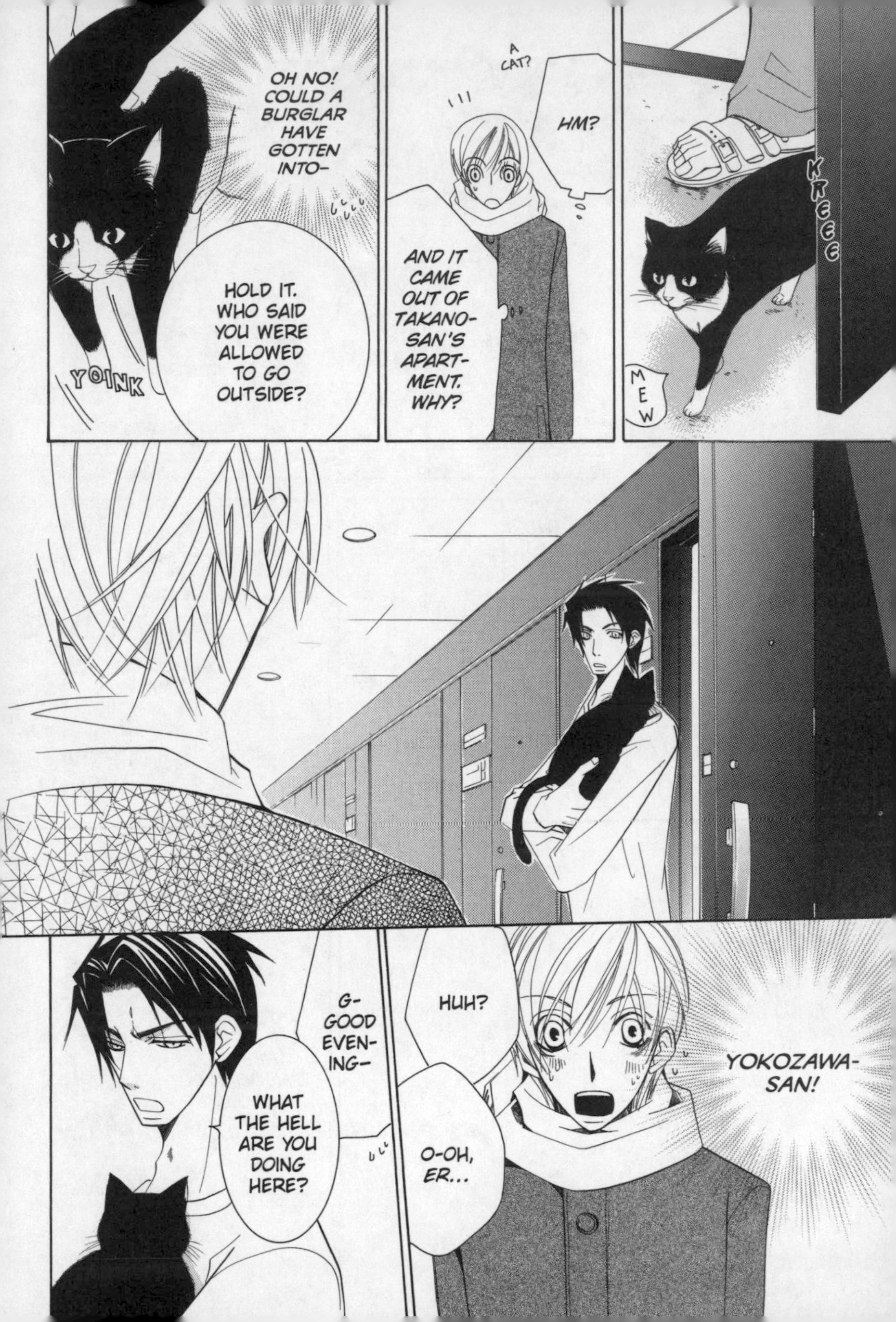
KREEE
MEW
A CAT?
HM?
AND IT CAME OUT OF TAKANO-SAN'S APARTMENT. WHY?
OH NO! COULD A BURGLAR HAVE GOTTEN INTO-
HOLD IT. WHO SAID YOU WERE ALLOWED TO GO OUTSIDE?
YOINK
YOKOZAWA-SAN!
HUH?
O-OH, ER...
G-GOOD EVENING-
WHAT THE HELL ARE YOU DOING HERE?

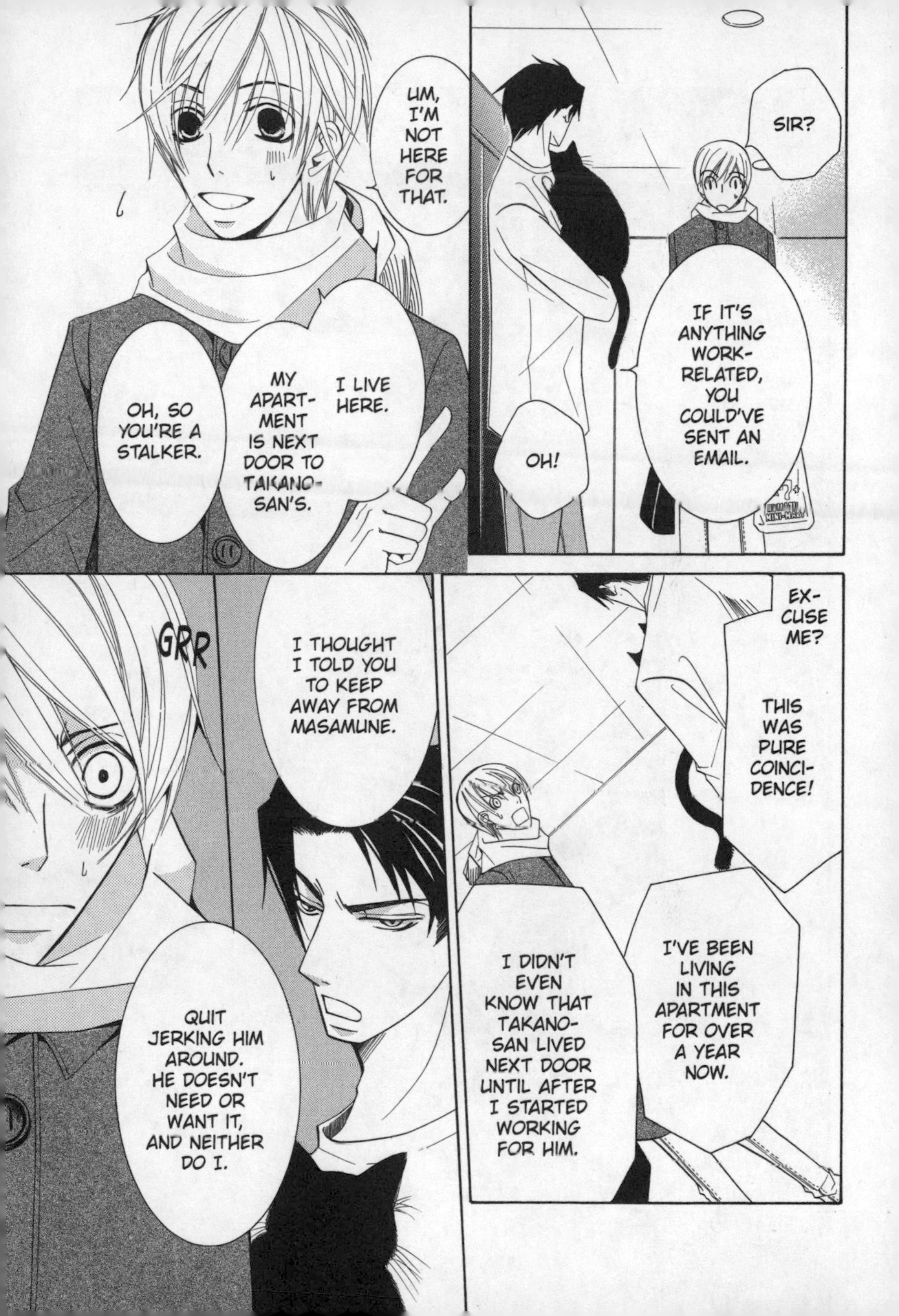
SIR?
IF IT'S ANYTHING WORK-RELATED, YOU COULD'VE SENT AN EMAIL.
OH!
UM, I'M NOT HERE FOR THAT.
I LIVE HERE.
MY APARTMENT IS NEXT DOOR TO TAKANO-SAN'S.
OH, SO YOU'RE A STALKER.
EXCUSE ME?
THIS WAS PURE COINCIDENCE!
I'VE BEEN LIVING IN THIS APARTMENT FOR OVER A YEAR NOW.
I DIDN'T EVEN KNOW THAT TAKANO-SAN LIVED NEXT DOOR UNTIL AFTER I STARTED WORKING FOR HIM.
I THOUGHT I TOLD YOU TO KEEP AWAY FROM MASAMUNE.
GRR
QUIT JERKING HIM AROUND. HE DOESN'T NEED OR WANT IT, AND NEITHER DO I.

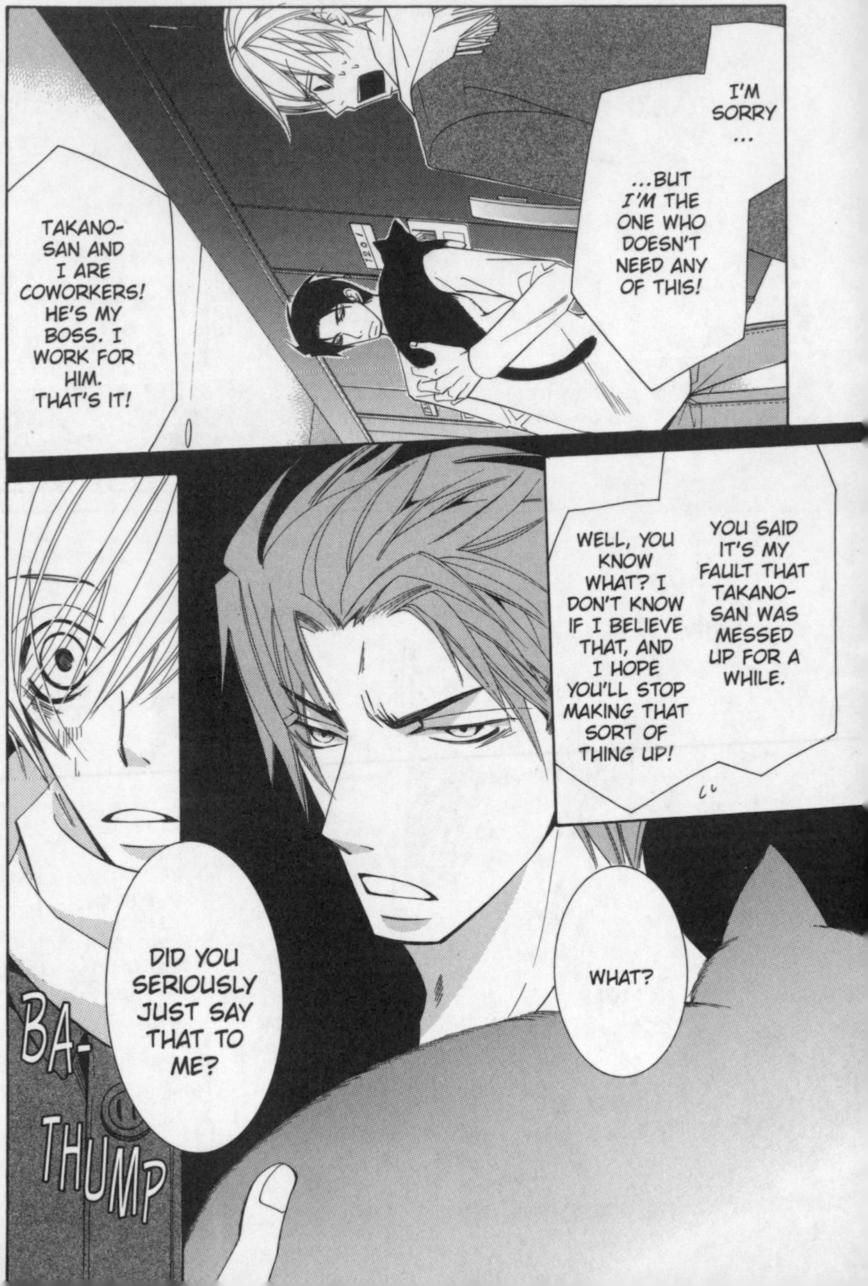
I'M SORRY ...
...BUT *I'M* THE ONE WHO DOESN'T NEED ANY OF THIS!
TAKANO-SAN AND I ARE COWORKERS! HE'S MY BOSS. I WORK FOR HIM. THAT'S IT!
YOU SAID IT'S MY FAULT THAT TAKANO-SAN WAS MESSED UP FOR A WHILE.
WELL, YOU KNOW WHAT? I DON'T KNOW IF I BELIEVE THAT, AND I HOPE YOU'LL STOP MAKING THAT SORT OF THING UP!
WHAT?
DID YOU SERIOUSLY JUST SAY THAT TO ME?
BA-THUMP

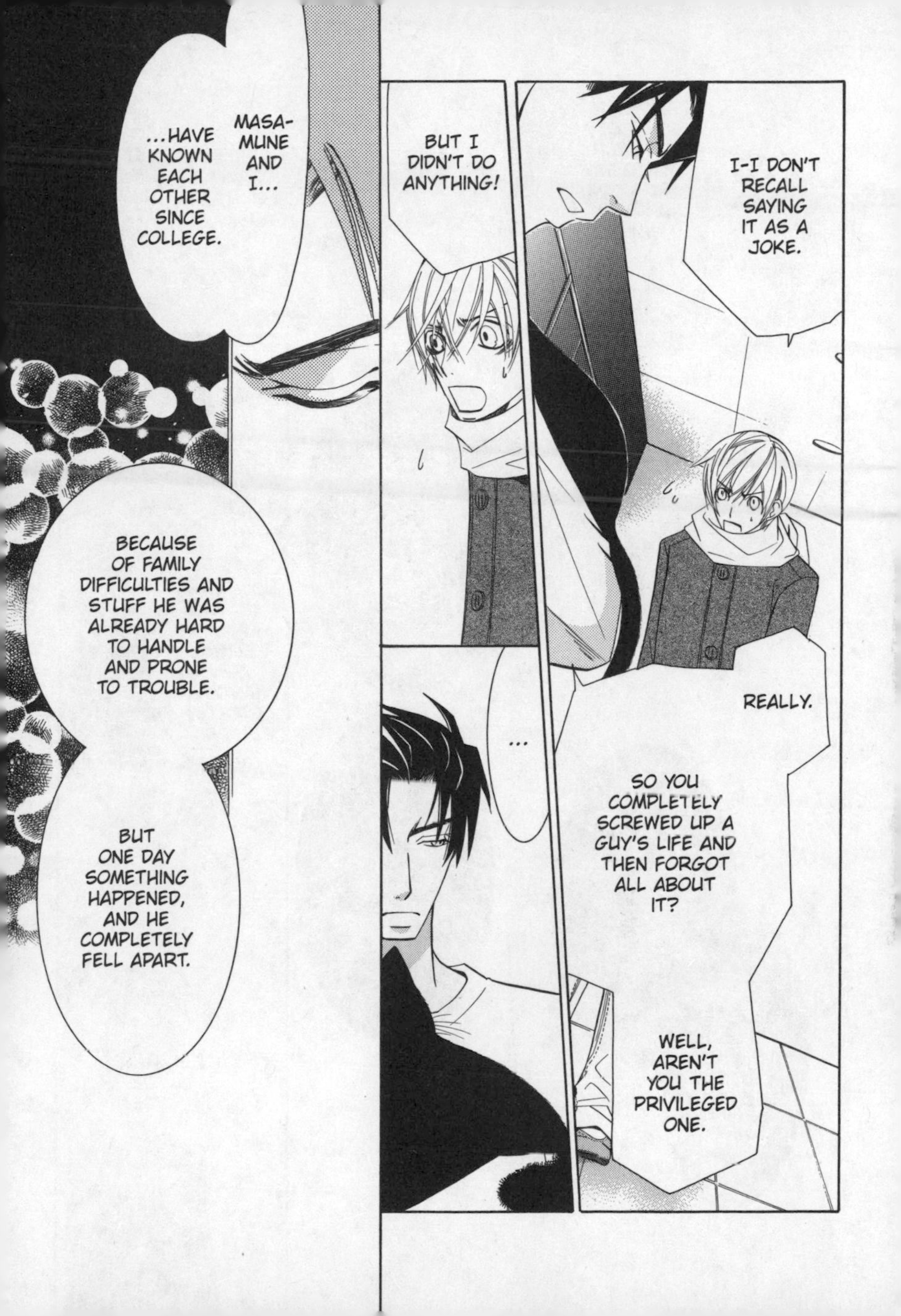
I-I DON'T RECALL SAYING IT AS A JOKE.
BUT I DIDN'T DO ANYTHING!
REALLY.
SO YOU COMPLETELY SCREWED UP A GUY'S LIFE AND THEN FORGOT ALL ABOUT IT?
WELL, AREN'T YOU THE PRIVILEGED ONE.
...
MASA-MUNE AND I...
...HAVE KNOWN EACH OTHER SINCE COLLEGE.
BECAUSE OF FAMILY DIFFICULTIES AND STUFF HE WAS ALREADY HARD TO HANDLE AND PRONE TO TROUBLE.
BUT ONE DAY SOMETHING HAPPENED, AND HE COMPLETELY FELL APART.

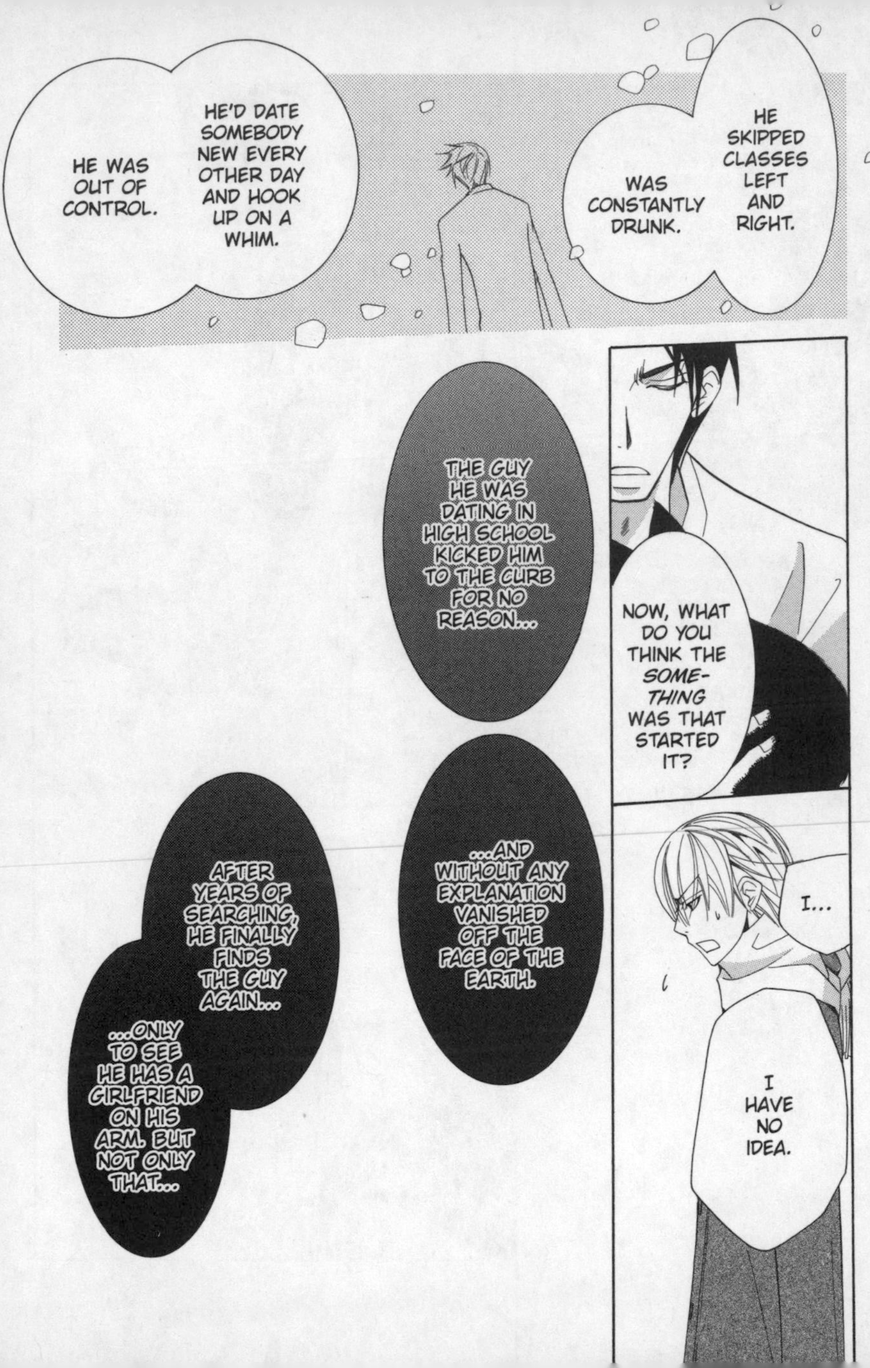
HE SKIPPED CLASSES LEFT AND RIGHT.
WAS CONSTANTLY DRUNK.
HE'D DATE SOMEBODY NEW EVERY OTHER DAY AND HOOK UP ON A WHIM.
HE WAS OUT OF CONTROL.
NOW, WHAT DO YOU THINK THE *SOMETHING* WAS THAT STARTED IT?
I...
I HAVE NO IDEA.
THE GUY HE WAS DATING IN HIGH SCHOOL KICKED HIM TO THE CURB FOR NO REASON...
...AND WITHOUT ANY EXPLANATION VANISHED OFF THE FACE OF THE EARTH.
AFTER YEARS OF SEARCHING, HE FINALLY FINDS THE GUY AGAIN...
...ONLY TO SEE HE HAS A GIRLFRIEND ON HIS ARM. BUT NOT ONLY THAT...

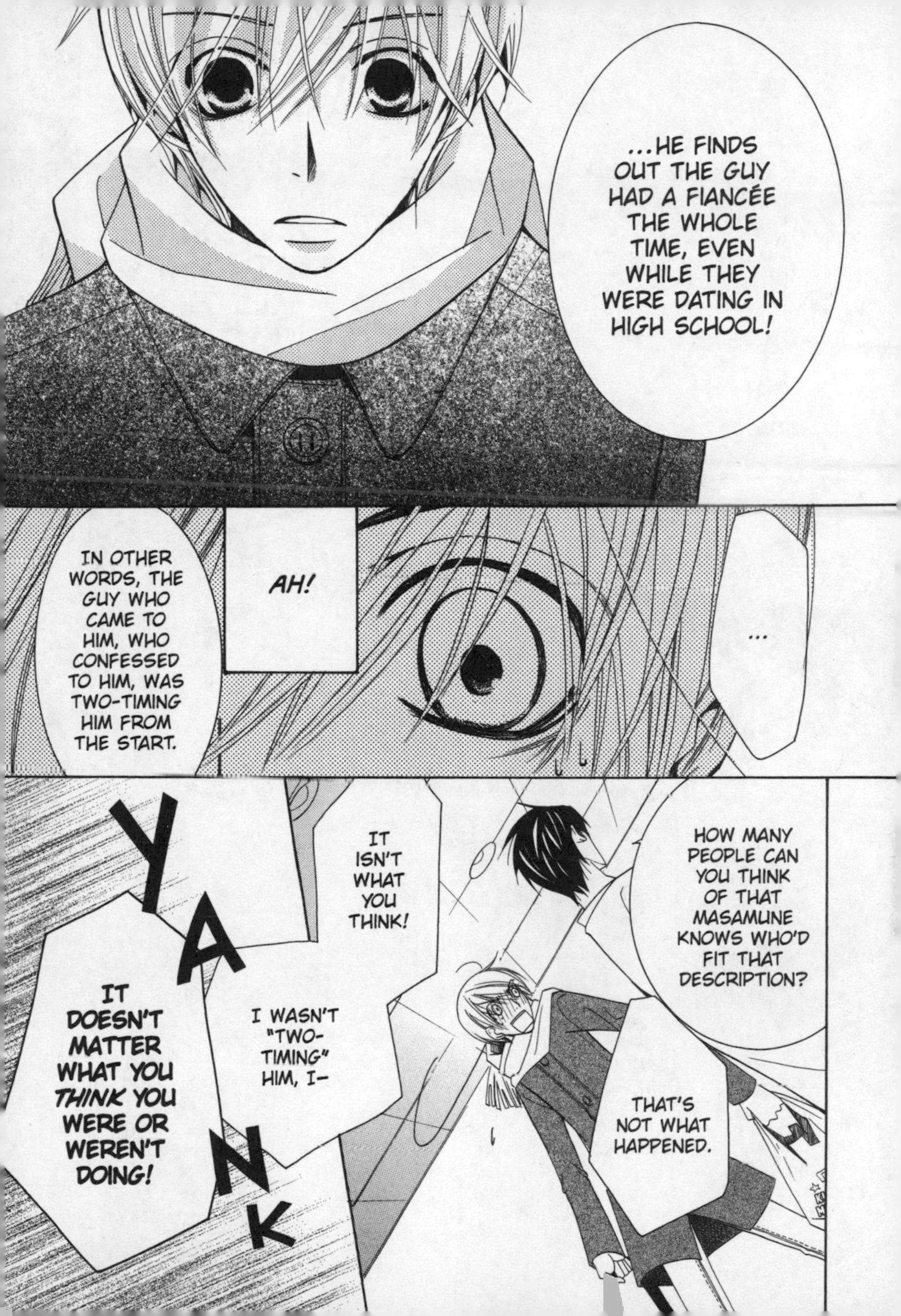
...HE FINDS OUT THE GUY HAD A FIANCÉE THE WHOLE TIME, EVEN WHILE THEY WERE DATING IN HIGH SCHOOL!
...
AH!
IN OTHER WORDS, THE GUY WHO CAME TO HIM, WHO CONFESSED TO HIM, WAS TWO-TIMING HIM FROM THE START.
HOW MANY PEOPLE CAN YOU THINK OF THAT MASAMUNE KNOWS WHO'D FIT THAT DESCRIPTION?
IT ISN'T WHAT YOU THINK!
YANK
THAT'S NOT WHAT HAPPENED.
I WASN'T "TWO-TIMING" HIM, I–
IT DOESN'T MATTER WHAT YOU *THINK* YOU WERE OR WEREN'T DOING!

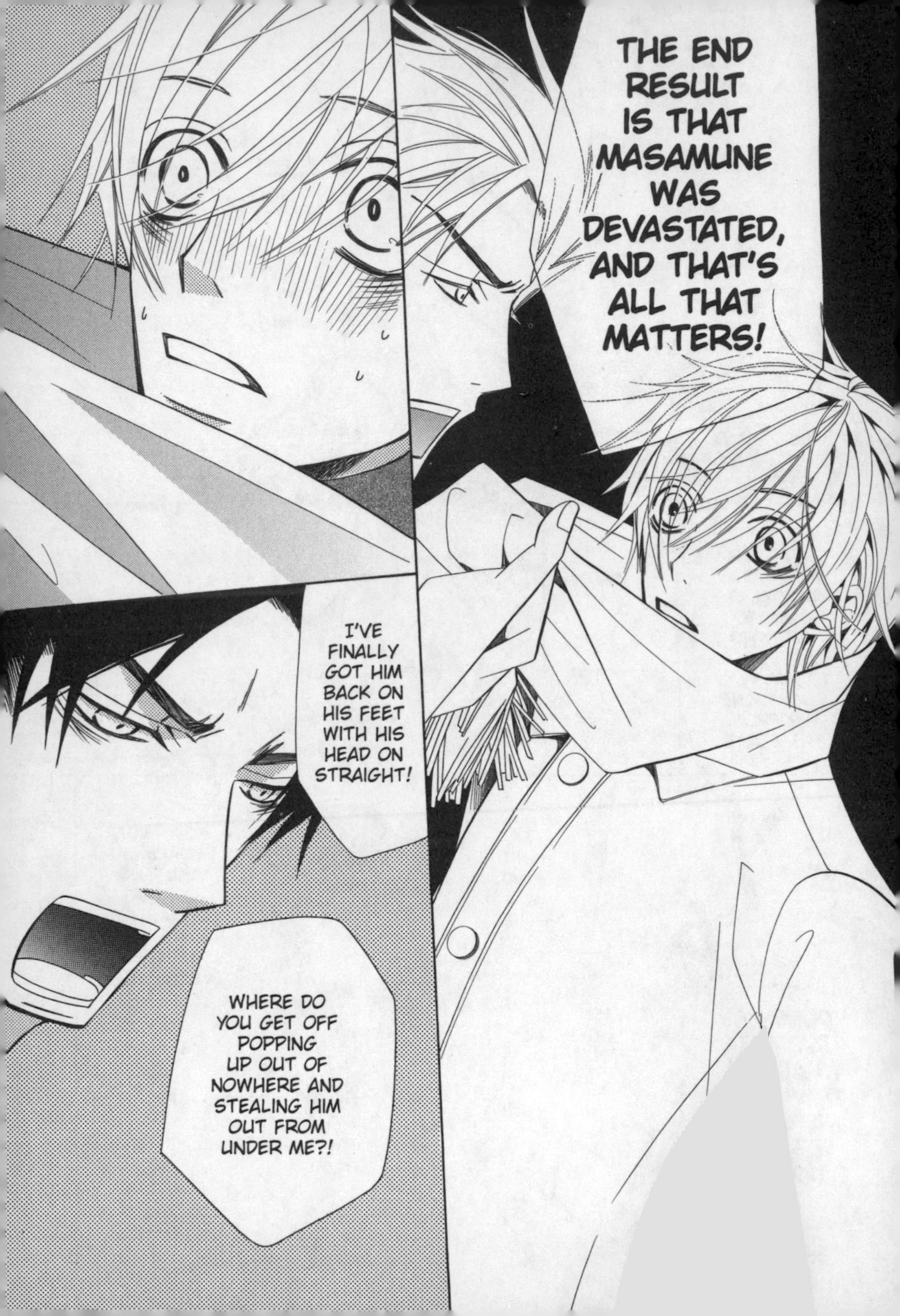
THE END RESULT IS THAT MASAMUNE WAS DEVASTATED, AND THAT'S ALL THAT MATTERS!
I'VE FINALLY GOT HIM BACK ON HIS FEET WITH HIS HEAD ON STRAIGHT!
WHERE DO YOU GET OFF POPPING UP OUT OF NOWHERE AND STEALING HIM OUT FROM UNDER ME?!

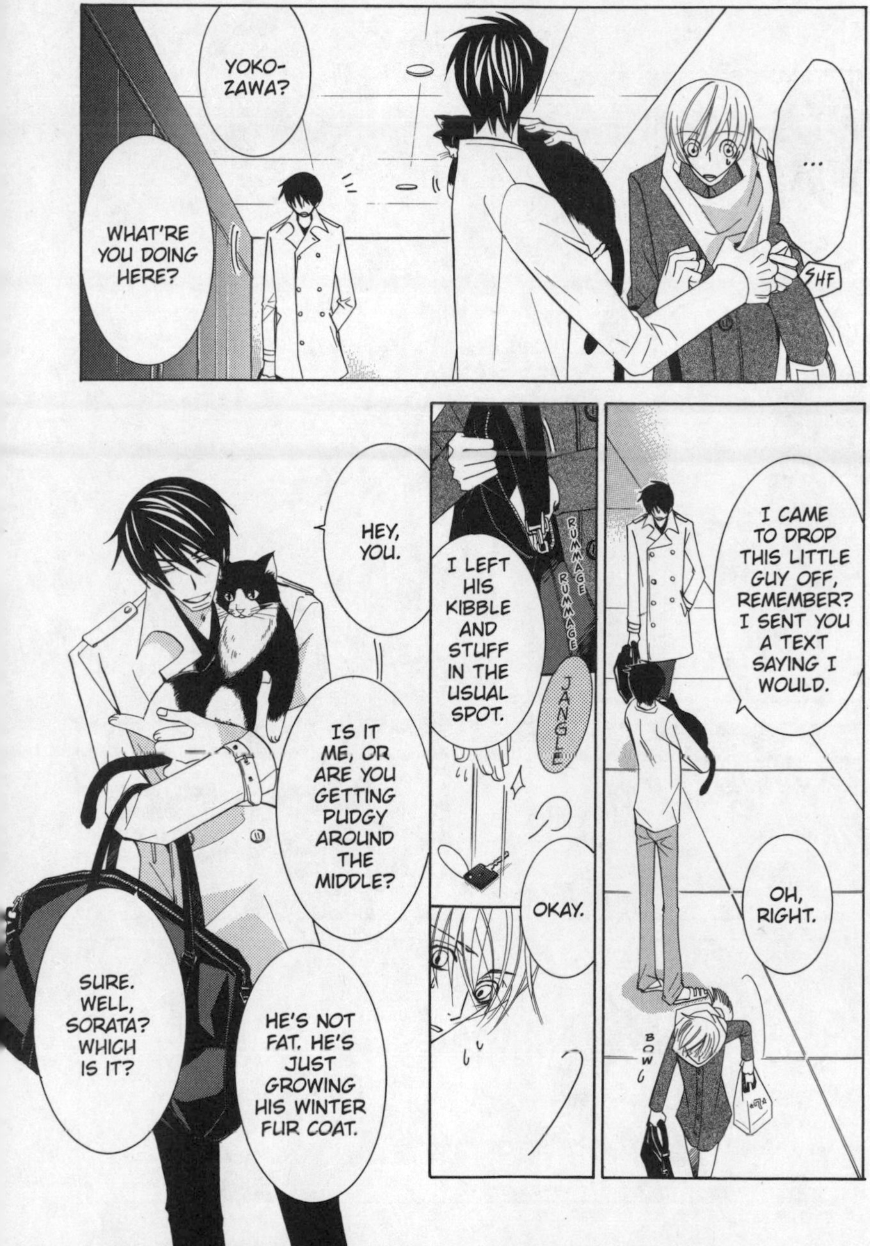
...
YOKO-ZAWA?
SHF
WHAT'RE YOU DOING HERE?
I CAME TO DROP THIS LITTLE GUY OFF, REMEMBER? I SENT YOU A TEXT SAYING I WOULD.
OH, RIGHT.
BOW
RUMMAGE RUMMAGE
I LEFT HIS KIBBLE AND STUFF IN THE USUAL SPOT.
JANGLE
OKAY.
HEY, YOU.
IS IT ME, OR ARE YOU GETTING PUDGY AROUND THE MIDDLE?
HE'S NOT FAT. HE'S JUST GROWING HIS WINTER FUR COAT.
SURE. WELL, SORATA? WHICH IS IT?

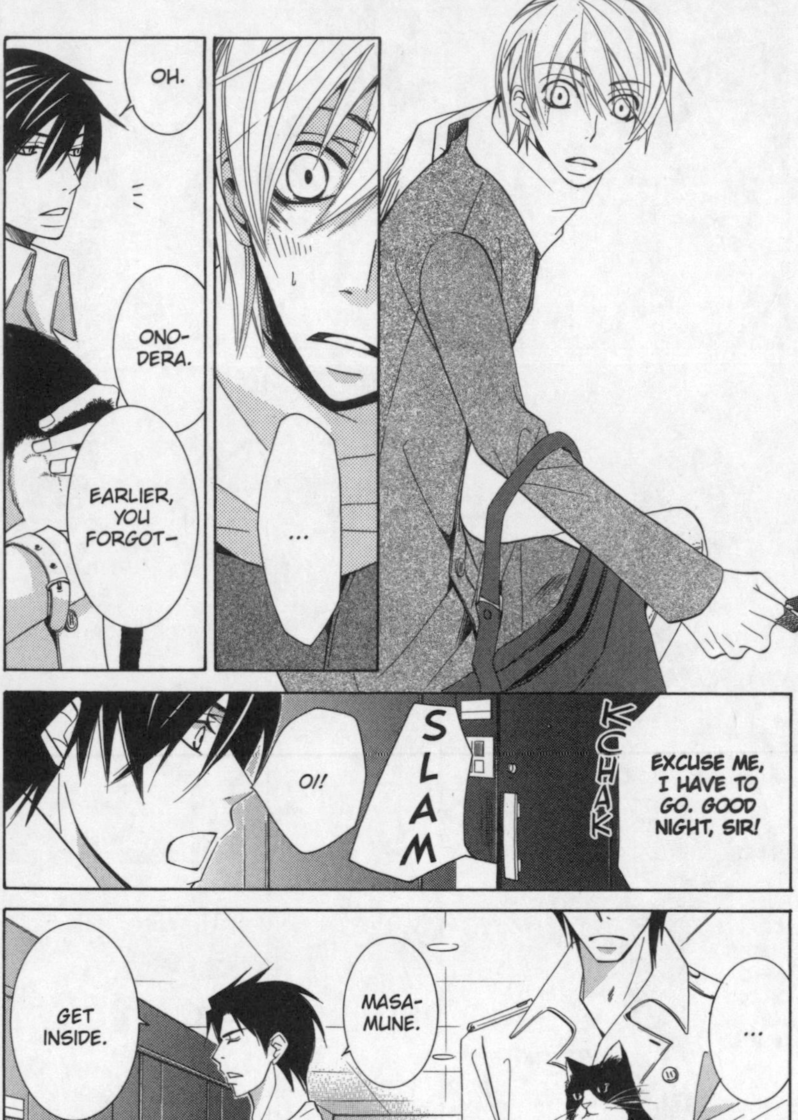
...
OH.
ONO-DERA.
EARLIER, YOU FORGOT-
KCHAK
EXCUSE ME, I HAVE TO GO. GOOD NIGHT, SIR!
SLAM
OI!
...
MASA-MUNE.
GET INSIDE.

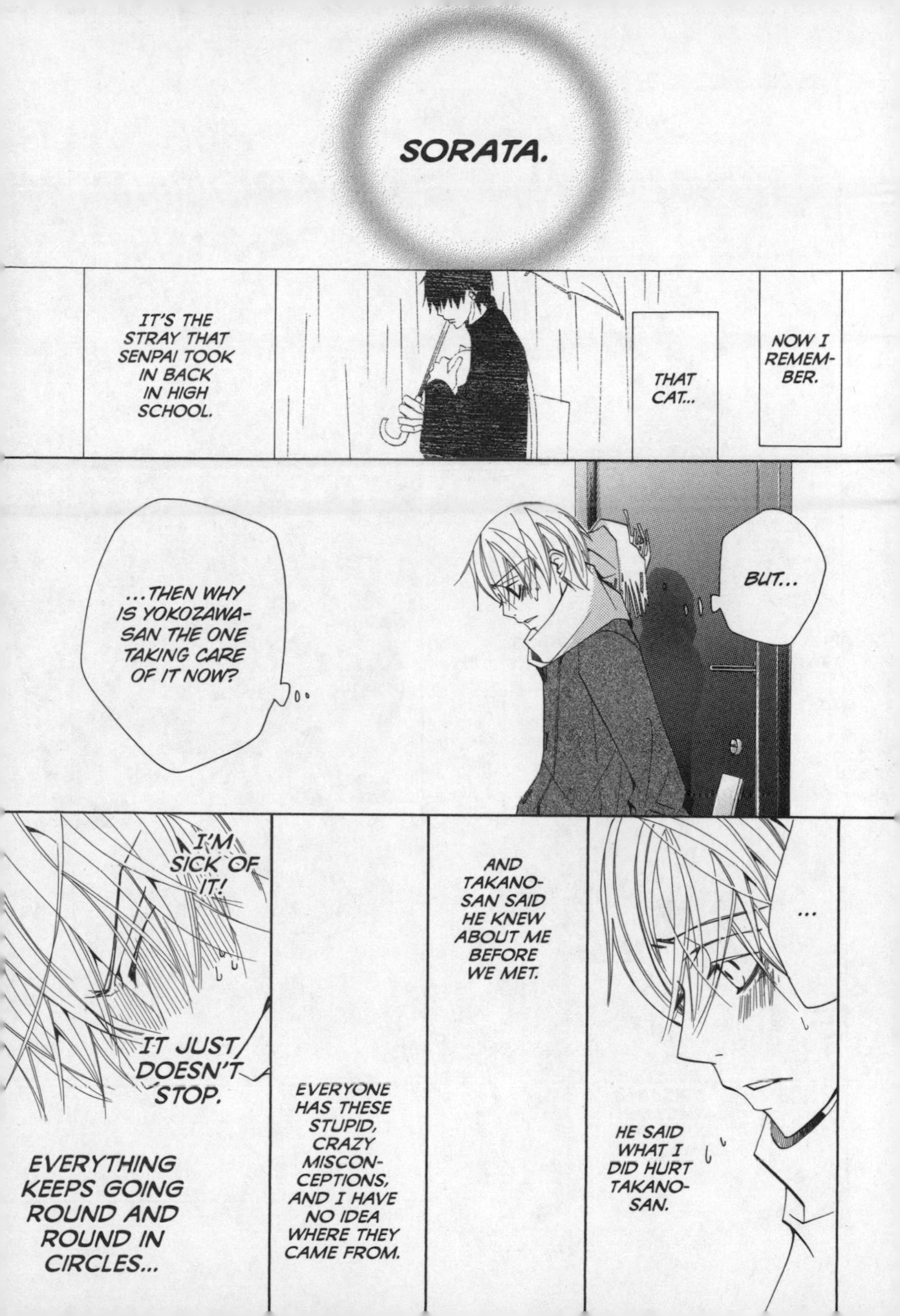
SORATA.
NOW I REMEMBER.
THAT CAT...
IT'S THE STRAY THAT SENPAI TOOK IN BACK IN HIGH SCHOOL.
BUT...
...THEN WHY IS YOKOZAWA-SAN THE ONE TAKING CARE OF IT NOW?
...
HE SAID WHAT I DID HURT TAKANO-SAN.
AND TAKANO-SAN SAID HE KNEW ABOUT ME BEFORE WE MET.
EVERYONE HAS THESE STUPID, CRAZY MISCONCEPTIONS, AND I HAVE NO IDEA WHERE THEY CAME FROM.
I'M SICK OF IT!
IT JUST DOESN'T STOP.
EVERYTHING KEEPS GOING ROUND AND ROUND IN CIRCLES...

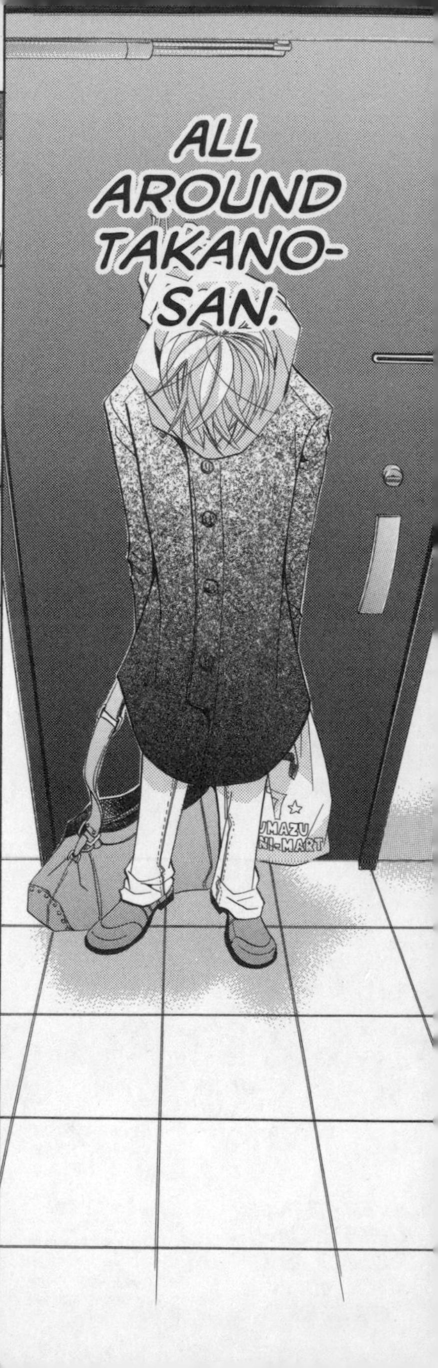
ALL AROUND TAKANO-SAN.

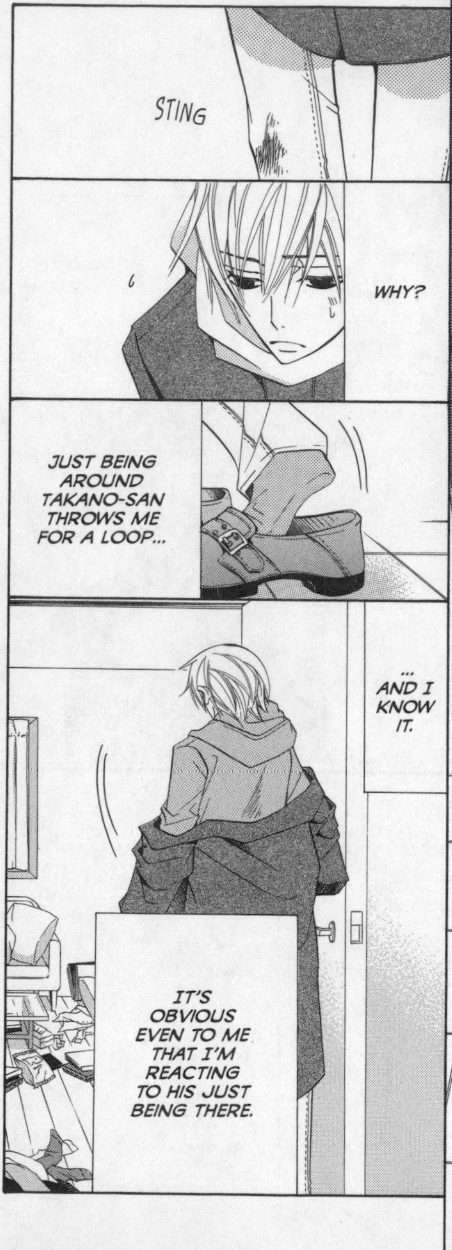
STING
WHY?
JUST BEING AROUND TAKANO-SAN THROWS ME FOR A LOOP...
...AND I KNOW IT.
IT'S OBVIOUS EVEN TO ME THAT I'M REACTING TO HIS JUST BEING THERE.

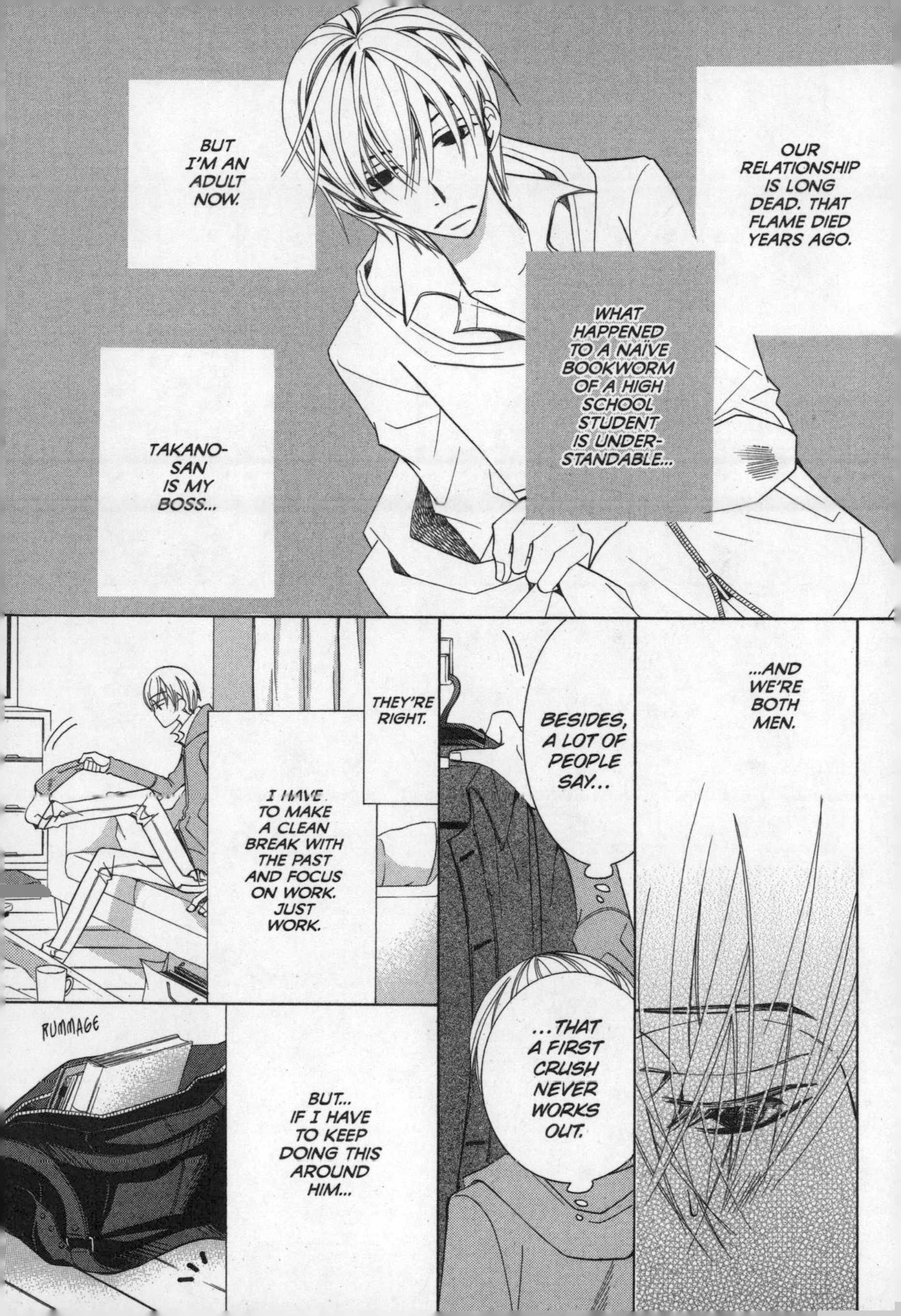
OUR RELATIONSHIP IS LONG DEAD. THAT FLAME DIED YEARS AGO.
WHAT HAPPENED TO A NAÏVE BOOKWORM OF A HIGH SCHOOL STUDENT IS UNDER-STANDABLE...
BUT I'M AN ADULT NOW.
TAKANO-SAN IS MY BOSS...
...AND WE'RE BOTH MEN.
BESIDES, A LOT OF PEOPLE SAY...
...THAT A FIRST CRUSH NEVER WORKS OUT.
THEY'RE RIGHT.
I HAVE TO MAKE A CLEAN BREAK WITH THE PAST AND FOCUS ON WORK. JUST WORK.
BUT... IF I HAVE TO KEEP DOING THIS AROUND HIM...
RUMMAGE

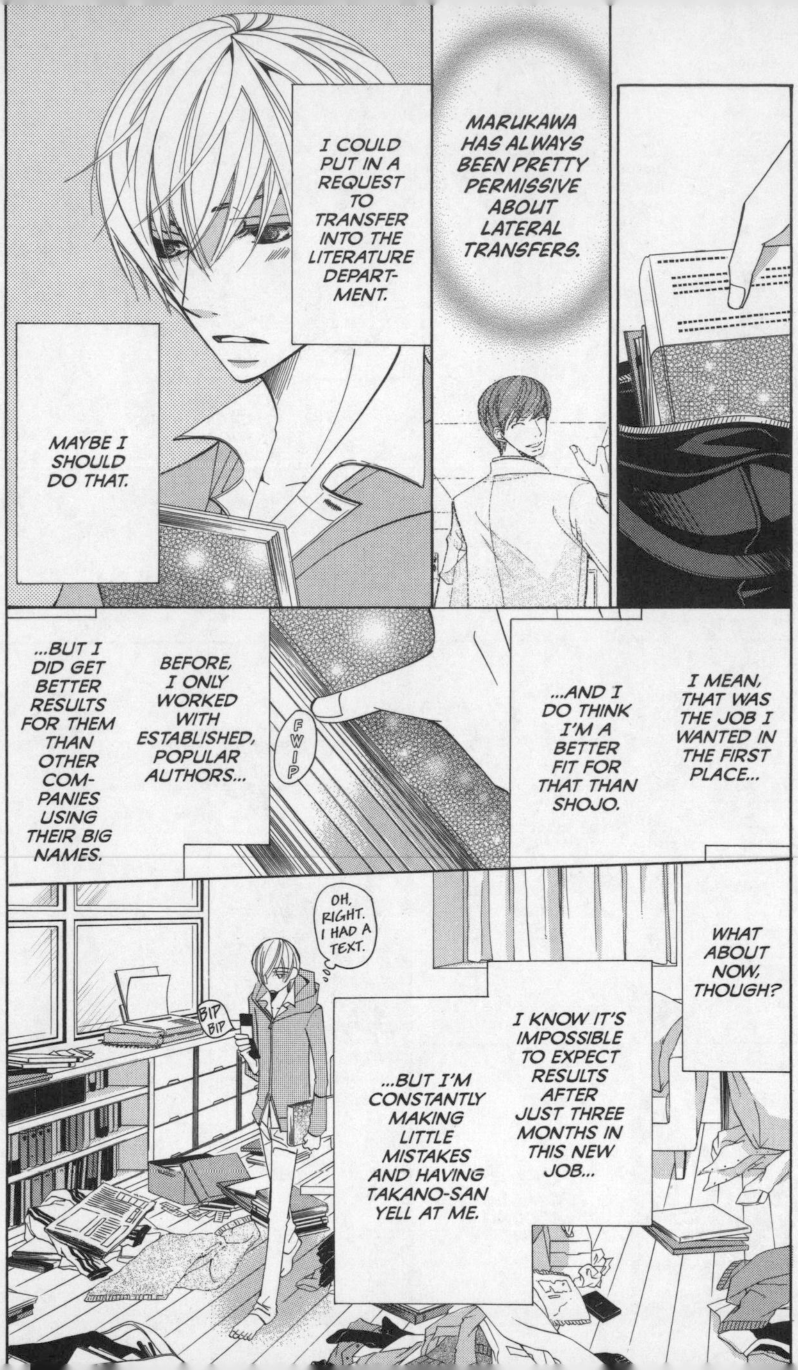
MARUKAWA HAS ALWAYS BEEN PRETTY PERMISSIVE ABOUT LATERAL TRANSFERS.
I COULD PUT IN A REQUEST TO TRANSFER INTO THE LITERATURE DEPARTMENT.
MAYBE I SHOULD DO THAT.
I MEAN, THAT WAS THE JOB I WANTED IN THE FIRST PLACE...
...AND I DO THINK I'M A BETTER FIT FOR THAT THAN SHOJO.
FWIP
BEFORE, I ONLY WORKED WITH ESTABLISHED, POPULAR AUTHORS...
...BUT I DID GET BETTER RESULTS FOR THEM THAN OTHER COMPANIES USING THEIR BIG NAMES.
WHAT ABOUT NOW, THOUGH?
I KNOW IT'S IMPOSSIBLE TO EXPECT RESULTS AFTER JUST THREE MONTHS IN THIS NEW JOB...
...BUT I'M CONSTANTLY MAKING LITTLE MISTAKES AND HAVING TAKANO-SAN YELL AT ME.
OH, RIGHT. I HAD A TEXT.
BIP BIP

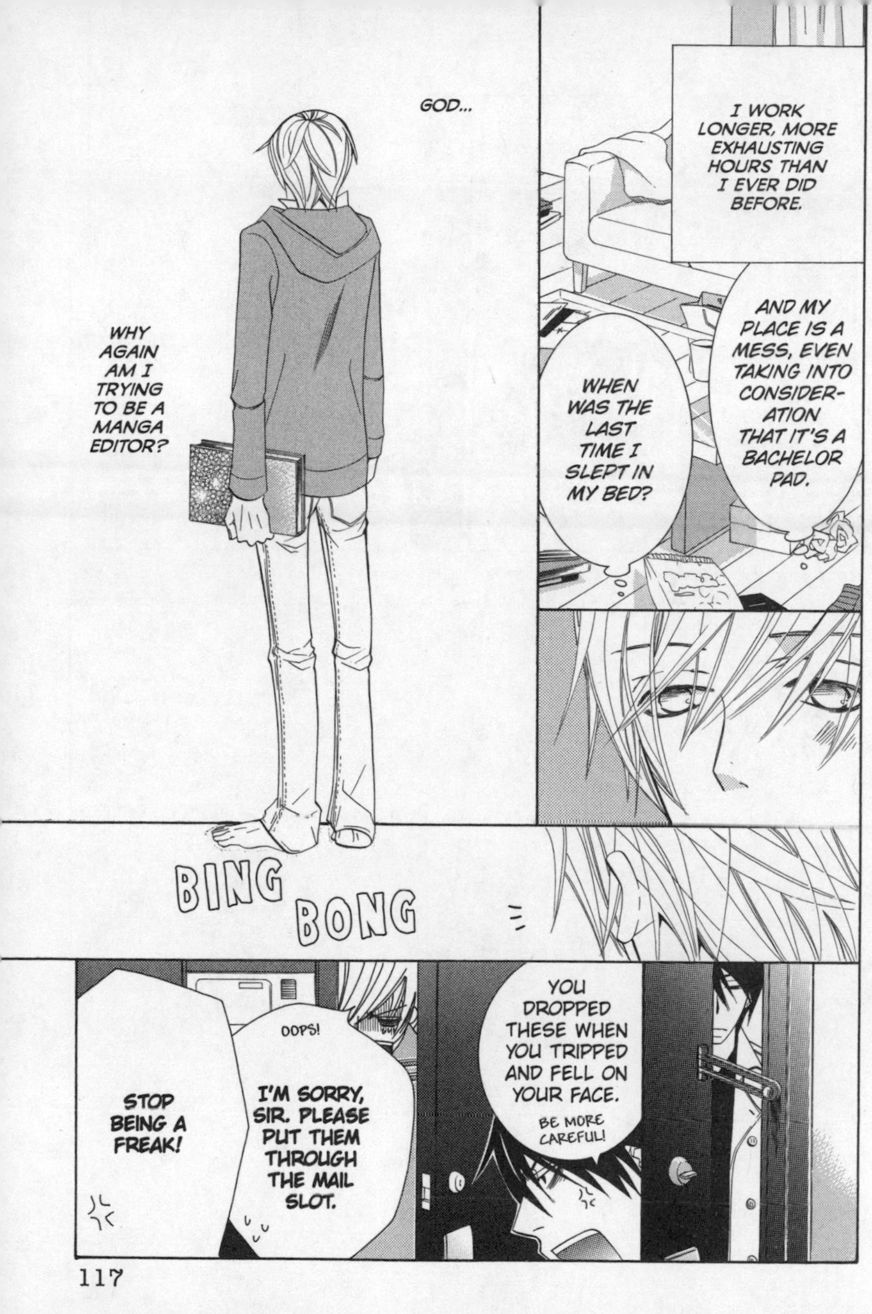
I WORK LONGER, MORE EXHAUSTING HOURS THAN I EVER DID BEFORE.
AND MY PLACE IS A MESS, EVEN TAKING INTO CONSIDER-ATION THAT IT'S A BACHELOR PAD.
WHEN WAS THE LAST TIME I SLEPT IN MY BED?
GOD...
WHY AGAIN AM I TRYING TO BE A MANGA EDITOR?
BING BONG
YOU DROPPED THESE WHEN YOU TRIPPED AND FELL ON YOUR FACE.
BE MORE CAREFUL!
OOPS!
I'M SORRY, SIR. PLEASE PUT THEM THROUGH THE MAIL SLOT.
STOP BEING A FREAK!

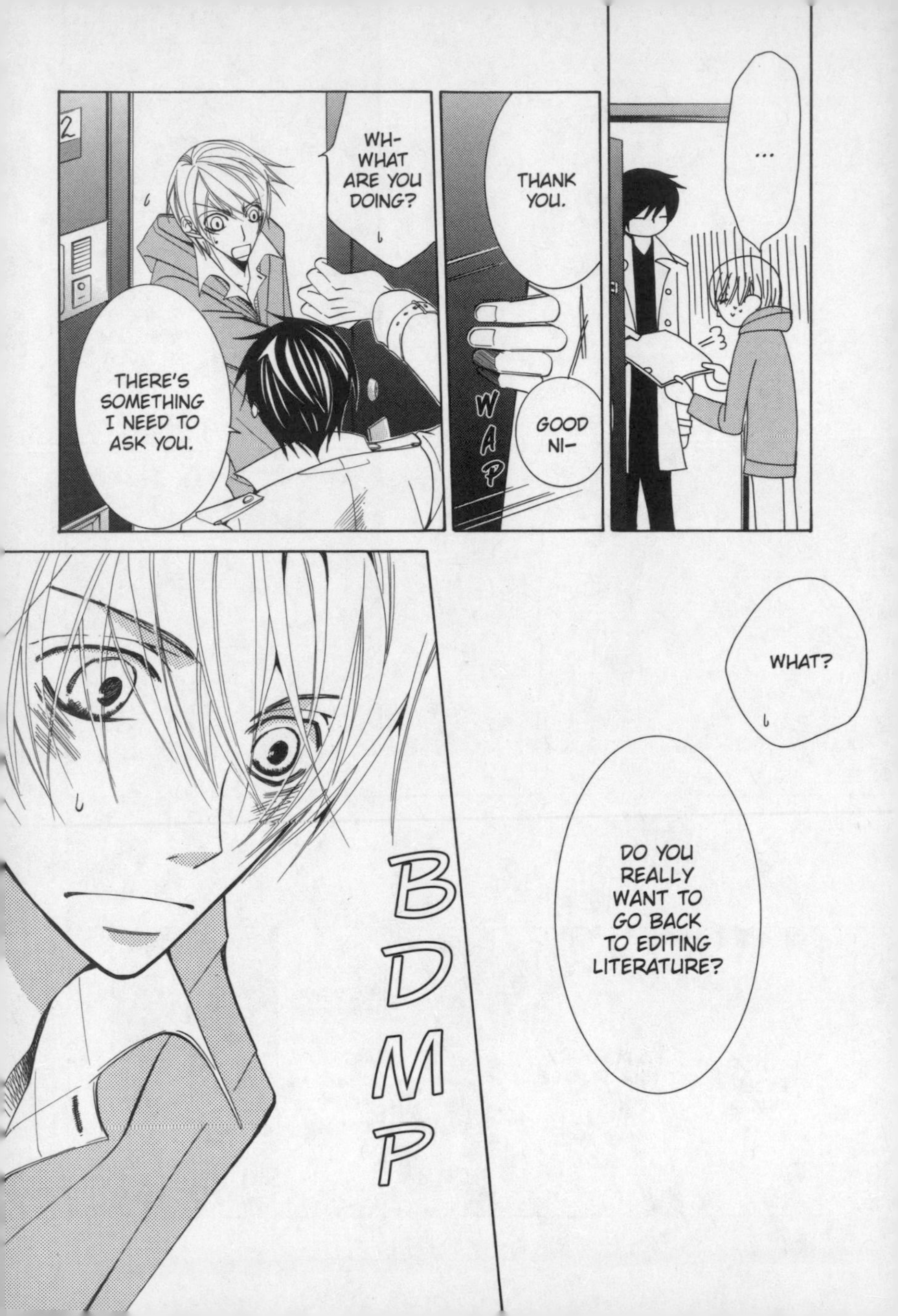
...
THANK YOU.
GOOD NI-
WAP
WH- WHAT ARE YOU DOING?
THERE'S SOMETHING I NEED TO ASK YOU.
WHAT?
DO YOU REALLY WANT TO GO BACK TO EDITING LITERATURE?
BDMP

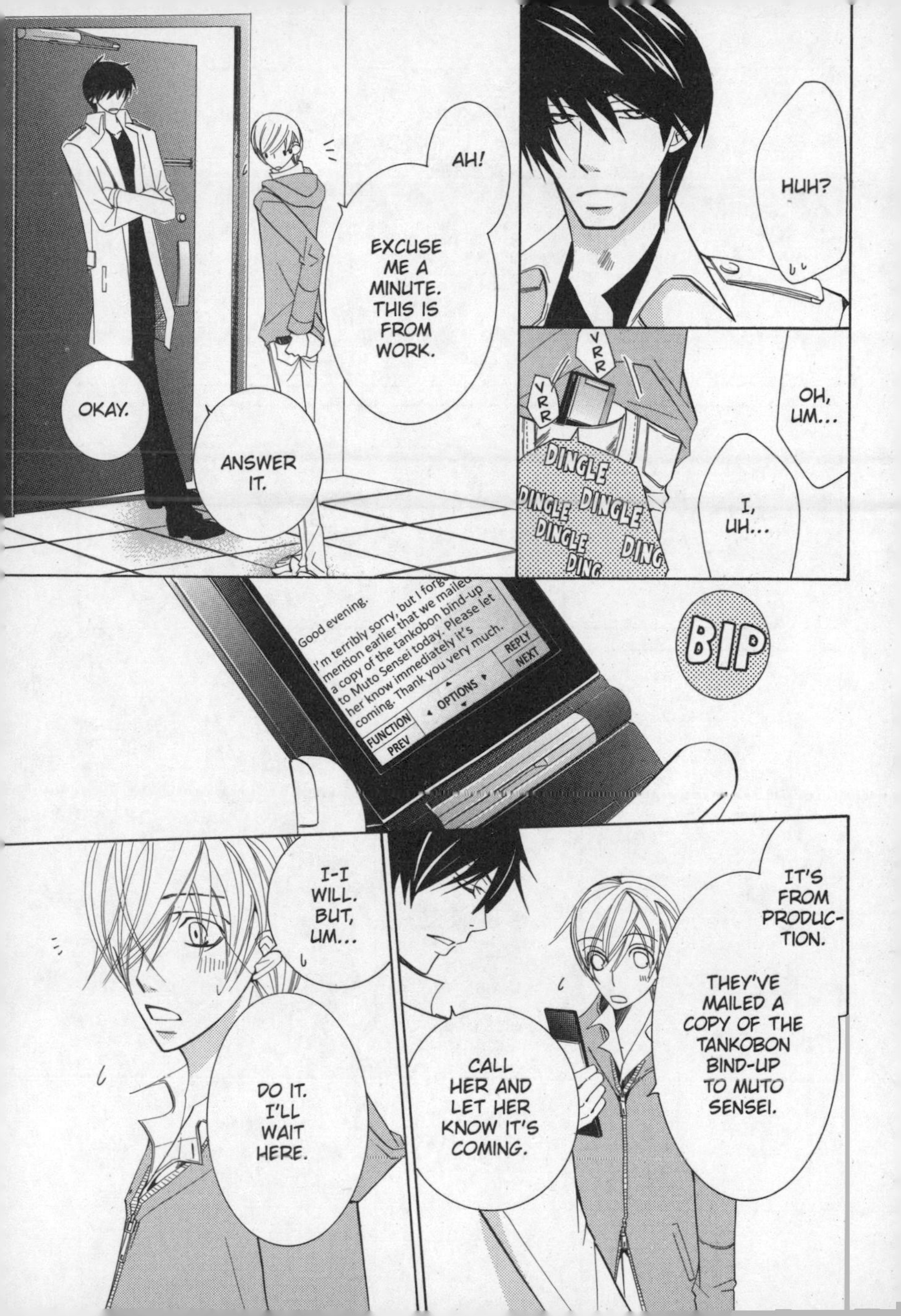
HUH?
VRR
VRR
OH, UM...
I, UH...
DINGLE DINGLE DINGLE DINGLE DING DING
AH!
EXCUSE ME A MINUTE. THIS IS FROM WORK.
OKAY.
ANSWER IT.
BIP
Good evening.
I'm terribly sorry, but I forgot to mention earlier that we mailed a copy of the tankobon bind-up to Muto Sensei today. Please let her know immediately it's coming. Thank you very much.
REPLY
NEXT
OPTIONS
FUNCTION
PREV
IT'S FROM PRODUCTION.
THEY'VE MAILED A COPY OF THE TANKOBON BIND-UP TO MUTO SENSEI.
CALL HER AND LET HER KNOW IT'S COMING.
I-I WILL. BUT, UM...
DO IT. I'LL WAIT HERE.

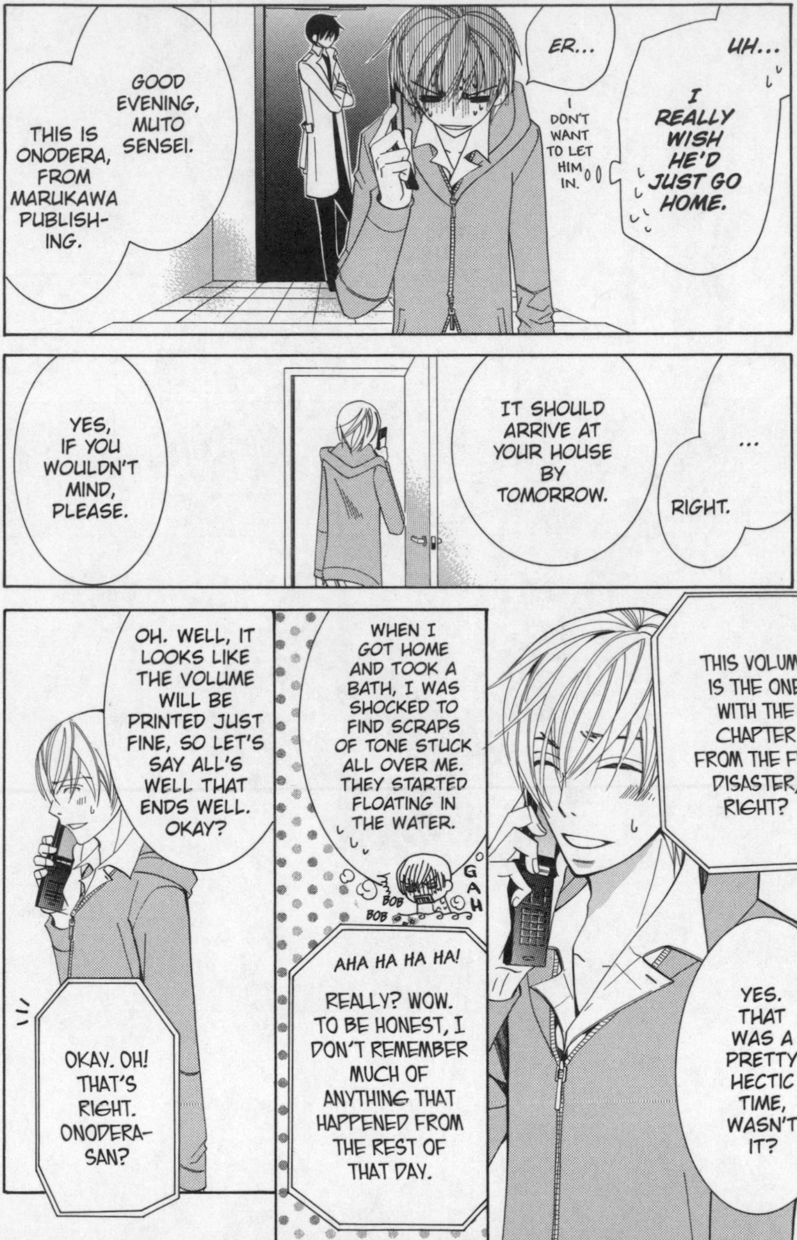

UH...
ER...
I REALLY WISH HE'D JUST GO HOME.
I DON'T WANT TO LET HIM IN.
GOOD EVENING, MUTO SENSEI.
THIS IS ONODERA, FROM MARUKAWA PUBLISHING.
... RIGHT.
IT SHOULD ARRIVE AT YOUR HOUSE BY TOMORROW.
YES, IF YOU WOULDN'T MIND, PLEASE.
THIS VOLUME IS THE ONE WITH THE CHAPTER FROM THE FLU DISASTER, RIGHT?
YES. THAT WAS A PRETTY HECTIC TIME, WASN'T IT?
WHEN I GOT HOME AND TOOK A BATH, I WAS SHOCKED TO FIND SCRAPS OF TONE STUCK ALL OVER ME. THEY STARTED FLOATING IN THE WATER.
GAH
BOB BOB
AHA HA HA HA!
REALLY? WOW. TO BE HONEST, I DON'T REMEMBER MUCH OF ANYTHING THAT HAPPENED FROM THE REST OF THAT DAY.
OH. WELL, IT LOOKS LIKE THE VOLUME WILL BE PRINTED JUST FINE, SO LET'S SAY ALL'S WELL THAT ENDS WELL. OKAY?
OKAY. OH! THAT'S RIGHT. ONODERA-SAN?

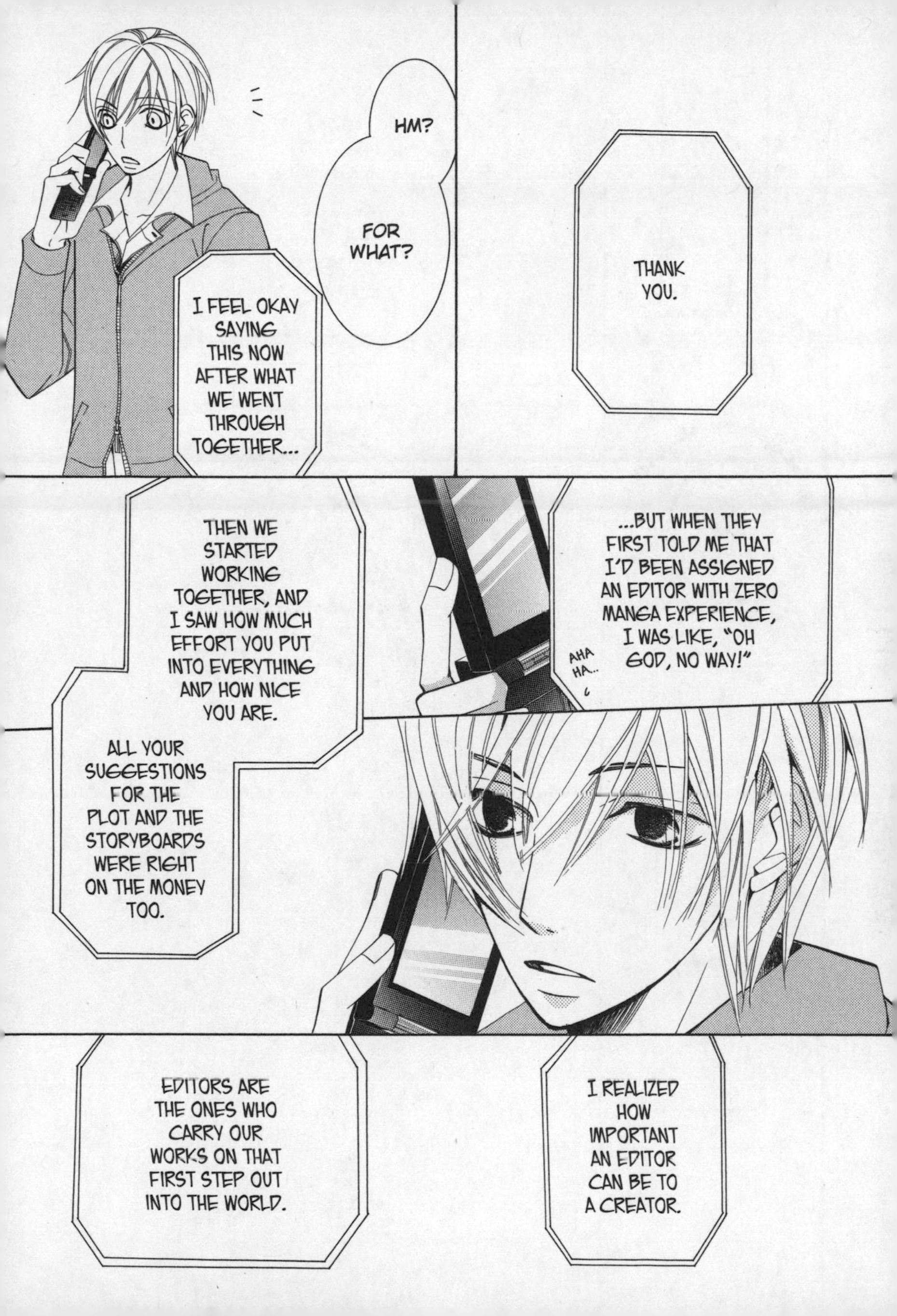
THANK YOU.
HM?
FOR WHAT?
I FEEL OKAY SAYING THIS NOW AFTER WHAT WE WENT THROUGH TOGETHER...
...BUT WHEN THEY FIRST TOLD ME THAT I'D BEEN ASSIGNED AN EDITOR WITH ZERO MANGA EXPERIENCE, I WAS LIKE, "OH GOD, NO WAY!"
AHA HA...
THEN WE STARTED WORKING TOGETHER, AND I SAW HOW MUCH EFFORT YOU PUT INTO EVERYTHING AND HOW NICE YOU ARE.
ALL YOUR SUGGESTIONS FOR THE PLOT AND THE STORYBOARDS WERE RIGHT ON THE MONEY TOO.
I REALIZED HOW IMPORTANT AN EDITOR CAN BE TO A CREATOR.
EDITORS ARE THE ONES WHO CARRY OUR WORKS ON THAT FIRST STEP OUT INTO THE WORLD.

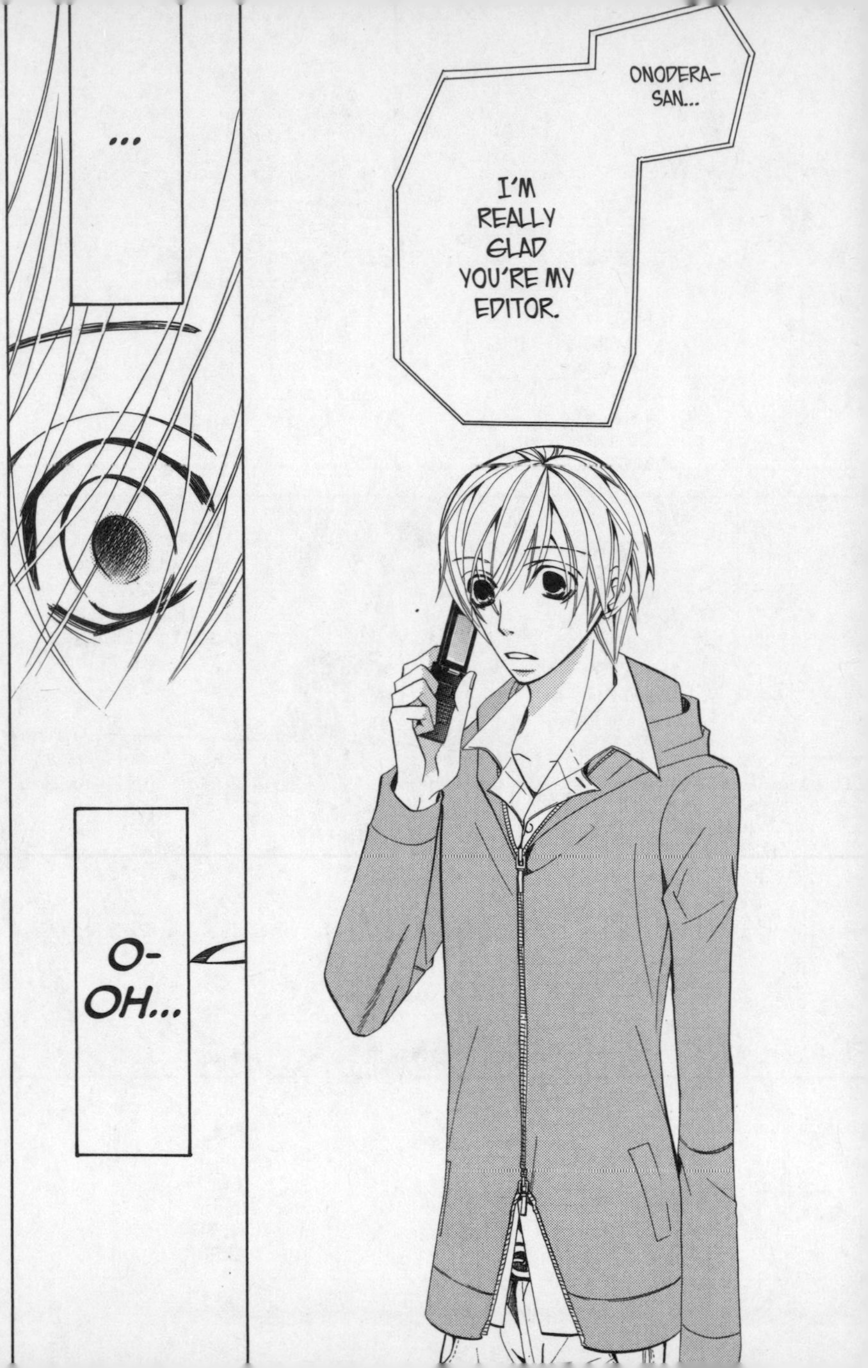
ONODERA-SAN...
I'M REALLY GLAD YOU'RE MY EDITOR.
...
O-OH...

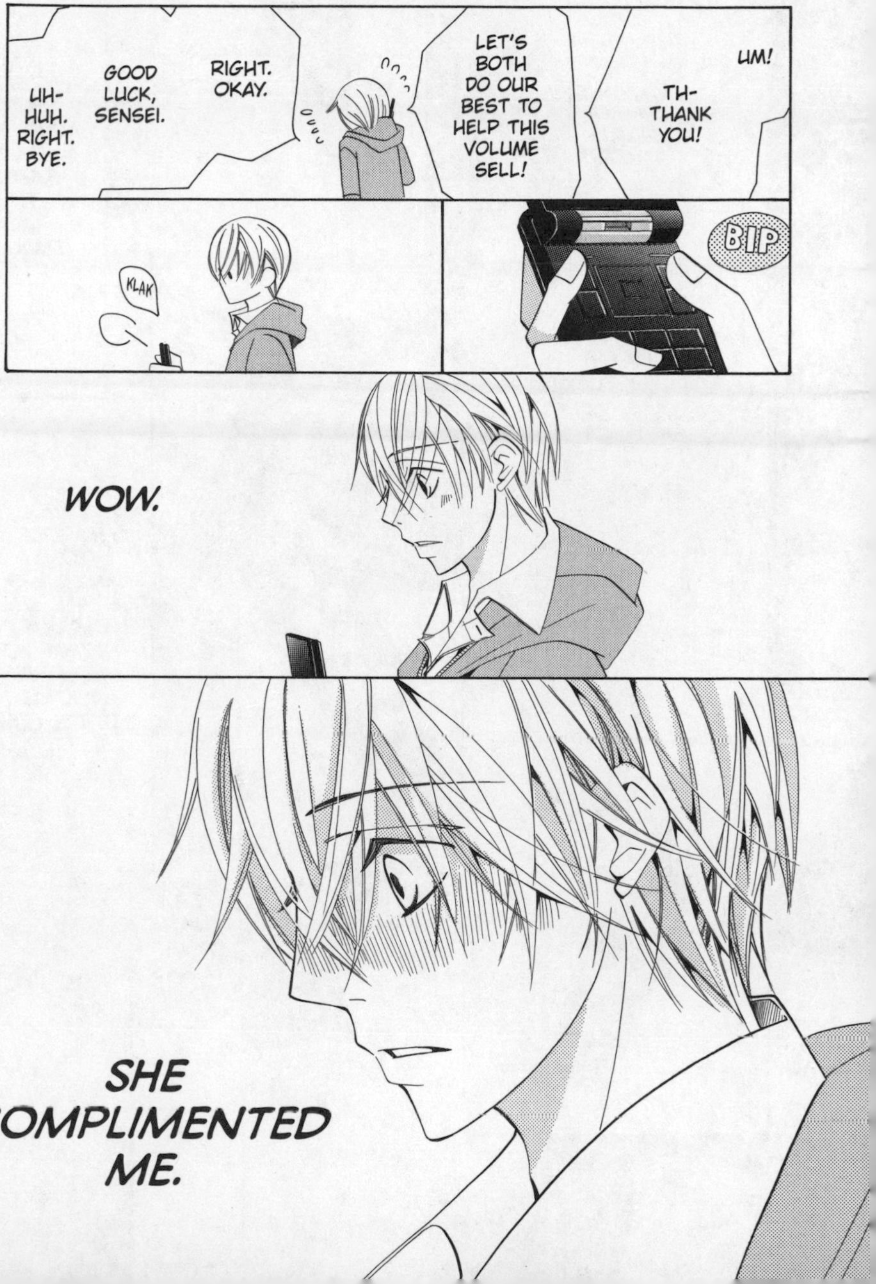
UM!
TH- THANK YOU!
LET'S BOTH DO OUR BEST TO HELP THIS VOLUME SELL!
RIGHT. OKAY.
GOOD LUCK, SENSEI.
UH-HUH. RIGHT. BYE.
BIP
KLAK
WOW.
SHE COMPLIMENTED ME.

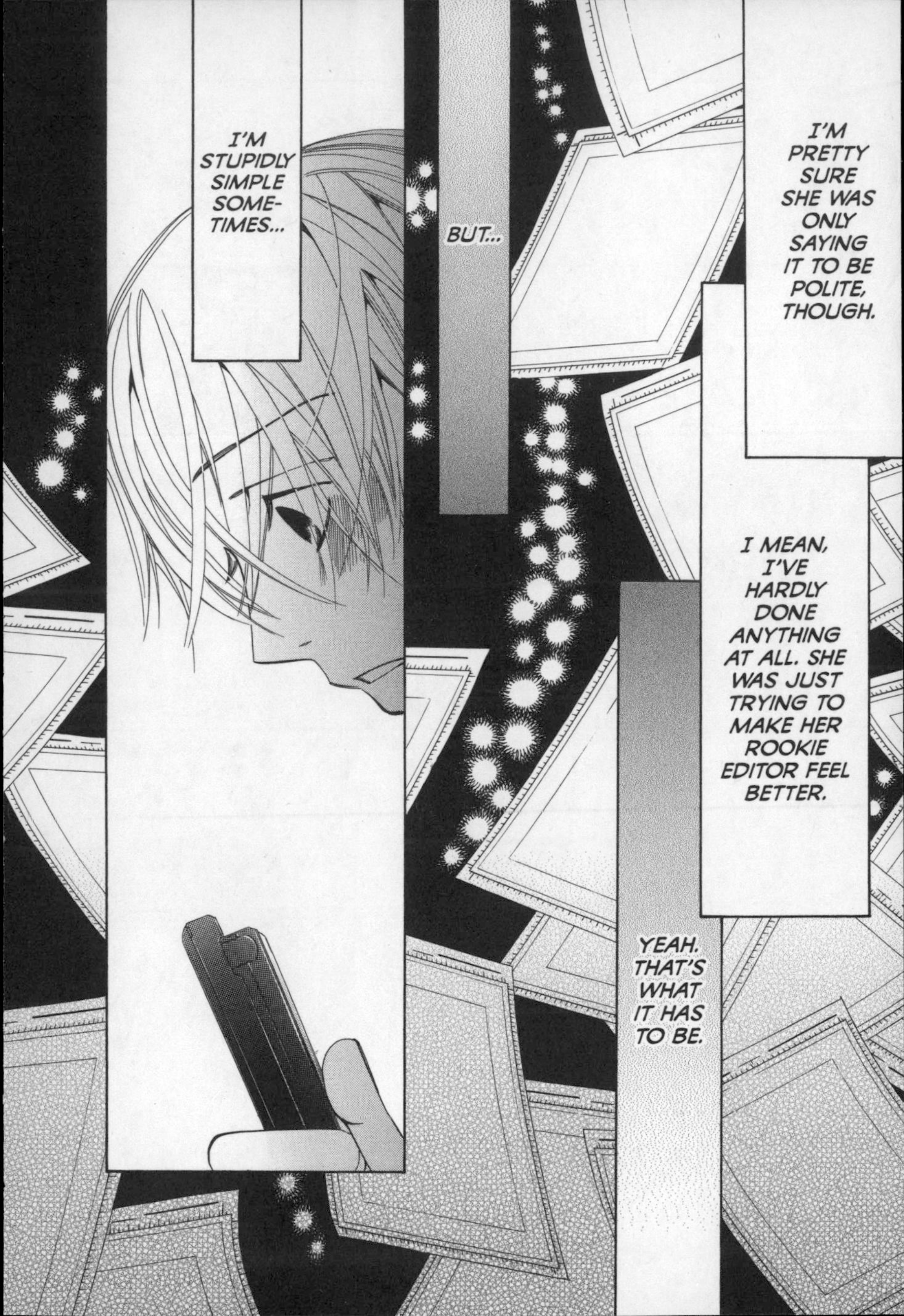
I'M PRETTY SURE SHE WAS ONLY SAYING IT TO BE POLITE, THOUGH.
I MEAN, I'VE HARDLY DONE ANYTHING AT ALL. SHE WAS JUST TRYING TO MAKE HER ROOKIE EDITOR FEEL BETTER.
YEAH. THAT'S WHAT IT HAS TO BE.
BUT...
I'M STUPIDLY SIMPLE SOME-TIMES...

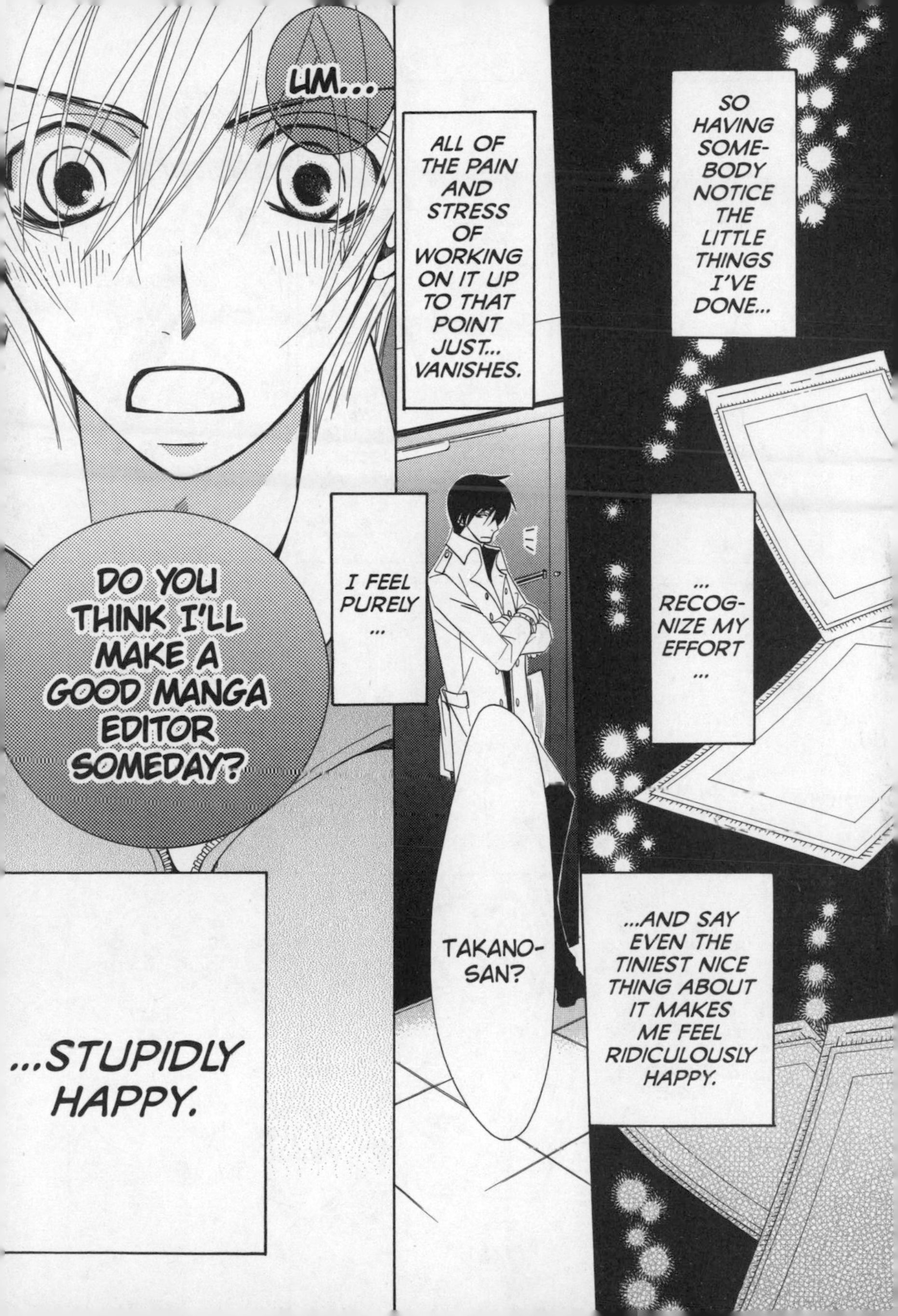
SO HAVING SOME-BODY NOTICE THE LITTLE THINGS I'VE DONE...
...RECOG-NIZE MY EFFORT...
...AND SAY EVEN THE TINIEST NICE THING ABOUT IT MAKES ME FEEL RIDICULOUSLY HAPPY.
ALL OF THE PAIN AND STRESS OF WORKING ON IT UP TO THAT POINT JUST... VANISHES.
I FEEL PURELY...
TAKANO-SAN?
UM...
DO YOU THINK I'LL MAKE A GOOD MANGA EDITOR SOMEDAY?
...STUPIDLY HAPPY.

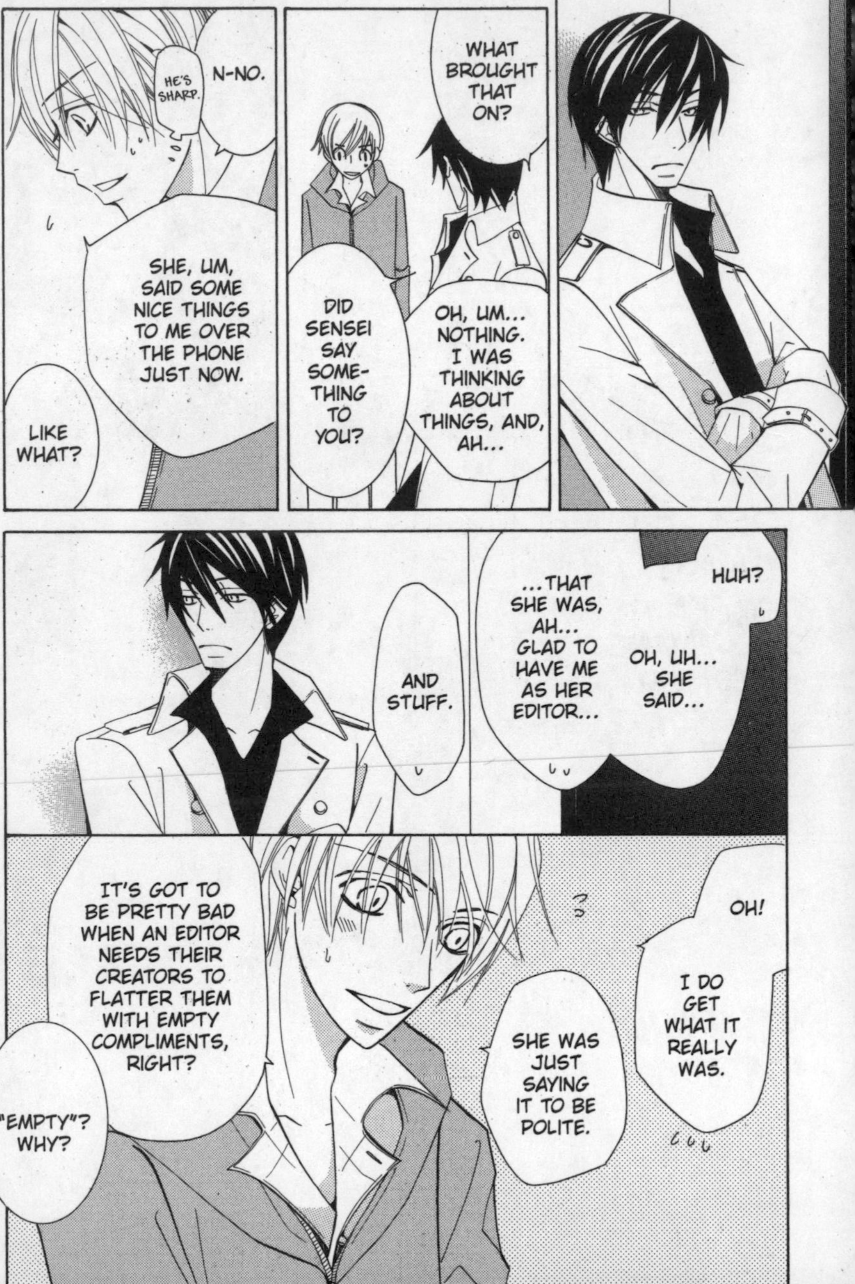
WHAT BROUGHT THAT ON?
OH, UM... NOTHING. I WAS THINKING ABOUT THINGS, AND, AH...
DID SENSEI SAY SOMETHING TO YOU?
N-NO.
HE'S SHARP.
SHE, UM, SAID SOME NICE THINGS TO ME OVER THE PHONE JUST NOW.
LIKE WHAT?
HUH?
OH, UH... SHE SAID...
...THAT SHE WAS, AH... GLAD TO HAVE ME AS HER EDITOR...
AND STUFF.
OH!
I DO GET WHAT IT REALLY WAS.
SHE WAS JUST SAYING IT TO BE POLITE.
IT'S GOT TO BE PRETTY BAD WHEN AN EDITOR NEEDS THEIR CREATORS TO FLATTER THEM WITH EMPTY COMPLIMENTS, RIGHT?
"EMPTY"? WHY?

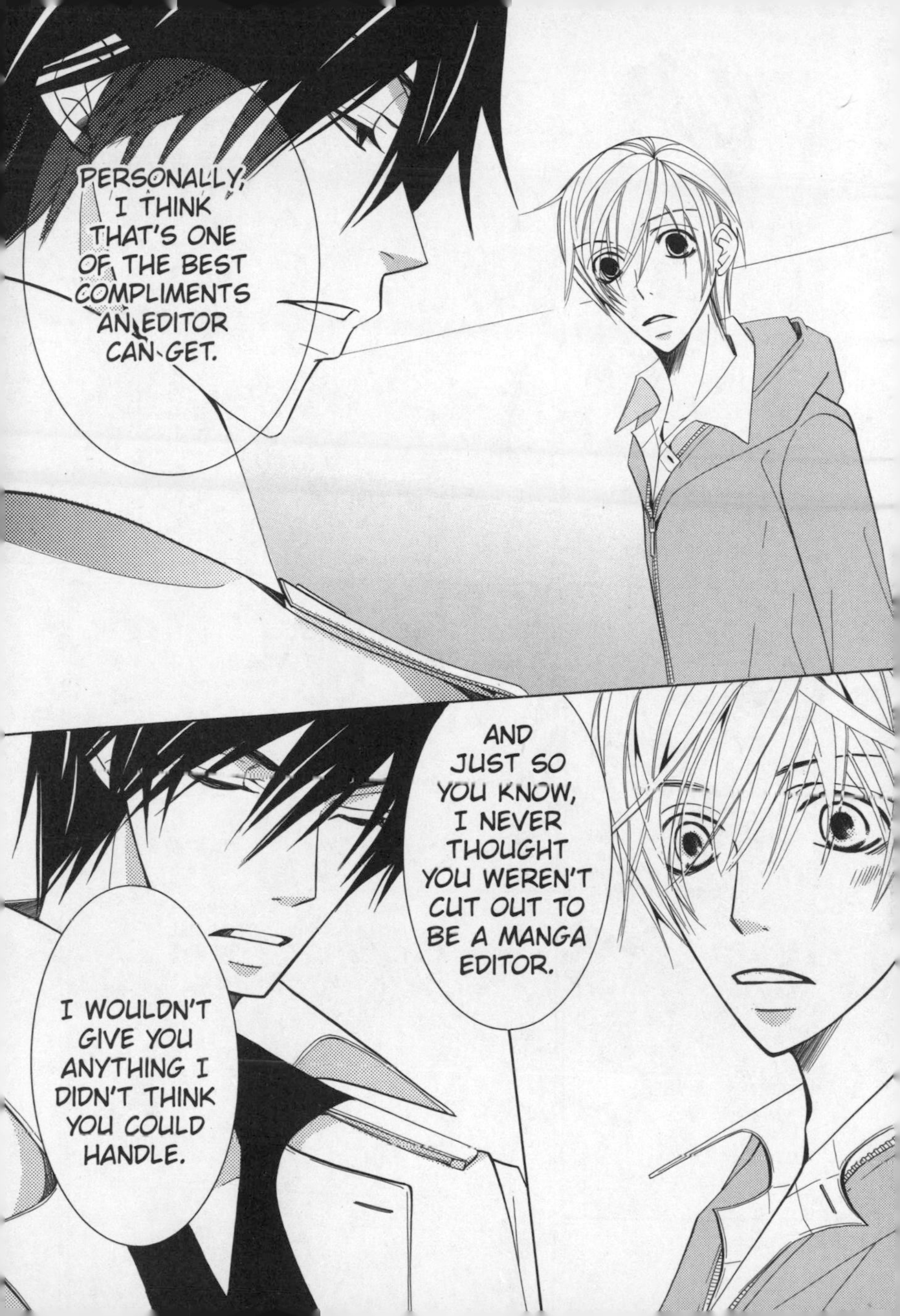
PERSONALLY, I THINK THAT'S ONE OF THE BEST COMPLIMENTS AN EDITOR CAN GET.
AND JUST SO YOU KNOW, I NEVER THOUGHT YOU WEREN'T CUT OUT TO BE A MANGA EDITOR.
I WOULDN'T GIVE YOU ANYTHING I DIDN'T THINK YOU COULD HANDLE.

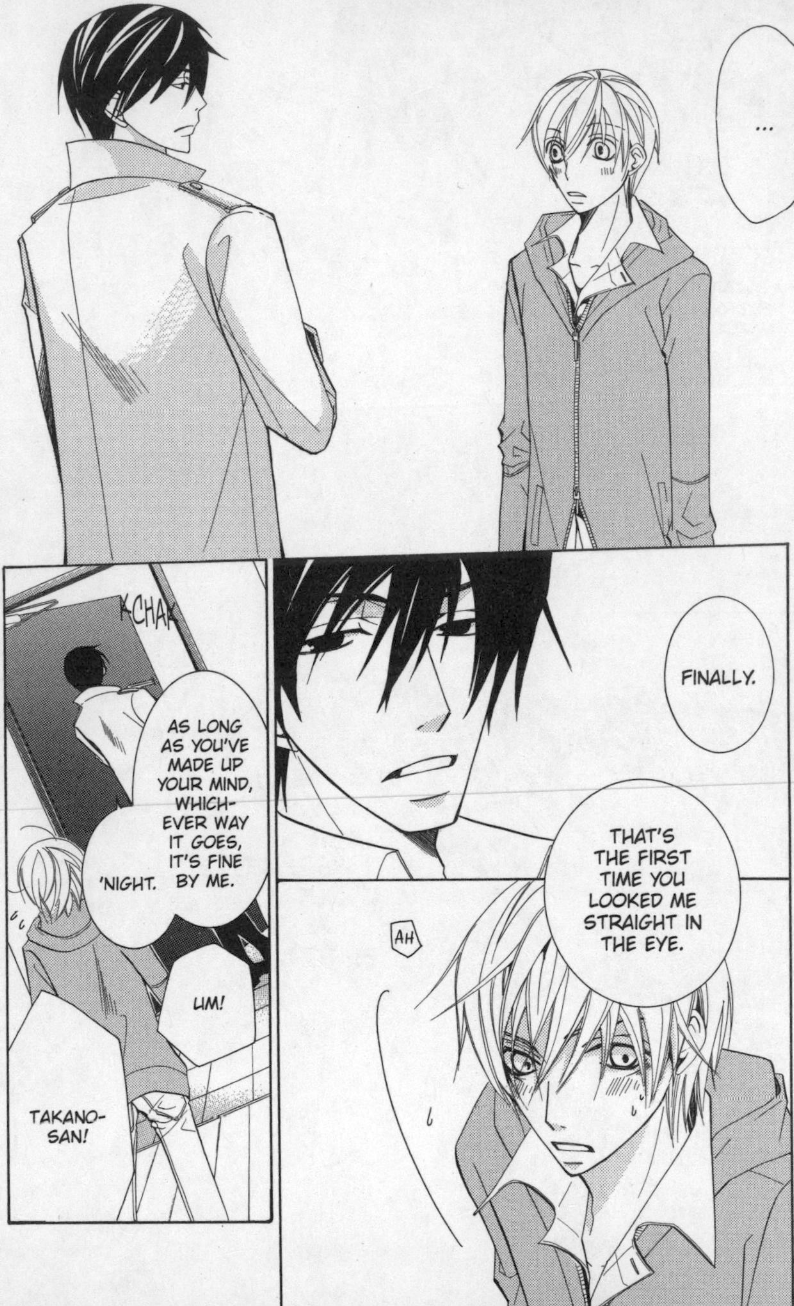
...
FINALLY.
THAT'S THE FIRST TIME YOU LOOKED ME STRAIGHT IN THE EYE.
AH
KCHA
AS LONG AS YOU'VE MADE UP YOUR MIND, WHICH-EVER WAY IT GOES, IT'S FINE BY ME.
'NIGHT.
UM!
TAKANO-SAN!

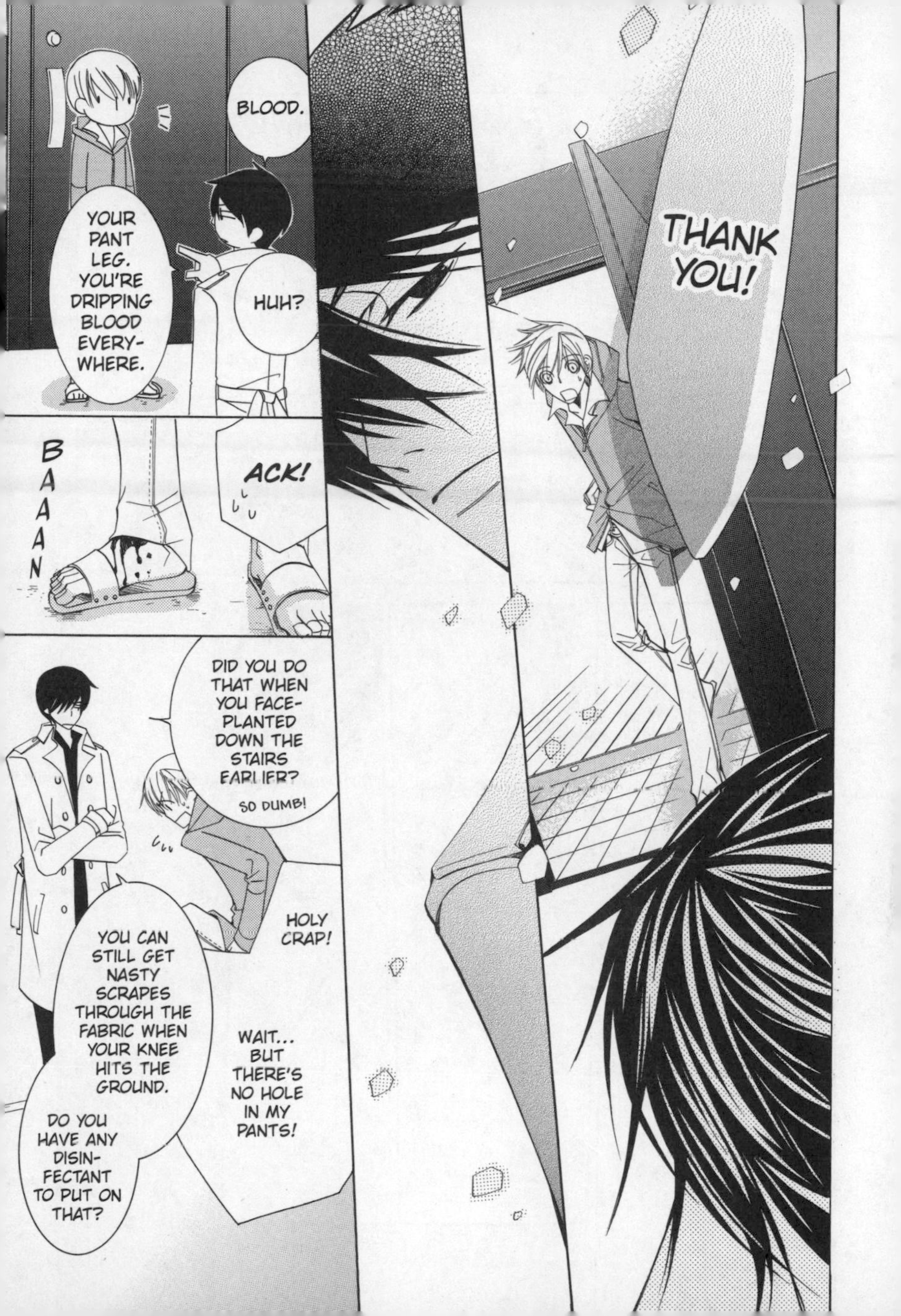

THANK YOU!
BLOOD.
YOUR PANT LEG. YOU'RE DRIPPING BLOOD EVERY-WHERE.
HUH?
ACK!
BAAAAN
DID YOU DO THAT WHEN YOU FACE-PLANTED DOWN THE STAIRS EARLIER?
SO DUMB!
HOLY CRAP!
YOU CAN STILL GET NASTY SCRAPES THROUGH THE FABRIC WHEN YOUR KNEE HITS THE GROUND.
WAIT... BUT THERE'S NO HOLE IN MY PANTS!
DO YOU HAVE ANY DISIN-FECTANT TO PUT ON THAT?

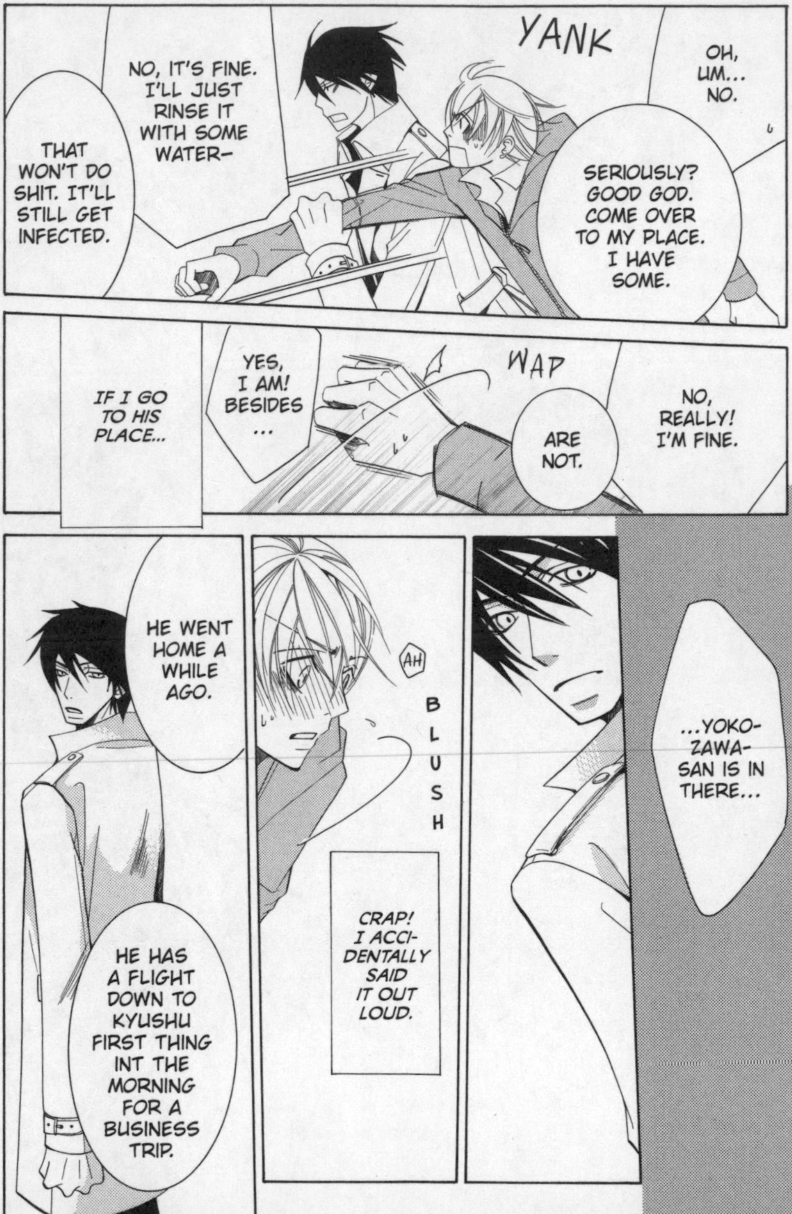
OH, UM... NO.
YANK
SERIOUSLY? GOOD GOD. COME OVER TO MY PLACE. I HAVE SOME.
NO, IT'S FINE. I'LL JUST RINSE IT WITH SOME WATER—
THAT WON'T DO SHIT. IT'LL STILL GET INFECTED.
NO, REALLY! I'M FINE.
WAP
ARE NOT.
YES, I AM! BESIDES...
IF I GO TO HIS PLACE...
...YOKO-ZAWA-SAN IS IN THERE...
AH
BLUSH
CRAP! I ACCI-DENTALLY SAID IT OUT LOUD.
HE WENT HOME A WHILE AGO.
HE HAS A FLIGHT DOWN TO KYUSHU FIRST THING INT THE MORNING FOR A BUSINESS TRIP.

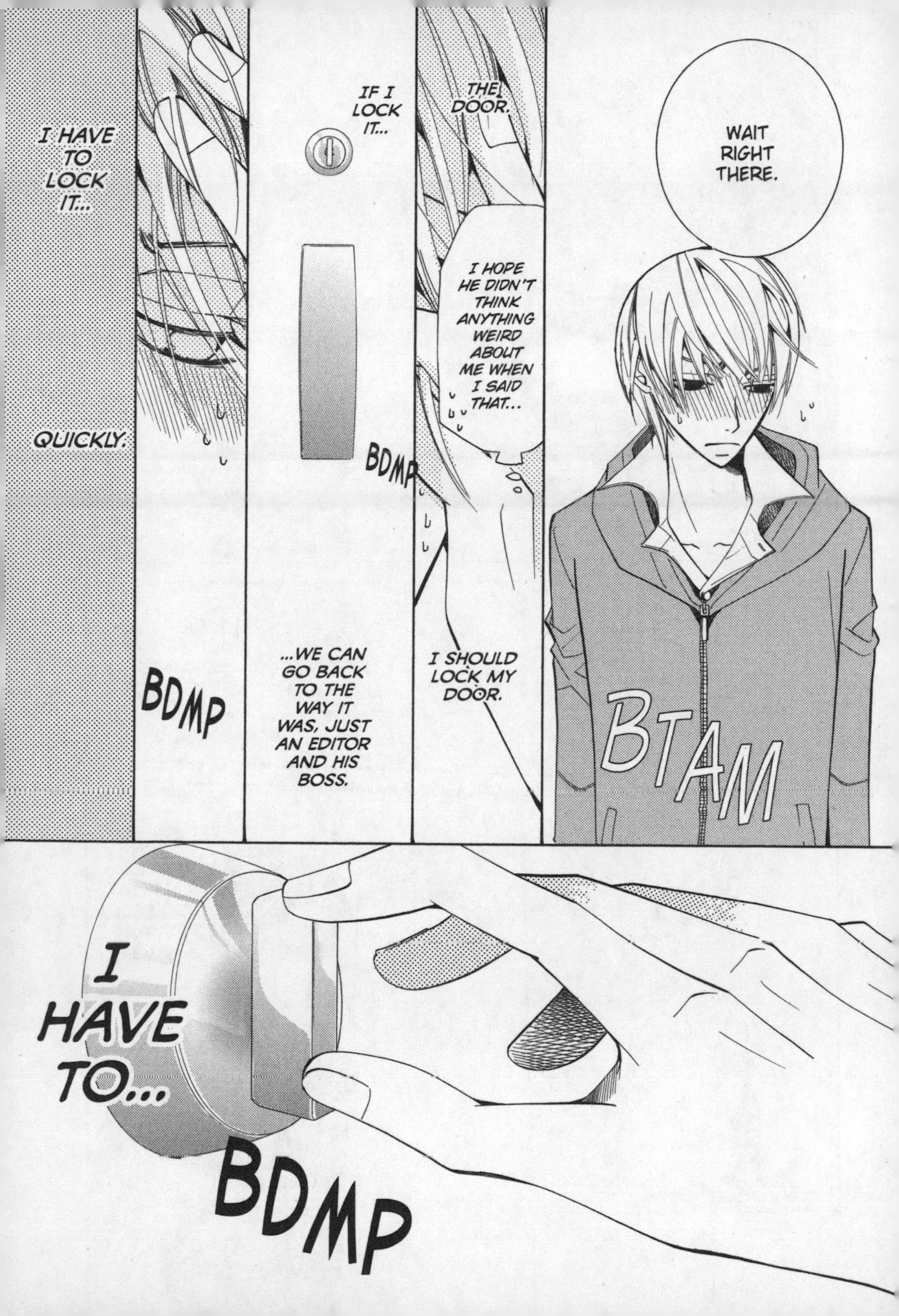
WAIT RIGHT THERE.
BTAM
THE DOOR.
I HOPE HE DIDN'T THINK ANYTHING WEIRD ABOUT ME WHEN I SAID THAT...
I SHOULD LOCK MY DOOR.
BDMP
IF I LOCK IT...
...WE CAN GO BACK TO THE WAY IT WAS, JUST AN EDITOR AND HIS BOSS.
BDMP
I HAVE TO LOCK IT...
QUICKLY.
I HAVE TO...
BDMP

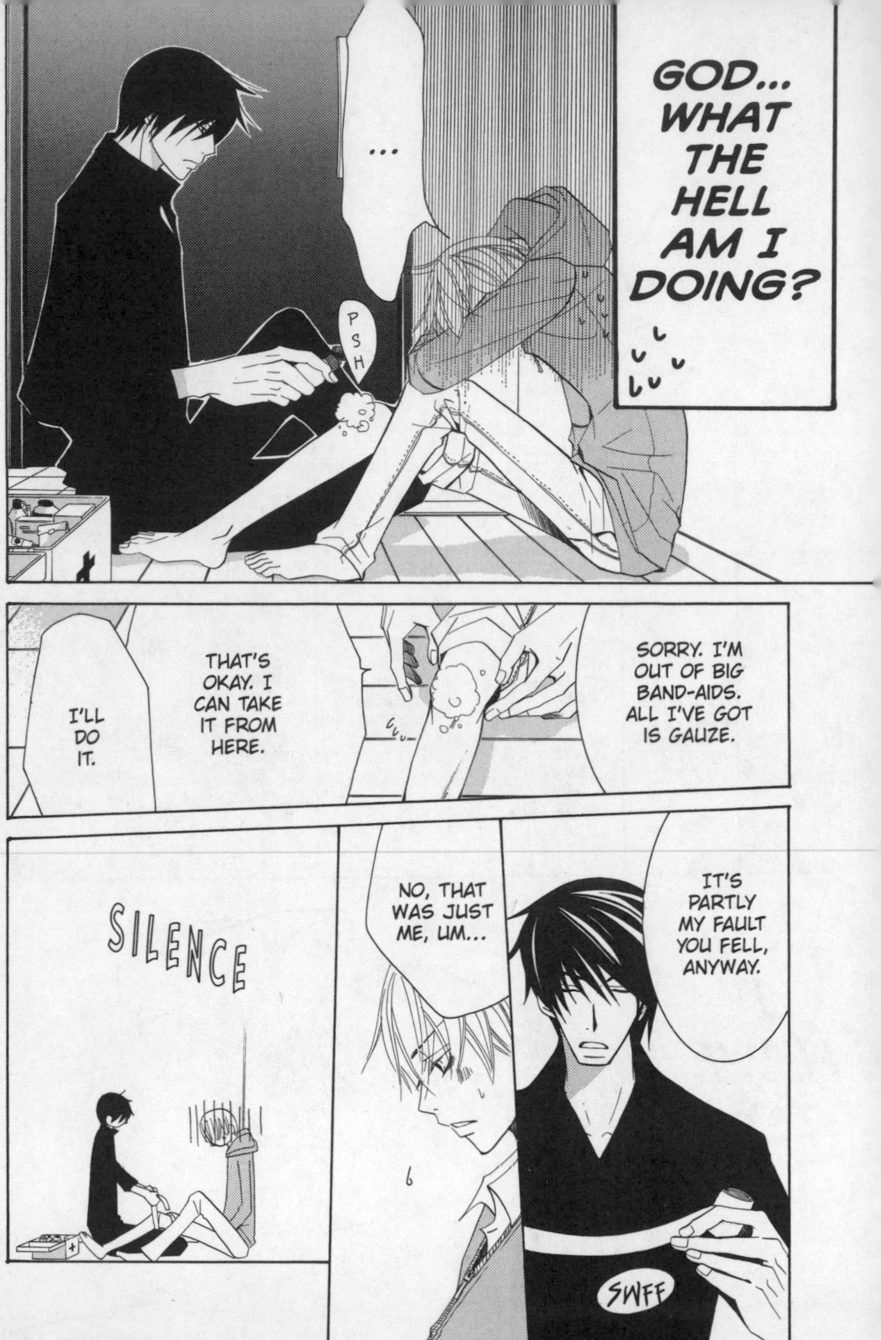
GOD... WHAT THE HELL AM I DOING?
...
PSH
SORRY. I'M OUT OF BIG BAND-AIDS. ALL I'VE GOT IS GAUZE.
THAT'S OKAY. I CAN TAKE IT FROM HERE.
I'LL DO IT.
IT'S PARTLY MY FAULT YOU FELL, ANYWAY.
NO, THAT WAS JUST ME, UM...
SWFF
SILENCE

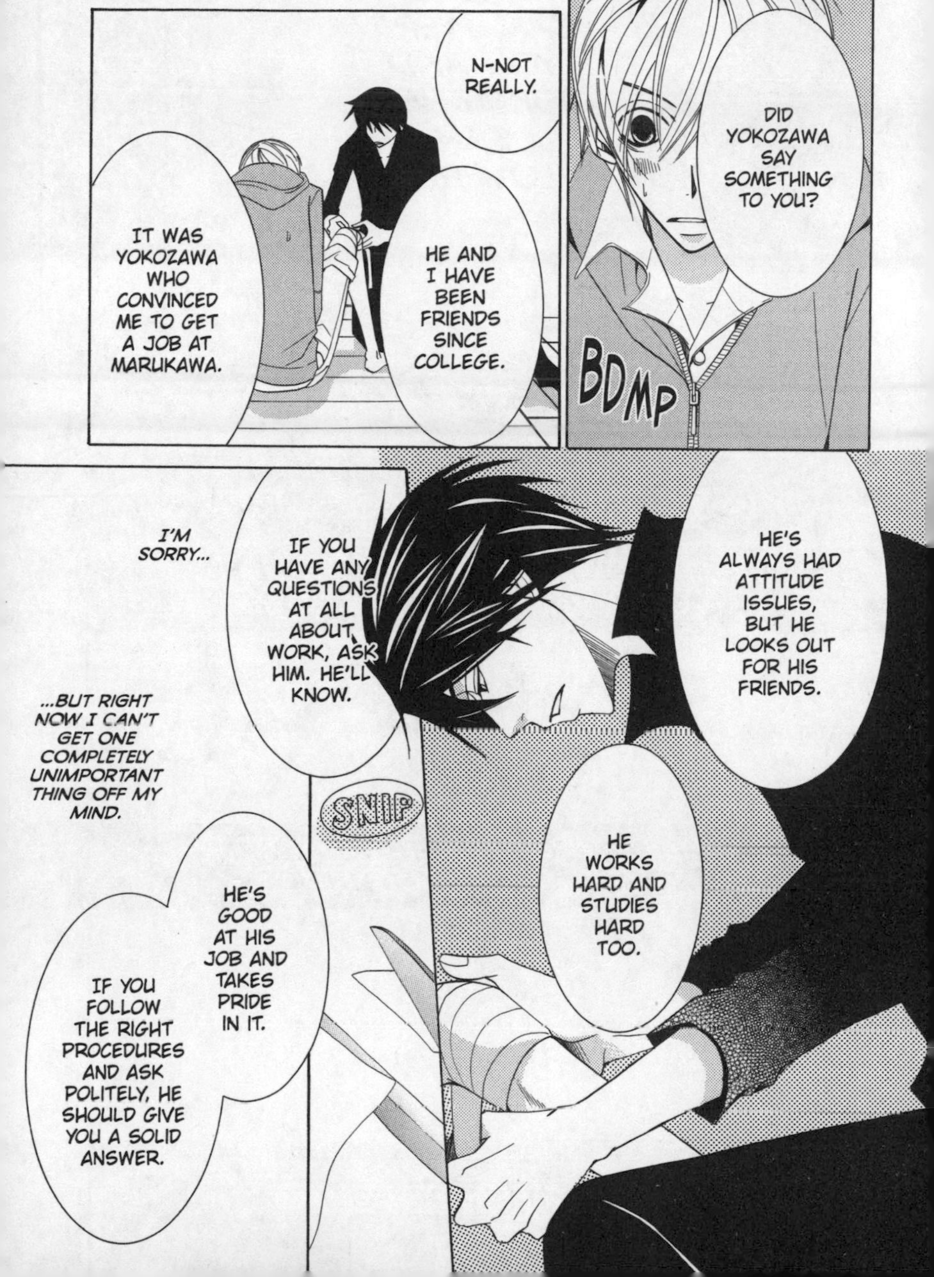
DID YOKOZAWA SAY SOMETHING TO YOU?
BDMP
N-NOT REALLY.
HE AND I HAVE BEEN FRIENDS SINCE COLLEGE.
IT WAS YOKOZAWA WHO CONVINCED ME TO GET A JOB AT MARUKAWA.
HE'S ALWAYS HAD ATTITUDE ISSUES, BUT HE LOOKS OUT FOR HIS FRIENDS.
HE WORKS HARD AND STUDIES HARD TOO.
IF YOU HAVE ANY QUESTIONS AT ALL ABOUT WORK, ASK HIM. HE'LL KNOW.
I'M SORRY...
SNIP
HE'S GOOD AT HIS JOB AND TAKES PRIDE IN IT.
IF YOU FOLLOW THE RIGHT PROCEDURES AND ASK POLITELY, HE SHOULD GIVE YOU A SOLID ANSWER.
...BUT RIGHT NOW I CAN'T GET ONE COMPLETELY UNIMPORTANT THING OFF MY MIND.

TAKANO-SAN, WERE YOU AND YOKOZAWA-SAN LOVERS?

WHY DOES HE HAVE A KEY TO YOUR APARTMENT?

WAS IT REALLY MY FAULT YOU WERE HURT AS BADLY AS HE MAKES IT SEEM?

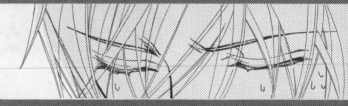

THERE ARE SO MANY THINGS I WANT TO ASK... TOO MANY THINGS.

ONODERA?

BUT WHAT'S THE POINT?

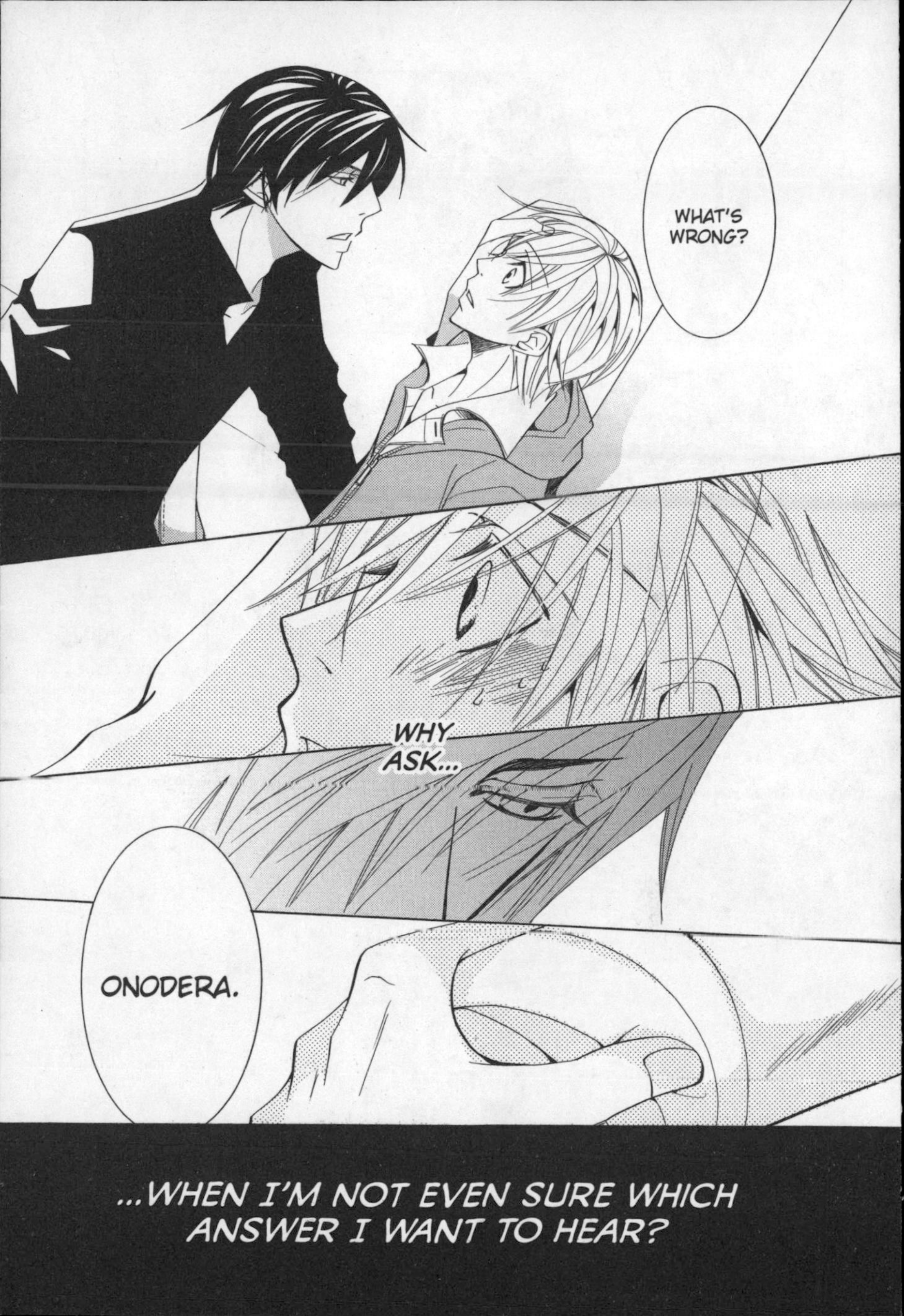
WHAT'S WRONG?
WHY ASK...
ONODERA.
...WHEN I'M NOT EVEN SURE WHICH ANSWER I WANT TO HEAR?

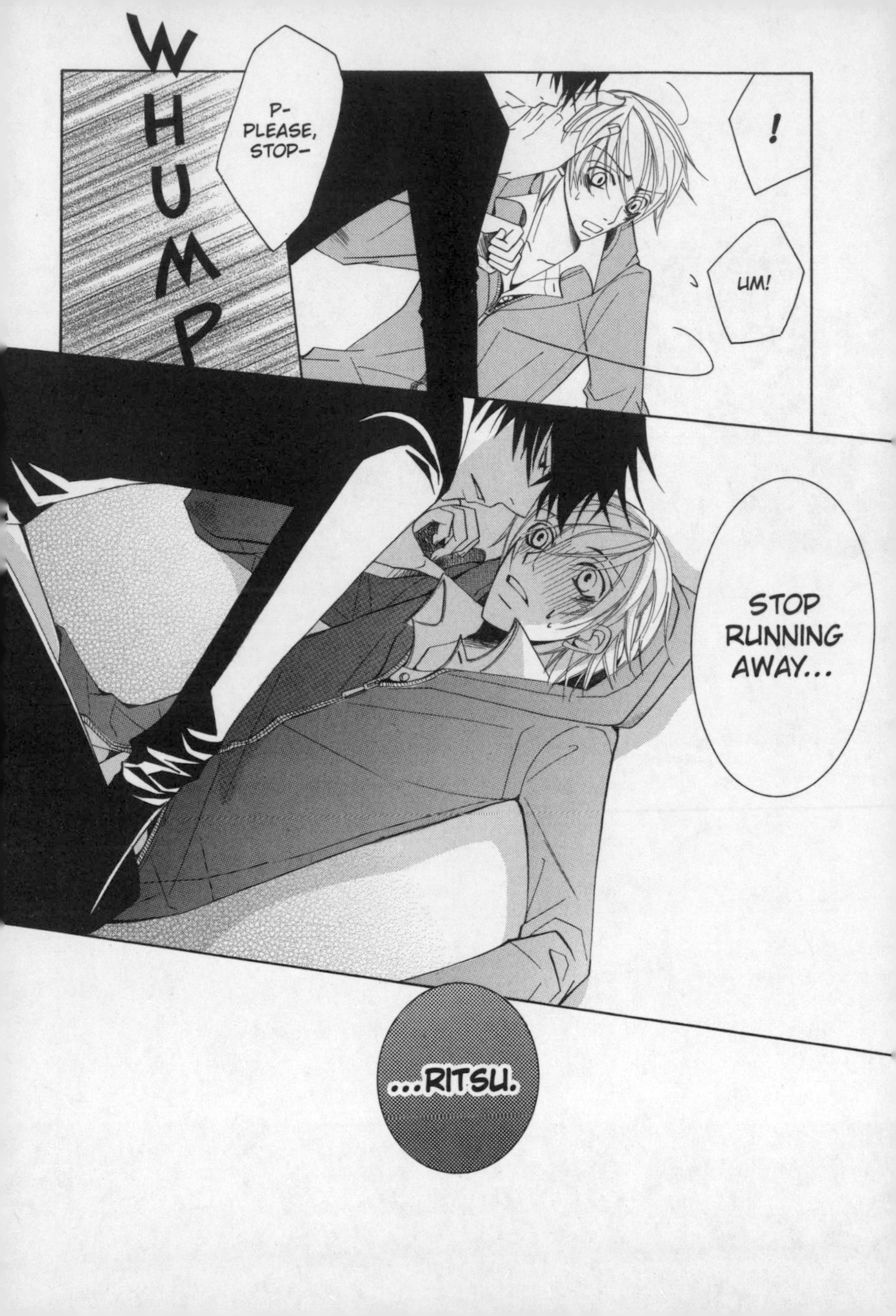
!
P-PLEASE, STOP-
UM!
WHUMP
STOP RUNNING AWAY...
...RITSU.

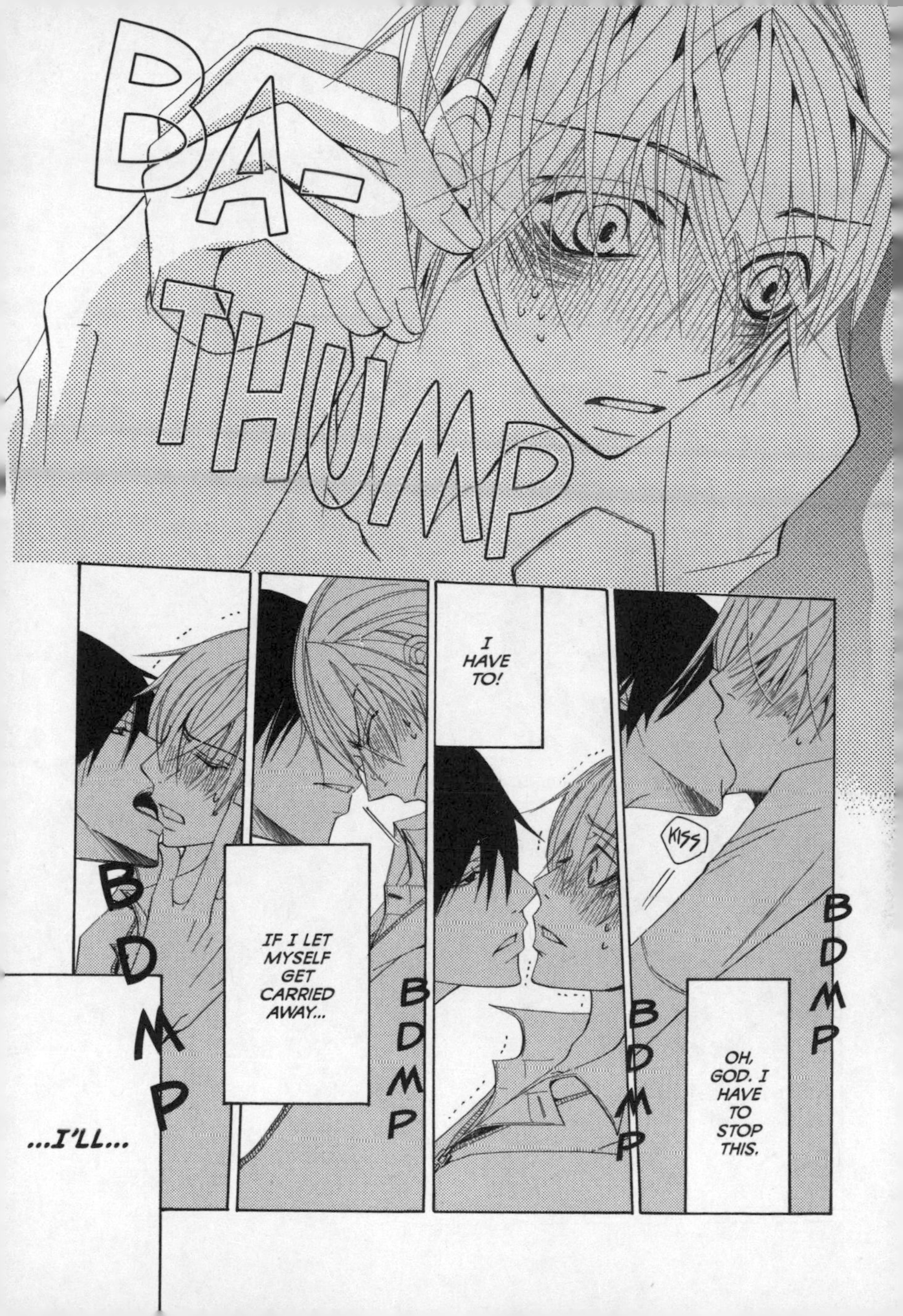
BA-THUMP
KISS
BDMP
OH, GOD. I HAVE TO STOP THIS.
I HAVE TO!
BDMP
BDMP
IF I LET MYSELF GET CARRIED AWAY...
BDMP
...I'LL...

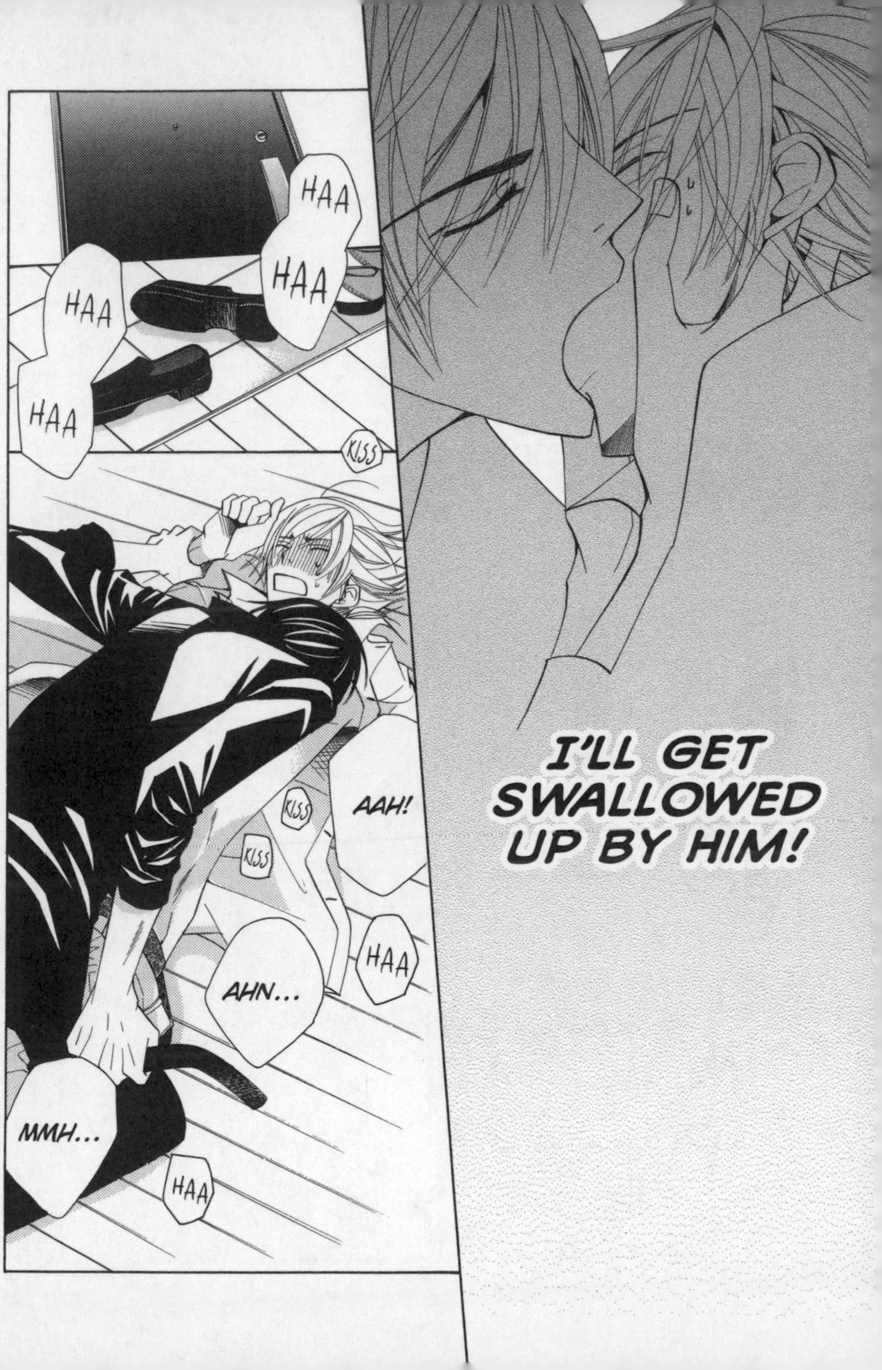
I'LL GET SWALLOWED UP BY HIM!
HAA
HAA
HAA
HAA
KISS
AAH!
KISS
KISS
HAA
AHN...
MMH...
HAA

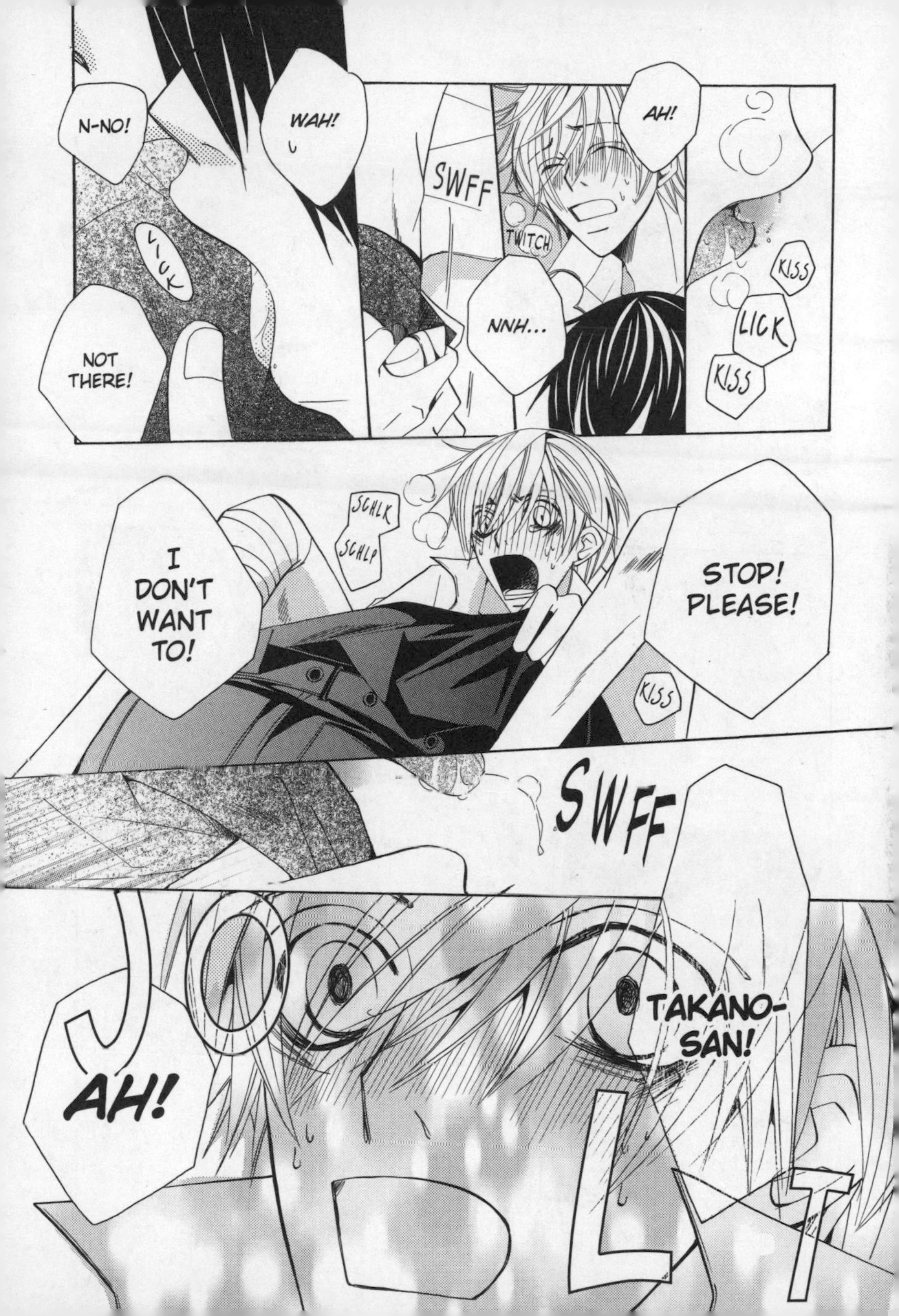
KISS
LICK
KISS
AH!
SWFF
TWITCH
NNH...
WAH!
N-NO!
LICK
NOT THERE!
STOP! PLEASE!
SCHLK
SCHLP
KISS
I DON'T WANT TO!
SWFF
TAKANO-SAN!
JOLT
AH!

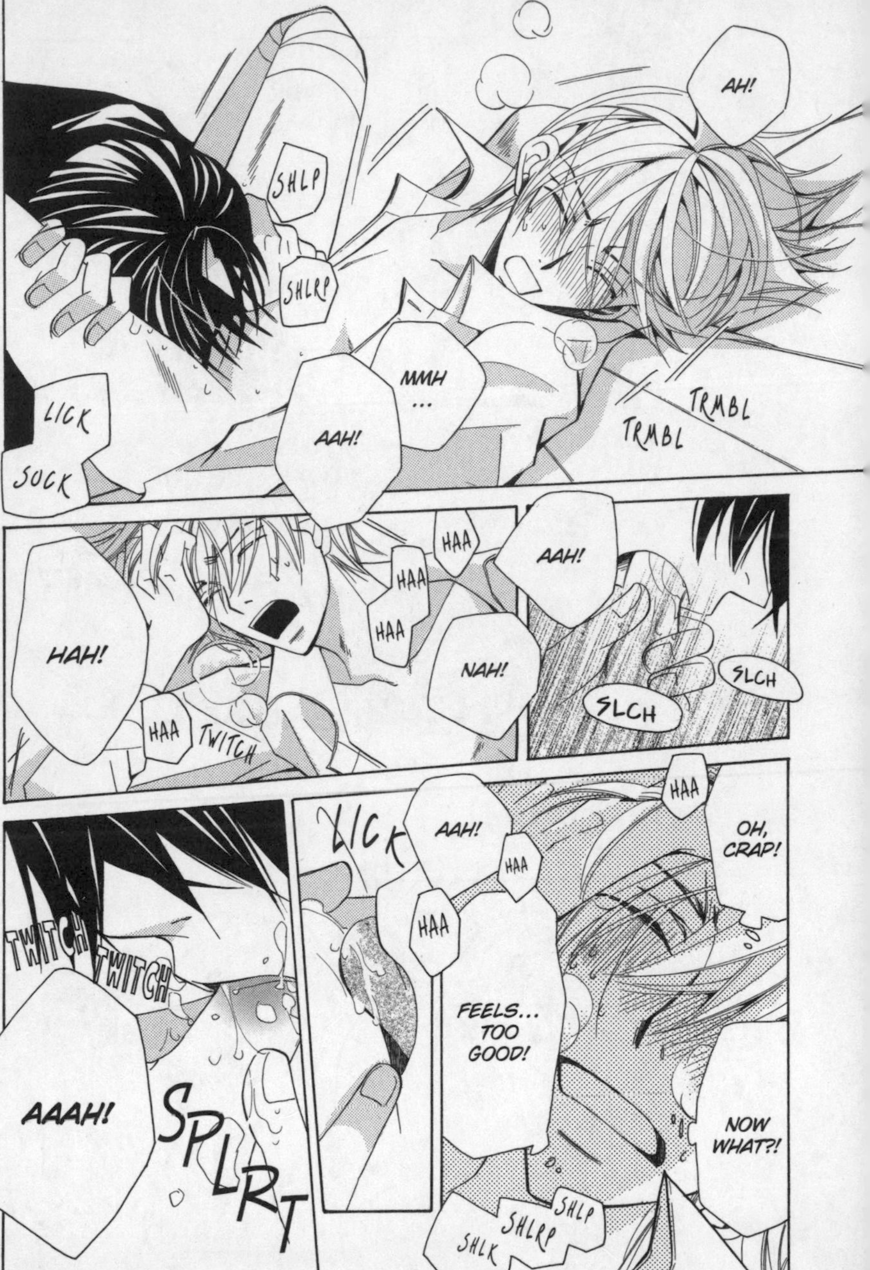
AH!
SHLP
SHLRP
MMH …
TRMBL
TRMBL
AAH!
LICK
SUCK
AAH!
SLCH
SLCH
HAA
HAA
HAA
NAH!
HAH!
HAA
TWITCH
HAA
OH, CRAP!
FEELS… TOO GOOD!
NOW WHAT?!
SHLP
SHLRP
SHLK
AAH!
HAA
HAA
LICK
TWITCH
TWITCH
AAAH!
SPLRT

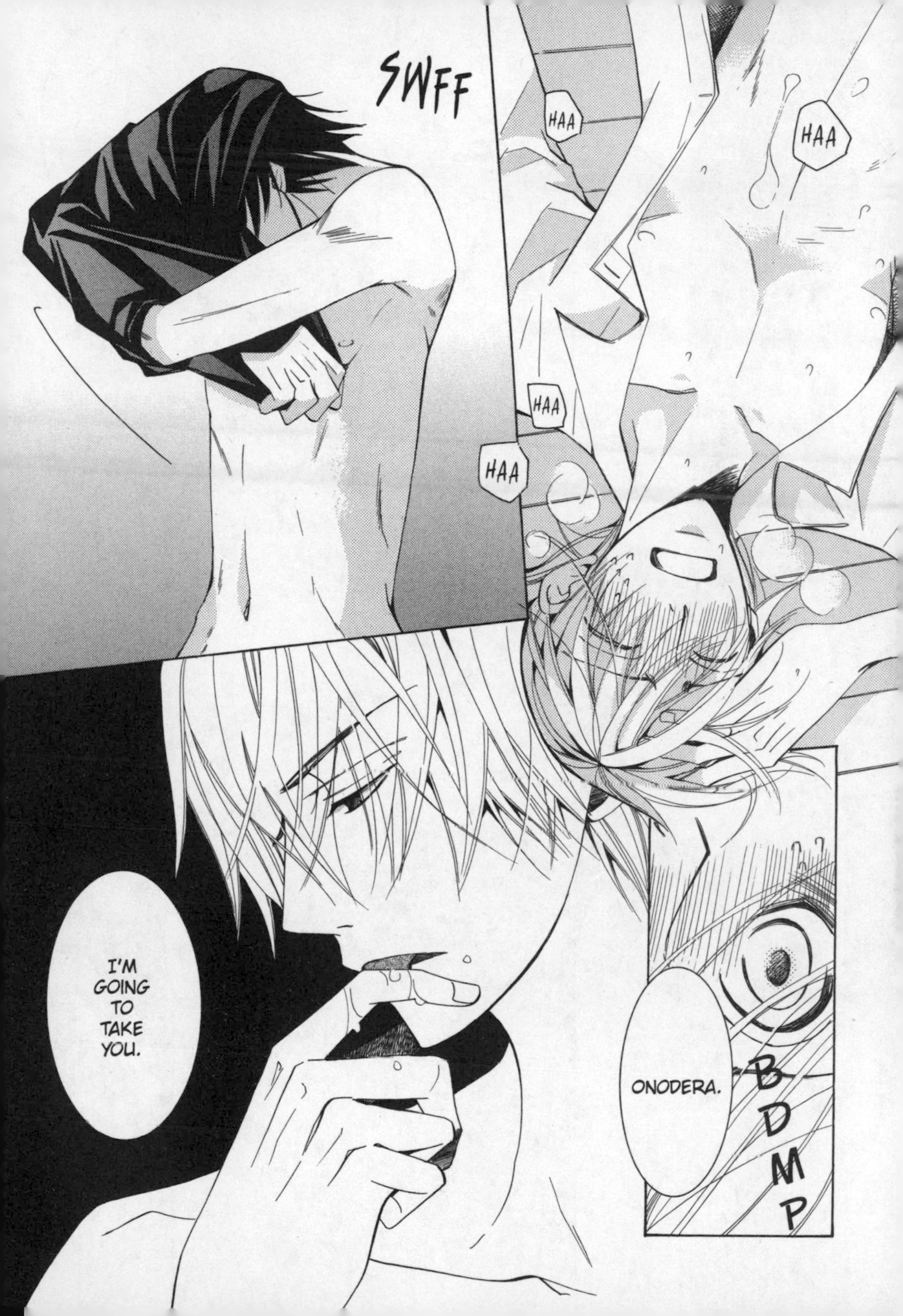
HAA
HAA
HAA
HAA
SWFF
ONODERA.
BDMP
I'M GOING TO TAKE YOU.

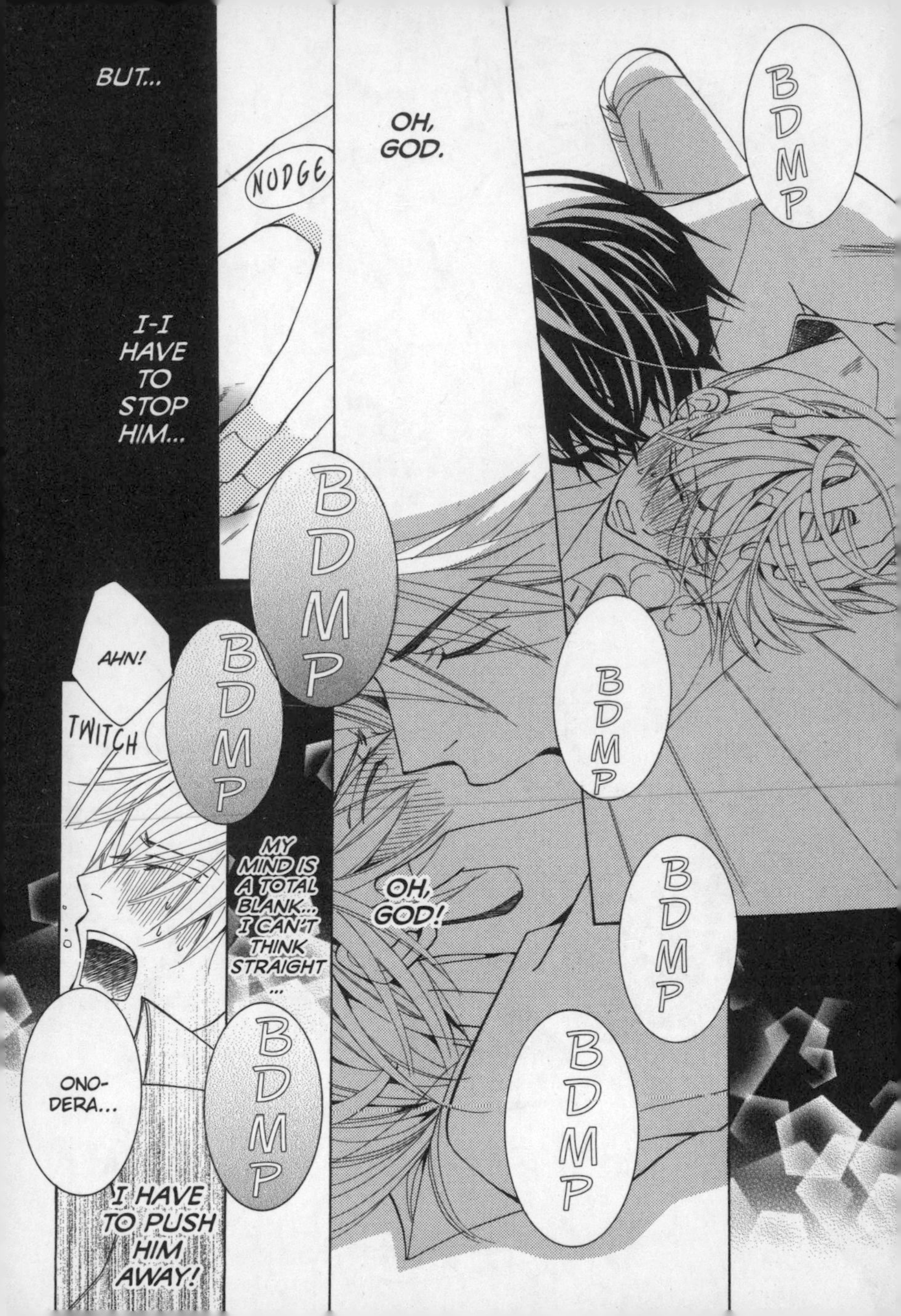
BDMP
OH, GOD.
BUT...
NUDGE
I-I HAVE TO STOP HIM...
BDMP
BDMP
BDMP
BDMP
OH, GOD!
MY MIND IS A TOTAL BLANK... I CAN'T THINK STRAIGHT...
BDMP
BDMP
AHN!
TWITCH
ONO-DERA...
I HAVE TO PUSH HIM AWAY!

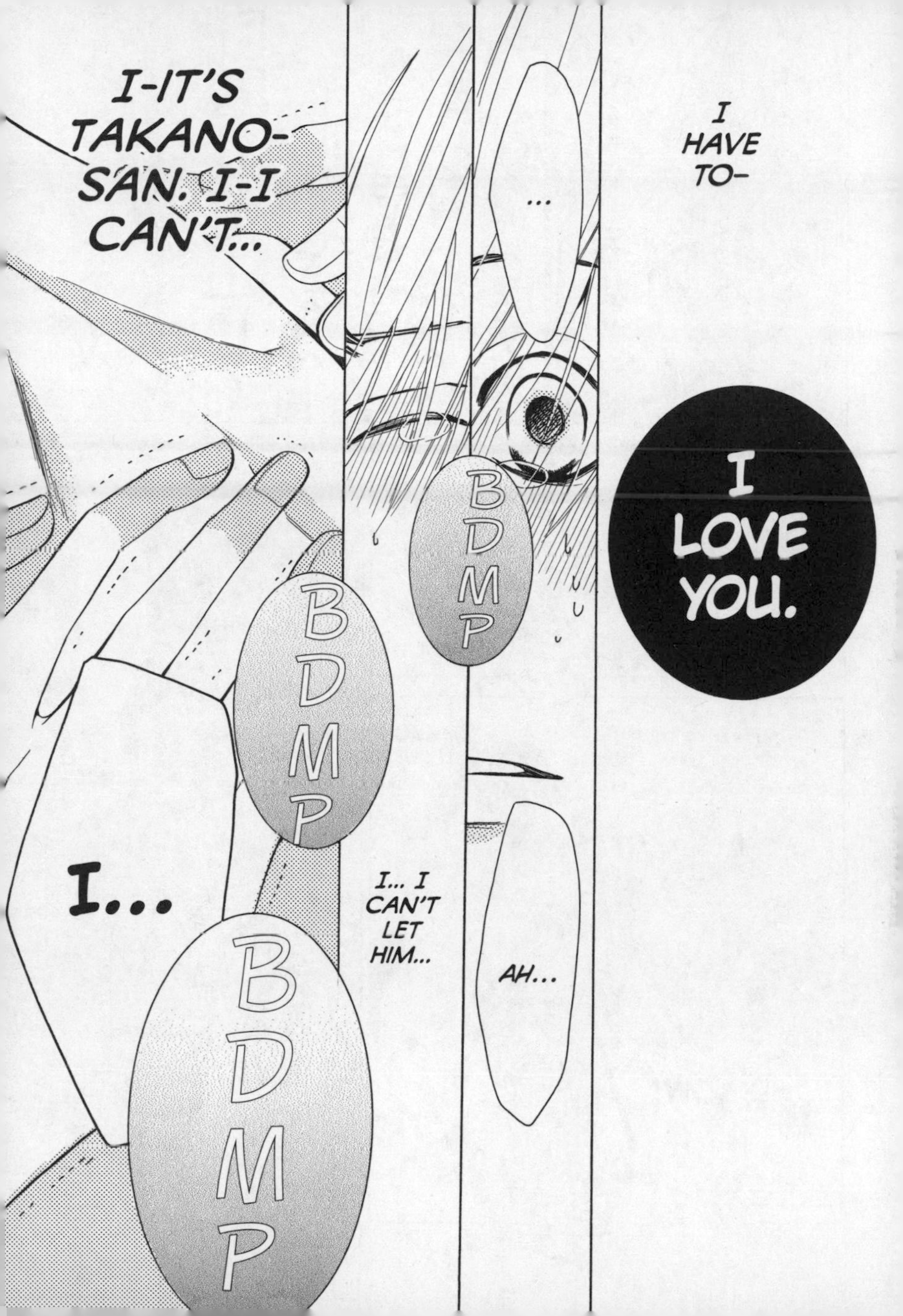
I HAVE TO-
I LOVE YOU.
...
BDMP
AH...
I... I CAN'T LET HIM...
I-IT'S TAKANO-SAN. I-I CAN'T...
BDMP
I...
BDMP

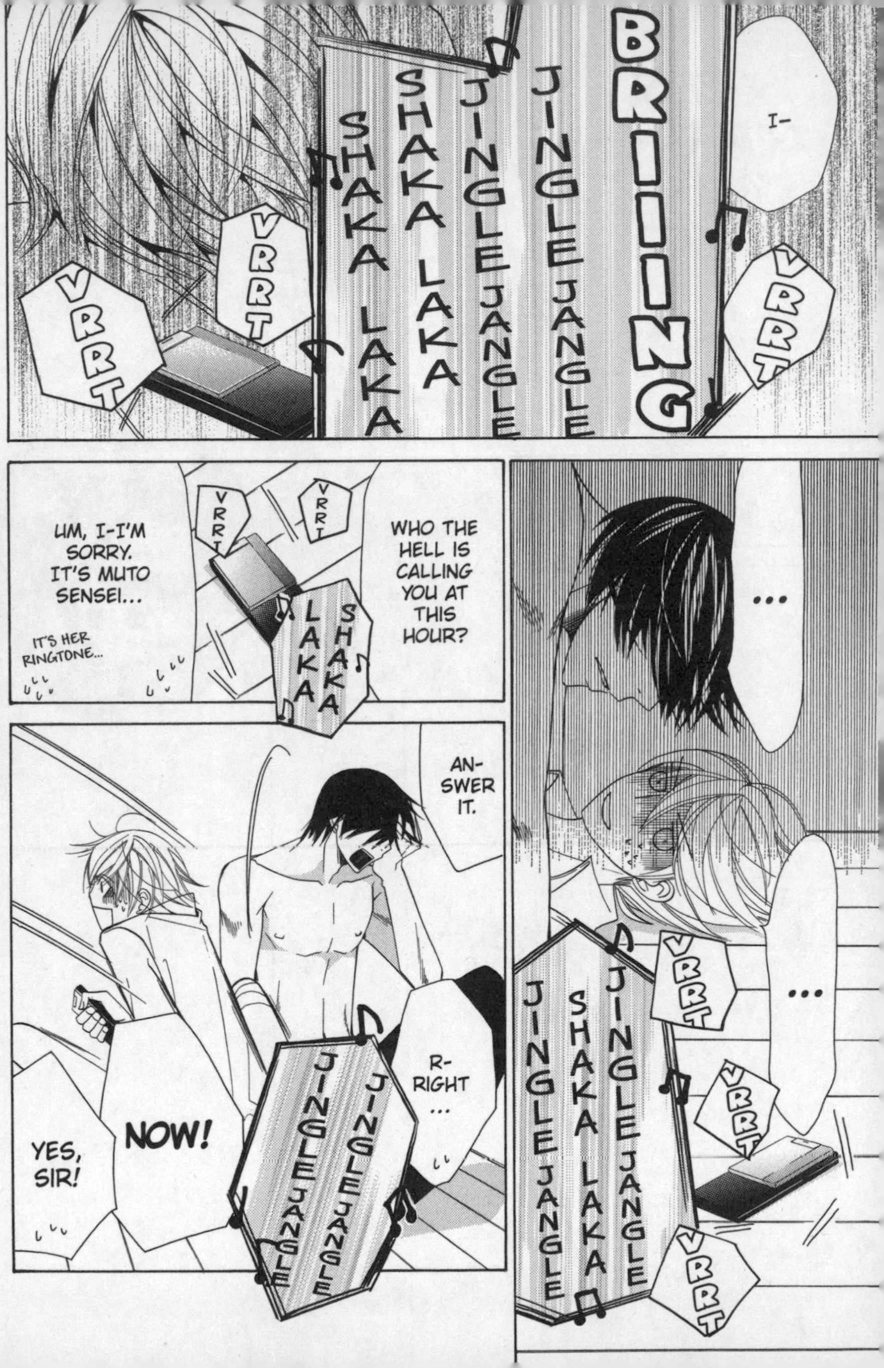
I-
VRRT
BRIIING
JINGLE JANGLE
JINGLE JANGLE
SHAKA LAKA
SHAKA LAKA
VRRT
VRRT
...
...
VRRT
JINGLE JANGLE
SHAKA LAKA
JINGLE JANGLE
VRRT
VRRT
WHO THE HELL IS CALLING YOU AT THIS HOUR?
VRRI
VRRI
SHAKA LAKA
UM, I-I'M SORRY. IT'S MUTO SENSEI...
IT'S HER RINGTONE...
ANSWER IT.
R-RIGHT...
JINGLE JANGLE
JINGLE JANGLE
NOW!
YES, SIR!

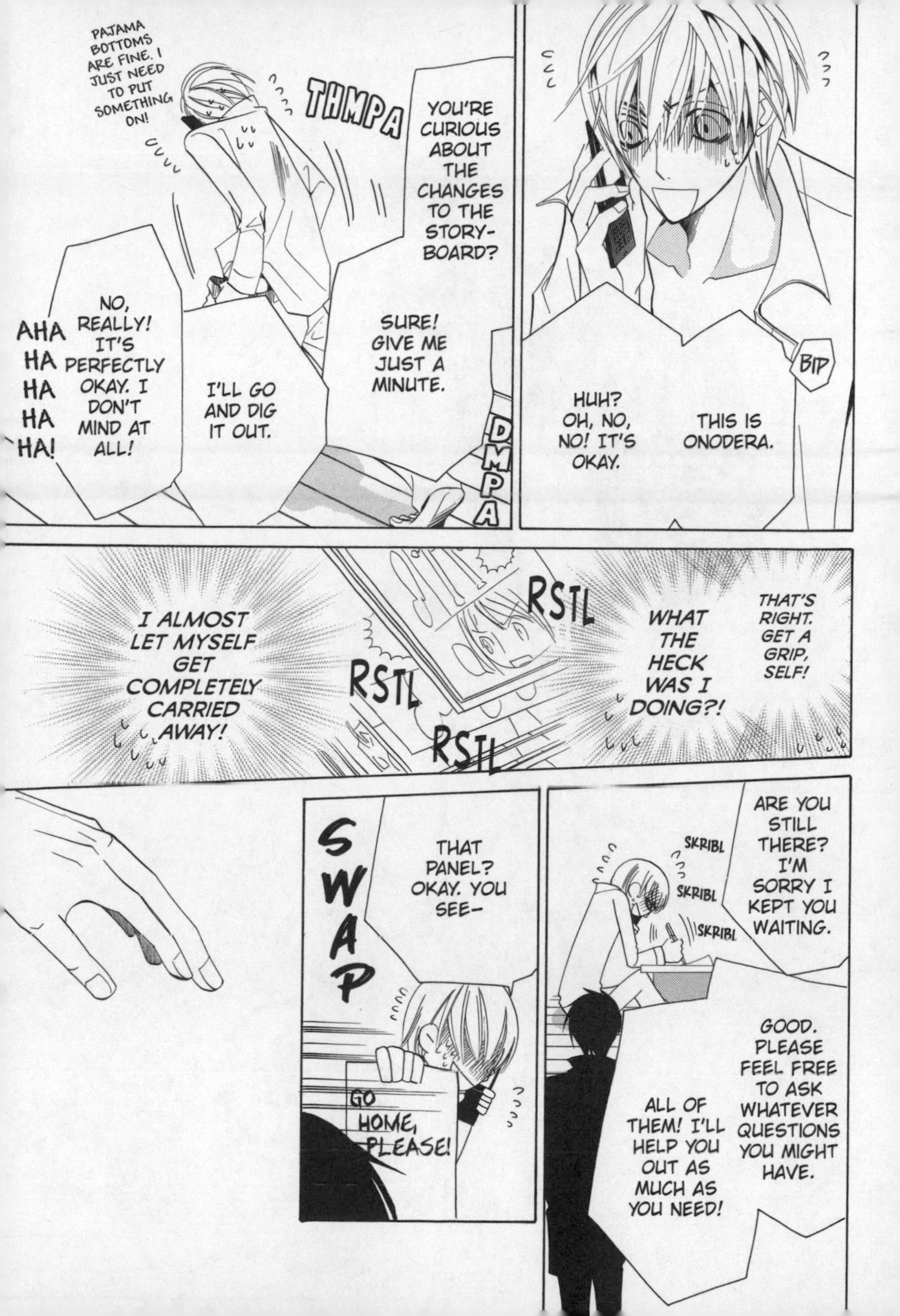
BIP
THIS IS ONODERA.
HUH? OH, NO, NO! IT'S OKAY.
THMPA
YOU'RE CURIOUS ABOUT THE CHANGES TO THE STORY-BOARD?
SURE! GIVE ME JUST A MINUTE.
DMPA
PAJAMA BOTTOMS ARE FINE. I JUST NEED TO PUT SOMETHING ON!
I'LL GO AND DIG IT OUT.
NO, REALLY! IT'S PERFECTLY OKAY. I DON'T MIND AT ALL!
AHA HA HA HA HA!
THAT'S RIGHT. GET A GRIP, SELF!
WHAT THE HECK WAS I DOING?!
RSTL
RSTL
RSTL
I ALMOST LET MYSELF GET COMPLETELY CARRIED AWAY!
ARE YOU STILL THERE? I'M SORRY I KEPT YOU WAITING.
SKRIBL
SKRIBL
SKRIBL
GOOD. PLEASE FEEL FREE TO ASK WHATEVER QUESTIONS YOU MIGHT HAVE.
ALL OF THEM! I'LL HELP YOU OUT AS MUCH AS YOU NEED!
THAT PANEL? OKAY. YOU SEE-
SWAP
GO HOME, PLEASE!

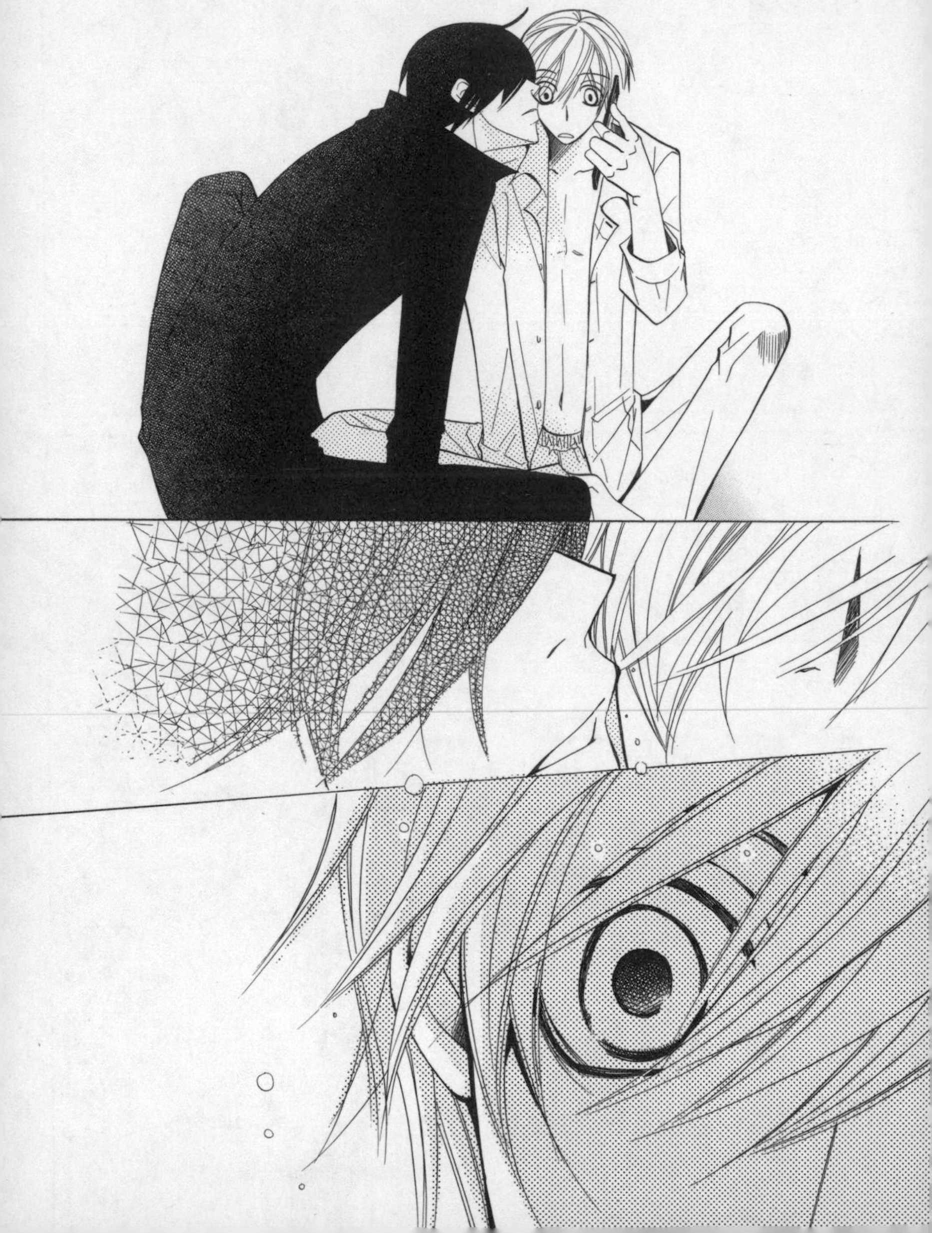

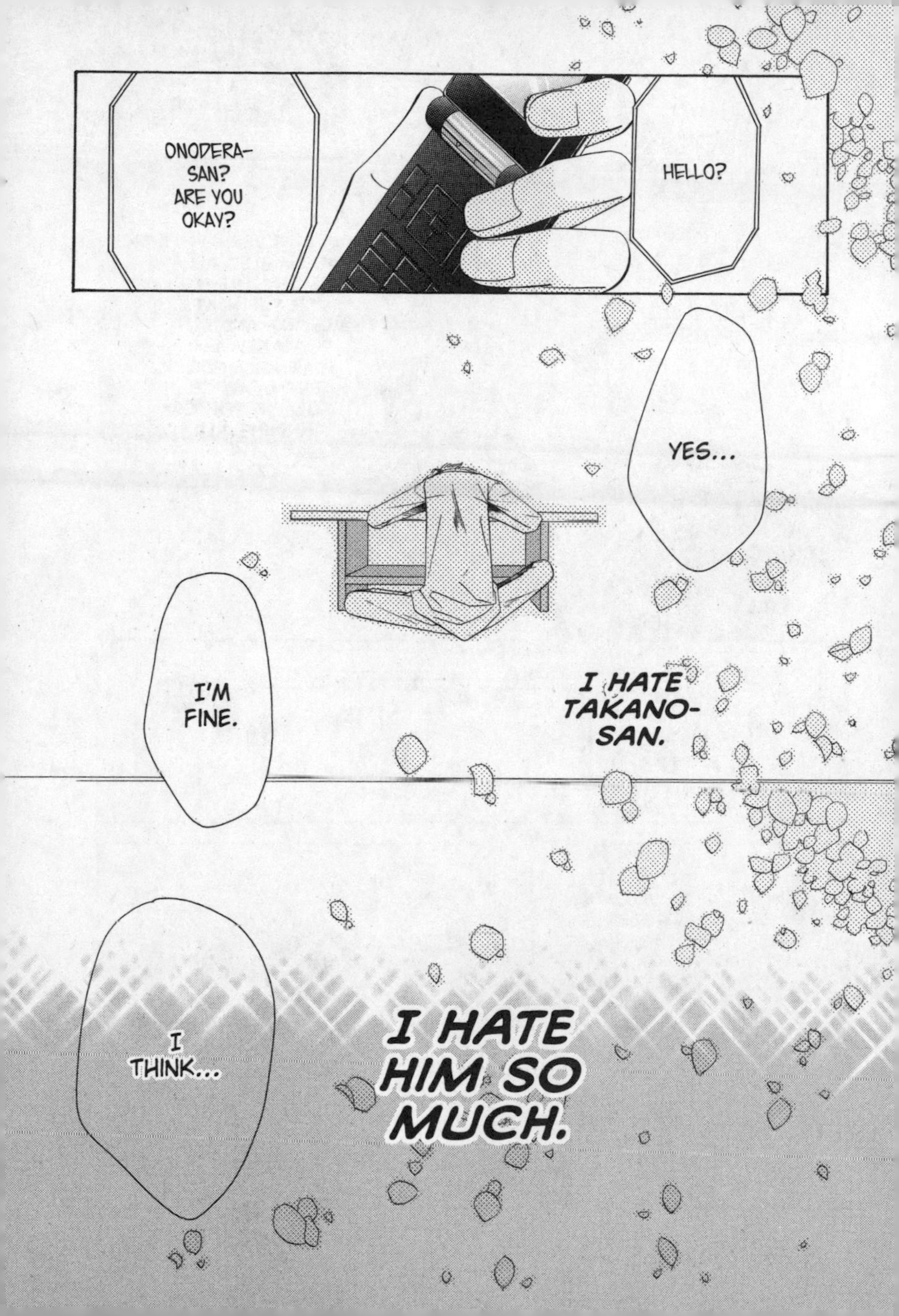
HELLO?
ONODERA-SAN? ARE YOU OKAY?
YES...
I'M FINE.
I HATE TAKANO-SAN.
I THINK...
I HATE HIM SO MUCH.

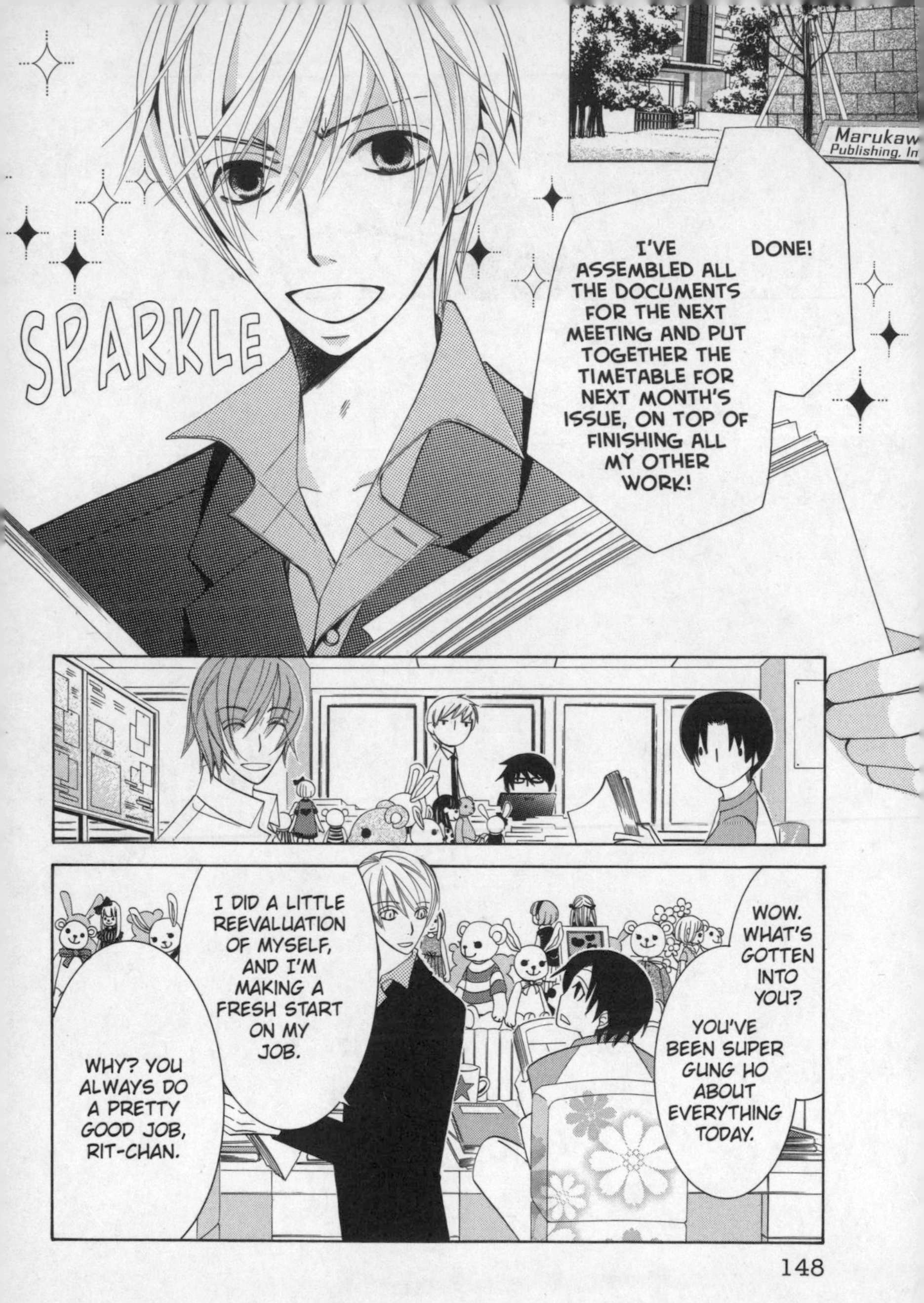
Marukaw
Publishing, In
DONE!
I'VE ASSEMBLED ALL THE DOCUMENTS FOR THE NEXT MEETING AND PUT TOGETHER THE TIMETABLE FOR NEXT MONTH'S ISSUE, ON TOP OF FINISHING ALL MY OTHER WORK!
SPARKLE
WOW. WHAT'S GOTTEN INTO YOU?
YOU'VE BEEN SUPER GUNG HO ABOUT EVERYTHING TODAY.
I DID A LITTLE REEVALUATION OF MYSELF, AND I'M MAKING A FRESH START ON MY JOB.
WHY? YOU ALWAYS DO A PRETTY GOOD JOB, RIT-CHAN.

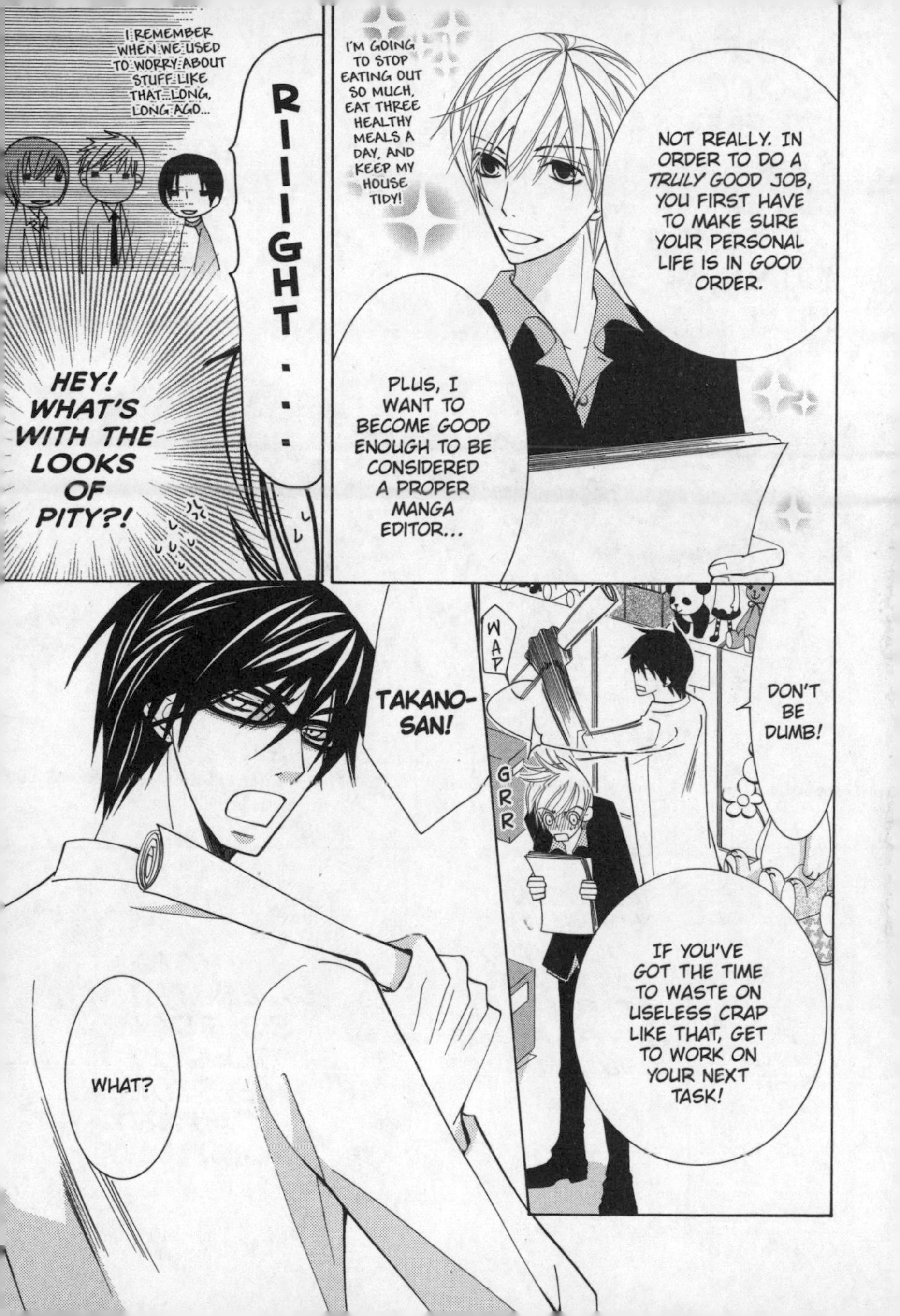
NOT REALLY. IN ORDER TO DO A *TRULY* GOOD JOB, YOU FIRST HAVE TO MAKE SURE YOUR PERSONAL LIFE IS IN GOOD ORDER.
I'M GOING TO STOP EATING OUT SO MUCH, EAT THREE HEALTHY MEALS A DAY, AND KEEP MY HOUSE TIDY!
PLUS, I WANT TO BECOME GOOD ENOUGH TO BE CONSIDERED A PROPER MANGA EDITOR...
RIIIGHT...
I REMEMBER WHEN WE USED TO WORRY ABOUT STUFF LIKE THAT LONG, LONG AGO...
HEY! WHAT'S WITH THE LOOKS OF PITY?!
DON'T BE DUMB!
WAP
GRR
IF YOU'VE GOT THE TIME TO WASTE ON USELESS CRAP LIKE THAT, GET TO WORK ON YOUR NEXT TASK!
TAKANO-SAN!
WHAT?

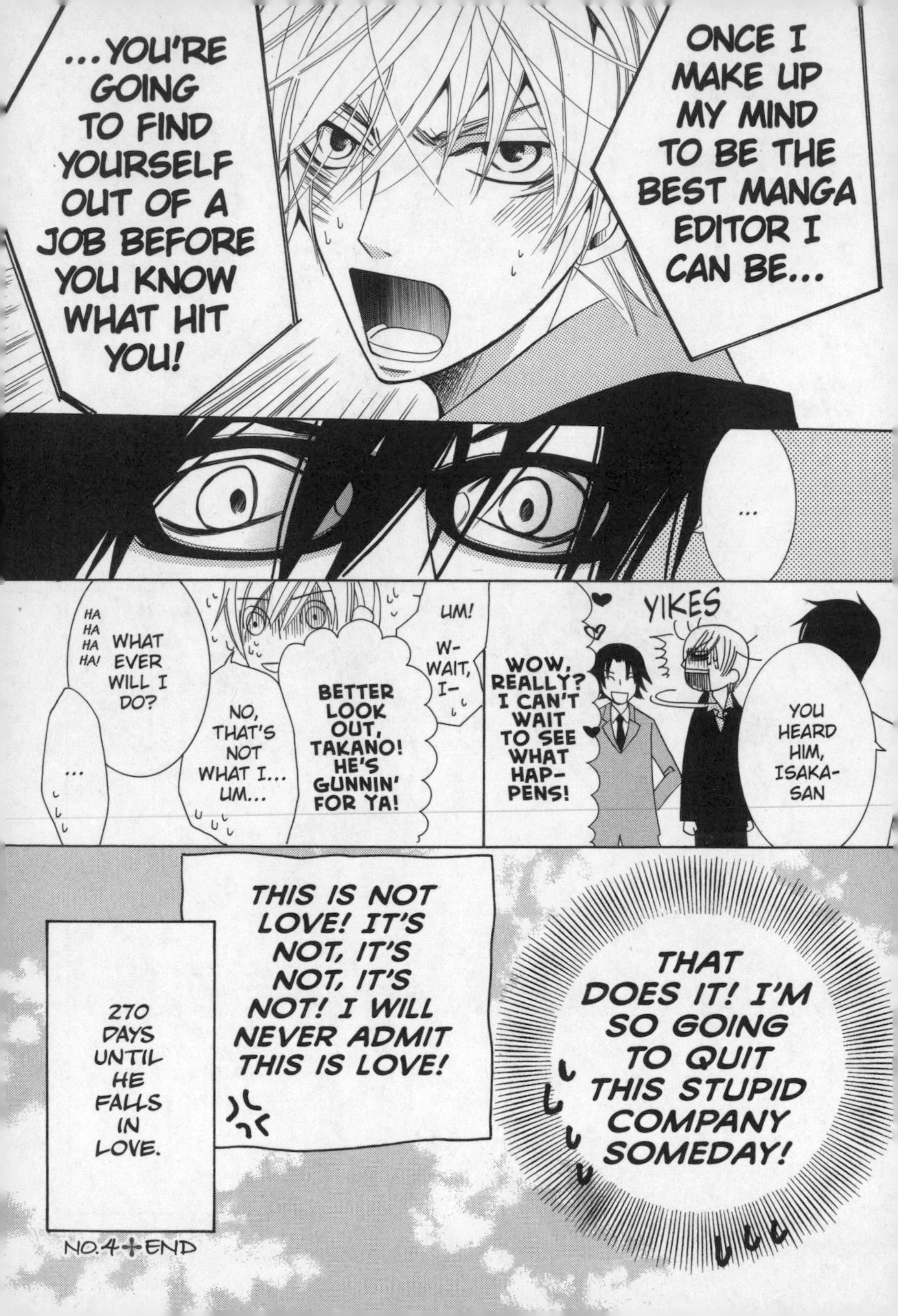
ONCE I MAKE UP MY MIND TO BE THE BEST MANGA EDITOR I CAN BE...
...YOU'RE GOING TO FIND YOURSELF OUT OF A JOB BEFORE YOU KNOW WHAT HIT YOU!
...
YOU HEARD HIM, ISAKA-SAN
YIKES
WOW, REALLY? I CAN'T WAIT TO SEE WHAT HAP-PENS!
UM!
W-WAIT, I-
BETTER LOOK OUT, TAKANO! HE'S GUNNIN' FOR YA!
NO, THAT'S NOT WHAT I... UM...
HA HA HA HA! WHAT EVER WILL I DO?
...
THAT DOES IT! I'M SO GOING TO QUIT THIS STUPID COMPANY SOMEDAY!
THIS IS NOT LOVE! IT'S NOT, IT'S NOT, IT'S NOT! I WILL NEVER ADMIT THIS IS LOVE!
270 DAYS UNTIL HE FALLS IN LOVE.
NO.4 END

MARUKAWA PUBLISHING TERMINOLOGY & JARGON (PART 7)

***NOTE:** ALL OF THE TERMINOLOGY LISTED HEREIN IS SPECIFIC TO MARUKAWA PUBLISHING AND MAY NOT BE APPLICABLE TO THE GENERAL PUBLISHING INDUSTRY.

[ONODERA PUBLICATIONS]

ONODERA PUBLICATIONS IS A LARGE BOOK PUBLISHER ON PAR WITH MARUKAWA PUBLISHING. LIKE MARUKAWA, ONODERA PUBLICATIONS PUBLISHES BOTH BOOKS AND MANGA AND HAS SEVERAL BEST SELLERS. RITSU, THE SON OF THE C.E.O. OF ONODERA PUBLICATIONS, IS CURRENTLY A ROOKIE EDITOR WITH MARUKAWA'S SHOJO MANGA IMPRINT, *EMERALD.*

[DEADLINE]

A DATE OR TIME DETERMINED IN ADVANCE BY WHEN A JOB OR PROJECT MUST BE COMPLETED OR SUBMITTED. THE *EMERALD* EDITORS GENERALLY SET DEADLINES FOR COPY SUBMISSION FROM CREATORS, COPY SUBMISSION TO THE PRINTERS, FORM COMPLETION, AND OTHER THINGS. DEADLINES ARE MEANT TO BE KEPT AND SHOULD NOT BE BROKEN.

[PEOPLE INVOLVED IN MAKING MANGA]

THE NAME OF THE FLOWCHART DEPICTING THE STAGES OF MANGA CREATION THAT ONODERA PUBLICATIONS MANGA EDITOR SAEKI ATTEMPTED TO MAKE. HER BOSS GOT MAD AT HER ABOUT IT AND MADE HER ABANDON THE PROJECT. IT WAS INTENDED TO SHOW A DEADLINE-BREAKING MANGAKA HOW MANY PEOPLE WERE INCONVENIENCED BY HER LATENESS.

The World's Greatest First Love
The Case of Ritsu Onodera

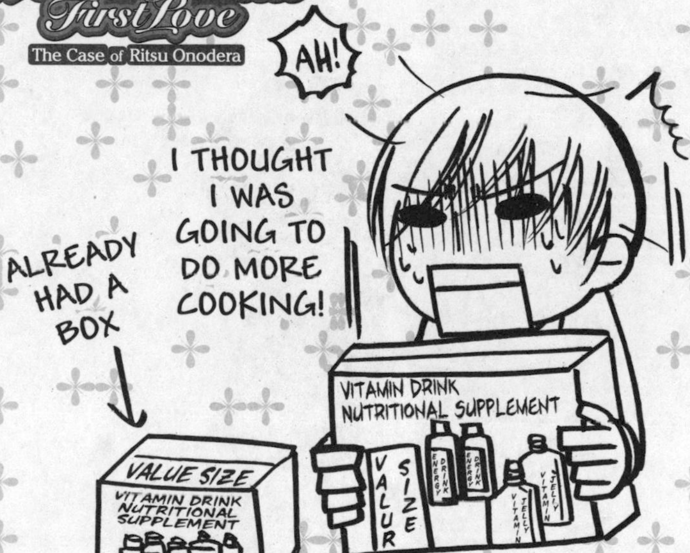
AH!
I THOUGHT I WAS GOING TO DO MORE COOKING!
ALREADY HAD A BOX
VITAMIN DRINK NUTRITIONAL SUPPLEMENT
VALUR SIZE
ENERGY DRINK
ENERGY DRINK
VITAMIN JELLY
VITAMIN JELLY
VALUE SIZE
VITAMIN DRINK NUTRITIONAL SUPPLEMENT

MARUKAWA PUBLISHING TERMINOLOGY & JARGON (PART 8)

***NOTE:** ALL OF THE TERMINOLOGY LISTED HEREIN IS SPECIFIC TO MARUKAWA PUBLISHING AND MAY NOT BE APPLICABLE TO THE GENERAL PUBLISHING INDUSTRY.

[MARUKAWA PUBLISHING EXECUTIVE DIRECTOR]

THE CURRENT EXECUTIVE DIRECTOR FOR MARUKAWA PUBLISHING IS RYUICHI ISAKA, THE SON OF MARUKAWA'S C.E.O. RYUICHI FIRST WORKED AS AN EDITOR AND IS CREDITED WITH SEVERAL BEST SELLERS. HE IS CHILDHOOD FRIENDS OF THE USAMI BROTHERS—HARUHIKO, HEIR TO THE USAMI GROUP, AND AKIHIKO, THE WIDELY POPULAR NOVELIST.

[STORYBOARD]

AFTER ESTABLISHING A PLOT OUTLINE, THE NEXT STAGE IN CREATING A MANGA IS THE STORYBOARD. PANEL LAYOUTS ARE SKETCHED AND ROUGH DIALOGUE INCLUDED SO AS TO GET A FEEL FOR THE OVERALL FLOW OF THE PIECE. THIS STEP CAN ALSO BE CALLED THE PANEL-LAYOUT STAGE OR SIMPLY THE ROUGH DRAFT.

[FOYER]

THE FOYER IS WHAT *EMERALD*'S NEWEST ROOKIE EDITOR, RITSU ONODERA, HAS BEEN USING AS HIS BED OF LATE. SO THOROUGHLY EXHAUSTED BY HIS JOB, HE WILL CLOSE THE DOOR TO HIS APARTMENT AND PROMPTLY COLLAPSE ON THE NEAREST PIECE OF OPEN FLOOR. IT IS SUGGESTED THAT READERS DO NOT FOLLOW HIS EXAMPLE, AS SLEEPING ON THE FLOOR WILL LEAVE YOU VERY SORE IN THE MORNING. PLEASE SLEEP ON A PROPER BED. FOYERS ARE TYPICALLY THE ENTRANCE TO A HOME OR APARTMENT.

The World's Greatest First Love
The Case of Ritsu Onodera

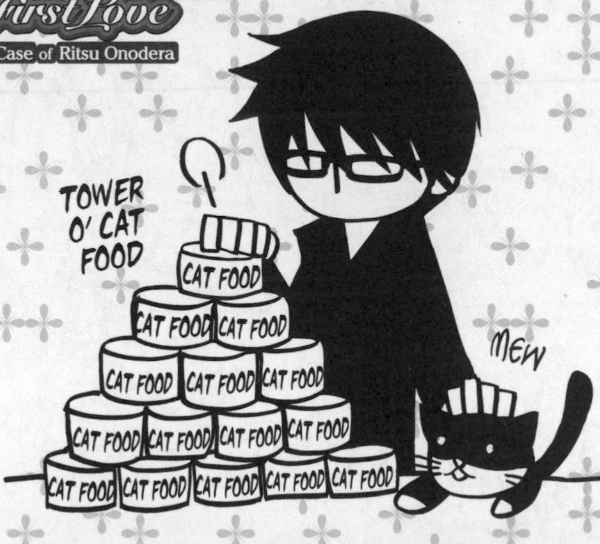
TOWER O' CAT FOOD
CAT FOOD
MEW

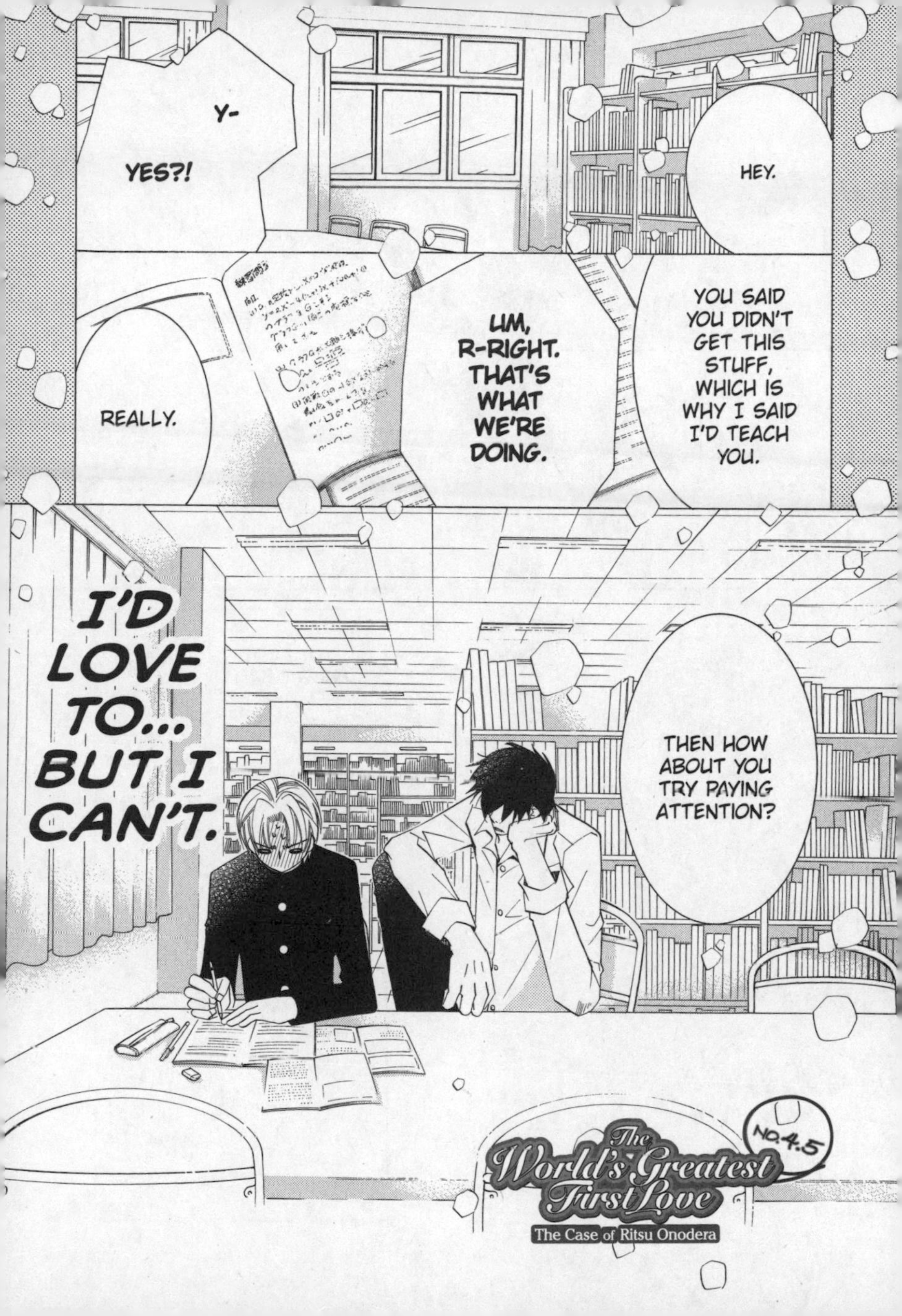
HEY.
Y-
YES?!
YOU SAID YOU DIDN'T GET THIS STUFF, WHICH IS WHY I SAID I'D TEACH YOU.
UM, R-RIGHT. THAT'S WHAT WE'RE DOING.
REALLY.
THEN HOW ABOUT YOU TRY PAYING ATTENTION?
I'D LOVE TO... BUT I CAN'T.
NO.4.5
The World's Greatest First Love
The Case of Ritsu Onodera

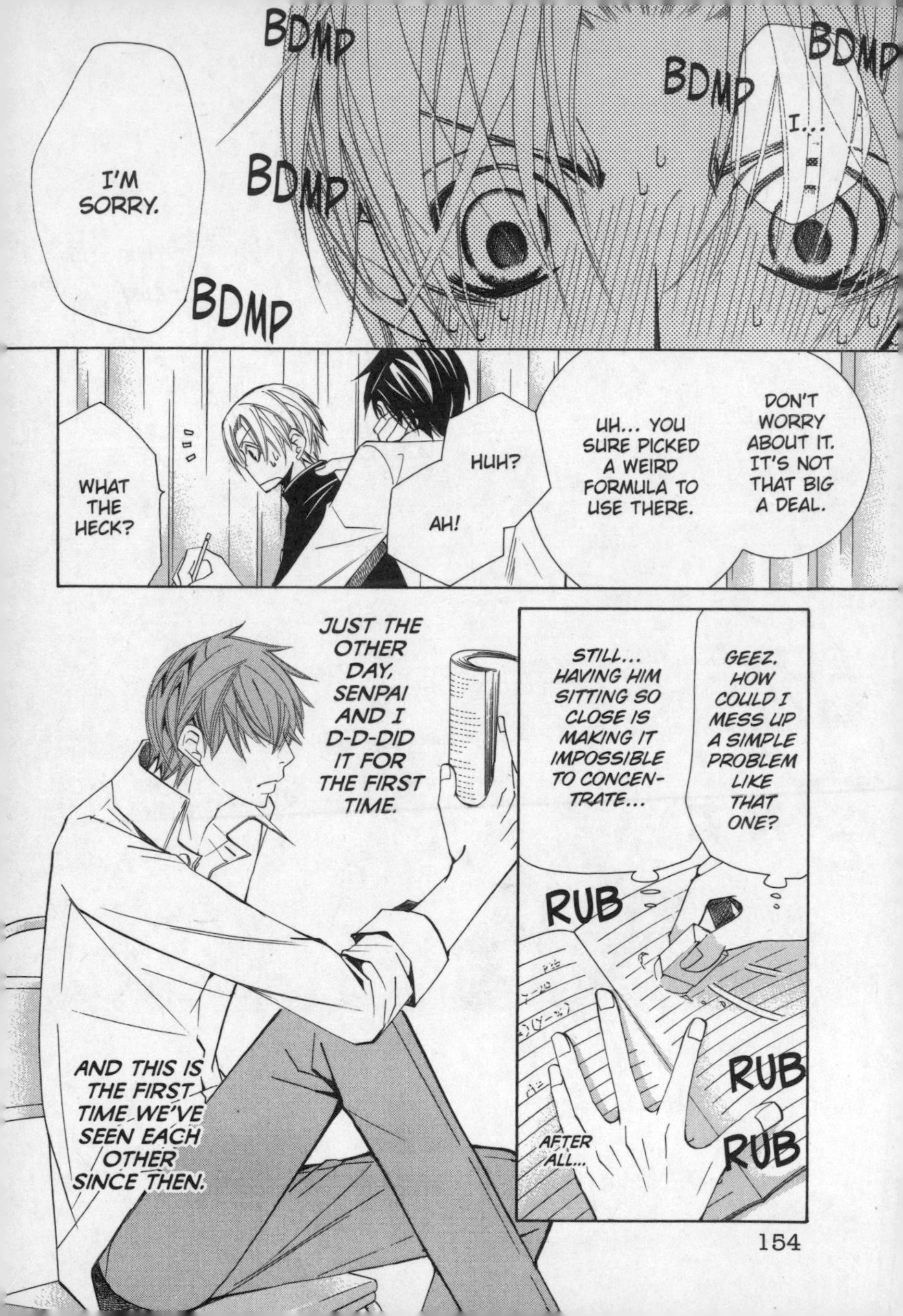
BDMP
BDMP
I...
BDMP
I'M SORRY.
BDMP
DON'T WORRY ABOUT IT. IT'S NOT THAT BIG A DEAL.
UH... YOU SURE PICKED A WEIRD FORMULA TO USE THERE.
HUH?
AH!
WHAT THE HECK?
GEEZ. HOW COULD I MESS UP A SIMPLE PROBLEM LIKE THAT ONE?
STILL... HAVING HIM SITTING SO CLOSE IS MAKING IT IMPOSSIBLE TO CONCENTRATE...
RUB
RUB
RUB
AFTER ALL...
JUST THE OTHER DAY, SENPAI AND I D-D-DID IT FOR THE FIRST TIME.
AND THIS IS THE FIRST TIME WE'VE SEEN EACH OTHER SINCE THEN.

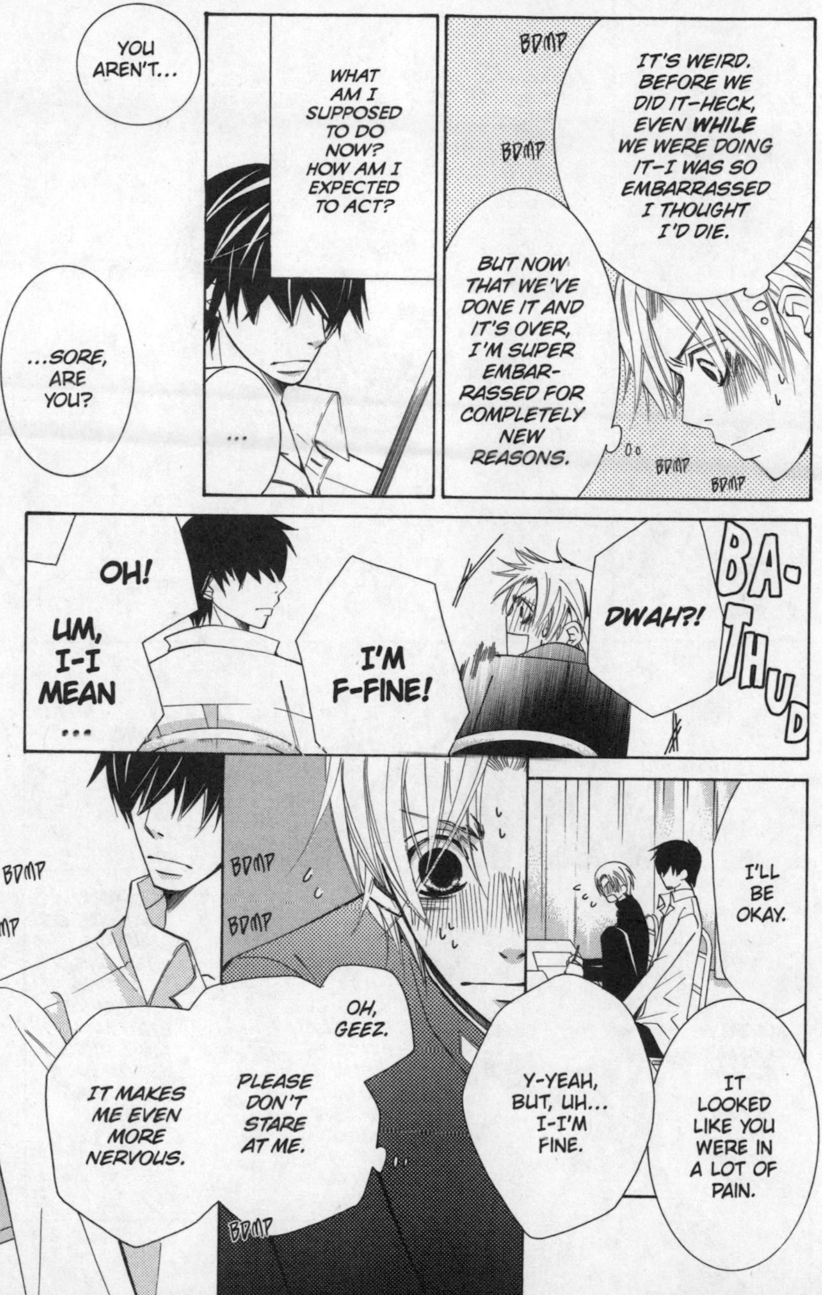
BDMP
IT'S WEIRD. BEFORE WE DID IT—HECK, EVEN WHILE WE WERE DOING IT—I WAS SO EMBARRASSED I THOUGHT I'D DIE.
BDMP
BUT NOW THAT WE'VE DONE IT AND IT'S OVER, I'M SUPER EMBAR-RASSED FOR COMPLETELY NEW REASONS.
BDMP
BDMP
WHAT AM I SUPPOSED TO DO NOW? HOW AM I EXPECTED TO ACT?
...
YOU AREN'T...
...SORE, ARE YOU?
BA-THUD
DWAH?!
I'M F-FINE!
OH!
UM, I-I MEAN...
I'LL BE OKAY.
IT LOOKED LIKE YOU WERE IN A LOT OF PAIN.
Y-YEAH, BUT, UH... I-I'M FINE.
BDMP
BDMP
BDMP
BDMP
OH, GEEZ.
PLEASE DON'T STARE AT ME.
IT MAKES ME EVEN MORE NERVOUS.
BDMP

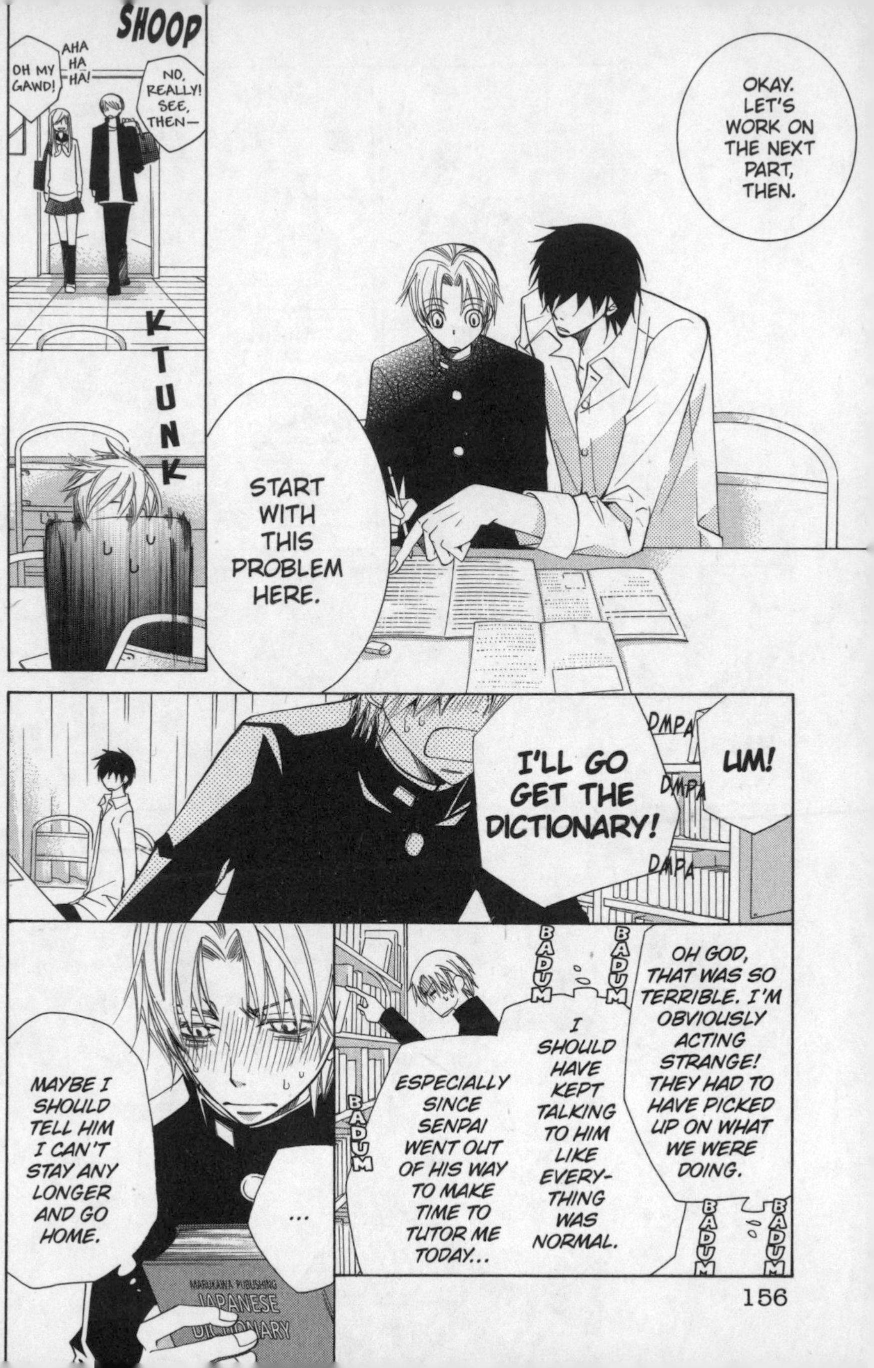
OKAY. LET'S WORK ON THE NEXT PART, THEN.
START WITH THIS PROBLEM HERE.
SHOOP
AHA HA HA!
NO, REALLY! SEE, THEN—
OH MY GAWD!
KTUNK
UM!
DMPA
DMPA
DMPA
I'LL GO GET THE DICTIONARY!
BADUM
OH GOD, THAT WAS SO TERRIBLE. I'M OBVIOUSLY ACTING STRANGE! THEY HAD TO HAVE PICKED UP ON WHAT WE WERE DOING.
BADUM
I SHOULD HAVE KEPT TALKING TO HIM LIKE EVERY-THING WAS NORMAL.
ESPECIALLY SINCE SENPAI WENT OUT OF HIS WAY TO MAKE TIME TO TUTOR ME TODAY...
BADUM
BADUM
BADUM
...
MAYBE I SHOULD TELL HIM I CAN'T STAY ANY LONGER AND GO HOME.
MARUKAWA PUBLISHING
JAPANESE DICTIONARY

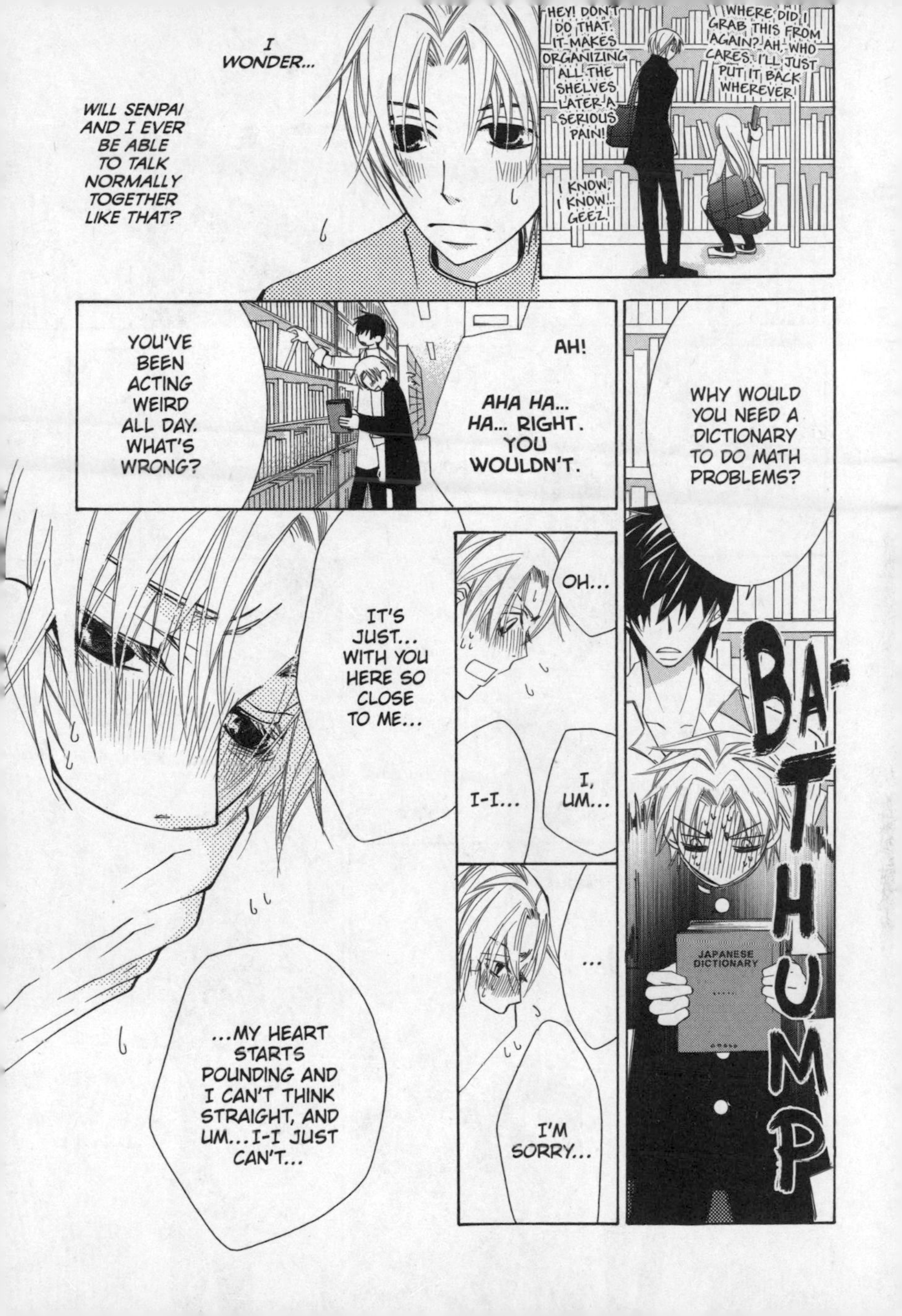
WHERE DID I GRAB THIS FROM AGAIN? AH, WHO CARES. I'LL JUST PUT IT BACK WHEREVER!
HEY! DON'T DO THAT. IT MAKES ORGANIZING ALL THE SHELVES LATER A SERIOUS PAIN!
I KNOW. I KNOW... GEEZ.
I WONDER...
WILL SENPAI AND I EVER BE ABLE TO TALK NORMALLY TOGETHER LIKE THAT?
WHY WOULD YOU NEED A DICTIONARY TO DO MATH PROBLEMS?
BA-THUMP
JAPANESE DICTIONARY
AH!
AHA HA... HA... RIGHT. YOU WOULDN'T.
YOU'VE BEEN ACTING WEIRD ALL DAY. WHAT'S WRONG?
OH...
I, UM...
I-I...
...
I'M SORRY...
IT'S JUST... WITH YOU HERE SO CLOSE TO ME...
...MY HEART STARTS POUNDING AND I CAN'T THINK STRAIGHT, AND UM...I-I JUST CAN'T...

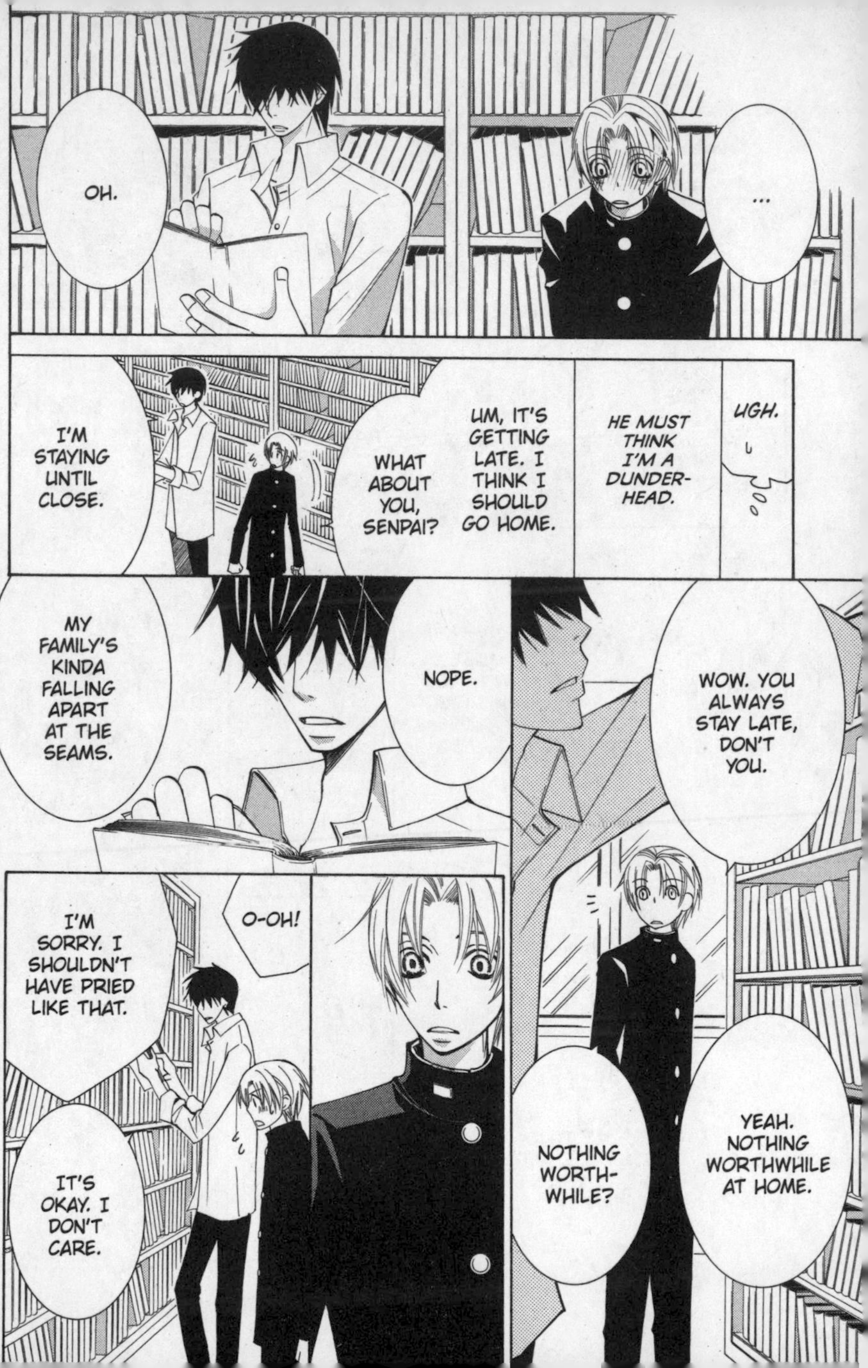
...
OH.
UGH.
HE MUST THINK I'M A DUNDER-HEAD.
UM, IT'S GETTING LATE. I THINK I SHOULD GO HOME.
WHAT ABOUT YOU, SENPAI?
I'M STAYING UNTIL CLOSE.
WOW. YOU ALWAYS STAY LATE, DON'T YOU.
YEAH. NOTHING WORTHWHILE AT HOME.
NOTHING WORTH-WHILE?
NOPE.
MY FAMILY'S KINDA FALLING APART AT THE SEAMS.
O-OH!
I'M SORRY. I SHOULDN'T HAVE PRIED LIKE THAT.
IT'S OKAY. I DON'T CARE.

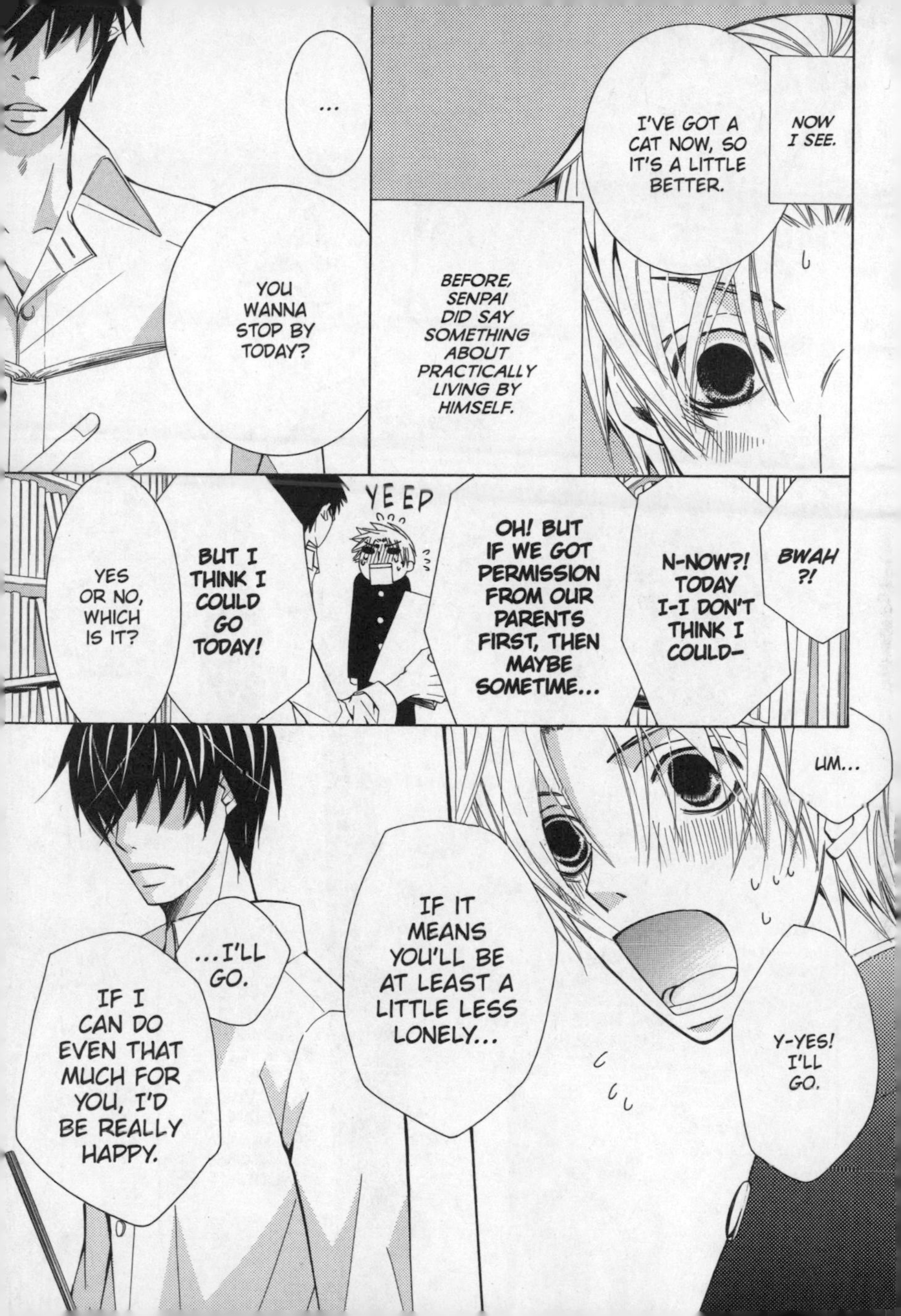
NOW I SEE.
I'VE GOT A CAT NOW, SO IT'S A LITTLE BETTER.
BEFORE, SENPAI DID SAY SOMETHING ABOUT PRACTICALLY LIVING BY HIMSELF.
...
YOU WANNA STOP BY TODAY?
BWAH ?!
N-NOW?! TODAY I-I DON'T THINK I COULD-
OH! BUT IF WE GOT PERMISSION FROM OUR PARENTS FIRST, THEN MAYBE SOMETIME...
YEEP
BUT I THINK I COULD GO TODAY!
YES OR NO, WHICH IS IT?
UM...
Y-YES! I'LL GO.
IF IT MEANS YOU'LL BE AT LEAST A LITTLE LESS LONELY...
...I'LL GO.
IF I CAN DO EVEN THAT MUCH FOR YOU, I'D BE REALLY HAPPY.

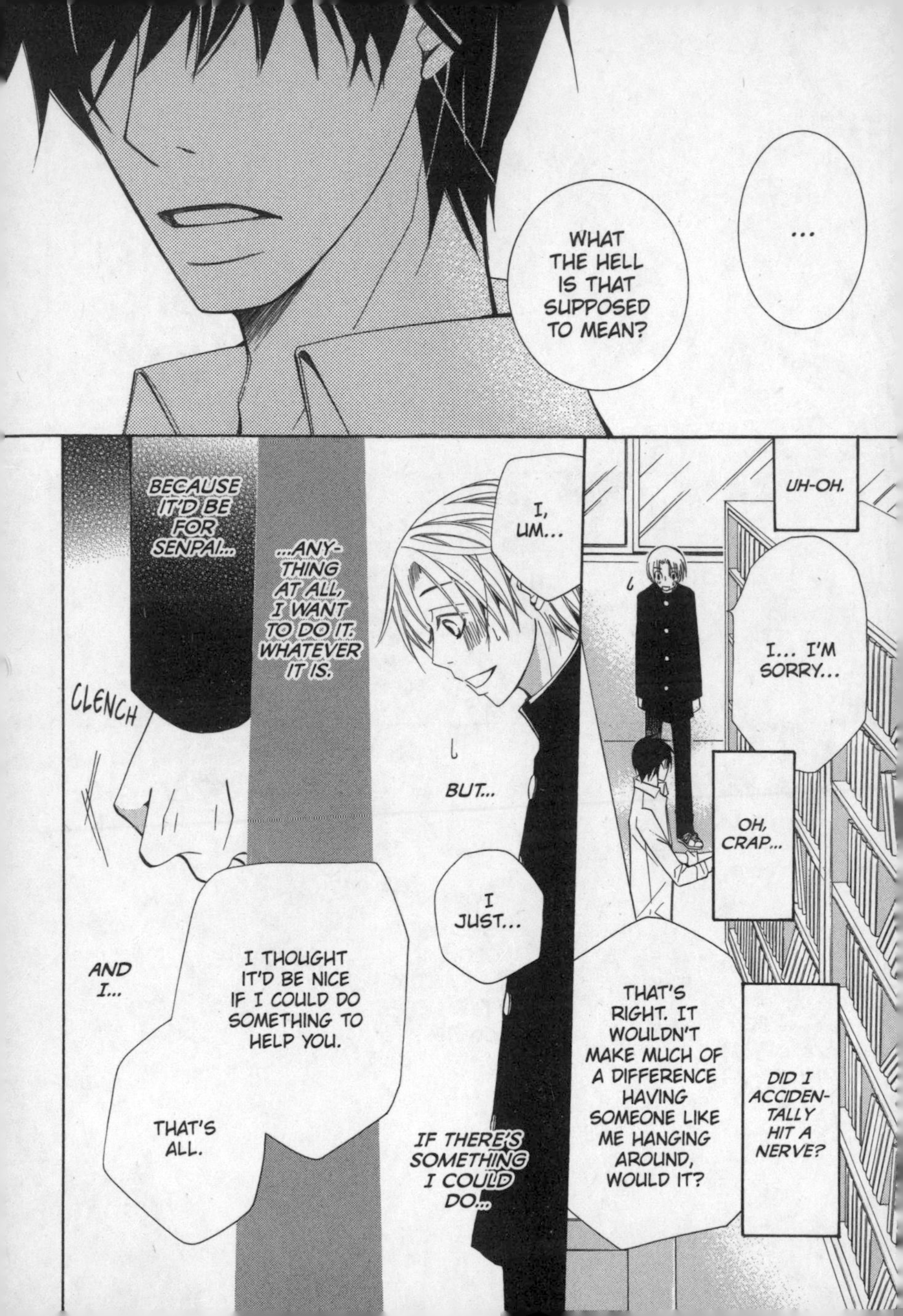
...
WHAT THE HELL IS THAT SUPPOSED TO MEAN?
UH-OH.
I... I'M SORRY...
OH, CRAP...
DID I ACCIDEN-TALLY HIT A NERVE?
I, UM...
BUT...
I JUST...
THAT'S RIGHT. IT WOULDN'T MAKE MUCH OF A DIFFERENCE HAVING SOMEONE LIKE ME HANGING AROUND, WOULD IT?
IF THERE'S SOMETHING I COULD DO...
...ANY-THING AT ALL, I WANT TO DO IT. WHATEVER IT IS.
BECAUSE IT'D BE FOR SENPAI...
CLENCH
I THOUGHT IT'D BE NICE IF I COULD DO SOMETHING TO HELP YOU.
AND I...
THAT'S ALL.

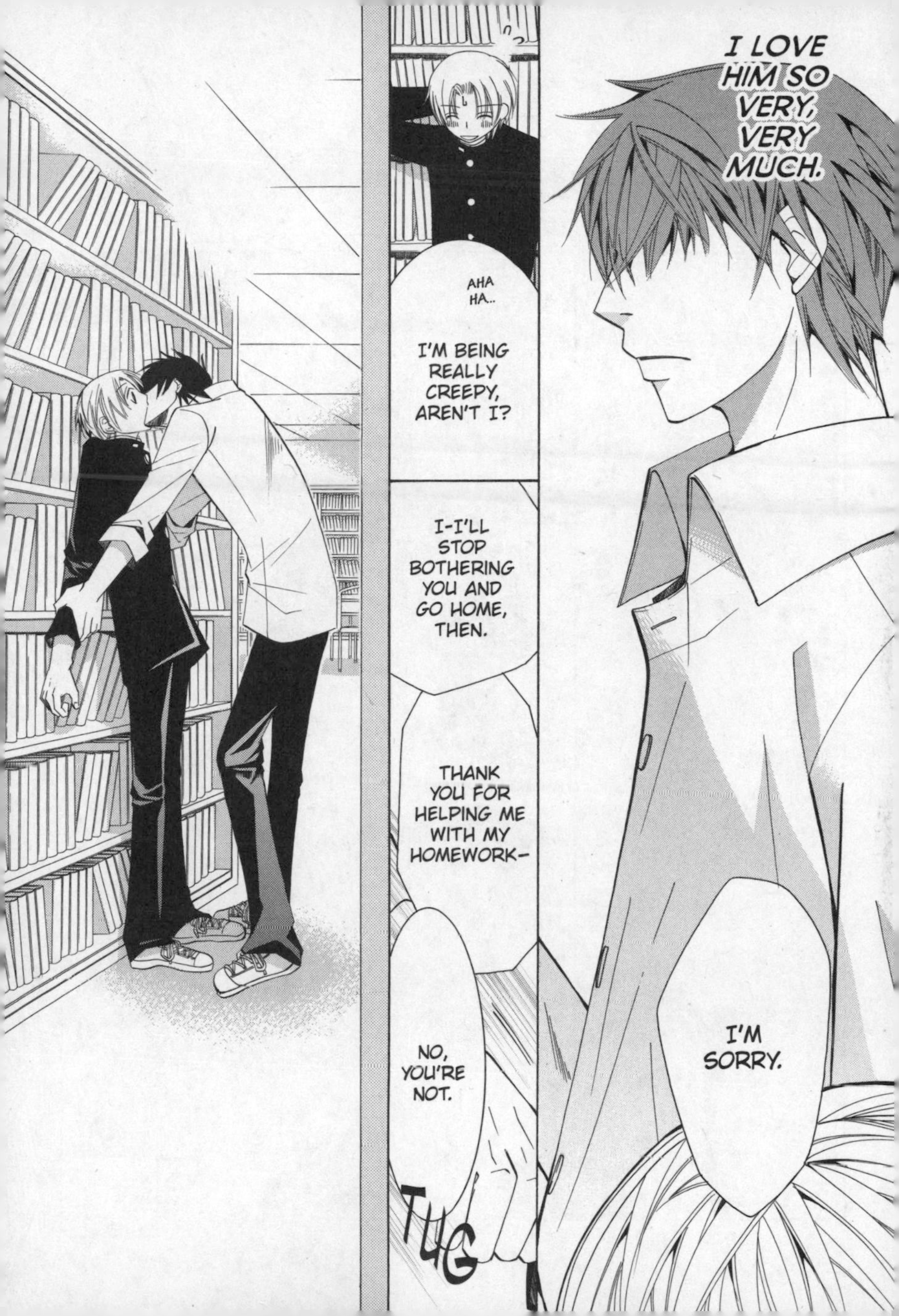
I LOVE HIM SO VERY, VERY MUCH.
I'M SORRY.
AHA HA...
I'M BEING REALLY CREEPY, AREN'T I?
I-I'LL STOP BOTHERING YOU AND GO HOME, THEN.
THANK YOU FOR HELPING ME WITH MY HOMEWORK-
NO, YOU'RE NOT.
TUG

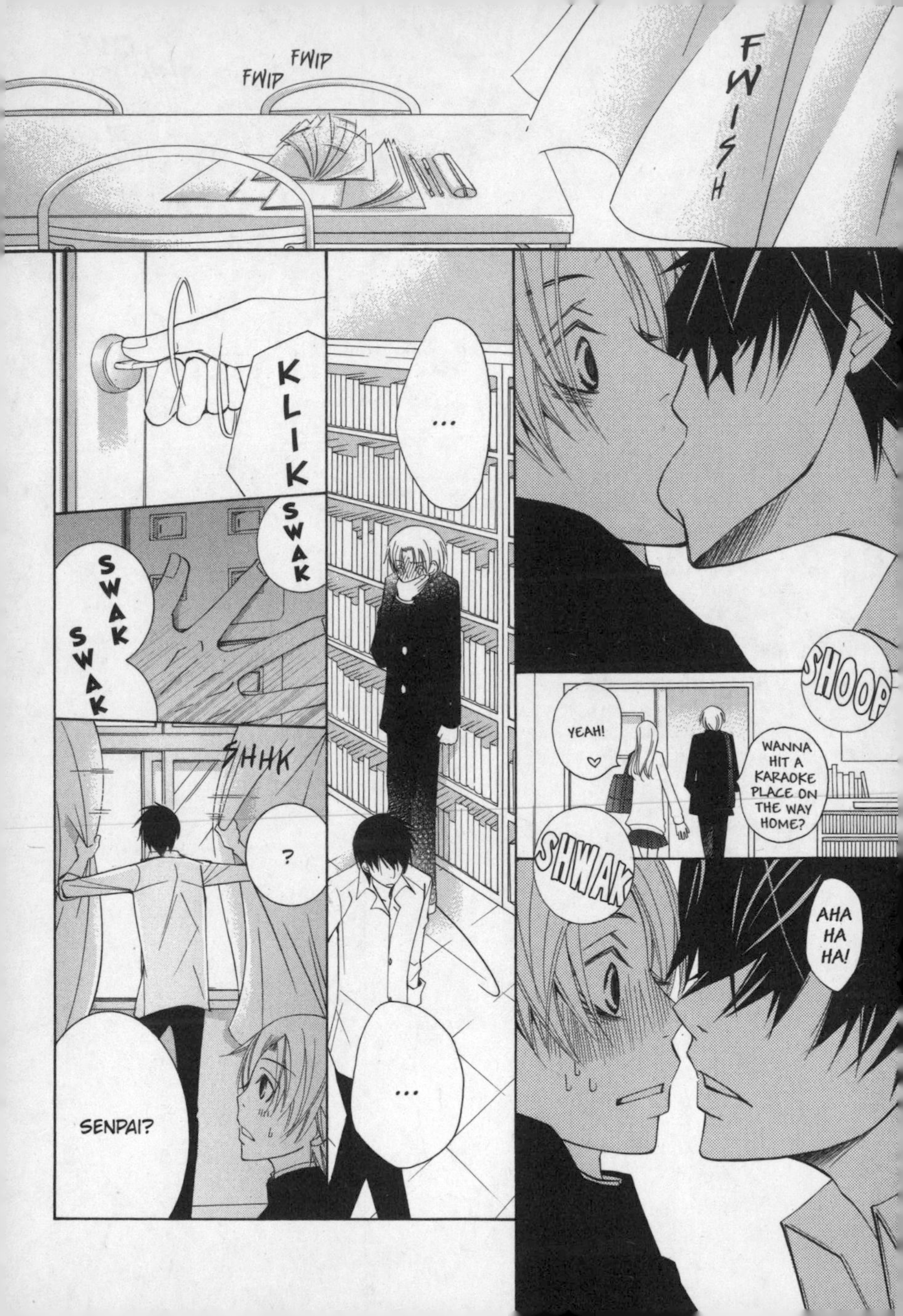

FWISH
FWIP
FWIP
SHOOP
WANNA HIT A KARAOKE PLACE ON THE WAY HOME?
YEAH! ♥
SHWAK
AHA HA HA!
...
KLIK
SWAK
SWAK
SWAK
SHHK
?
...
SENPAI?

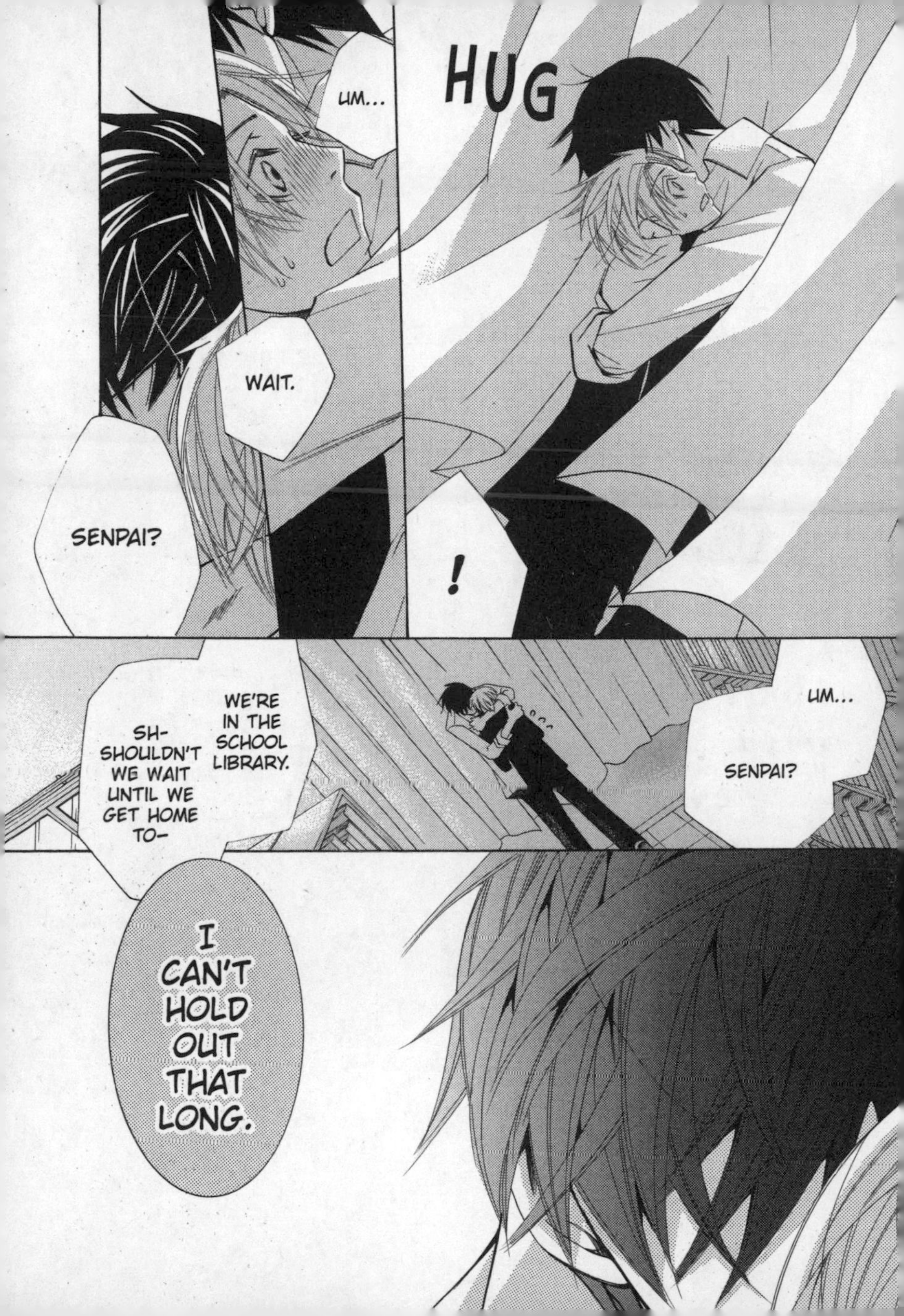
HUG
!
UM...
WAIT.
SENPAI?
UM... SENPAI?
WE'RE IN THE SCHOOL LIBRARY.
SH-SHOULDN'T WE WAIT UNTIL WE GET HOME TO—
I CAN'T HOLD OUT THAT LONG.

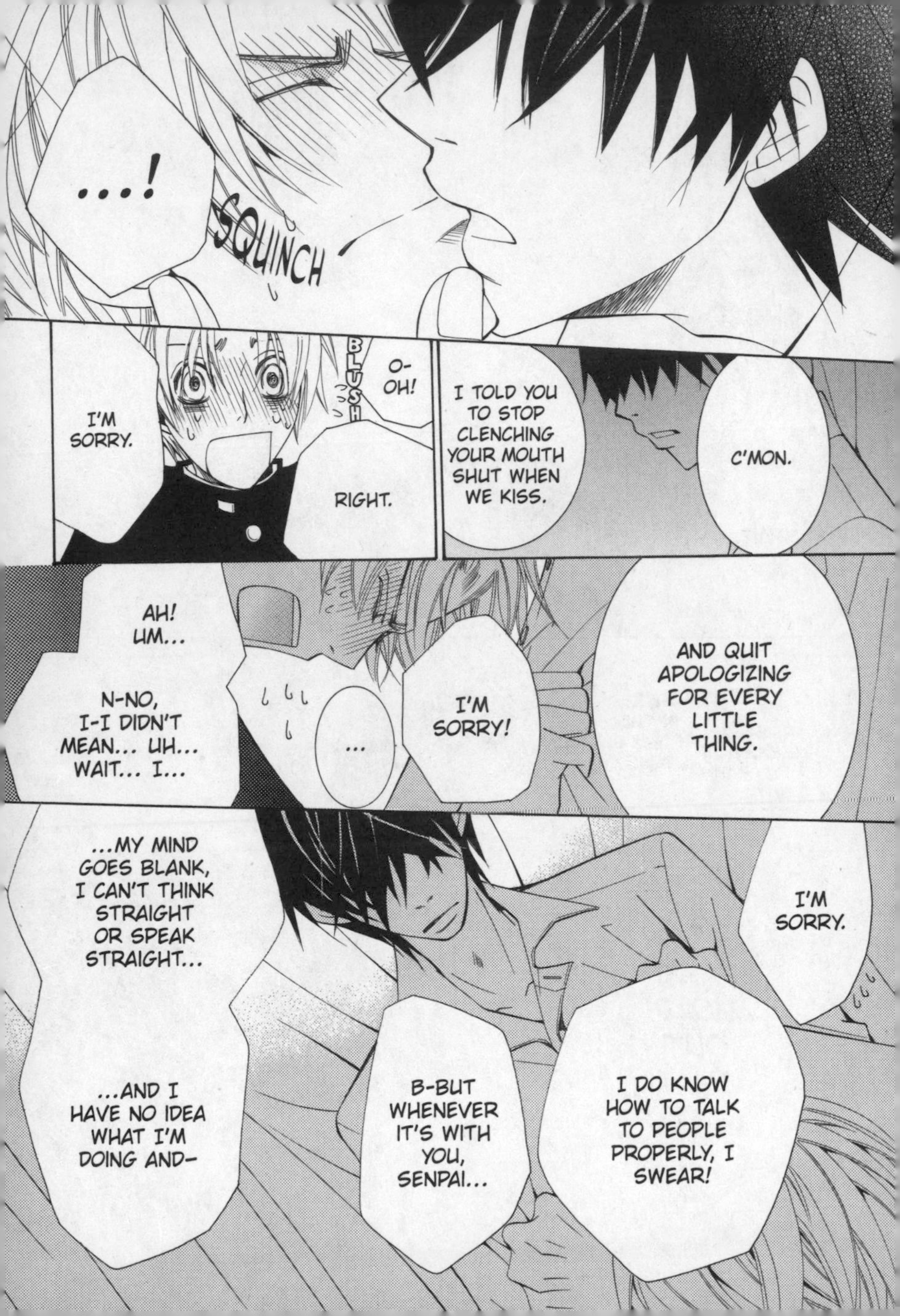
...!
SQUINCH
I TOLD YOU TO STOP CLENCHING YOUR MOUTH SHUT WHEN WE KISS.
C'MON.
O-OH!
BLUSH
RIGHT.
I'M SORRY.
AND QUIT APOLOGIZING FOR EVERY LITTLE THING.
I'M SORRY!
...
AH! UM...
N-NO, I-I DIDN'T MEAN... UH... WAIT... I...
I'M SORRY.
I DO KNOW HOW TO TALK TO PEOPLE PROPERLY, I SWEAR!
B-BUT WHENEVER IT'S WITH YOU, SENPAI...
...MY MIND GOES BLANK, I CAN'T THINK STRAIGHT OR SPEAK STRAIGHT...
...AND I HAVE NO IDEA WHAT I'M DOING AND-

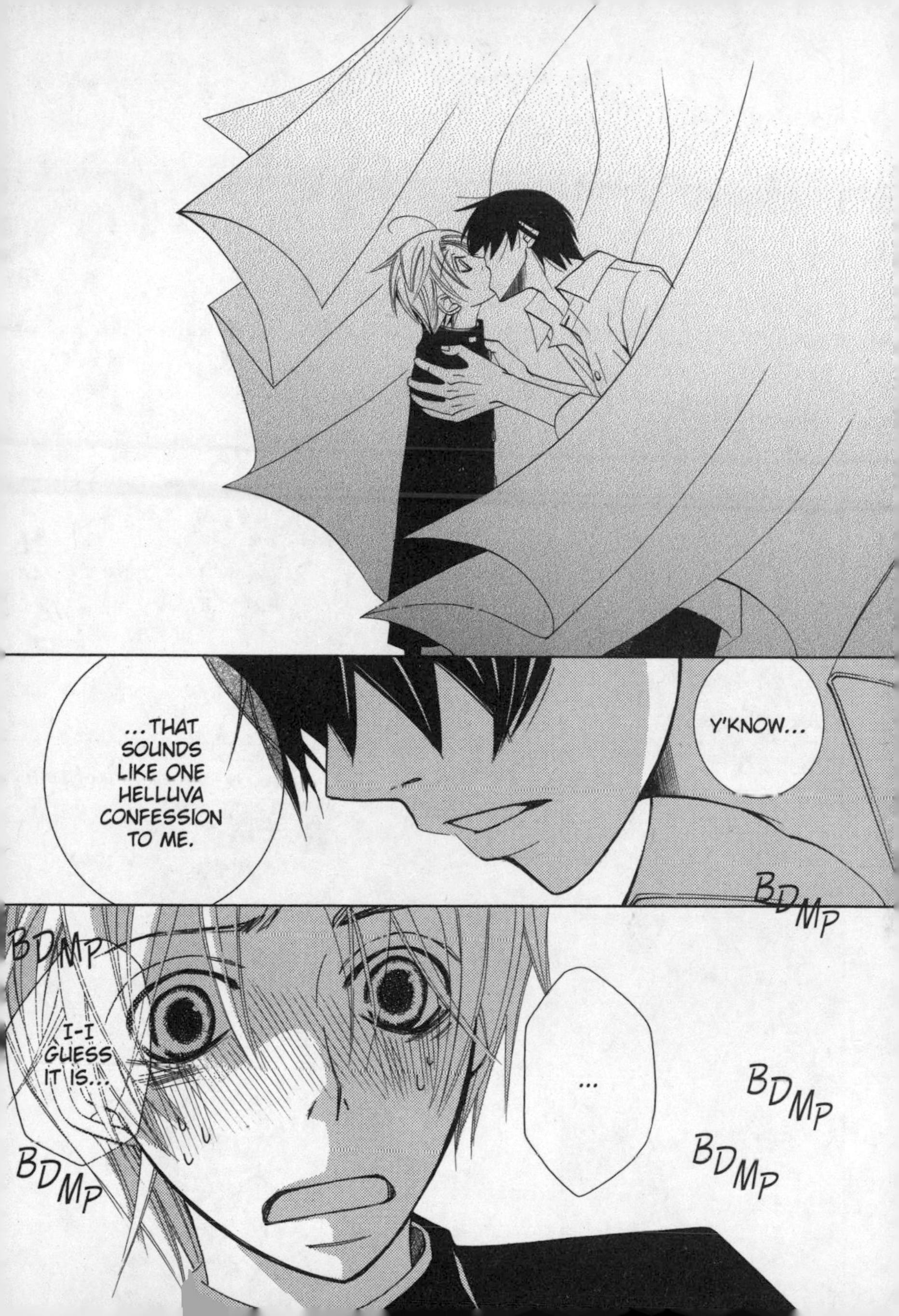
Y'KNOW...
...THAT SOUNDS LIKE ONE HELLUVA CONFESSION TO ME.
BDMP
BDMP
BDMP
BDMP
...
I-I GUESS IT IS...
BDMP

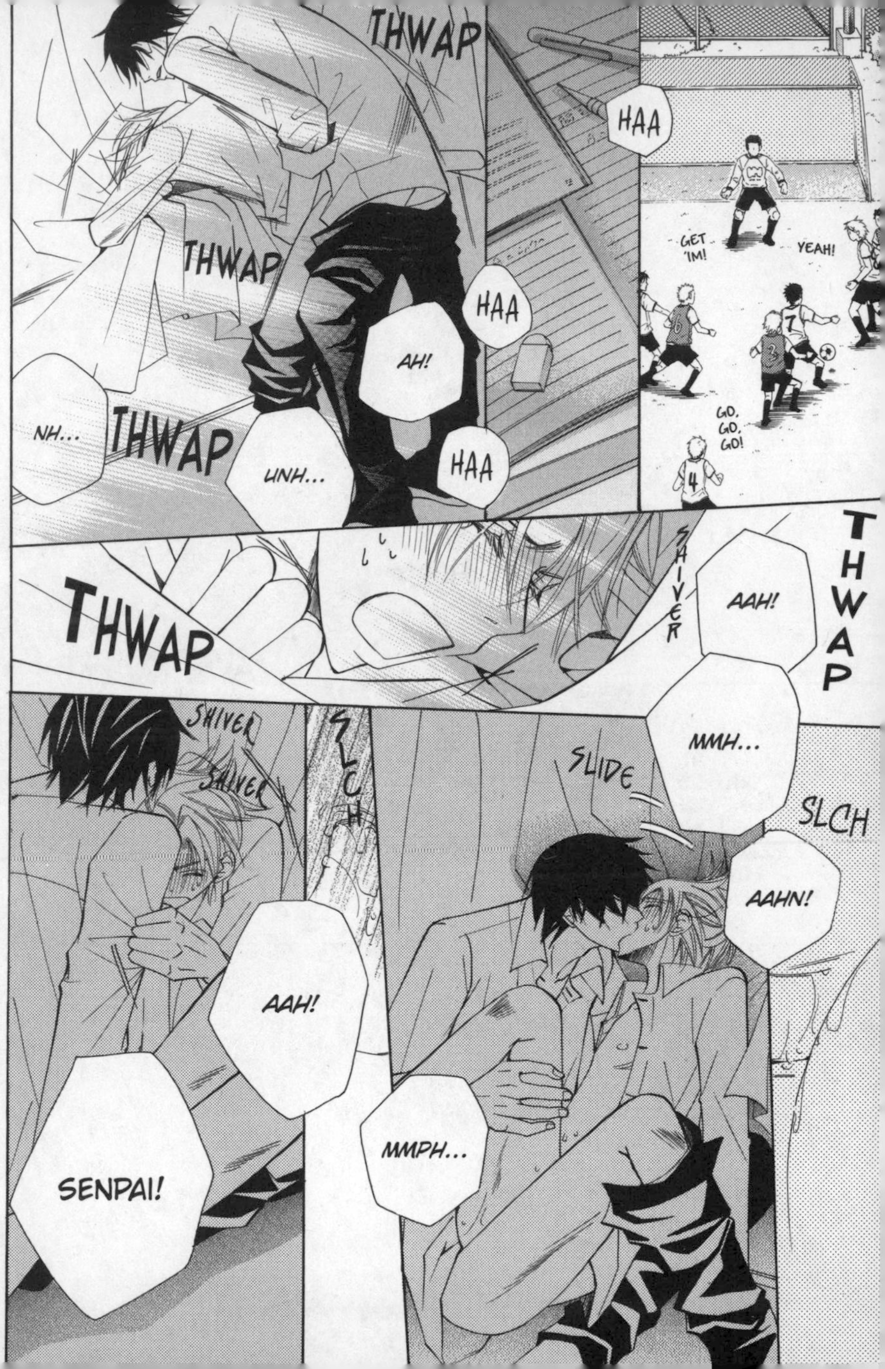
HAA
YEAH!
GET 'IM!
GO, GO, GO!
THWAP
HAA
AH!
HAA
THWAP
UNH...
THWAP
NH...
THWAP
AAH!
SHIVER
THWAP
MMH...
SLCH
SLIDE
AAHN!
MMPH...
SLCH
SHIVER
SHIVER
AAH!
SENPAI!

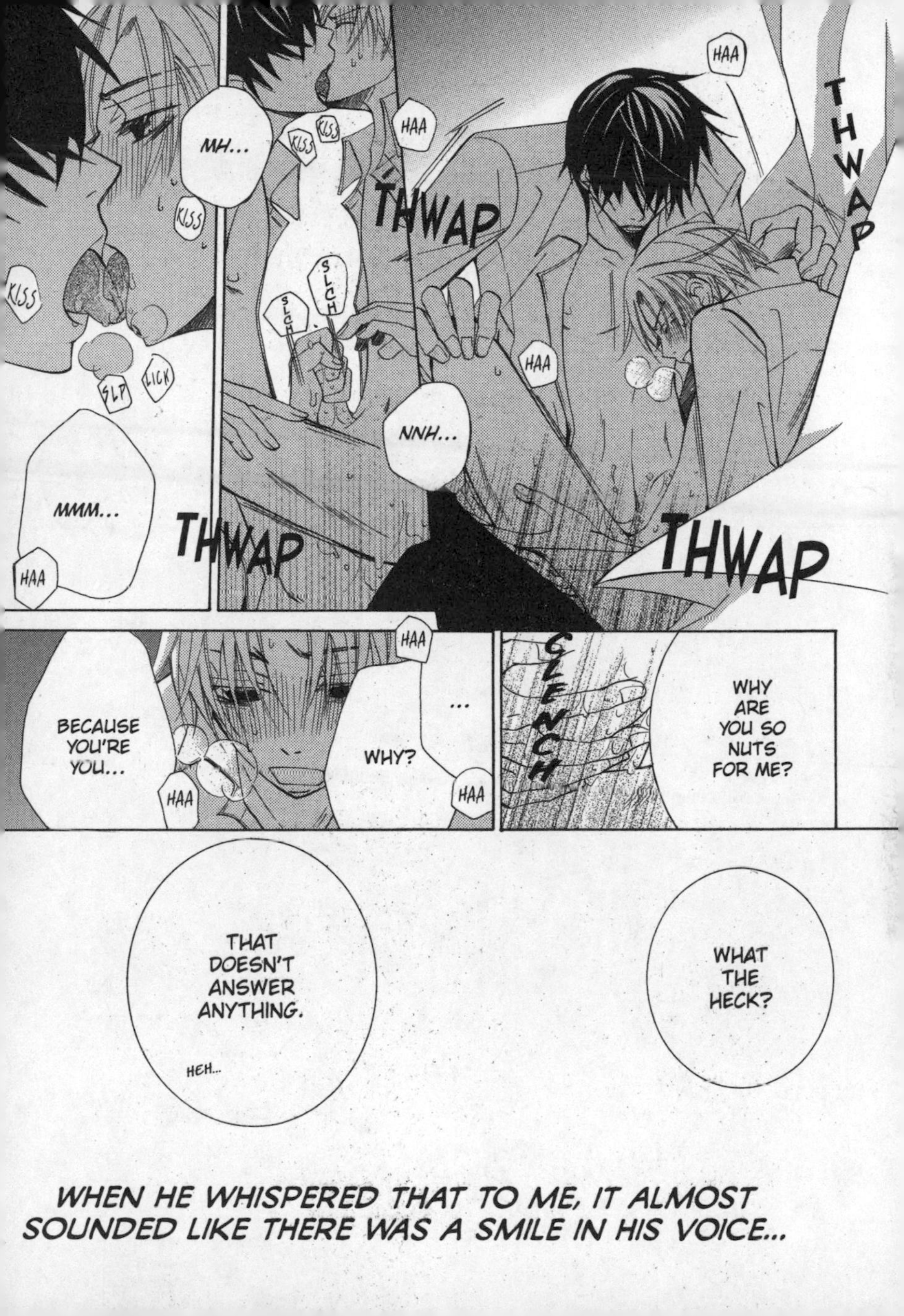
HAA
THWAP
HAA
THWAP
KISS
KISS
HAA
MH...
THWAP
SLCH
SLCH
NNH...
THWAP
KISS
KISS
LICK
SLP
MMM...
HAA
WHY ARE YOU SO NUTS FOR ME?
CLENCH
HAA
...
WHY?
HAA
BECAUSE YOU'RE YOU...
HAA
WHAT THE HECK?
THAT DOESN'T ANSWER ANYTHING.
HEH...
WHEN HE WHISPERED THAT TO ME, IT ALMOST SOUNDED LIKE THERE WAS A SMILE IN HIS VOICE...

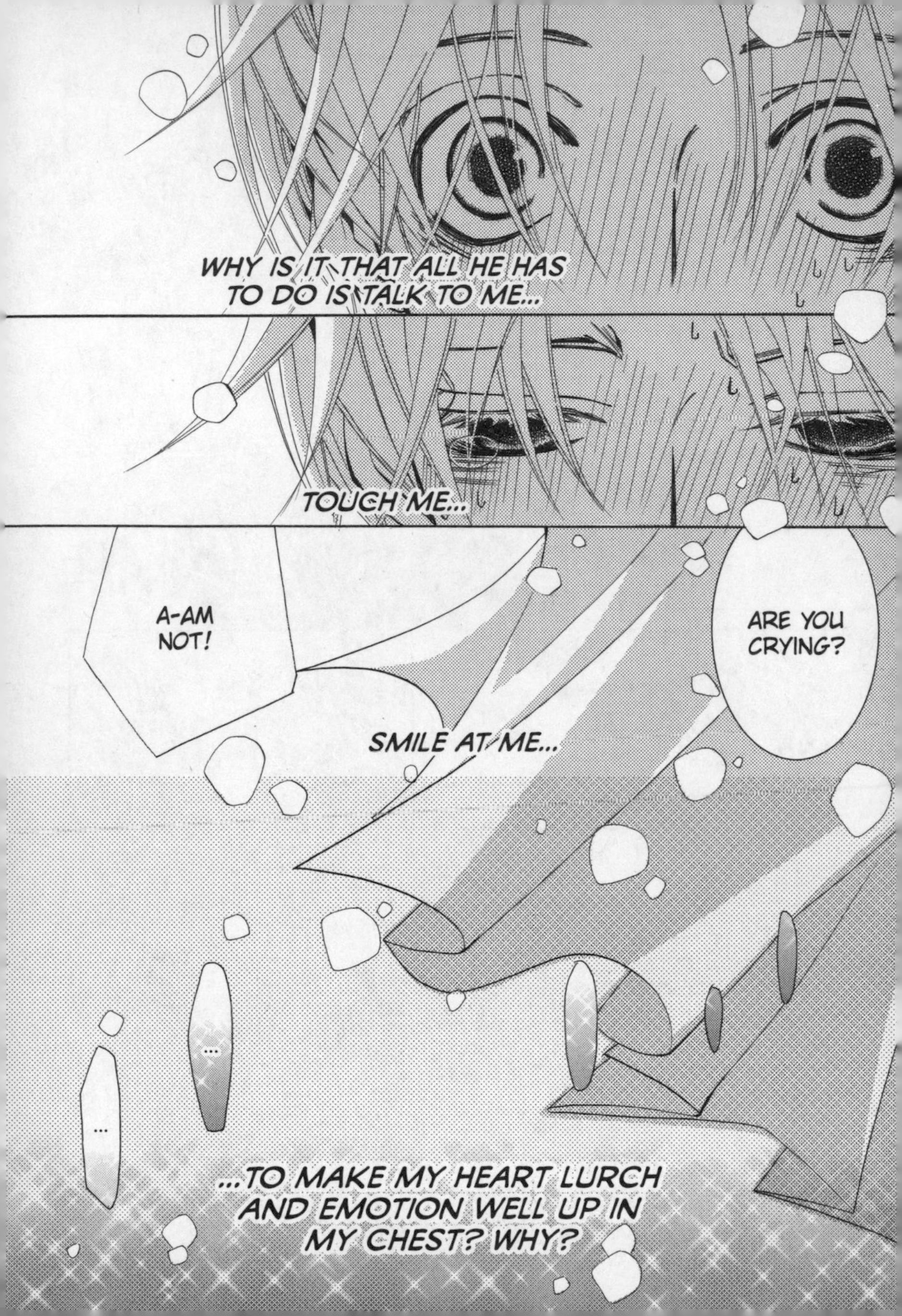
WHY IS IT THAT ALL HE HAS TO DO IS TALK TO ME...
TOUCH ME...
ARE YOU CRYING?
A-AM NOT!
SMILE AT ME...
...
...
...TO MAKE MY HEART LURCH AND EMOTION WELL UP IN MY CHEST? WHY?

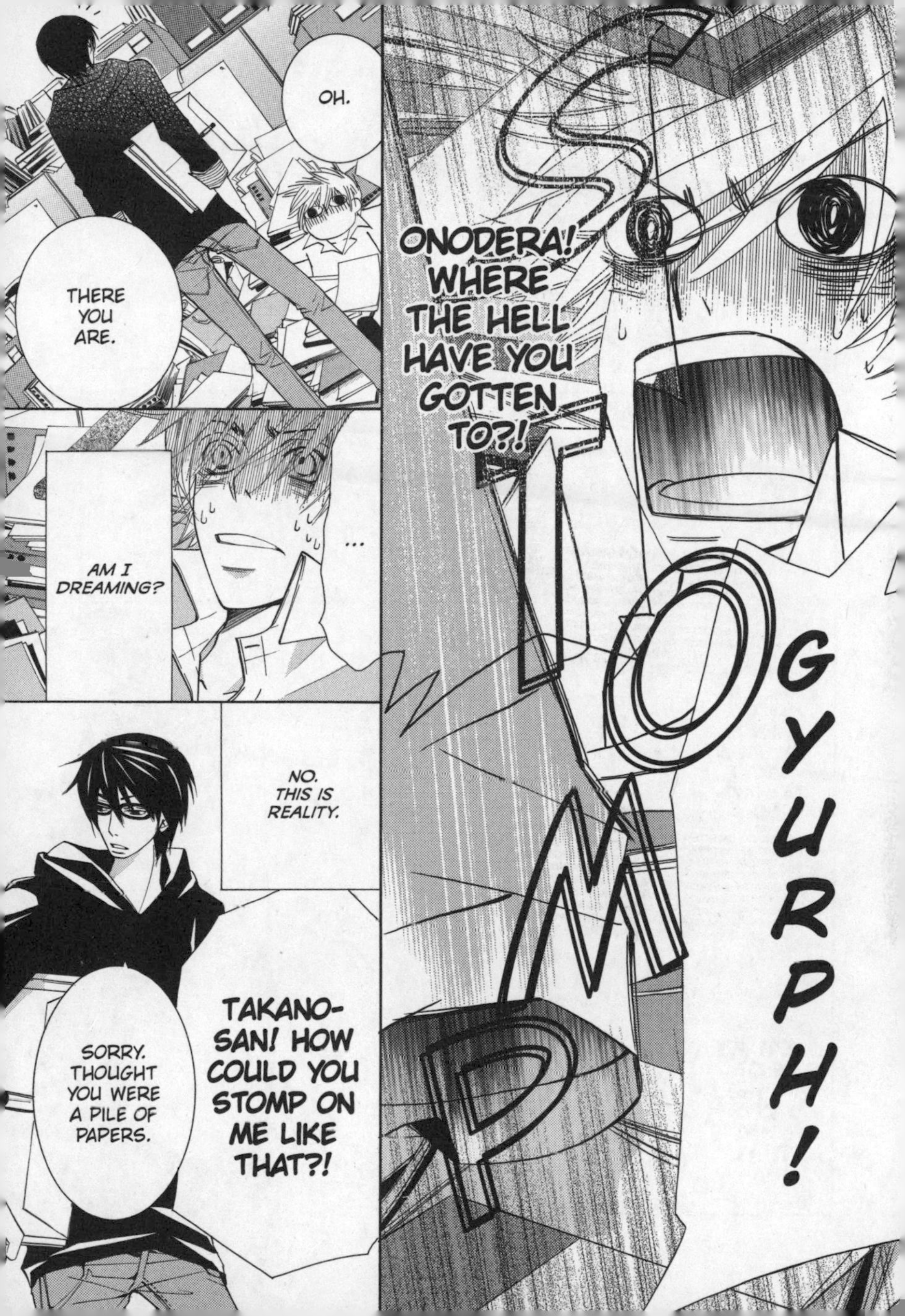
ONODERA! WHERE THE HELL HAVE YOU GOTTEN TO?!
STOMP
GYURPH!
OH.
THERE YOU ARE.
...
AM I DREAMING?
NO. THIS IS REALITY.
TAKANO-SAN! HOW COULD YOU STOMP ON ME LIKE THAT?!
SORRY. THOUGHT YOU WERE A PILE OF PAPERS.

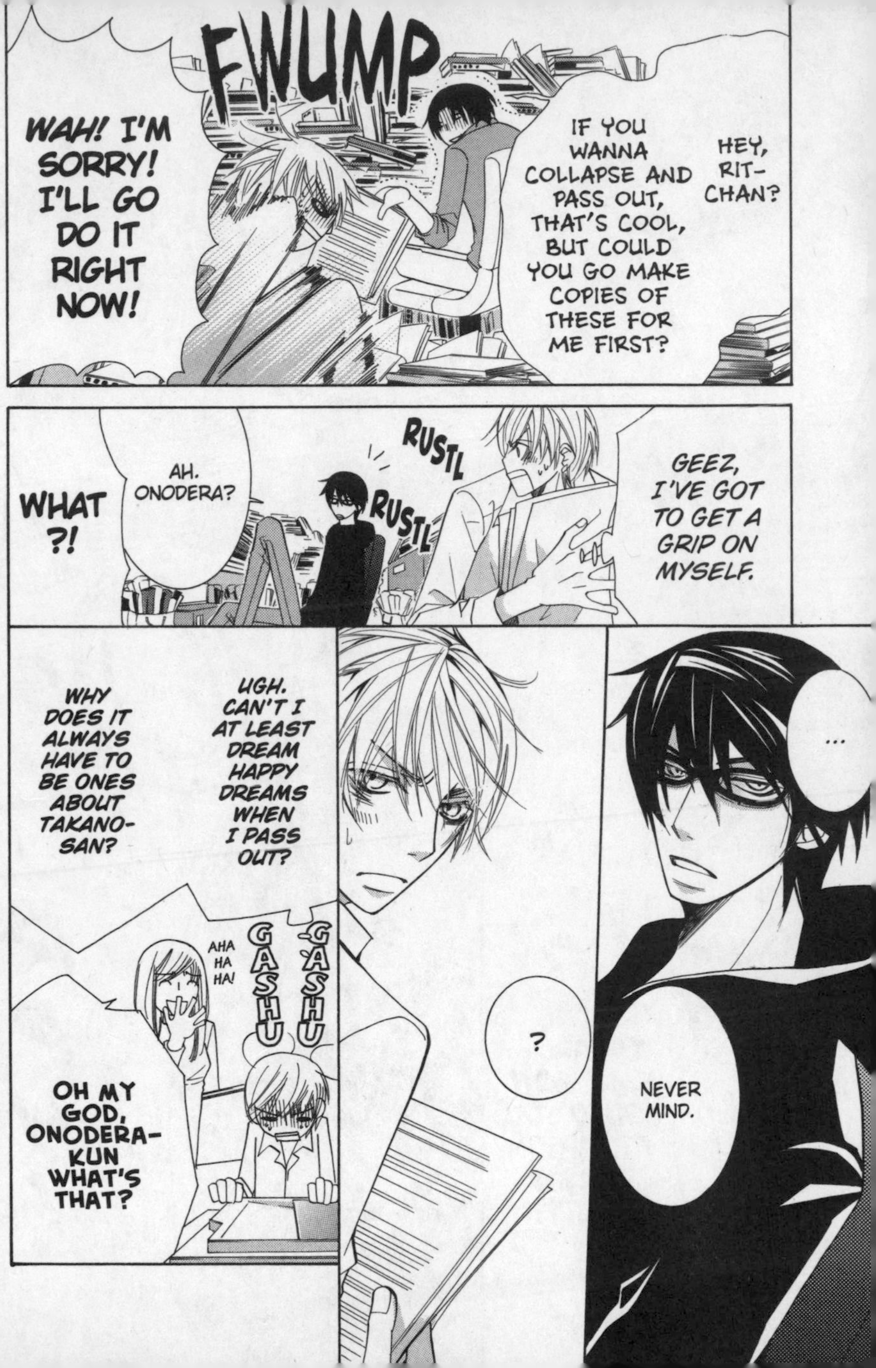
HEY, RIT-CHAN?
IF YOU WANNA COLLAPSE AND PASS OUT, THAT'S COOL, BUT COULD YOU GO MAKE COPIES OF THESE FOR ME FIRST?
FWUMP
WAH! I'M SORRY! I'LL GO DO IT RIGHT NOW!
GEEZ, I'VE GOT TO GET A GRIP ON MYSELF.
RUSTL
RUSTL
AH. ONODERA?
WHAT?!
...
?
NEVER MIND.
UGH. CAN'T I AT LEAST DREAM HAPPY DREAMS WHEN I PASS OUT?
WHY DOES IT ALWAYS HAVE TO BE ONES ABOUT TAKANO-SAN?
GASHU
GASHU
AHA HA HA!
OH MY GOD, ONODERA-KUN WHAT'S THAT?

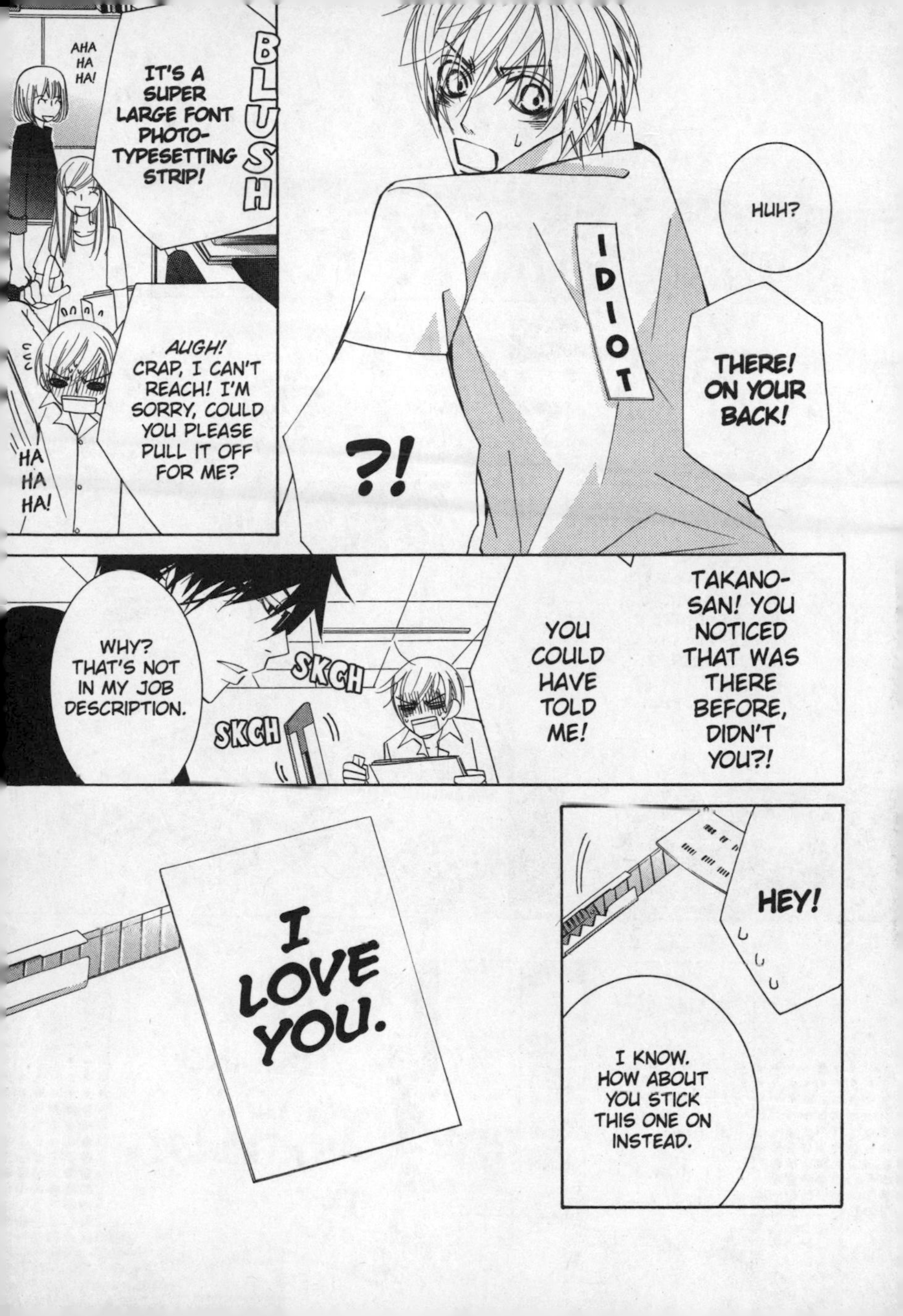
HUH?
IDIOT
THERE! ON YOUR BACK!
?!
BLUSH
IT'S A SUPER LARGE FONT PHOTO-TYPESETTING STRIP!
AHA HA HA!
AUGH! CRAP, I CAN'T REACH! I'M SORRY, COULD YOU PLEASE PULL IT OFF FOR ME?
HA HA HA!
TAKANO-SAN! YOU NOTICED THAT WAS THERE BEFORE, DIDN'T YOU?!
YOU COULD HAVE TOLD ME!
SKCH
SKCH
WHY? THAT'S NOT IN MY JOB DESCRIPTION.
HEY!
I KNOW. HOW ABOUT YOU STICK THIS ONE ON INSTEAD.
I LOVE YOU.

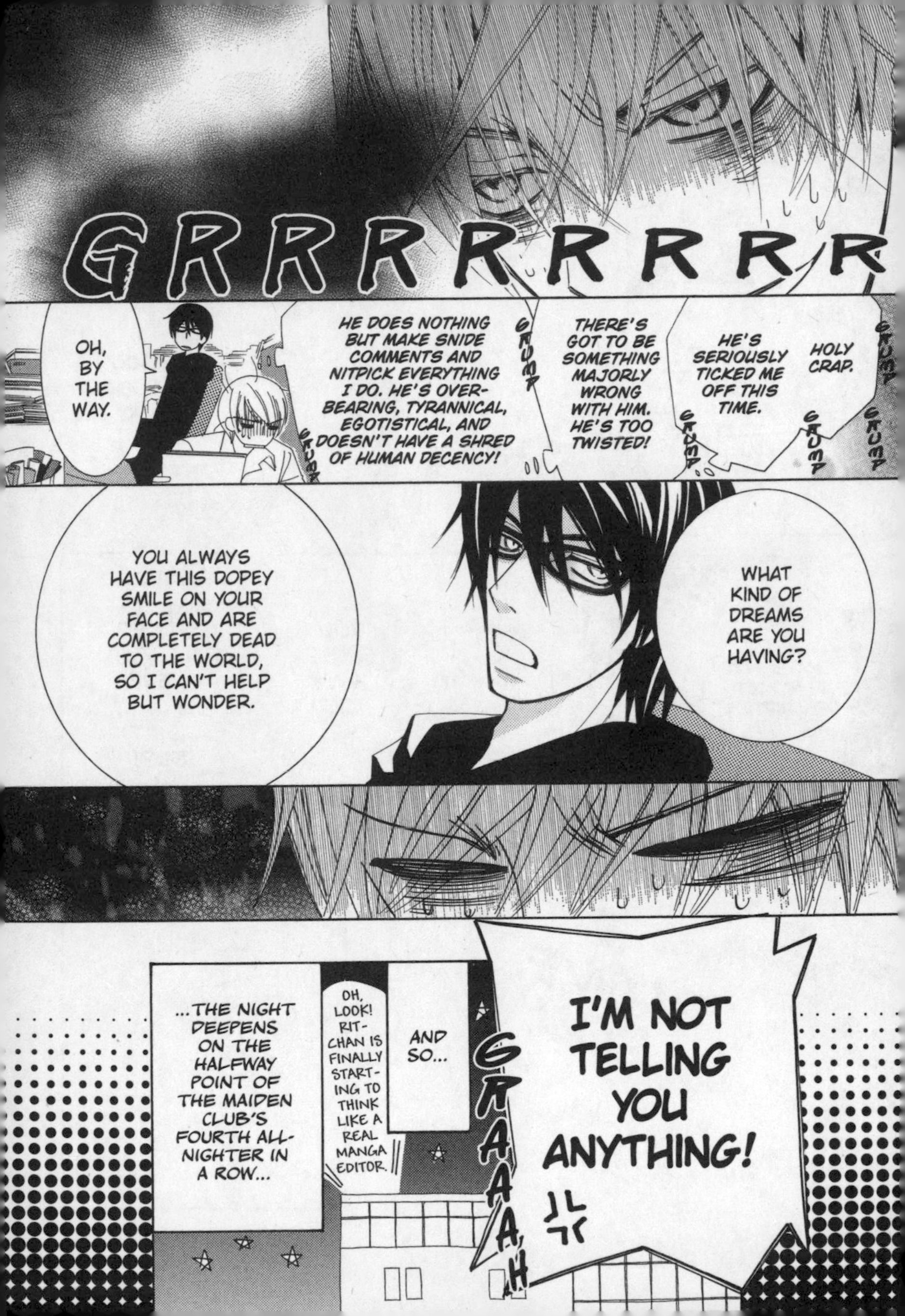
GRRRRRRRRR
HOLY CRAP.
GRUMP
HE'S SERIOUSLY TICKED ME OFF THIS TIME.
GRUMP
GRUMP
GRUMP
THERE'S GOT TO BE SOMETHING MAJORLY WRONG WITH HIM. HE'S TOO TWISTED!
GRUMP
HE DOES NOTHING BUT MAKE SNIDE COMMENTS AND NITPICK EVERYTHING I DO. HE'S OVER-BEARING, TYRANNICAL, EGOTISTICAL, AND DOESN'T HAVE A SHRED OF HUMAN DECENCY!
OH, BY THE WAY.
WHAT KIND OF DREAMS ARE YOU HAVING?
YOU ALWAYS HAVE THIS DOPEY SMILE ON YOUR FACE AND ARE COMPLETELY DEAD TO THE WORLD, SO I CAN'T HELP BUT WONDER.
I'M NOT TELLING YOU ANYTHING!
GRAAAAH
AND SO...
OH, LOOK! RIT-CHAN IS FINALLY START-ING TO THINK LIKE A REAL MANGA EDITOR.
...THE NIGHT DEEPENS ON THE HALFWAY POINT OF THE MAIDEN CLUB'S FOURTH ALL-NIGHTER IN A ROW...

Hello. It's nice to meet you! My name is Shungiku Nakamura. Thanks to everyone's generous help and support, we were able to publish Volume 2!

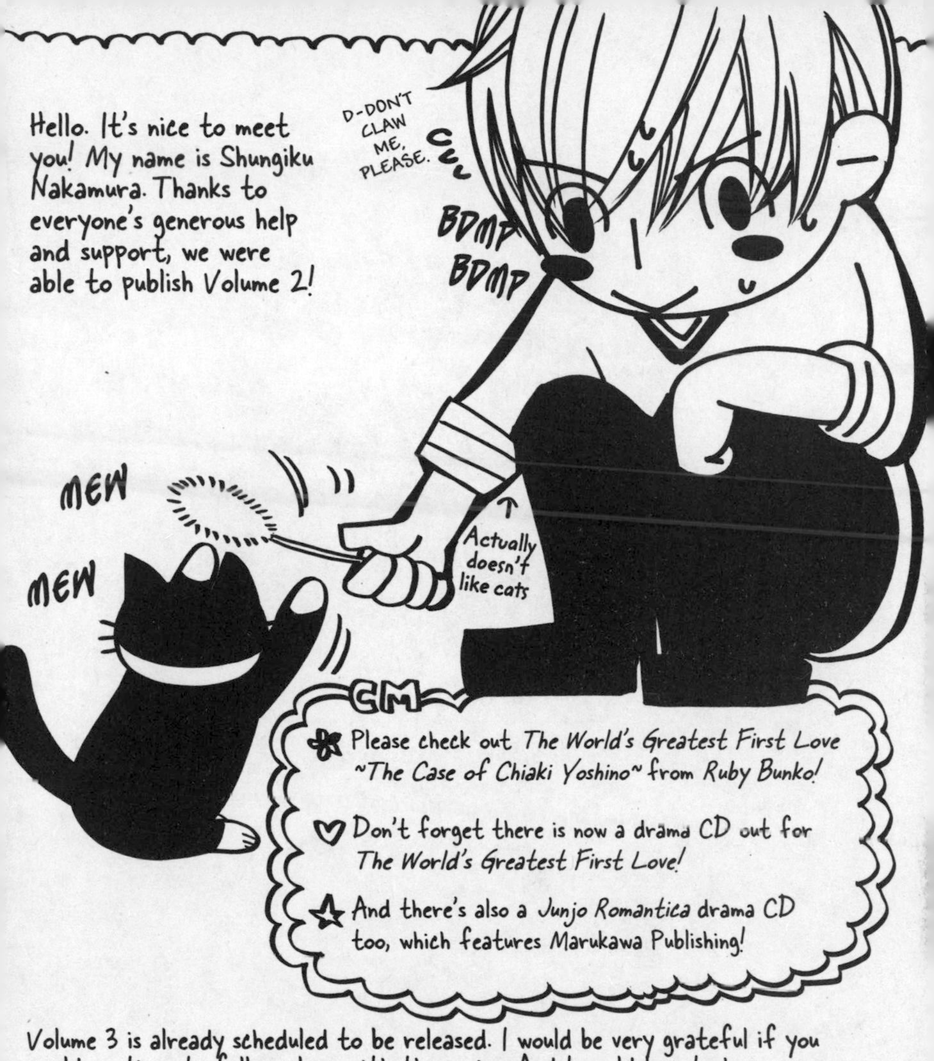
D-DON'T CLAW ME, PLEASE.
BDMP BDMP
MEW MEW
Actually doesn't like cats

CM

- Please check out *The World's Greatest First Love ~The Case of Chiaki Yoshino~* from *Ruby Bunko*!
- Don't forget there is now a drama CD out for *The World's Greatest First Love*!
- And there's also a *Junjo Romantica* drama CD too, which features Marukawa Publishing!

Volume 3 is already scheduled to be released. I would be very grateful if you would continue to follow along with the series. And I would love to hear any of your thoughts and comments! See you next volume!

Nakamura 2009

Current Situation: I slept funny, and now I'm stuck walking around like a robot. How does that happen?

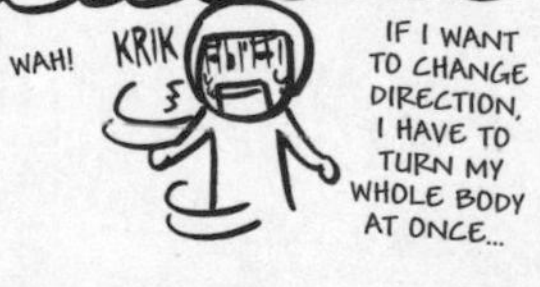
WAH!
KRIK
IF I WANT TO CHANGE DIRECTION, I HAVE TO TURN MY WHOLE BODY AT ONCE...

I bought a whole bunch of cute masking tape rolls on impulse. They're so cute I don't want to waste them, so I've hardly used them at all.

About the Author

Shungiku Nakamura
DOB December 13
Sagittarius
Blood Type O

The World's Greatest
First Love:
The Case of Ritsu Onodera
Volume 2
SuBLime Manga Edition

Story and Art by **Shungiku Nakamura**

Translation—**Adrienne Beck**
Touch-up Art and Lettering—**NRP Studios**
Cover and Graphic Design—**Fawn Lau**
Editor—**Jennifer LeBlanc**

SEKAIICHI HATSUKOI ~ONODERA RITSU NO BAAI~ Volume 2
© Shungiku NAKAMURA 2009
First published in Japan in 2009 by KADOKAWA CORPORATION, Tokyo.
English translation rights arranged with KADOKAWA CORPORATION, Tokyo.

**ASUKA
COMICS
CL** D X

Printed in the U.S.A.

Published by SuBLime Manga
P.O. Box 77010
San Francisco, CA 94107

10 9 8 7 6 5 4
First printing, June 2015
Fourth printing, February 2022

 PARENTAL ADVISORY
THE WORLD'S GREATEST FIRST LOVE is rated M for Mature and is
recommended for mature readers. This volume contains graphic
MATURE imagery and mature themes.

www.SuBLimeManga.com

Downloading is as easy as: